OFFICIAL
Netscape Navigator 3.0
BOOK

MACINTOSH EDITION

**The definitive guide
to the world's most
popular Internet navigator**

Phil James

Contributing Author:
John Trebnik

An imprint of Ventana Communications Group

Official Netscape Navigator 3.0 Book, Macintosh Edition: The definitive guide to the world's most popular Internet navigator

Library of Congress Cataloging-in-Publication Data

James, Phil.
        Official Netscape Navigator 3.0 Book: The definitive guide to the world's most popular Internet navigator / Phil James. —Macintosh ed.
            p.   cm.
        Includes index.
        ISBN 1-56604-512-6
        1. Netscape. 2. World Wide Web (Information retrieval system) I. Title.
    TK5105.883.N48J35 1996
    005.7'1369—dc20   96-26457
                                          CIP

First Edition 9 8 7 6 5 4 3 2 1

Printed in the United States of America

Published and distributed to the trade by Ventana Communications Group, Inc.
P.O. Box 13964, Research Triangle Park, NC 27709-3964
919.544.9404
FAX 919.544.9472
http://www.vmedia.com

Chief Executive Officer
Josef Woodman

Vice President of
Content Development
Karen A. Bluestein

Managing Editor
Lois J. Principe

Production Manager
John Cotterman

Technology Operations Manager
Kerry L. B. Foster

Product Marketing Manager
Jamie Jaeger

Creative Services Manager
Diane Lennox

Art Director
Marcia Webb

Acquisitions Editor
JJ Hohn

Project Editor
Amy E. Moyers

Copy Editor
Angela Anderson

Assistant Editor
Paul Cory

Technical Director
Dan Brown

Desktop Publisher
Scott Hosa

Proofreader
Kortney Trebnik

Indexer
Sharon Hilgenberg

Cover Designers
Charles Overbeck
Laura Stalzer

About the Author

Phil James has been wandering around cyberspace—often aimlessly—for more than a decade. He is a software design consultant, performance artist, part-time musician, and author of several other Ventana books including the bestselling *Official Netscape Navigator 2.0 Book*. As a literary writer, his stories have appeared in a variety of print and electronic zines. Currently, he is working on a series of one-note operas.

ACKNOWLEDGMENTS

I can't tell you how many people helped me out on this one. But I would like to thank all the hard-working Netscape Press people who made this my smoothest, most hassle-free project yet, especially JJ Hohn, Amy Moyers, John Cotterman, Dan Brown, Jamie Jaeger, Laura Stalzer, and Scott Hosa.

I also want to thank my contributing author, John Trebnik, and the contributing writers who helped out on the 2.0 version of the book: Mark Chambers, Clay Shirky, and Walt Bruce.

I couldn't have won this Academy Award without the unflagging dedication and support of my Internet Service Provider, Computerland. Oops, wrong speech. Anyway, their URL is http://www.computerland.net, and they're good people and they'd be happy to sell you stuff.

Lastly, a great big thank you to my wife and kids, who are always the light at the end of the tunnel of words.

—*Phil James*

Contents

Chapter 10 Commerce & Security 359

Chapter 11 Your Personal Workspace & Web Page 397

Chapter 12 Our Favorite Net Resources 429

Foreword

When Netscape Navigator 2.0 came out eight months ago, it was a time of transition for many of us. Companies of all sizes were just starting to set up Web servers so they could distribute information to their own employees as well as to the world at large. Online commerce was beginning to take off, and consumers were finally able to purchase a wide variety of goods and services on the Web. And through Java and other new technologies, the Internet was at last making good on its multimedia promises.

Over the months since then, part of what we've been doing at Netscape is making the extraordinary commonplace. Thanks to the advanced security features incorporated in Navigator 3.0 as well as in our server products, online commerce is now both safe and convenient. Because 3.0 internally supports video, sound, and even interactive virtual 3D worlds, you no longer have to configure third-party software in order to experience the full range of rich Web content. And with the Internet telephony and graphical collaboration tools included in 3.0, your home or office computer becomes a full-fledged interactive communications center.

These are obvious enhancements that you notice right away. But what I consider some of the most important improvements may not be apparent the first time you launch the program. New HTML tags for multi-column text, font support, table background colors, spacers, and autoscrolling frames let Web developers deliver more flexible and dynamic content. Our LiveConnect technology lets Navigator plug-ins, Java applets, and JavaScript interact seamlessly, so that Web pages can even send you different content depending on what plug-ins you have installed. And as in each new version of Navigator, both the user interface and performance have been improved throughout.

There is one more area that occupies plenty of our time, though you might not even be aware of it. From the beginning, we've been committed to making Navigator a universal platform. That means it is extensible via open standards and protocols rather than proprietary tricks. There are dozens of books that show you how to extend Netscape's power with Java, which is a well-known and standard language. You can download the SSL security specification right from our home site. And when we develop new HTML tags, we work closely with both our customers and the international standards committees to make sure we are adding features that will benefit the broadest range of users. Open standards and interoperability are just as important to us as having the most exciting software on the planet.

The *Official Netscape Navigator 3.0 Book* is a broad, hands-on introduction to what we think is Netscape's most forward-looking product yet. As the Web continues to change our ways of doing business, gathering information, and even communicating with friends, this next year promises to be as full of transitions as the last. Navigator 3.0 will ensure that you keep up!

Marc Andreessen
Vice President of Technology
Netscape Communications Corporation

Introduction

Just a couple of years ago I wrote in the introduction to a book that exploring the Internet made you a pioneer, a rugged individualist blazing new information trails. Well, you can take off that buckskin jacket now: the pioneering days are over. The territory has been surveyed and subdivided, the electronic carpenters are busy with their virtual hammers and saws, and that sure sign of progress—advertising—is springing up all over the Net. Having an Internet connection these days is about like owning a TV in the late 1940's.

The mainstreaming of the Net, though, has in no way diminished its excitement. As content providers familiar with other media started moving in, they pushed the boundaries of what is possible on the Net. The world of monochrome text that I was used to suddenly became an electronic amusement park full of images, sounds, and interactivity. New ways of presenting information have demanded new technologies, and new technologies have inspired new ways of delivering information. This feedback loop between the content people and the technical people has sped up the pace of innovation so much that I don't even get a break between writing new versions of this book!

Netscape remains the leader when it comes to innovation. There are not many companies that have grown so quickly, and there are even fewer that have earned so much respect from the industry. If you wanted to start exploring the Internet two years ago, your head would have been buzzing with arcane terminology. (I even wrote a book or two full of arcane terminology!) But now a new Internet user needs to add only a few words to his or her vocabulary, and certainly the most prominent of these is *Netscape*.

Netscape's success is not simply an artifact of our celebrity culture, in which people and businesses step up to the plate for their 15 minutes of fame. No, in this case, there are more substantial factors. First of all, there's the "right time, right place" factor. The founders of Netscape knew that a graphical World Wide Web browser was the single most important piece of software you could produce right now. Secondly, they knew that to succeed, they must integrate a full range of Internet services. Netscape Navigator is aimed at a public that no longer wants—and will no longer tolerate—the dozens of little applications that used to be necessary to perform even the most routine Internet tasks. Finally, Netscape recognized the importance of open platforms. With its support for plug-ins and other extensions, Netscape Navigator 3.0 is positioned to follow the curving path into the future for many years to come.

Let's take a moment to look at what Netscape's latest release, Netscape Navigator 3.0, means to you:

- You can browse through the enormous range of multimedia information available on the World Wide Web. You can do advanced research without flying off to some university library, you can read the latest stock quotes, you can listen to clips of songs before you go out and plunk down $15 for a CD, you can probably even learn to dance the lambada with animated step-by-step lessons. Remember the lambada?

- You can access all the older, less flashy repositories of information: specialized Gopher and Telnet sites, vast file archives, and databases full of bizarre and arcane data.

■ You can exchange electronic mail quickly and reliably with Internet users around the world. You can even exchange messages with users of private online services connected to the Net. Fire up Netscape Navigator 3.0 and you are almost by default a "global citizen." And if you want to be a very flashy global citizen, Navigator lets you incorporate multimedia right into your e-mail messages.

■ You can join the ranks of thousands of electronic consumers and actually make purchases online. And with Netscape Navigator 3.0's built-in security features, transferring sensitive financial data is safer than it ever has been.

But wait a minute: what if you're on an office *intranet* rather than the Internet? What if you want to access your corporate information by clicking your mouse instead of digging through files and databases? No problem! Netscape is the perfect intranet tool. All of the exciting new features in version 3.0 can be used just as well on an intranet as on the Net.

WHO CAN USE THIS BOOK

This book is aimed at anyone who knows how to use some version of Apple's Macintosh computers and wants to get busy on the Net. It's also aimed at anyone who's been on the Net for a while but wants to upgrade to Netscape Navigator 3.0. Here's what you need:

■ A Macintosh 68000 (68020 minimum) running System 7 or higher, or a more current Macintosh PowerPC or Power Macintosh, with at least 8MB of RAM for the most limited configuration of Navigator 3.0. Netscape's recommendation for minimum memory is 9MB of RAM, but you will want to operate with at least 16MB in order to use some of the new features and functions of this exciting product.

■ If you haven't already installed Netscape Navigator 3.0, about 8MB of space on your hard drive for a full installation of the smallest application configuration and about 15MB for a full installation of the Windows 95 or Windows NT version.

- For the version of this book that comes with a CD-ROM, a CD-ROM drive.

- A TCP/IP local area network (LAN) or a way to get on the Internet.

- For home access via an Internet access provider, a modem, preferably one that can run at 28.8 kbps. (Don't skimp here—get the fastest modem you can afford.)

The last two requirements need some explanation. First of all, you can gather from what I said earlier that Internet access is not really necessary in all cases. Thousands of people are using Netscape Navigator 3.0 to share multimedia information within their own companies. This use relies not on the Internet but on intranets, enterprise-wide networks that a local system administrator sets up. All that's needed is a LAN or wide area network (WAN) that can run the TCP/IP protocols (if you don't know what that means, don't worry: your system administrator will).

But let's say you're a home user who wants to get out into the big Internet ocean. Chances are that unless you're a very ambitious and wealthy computer nerd (no longer an oxymoron in the age of Gates), you don't have a direct connection to the Net. That means you need a modem and an account with an Internet service provider. Neither is hard to get or very expensive any more. Of course, you should get the fastest modem you can afford, preferably one that can run at 28.8 kbps, but a 14.4 kbps modem will still (barely) do the job.

For those of you who bought the version of this book that has a CD-ROM inside the back cover, here's something you *don't* need: Netscape Navigator 3.0 itself. That's right, the CD includes the official software right from Netscape!

HOW THIS BOOK IS ORGANIZED

Chapter 1, "The Web & the Net," provides an overview of the Internet: where it came from, some of its features, and where it's going. You'll learn what the difference really is between the Internet and the World Wide Web, and you'll learn enough about the technical underpinnings of the Net to understand any other technical discussions in the book. We'll even throw in some hints on using the Net so that the natives don't spot you as a "newbie."

In **Chapter 2, "Getting Started,"** you will actually install and configure the Netscape Navigator 3.0 software. This chapter includes hints on selecting an Internet access provider, and it goes pretty deeply into configuring your Macintosh system for Internet access. Once you work through the instructions here, you'll be ready to start exploring.

Chapter 3, "A Quick Look Around," introduces you to the Netscape Navigator 3.0 interface and the basics of navigating the Web. In a few short minutes, you'll be cruising, surfing, or whatever the term is this year.

Electronic mail is one of the most important "meat and potatoes" Internet applications, and **Chapter 4, "Netscape Mail,"** covers it fully. Step-by-step tutorials guide you through the excellent e-mail facilities that are built right into Netscape Navigator 3.0, and in no time you'll be zipping off messages as if you'd been doing it for years. And with Navigator 3.0's advanced e-mail features, you can even make your messages look just like mini Web pages!

Chapter 5, "Newsgroups," introduces you to one of the most fascinating services available on the Net. Usenet newsgroups are forums where Internet users with particular interests trade information, insights, and even files. There are groups devoted to everything from astrophysics to zydeco, and with the excellent newsgroup functionality built right into the Netscape software, you'll be able to join in quickly.

In **Chapter 6, "Getting Files via FTP,"** you'll learn how to explore file archives and download files via FTP, the standard file transfer protocol on the Net. There are archives of informational files, technical files, shareware and freeware programs, games, graphics, video clips. . . . *Warning:* Get a bigger hard drive. You're not going to believe what's available.

Chapter 7, "Gopher & Telnet," introduces you to two old Internet friends: Gopher and Telnet. These Internet services have been around for quite a while, but are still useful tools in certain situations. Netscape Navigator 3.0 includes support for both.

Of course the real *fun* of the World Wide Web is its multimedia capabilities. **Chapter 8, "Sound, Graphics & Video,"** explains how Netscape Navigator 3.0 makes your computer screen look more and more like a TV screen. We show you some of what's available out there, and we walk you through configuring Netscape Navigator 3.0 so that it uses your system optimally in dealing with these new types of information.

In **Chapter 9, "Power Navigator 3.0,"** we go beyond the basics and show you some of the more forward-looking extensions to a forward-looking piece of software. Don't be scared off by the word "advanced": none of these features are difficult to use. In this chapter we explore VRML, Java, JavaScript, and plug-ins.

Want to do your banking on the Net? Before you do, you might want to read **Chapter 10, "Commerce & Security."** This chapter gives you the lowdown on Netscape Navigator 3.0's impressive security features. We'll never get rid of greed and crime, but Netscape's technology helps a lot.

Now that you know what's out there, you might want a convenient personalized way to store your links. **Chapter 11, "Your Personal Workspace & Web Page**," shows you how to design a special Web page that's ideal for your own use. And if you want to develop a page for others to access, I'll show you how to get started on that as well.

In **Chapter 12, "Our Favorite Sites,"** I tell you about some of my own favorite Internet resources. This list is not exhaustive, since that would require volumes—and literally constant updating. Instead, these are a few attractions that I've found exciting, informative, fun, or just plain weird. You can also think of them as jumping off places for your own explorations. If you have purchased the version of this book that has a companion CD-ROM inside the back cover, you also have an electronic version of Chapter 12. You can browse the listings electronically, simply clicking the links to visit sites in which you're interested in.

THE ONLINE COMPANION:
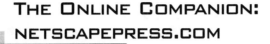
NETSCAPEPRESS.COM

To further enhance this book, we're providing an online companion for this and other Netscape Press titles. The online companion at netscapepress.com includes an area where you can download files we've mentioned; a Web version of Chapter 12, so that you don't have to type in all the Internet addresses we provide; and even a facility for sending us your comments on this book. Please feel free to log on as often as you want; there are no additional charges.

To get to netscapepress.com, simply point Netscape Navigator 3.0 to *http://www.netscapepress.com/.* (If you don't know what I'm talking about, you will by the end of Chapter 2.)

OK, enough introduction. Let's get busy exploring this vast new world of multimedia information!

The Net & the Web

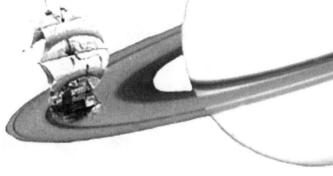

Internet. World Wide Web. Just about everywhere you go these days you overhear somebody using these words. And not just the words themselves, but dozens of phrases derived from them. If you pay attention to the mass media hype, you'd think that most people spend a significant portion of their time "cruising the Net," or "checking out Web sites," or even "surfing cyberspace" (now *there's* a mixed metaphor to make your old English professor cringe).

As with most new technologies, jargon precedes popular understanding. New terminology makes it possible to explore new ideas, but it also exacerbates the epidemic of Geek Answer Syndrome. There is no shortage of people who will blab on authoritatively but incorrectly about anything to do with information technology, flashing their vocabulary like bright plumage. Well now you can tell them to take a walk, because in the next few minutes we'll make sure that you *really* understand what the Net is, what the Web is, and how you can use these exciting new resources. By the time you've finished this chapter you won't be a cybergeek, but you'll be able to answer these questions and probably more:

- Just what *is* the Internet? How did it start? How did it evolve?

- What kinds of services and information are available on the Net?

- How does Internet addressing work?
- What is the World Wide Web? How is it related to the Net?
- What is hypertext? How about hypermedia?
- How does Netscape Navigator give you access to the Web and the rest of the Net?
- Are there any general guidelines for using the Internet?

ENTERPRISE NETSCAPING

This book concentrates on using Netscape Navigator 3.0 to cruise around the Internet, but there are other ways you can harness its power. For instance, if your office is on a LAN you can use Netscape Navigator 3.0 to share multimedia information among employees. You might want to create a colorful tutorial for coworkers, or your personnel department might want to enliven the company expense regulations with songs and animation. Everybody connected to the network could then view these multimedia files using Netscape Navigator 3.0. In addition, you could use Netscape Navigator 3.0 as a front-end for accessing *any* kind of files, not just multimedia ones. You can even use Netscape Navigator 3.0 for your company e-mail. Throughout this book I'll include occasional sidebars that point out interesting uses for Netscape Navigator 3.0 on enterprise-wide *intranets*.

WHAT IS THE INTERNET?

It's really a lot simpler than you'd guess. A network is a collection of computers that are connected together so they can share information, and the Internet is a network of networks. It lets individuals on one network share information with users on another network that may be thousands of miles away. The shared information can take many forms. For instance, you can use the

Internet to send e-mail messages, or to download files, or to view video clips, or listen to music. You can even use the Net for banking and shopping. It's a lot like the phone system, except that instead of just talking you can exchange all different kinds of information.

The physical Internet looks like a vast net of wires. A few high-speed "backbone" cables branch out into other cables, which in turn radiate outward into finer strands. Most of the developed areas of the world have already been wired, so by routing your information or requests through this vast system you can reach other Internet users all over the world. Fortunately the routing happens automatically, just as it does with telephone calls, so you don't need to know *how* data gets from your computer to a computer in Timbuktu.

And the system is democratic. Anyone can use it. You don't even need to have your own network in order to connect—you can communicate using the current infrastructure by plugging into somebody else's network. Maybe you're already doing this. If you have a Serial Line Internet Protocol (SLIP) or Point-to-Point Protocol (PPP) account (see Chapter 2, "Getting Started"), you simply connect via modem and phone line to your access provider's network site (known as a "point of presence"). The actual transmission of data is free, but you'll probably need to pay the access provider for the time you spend accessing its equipment.

There are hundreds of thousands of users sitting at their Macs right now, gathering information from far-flung reaches of the globe. Pretty soon the Internet will be accepted as a simple fact of modern life, and people will forget how it originated.

ORIGINS OF THE INTERNET

I'm not going to cover the Internet's history with any depth. There are other books, even a couple of mine, that cover the topic in more detail. But it may be useful for you to have a little background. If you really don't care about the history, just skip this section. On the other hand, if you want to be the hit of the next propeller-head party you attend, memorize the following four paragraphs:

As with many technological advances, the Internet began as a military research project. It was the early 1970s, a time full of menace to civilization as we knew it: leisure suits, wide ties, platform shoes, and the threat of nuclear war. The U.S. Defense Department implemented a network, called ARPAnet, that was designed so that even if part of its physical structure were destroyed, information could still be sent to any remaining destination.

In the early 1980s, local area networks at a variety of research institutions started hooking into ARPAnet. They were able to do this by using the same underlying technology that ARPAnet used to transfer data and make sure it got to the right place.

Then in the late 1980s, the National Science Foundation (NSF) established five supercomputer centers and connected them via their own network, NSFnet. Based on the same technology as ARPAnet, the sites were physically linked by special phone lines. Since the phone companies charged by the mile for these lines, it was very expensive to gather information from one of these centers. The NSF decided to create several regional networks with dozens of connected sites; any data could be passed along the line from one node to another, saving on the costly line charges.

The rest of the Internet's history is one of expansion. As new educational institutions and government agencies developed their own networks and joined NSFnet, the original wiring quickly became overloaded. Much faster lines were put in, faster computers were installed, and what is now known as the Internet, opened its virtual doors to most of the academic and government community. Universities from other nations, not to mention foreign governments, started joining the Net. In the early 1990s, commercial organizations began to jump on board, and it is now common for companies to promote, and even sell, all sorts of products and services over the Net.

The latest trend on the Internet is the rapid growth of personal information, with individuals making available all sorts of things they'd like to share with the world. I can almost guarantee you that somebody you know has a poem out on the Net, and that another friend has provided humanity with a picture of a favorite pet cat. And of course you can access all of this stuff with

Netscape Navigator 3.0. Andy Warhol predicted a time when everyone in the world would enjoy 15 minutes of fame. Well, notwithstanding Kato Kaelin, that hasn't quite happened, but we are fast approaching a time when everybody can enjoy 15 *kilobytes* of fame.

WHAT IS OUT THERE

What services does the Internet actually provide the average user right now? Let's take a slightly deeper look at a few that can have a real impact on your life:

ELECTRONIC MAIL

Thanks to the Internet, you can send messages to just about anybody who has a computer and a network connection or a modem. If the individual you want to contact is not directly on the Net, you can use Netscape Navigator 3.0 to send a message to him or her on one of the popular online services such as CompuServe or America Online.

There are a number of advantages to sending messages via e-mail instead of the U.S. Postal Service (known affectionately as "snail mail" by e-mail advocates). First of all, there's the speed. It may take only seconds for your message to reach somebody on the other side of the world. The recipient can read your text immediately on the screen, respond to it right away, save it for later, print it out, or quickly forward it to somebody else. You can create electronic mailing lists for sending notices to hundreds or even thousands of people at once. Messages you receive can be organized into convenient electronic folders and saved for as long as you want without taking up any office space. And with e-mail, it's possible to verify very quickly that your message has indeed arrived at its destination. Because of these advantages, and several others that you'll learn about in Chapter 4, "Netscape Mail," e-mail has become my principal means of communicating with the world. I receive several dozen e-mail messages a day and send about as many. In several months I generate more messages than all the old-fashioned paper letters I've written in my life!

Netscape Navigator 3.0 includes full-featured e-mail support, and Figure 1-1 shows what its main Mail window looks like.

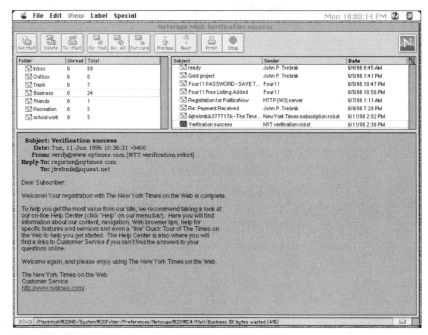

Figure 1-1: *E-mail in Netscape Navigator 3.0.*

RESEARCH

Locating specific information used to be a tedious and time-consuming process. Remember digging through library card catalogs and then wandering through dusty stacks of books, only to discover that what you needed wasn't even at this library? Now finding references to topics can be as simple as typing in a keyword and clicking a button—from the privacy of your own home! The Internet includes entire libraries of specialized information, and thousands of these are accessible, free of charge, to the general public.

The Internet also supports a variety of research techniques and styles. Suppose you're trying to come up with a topic for a speech you have to deliver. At first you might want to browse a variety of materials to refine your subject area. This process is much like going to an area in a library and starting to pull books off the shelf, except that on the Internet you can leap from library to library, following associative links or trains of thought. Once you've determined the exact subject of your speech, you may need to track down some very specific information, such as statistics to back up a particular point. (Statistics always make it sound like you know what you're talking about, don't they?) Once again there are Internet services that will help you; powerful search tools that will scurry around the Net and quickly find your needle in the information haystack. Netscape Navigator 3.0 gives you access to these tools through the Net Search feature on the Netscape home page, shown in Figure 1-2.

Figure 1-2: *Net Search gives you access to a variety of search tools from the Netscape home page.*

UNDER THE HOOD: TCP/IP

You can probably get through life just fine without understanding the technical underpinnings of the Net. But if you like the nuts and bolts stuff, boy have I got a sidebar for you!

TCP/IP really means "the TCP/IP protocol suite." It is a group of protocols that allows data to be transmitted correctly from one machine to another over the Net. And what exactly is a protocol? It's simply a set of standardized conventions for communication. In the human world, a typical protocol is saying "Your Honor" when you talk to a judge. In the world of data communications, a protocol might require that a sending machine include a special string of characters before and after every chunk of data so that the receiving machine can determine where that data begins and ends.

The TCP part of TCP/IP stands for Transmission Control Protocol. It divides any information you send into manageable blocks; conversely, it reconstructs received blocks into a stream of information. TCP does not require that all the blocks be received in the right sequence, since it attaches sequence numbers for reassembly. TCP also includes error checking; if blocks are missing or garbled, it requests that they be resent. When you run Internet applications you remain blissfully unaware of all of this activity, since the TCP software layer "sits below" the application software. Information is passed from the application software to TCP without any human intervention; at the other end, reassembled information is passed *from* TCP to the appropriate software program.

The IP part of TCP/IP stands for Internet Protocol. The Internet Protocol is the real workhorse of the Internet. When you send something over the Internet, TCP passes its packets on to IP. This is roughly like dropping a letter at the post office, because IP repackages the data and makes sure that all of it gets delivered from point to point on the Internet on its way to the final destination: the specified IP or domain name address. Conversely, when IP receives packets, it "delivers" them up to TCP. There are other low-level Internet protocols, but these are the two most important ones, the basis of most Internet communication.

NEWS & INFORMATION

This is the age of information, and success in many fields depends on getting the latest news as quickly as possible. The Internet provides numerous sources for specialized, up-to-date information. You may want to subscribe to an electronic mailing list, for instance, that keeps you posted on the latest developments in nanotechnology; you may want to get stock prices more current than those you can read in your local newspaper; or you may want to participate in a Usenet newsgroup where specialists in some arcane area of knowledge keep you abreast of what you need to know. Because of its scope and speed, the Internet is by far the most efficient way to make sure you maintain expert status in your little corner of the information universe. Netscape Navigator 3.0 gets you the information you need!

SOFTWARE

One of the most astounding features of the Internet is the availability of thousands and thousands of software programs that you can download at no charge. In fact, until recently you couldn't even buy commercial Internet client programs for Macs that were anywhere near as good as the freeware and shareware available on the Net. (For more information about freeware and shareware, see Chapter 6, "Getting Files via FTP.") That situation is starting to change, but there still are times when you need a program dedicated to a very specific task, such as playing a new kind of sound or video file.

Many of the sites that allow you to download programs are large, and most do not include descriptions of the files. Fortunately Netscape Navigator 3.0 helps you locate and download exactly what you need.

Figure 1-3 shows you some of the directories of files available at Netscape's own FTP site.

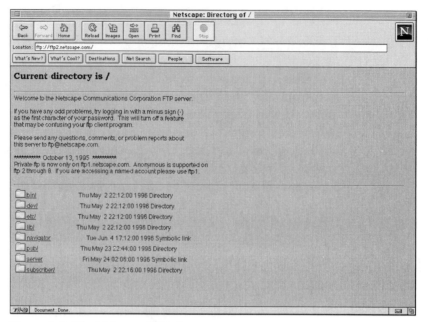

Figure 1-3: *The Netscape FTP site.*

PROMOTION, SHOPPING & ONLINE TRANSACTIONS

For years the Internet was a commerce-free zone. It was funded and monitored by dedicated bureaucrats and academicians who instituted strict usage policies restricting anything that smelled vaguely of money. Well, all that's changed. Now there are vast areas of cyberspace that look less like research libraries than like your local mall, and most major corporations maintain Web sites where they promote their products and services.

Figure 1-4 shows Open Market's Commercial Sites Index; a vast directory of commercial services and products (http://www.directory.net).

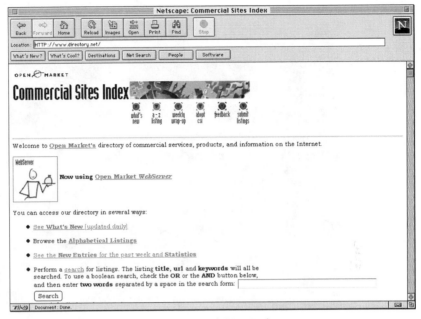

Figure 1-4: *Open Market's Commercial Sites Index.*

RECREATION

Planning a vacation? The Internet can provide current travel information on just about any area of the globe. Considering taking up a new sport? Want to find out about the latest foreign movies? The Internet can point you to the resources you need.

But the Internet not only supplies information *about* recreational activities, it also provides its own diversions and amusements. If you like interactive online games, for instance, you might be in danger of staying glued to your keyboard and monitor well into the wee hours. Figure 1-5 shows one of the many games sites available to you via the Web.

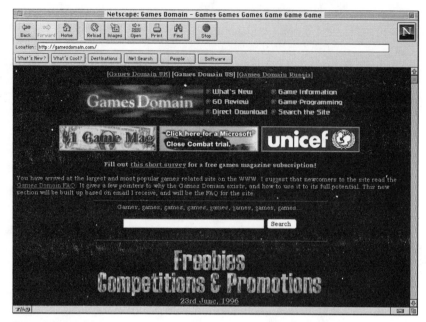

Figure 1-5: *The Games Domain site on the World Wide Web.*

And if you're a more cyber-gregarious person than I am, the Internet offers plenty of opportunities for meeting friends and chatting online. Then of course the World Wide Web, which we'll talk about later in this chapter, is full of unclassifiable forms of fun and nonsense, and Netscape Navigator 3.0 brings it all right into your own home.

But before discussing the Web, we need to take a quick look at how information actually gets from one place to another on the Web. A basic understanding of Internet addressing will make it easier for you to find the sites with information you're interested in.

INTERNET ADDRESSING

The whole basis of the Internet is that machines are constantly sending messages to other machines. Some of these messages are software commands, some are requests for data, and some include the human-readable data itself. Obviously there has to be a way for information to get to the proper recipient, and so the underlying suite of Internet protocols includes an addressing scheme. At the heart of the addressing scheme is the concept of domains.

DOMAINS & DOMAIN NAMES

By *domain*, we simply mean where a computer resides. For instance, a specific computer at the University of Missouri is in the *missouri* domain, which in turn is within the top-level *edu* domain, the domain that includes all Internet-connected colleges and universities in the United States. The complete domain name of a machine called *bigcat* at the University of Missouri, for instance, would be *bigcat.missouri.edu*. No other machine anywhere on the Internet has the same domain name. Every name is registered with a special Internet organization to ensure that it is unique.

I have an e-mail account on echonyc.com. To reach my account, all you need to do is add my username to the domain name. My username is pjames, so my full e-mail address is *pjames@echonyc.com*. If you wanted to visit the Web pages at echonyc.com, however, you'd simply tell Netscape Navigator 3.0 to get a document from the Web server machine at that site, www.echonyc.com.

At first these addresses might look impossible to pronounce, but pronunciation conventions have developed. Pjames@echonyc.com is pronounced "p-james at echo-n-y-c dot com," and ftp.vmedia. com is pronounced "f-t-p dot v-media dot com." Of course usernames don't have to be as simple as mine. If your LAN administrator or access provider lets you choose your own name, you might want to be zzzx_12_qwerty@serviceprovider.com. Then again you might not. Keep in mind that people who send you e-mail need to remember your address.

Fortunately, the Internet doesn't care about case-sensitivity in e-mail addresses. You can send a message to pJaMeS@EcHoNyC. cOm, and I will still get it. But most experienced Internet users stick with lowercase when typing addresses—it's just easier. If you use both uppercase and lowercase letters in your addresses, some of the old-timers will chuckle at the newcomer, more often called a "clueless newbie."

TIP

Even though Internet e-mail addresses are not case-sensitive, remember that URLs for Web pages and FTP directories are!

As I mentioned earlier, the last part of a domain name address is called the top-level domain. There are six standardized domain names corresponding to types of organizations, as shown in Table 1-1.

Domain	Type of Organization
com	Commercial entity
edu	Educational institution
gov	Government agency or department
mil	Military organization
net	Network resource
org	Other type of organization, usually a not-for-profit

Table 1-1: *Top-level domains.*

In addition, Internet sites outside the United States are identified by a special two-letter, top-level domain name. For instance, a computer in Finland would have a top-level domain name of *fi*, and a computer in Germany would have a top-level domain name of *de* (for Deutschland). As you start cruising around the Net, you will run into these foreign domain names on a daily basis. There is even a two-letter designation for the United States (you guessed it, *us*), but it is rarely used since the six "organization type" names are more descriptive.

IP ADDRESSES

Pretty simple, isn't it? Well, luckily for those of us who make a living explaining such things, it's not *quite* that simple. Domain name addresses are really easy-to-remember translations of the kind of addresses the Internet really uses, numeric *IP addresses*. IP stands for "Internet Protocol." You may have read about IP in the earlier sidebar, "Under the Hood: TCP/IP." For now, it's only important to understand the difference between the two kinds of addresses.

If you're my age, you probably remember when phone numbers always began with the name of the exchange, as in "Murray Hill Seven, Five Five Five Five." You can think of Murray Hill Seven, the exchange, as a top-level domain name. But in fact your telephone didn't really care about the words Murray Hill Seven, it simply transmitted down the line the fact that you had dialed the numbers 647. You can think of 647 as the top-level portion of the IP address. When you use a domain name address to attach to a Web server, for instance, a special Internet service known as a Domain Name Service (DNS) looks up the name and replaces it with an IP number. And as long as you're connected to the Net, you have your own IP address so that remote machines know how to send you the information you request.

IP addresses are structured very much like domain name addresses, but backwards. They consist of four numbers, each less than 256, separated by periods. The rightmost number specifies the actual machine, while those to the left identify the network and subnetwork. When I link to the Net via my PPP account with the access provider ThoughtPort, for instance, my IP address is 199.171.225.100. The "100" part of that address is my actual computer on the ThoughtPort network.

OK, that's enough technical talk for now. Let's move ahead to one of the most fascinating Internet resources available, the World Wide Web.

WHAT IS THE WORLD WIDE WEB?

There is a lot of confusion among the general public about what the Web really is, and especially about how it relates to the Internet as a whole. Let's clarify these issues right now.

The World Wide Web is, quite simply, a global hypermedia document that resides on and stretches across most of the Internet. Whoa! What the !@#$ am I talking about? To understand the Web you really need to know what we mean by hypertext and hypermedia.

HYPERTEXT AND HYPERMEDIA

Imagine you are reading this book on your computer screen instead of on the page. As you read along, you notice that some of the words are underlined and may appear in a different color or **font**, just like that. In this example, you try clicking your mouse on the word font. Magically, a new document appears on your screen, explaining what fonts are. This new document also contains words and phrases that you can click on, taking you to yet other documents or to other places in the same document. That's what *hypertext* is all about: the nonlinear presentation of text, letting you jump from idea to idea following your own associative pathways. The clickable words and phrases are known as links, and the activity of moving around through these linked documents is known as *browsing*.

Now imagine that when you click on the **font** link you don't just get a text explaining fonts. Instead, a fancy picture pops up, a colorful depiction of fonts through the ages from Guttenberg to Adobe. Perhaps you're even presented with a video clip complete with Charlton Heston narration and a corny John Williams score. Congratulations! You've just learned what *hypermedia* is: the nonlinear presentation not just of text, but of a variety of other media including graphics and sound.

HYPERMEDIA ON THE NET

So what's this got to do with the Internet? Well, this is where it gets interesting. When you click on a link, the document that you get—whether it's text, graphics, sound, or full-motion video—does not have to be on the same machine as the original document. Thanks to a special protocol known as *HyperText Transfer Protocol* (HTTP), the primary protocol for the World Wide Web, you can access documents on any public World Wide Web server on the Internet! The original document might be on your own computer, or on the Netscape site; the video clip about fonts might reside on a machine in Hollywood or Timbuktu. Now here's the conceptual leap that makes this new technology so exciting: you can think of the collection of all the documents linked together as one big hypermedia document.

Let's go back to our original definition of the Web: a global hypermedia document that resides on and stretches across most of the Internet. Make sense now?

WHAT'S SO GREAT ABOUT HYPERMEDIA?

Suppose you're reading one of those wonderful but frustrating Russian novels in which 36 major characters are introduced during the first two chapters. If you're anything like me, you'll continually find yourself flipping back and forth trying to keep track of who's who. Was Natasha Galanskaya the one who ran away with the Count against her father's wishes, or was that Natalia Balanchina? Wouldn't it be great if you could just push a button on a character's name and instantaneously be transported to a full description of that character's relevant history? Well, you can't do that in a book or a magazine or even a regular computer document, but the magic of hypermedia makes it possible.

Let's look at another example of how hypermedia can improve the communication process, and even make learning more fun and interesting. Suppose you're a high school student studying astrophysics. One option is to open your textbooks and review the mathematics of planetary motion in the abstract. Even if you enjoy solving a few motion problems, it's still a fairly boring exercise. But what if your physics lab computer is linked to the Web and takes you to a virtual textbook with animations that show the orbits of the bodies, in full color and motion? Or plays back short lectures on the day's exercises, by the foremost authority in the field? Educators and trainers know the power of multimedia to speed learning and increase students' retention levels. This type of presentation has become popular in education and corporate training environments, as it presents information in an interesting and entertaining format.

When we click on the graphics, video, and sound objects embedded in a compound-document Web page, we are fulfilling prophesies made years ago for a global information system. When you're up and running with Netscape Navigator 3.0, you'll see exactly what all the excitement's about.

SERVERS & BROWSERS

The Web utilizes what is sometimes called a client-server model. Special machines or software known as World Wide Web servers make the linked hypermedia documents available to the public. Individuals then move around through these documents using software known as Web clients or, more commonly, Web browsers. Obviously a Web browser has to be able to display or "play" a wide variety of hypermedia formats.

Because the World Wide Web uses a standardized protocol (HTTP) for transferring the information across the Internet, and because all Web software adheres to this protocol, any kind of Web browser will work with any kind of Web server. For instance, a site may decide to use one of the server packages developed by Netscape, but any World Wide Web browser will be able to access the information available at that site. Conversely, the browser we are discussing in this book, Netscape Navigator 3.0, can access hypermedia documents on any Web server anywhere in the world.

WHAT'S A HOME PAGE?

Once you start exploring the World Wide Web, you'll encounter the term *home page* or *homepage* over and over again, and it won't always be used the same way. Here are some of the things it can mean:

- A home page is the document that's displayed by a Web browser such as Netscape Navigator 3.0 when you first load the program. This document may be located on your local machine or at a remote site. In the case of Netscape Navigator, the default home page is a document located at Netscape's own Web site, but as with most other browsers, you can change this.

■ A home page is the top-level document at a particular Web site. For instance, a typical small business's home page would contain a title, a logo, some introductory information, and a bunch of links to more detailed marketing information.

■ A home page is a personal Web document created by an individual and made available to the public (Joe Blow's 15 kilobytes of fame). Many access providers now let users copy Web documents to their public Web servers, and the Net sprouts hundreds of new personal home pages every day. You'd be surprised who's out there!

■ In some contexts, a home page is simply any hypertext Web document, though I have to admit it bugs me when I hear people use the term this way.

A Quick Dip in Acronym Soup

OK, let's get all of our technical-sounding acronyms out of the way in OSF (one swell foop). There are only two you really need to worry about: HTML and URL. Not only will they give you a better handle on navigating around the Web, but if you pepper your conversation with them, many people will think you are really cool in a geeky sort of way.

HTML

All Web pages that contain text are written in a language called HTML, which stands for HyperText Markup Language. HTML is a subset of SGML (Standard Generalized Markup Language), a very generalized system originally designed for typesetting and document page description. HTML is simply ordinary ASCII text with embedded codes (usually referred to as *tags*) that represent instructions for displaying the text or for linking to other Web documents. For example, *<I>italic</I> or <B>bold</B>* in a Web document tells the browser to display the phrase "italic or bold" with the word "italic" in italics and the word "bold" in boldface. It is important to understand that HTML does *not* indicate exactly what the resulting text should look like—that is up to the browser software. On a system that can't display true italic or bold fonts, for instance, the browser might just display the words in a different color. When you author your own Web document, you simply label various text elements rather than specifying exactly what the text will look like. This makes HTML a universal language, ensuring that Web pages are displayable in one way or another on any conceivable machine or operating platform.

Figure 1-6 shows a typical Web page, and Figure 1-7 shows what some of the HTML source for it looks like.

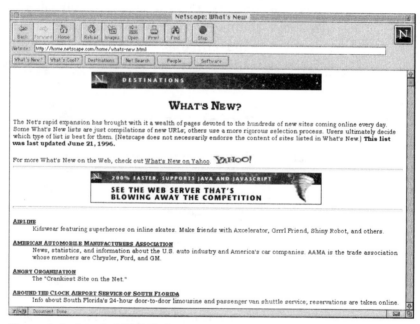

Figure 1-6: *A typical HTML document.*

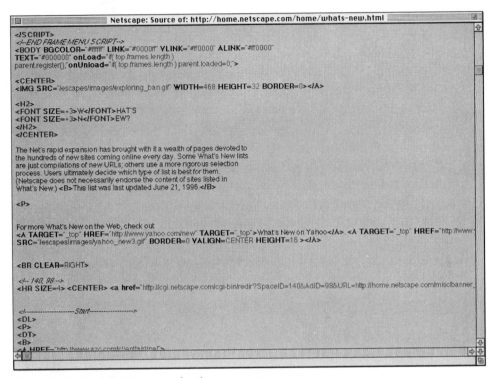

Figure 1-7: *The HTML source for the same page.*

TIP

Yes, Netscape Navigator 3.0 not only displays Web documents properly, it also lets you see the source for any document it displays! This is especially useful if you're learning how to create your own Web page. Simply select Document Source from the View menu.

HTML is an evolving language. Tim Berners-Lee of the European Particle Physical Laboratory (CERN) in Switzerland, started it all in 1990 by releasing an initial specification to the public. It was pretty basic, supporting only the basic text handling tags. Berners-Lee started an Internet mailing list to solicit suggestions for refining and adding to the language, and in 1992 Dan Connolly released a "level 1" HTML specification. As soon as it was released, work began on a level 2 specification that would contain more advanced text handling capabilities. HTML 2.0, now completed and approved by a standards body known as the Internet Engineering Task Force (IETF), also includes support for interactive forms and imagemaps. Interactive forms let you enter data on the screen that is then sent to the host site, and imagemaps let you link to other documents by clicking on "hot spots" within an image. Most good browsers now support the HTML 2.0 features.

HTML FILENAMES

Files that contain HTML tags are known as HTML files, and they always have an extension of either .HTM or .HTML. On UNIX and other systems that support long filenames, the extension is .HTML; on DOS-based systems, it's .HTM. This extension tells the browser it is dealing with a hypertext document rather than some other type of hypermedia document, such as an image or audio file.

What's next? HTML 3.0, of course! Netscape has been at the forefront of the collaborative design process in proposing *and implementing* new features for HTML 3.0. Many of these exciting new extensions are covered later in this book, particularly in Chapter 9, "Power Navigator 3.0."

MORE HISTORY

If you're the kind of person who likes to know all about the origins and evolution of new information technologies, here are some sites to try once you've learned how to use Netscape Navigator 3.0:

- About the World Wide Web (http://www.nmsi.ac.uk/usage/).

- World Wide Web and CERN (http://www1.cern.ch/CERN/ WorldWideWeb/WWWandCERN.html).

- The World Wide Web: Origins and Beyond (http:// homepage.seas.upenn.edu/~lzeltser/WWW/).

I mentioned before that HTML also includes the format for specifying links to other documents or to other areas of the same document. Here's what one of these links looks like:

```
<a href="http://www.faraway.com/explain-directory/
explain.html">Click here for an explanation</a>
```

Looks a little strange, doesn't it? That's OK. All you really need to know is that when you click the phrase "Click here for an explanation" a new HTML document (the file explain.html, which is located at a remote site) pops up. This will all make more sense when you learn about URLs, and so without further ado. . . .

URL

URL stands for Uniform Resource Locator. Back when $10 was worth something, that's what we used to call a bunch of $10 words, but it's really pretty simple. URLs are like signs pointing to hypermedia documents on the Web. They provide the protocol and addressing information that Netscape Navigator 3.0 or another browser uses to connect to the target document. The first part of a URL specifies the type of data or the protocol necessary to retrieve the data, the second part specifies the server where the information is located, and the optional third part specifies the exact path to that data. For instance, the URL http://www.vmedia.com/vvc/index.html tells Netscape Navigator 3.0 to retrieve the file index.html from the vvc directory at www.vmedia.com (Ventana Online's Web server) using the HTTP protocol, the basic support protocol on the Web. (See Chapters 6 and 7 for information about accessing resources available via other major Internet protocols, including FTP and Gopher.)

URLs are used in several different ways. First of all, they are part of the HTML tags that tell your browser to jump to a remote document. In the middle of an HTML file, for instance, the above URL might be used like this:

```
<a href="http://www.vmedia.com/vvc/index.html">Click here to
go to the Ventana Online home page!</a>
```

You can also type URLs directly into Netscape Navigator 3.0 to jump immediately to a remote document. And finally, you can add URLs to Netscape Navigator 3.0 as "bookmarks" for easy access at some later time.

NETSCAPE NAVIGATOR 3.0 & THE FUTURE OF THE WEB

Remember how I said that any Web browser can access hypermedia documents from anywhere on the Web? If that's true, why would you choose one browser over another, especially since there are a number of shareware and even freeware browsers available?

Well, here's the catch: while any browser can *access* available documents, different software packages vary greatly in their ability to *present* hypermedia information to you. For instance, some browsers are exclusively text-based. If you click on a link to a graphics document, all you'll get is a message saying something like "There is a picture here." But even among browsers that support a wide variety of hypermedia formats, there are still differences. For instance, different browsers support different versions or different features of HTML. Some browsers, for instance, will not let you enter information into interactive forms that may be essential for online shopping, or may not be able to display text in table format. As I mentioned earlier, Netscape Navigator 3.0 not only supports the full range of standard HTML features, it also supports a huge number of *proposed* HTML features; formatting options that are very likely to become standards in the next couple of years. With Netscape Navigator 3.0, you can view the future of the Web today.

WEB CONFERENCING

Some of you may be familiar with electronic BBS's, or Bulletin Board Systems, which allow users to post public messages in various discussion areas or forums. Others of you may be familiar with CompuServe or America Online, which also have discussion areas for people with similar interests. This format for electronic communications has been around since the mid-eighties, but ironically one of the newest trends on the Web is to emulate this approach with HTML forms. In other words, you can now use Netscape Navigator 3.0 to log onto what looks something like an old-fashioned BBS and then read and post messages. The Web pages, forms, and special scripts that support this kind of communication are often called *Web conferencing systems*. Web conferencing systems reside on Web servers. Though they are technically accessible using any forms-capable Web browser, they often require users to register before actually reading or posting messages.

To see a Web conferencing system in action, you might want to take a look around Utne Reader's Web "café," which is more like a salon where people discuss culture, politics, and art as well as the usual technical issues. You will have to go through a registration procedure, but it's worth it. The URL is: http://www.utne.com.

SOME POINTERS ON USING THE NET

OK, we talked about the Internet a little, then about the World Wide Web. We're going to end this chapter by focusing once more on the Internet as a whole. The Web, after all, is really only one feature—albeit a dazzling one—of the new information landscape. And remember, Netscape Navigator 3.0 is more than a Web browser, it is more like a luxury cruise-mobile for exploring *all* the resources of the Net. And so in this section, I'd like to give you some very general pointers on using the Net effectively and efficiently.

Some people view the Internet as an experiment in grassroots self-governance. There aren't many laws, and there aren't many cops, and the best way to keep it that way is with generosity and common sense. If the Internet is to stay the wide-open magical place it is today, users will have to keep concentrating on the welfare of the community as a whole instead of exploiting it for individual gain. The Net can be seen as an *information environment* in which everything is interconnected, and we should all practice our "Internet ecology."

The online culture has developed its own guidelines, and before actually exploring the Net, it's a good idea to get familiar with some of these mostly unwritten rules of the road. Here are just a few that will make your Internet travels more efficient, more pleasant, and more "ecological." I think these guidelines are so important that I try to include the following subsections in every book I write. (Sure took that Harlequin Romance editor by surprise!)

AVOID TRAFFIC JAMS

They call it a superhighway, but sometimes it's more like driving through Bombay. Every day several thousand clueless newbies start exploring the Net. (Don't worry, you're not one of them: you bought this book!) Servers can support only a certain number of clients, and routers start to seem "sludgy" when they're called upon to transfer packets of data for thousands of users. Certain sites are practically impossible to reach, especially those distributing the latest free software or pictures of naked people.

To avoid traffic jams, and to avoid creating them, follow these simple rules of thumb:

- Connect during nonbusiness hours whenever possible. (Since this is a world-wide system, remember to compensate for different time zones!)

- If you're unable to connect with a particular server—for instance, if you get an "unable to connect with host" message when you try to access a Web page—wait a while before trying again. Bombarding the Net with unsuccessful connection attempts only adds to the problem.

- Use what are known as "mirror sites" for downloading files via FTP. Since some of the large anonymous FTP servers are so busy, a number of hosts sprinkled around the Net have been kind enough to "mirror" the exact contents, keeping their file lists completely up-to-date. The original site usually informs you about these mirror sites in its sign-on message. FTPing to a mirror is just like FTPing to the original host, except that you'll be out of the heaviest traffic.

- Find the closest site that has what you need. Don't Telnet to Timbuktu if you can get the same information by FTPing to Peoria. When you access far-flung reaches of the globe, your packets of information must travel point-to-point through dozens of locations.

- Don't create unnecessary message traffic. This is especially important in Usenet newsgroups (see Chapter 5, "Newsgroups"). If you have something to say, by all means say it, but the Net provides a useful venue for practicing eloquent restraint. Don't send the text of your Great American Novel to the whole world, simply tell users where they can find it. And remember that even a short message like "Ha ha ha!" expands to several hundred bytes of control and addressing information, and may require the services of dozens of routers. Sending a message like this may look free to you, but it definitely costs the community as a whole.

- Follow any instructions that are given to you for logging off a particular site. If you don't follow the proper procedures for logging off from a Telnet site, for instance, a connection may be left open, perhaps making it difficult for others to log in.

UNDERSTAND ACCEPTABLE USE

Certain networks on the Internet, including the large backbones, have published standards for information that may be transmitted via their equipment and cabling. When you sign up with an access provider, you are mailed or e-mailed a document that outlines the acceptable use policies in effect for the networks used by that provider. You must adhere to these strictly! Besides the obvious prohibitions against using the network for trafficking in drugs and bombs, these policies usually make clear what kinds of commercial activities are permitted.

Here's a typical list of prohibitions from an acceptable use policy statement:

- Users may not transmit any data or programs that cause disruption of service for others.

- Users may not transmit any form of computer worm or virus.

- Users must not use the network to violate intellectual property laws by distributing copyrighted or otherwise protected information, documents, or software programs.

- Users may not distribute unsolicited advertising.

But the written policies are really only the beginning of acceptable use. Common sense and respect for others should be your guiding principles when communicating over the Net. The Internet is not a good place for personal attacks and threats, as they frequently escalate into full-blown "flame wars" that waste resources. It's not necessarily a good place for challenging local community ethical standards, either, since various factions are looking for excuses to impose more stringent regulation. Make sure that you post your materials at the appropriate sites.

RESPECT & PROTECT PRIVACY

Privacy is the big hot topic on the Internet today. To what extent should government agencies have access to private Internet communications? Should the content of public sites be regulated? Should there be safeguards against commercial entities adding you to electronic mailing lists? It remains to be seen how these issues will be decided, but it is very clear that the Internet community expects its citizens to respect the privacy of other individuals. Nothing will get you in more trouble than trying to "hack" somebody else's account, trying to take advantage of technological loopholes to access private data, or publishing confidential information.

At the same time, you should realize that in a culture as large as the Internet there are going to be occasional problems with privacy, and you should do what you can to protect yourself and others by keeping your accounts secure:

■ Always use good, specific passwords; your spouse's name or the name of a *Star Trek* character just won't cut it.

■ Change your passwords often.

■ Always inform the appropriate network administrators when you think there may have been a security breach.

■ If you're worried about particularly sensitive information, use some form of encryption such as Pretty Good Privacy (PGP), which is available on most large anonymous FTP sites.

■ And just in case, don't make any information available on the Net if you wouldn't want it to appear on the front page of *USA Today* or your hometown newspaper. Yes, I learned this lesson the hard way once, but we're not going to talk about that!

BE WILLING TO ASK FOR HELP

In my experience, the most annoying Internet users are those who "know just enough to be dangerous." They go crashing around the Internet, leaving a mess for others to clean up. Look, the Internet is full of *real* experts; if you don't know how to do something, just ask. You'll be amazed at how helpful and friendly the seasoned Net veterans can be. I've asked some pretty stupid questions on the Internet, but only rarely have I received a snooty response.

Of course, before asking questions of other users, you should look for available resources such as help files or appropriate technical documents. The Netscape site, which appears as soon as you load Netscape Navigator 3.0, is full of useful information. Many Usenet newsgroups even maintain files of frequently asked questions, called FAQs. But if you've exhausted other resources, there's nothing wrong with a plea for help.

DON'T BE AFRAID TO EXPLORE

On the other hand, one of the most valuable ways to learn how to use the Net is simply to explore. As long as you're not trying to do something too tricky or arcane, common sense will usually get you where you want to go. Half the fun of the Internet is wandering around, guided as much by your instincts as by a conscious plan. Certainly you can do no harm by getting out there and seeing the world!

MOVING ON

What makes Netscape Navigator 3.0 the premier product for accessing the Internet is not its slick interface, or its availability on a variety of platforms, or its solid reliability, or even its early support of forward-looking Web features. What really sets this product apart is that it lets you do *everything you need to do on the Net*. In addition to browsing the Web, you can use Netscape Navigator 3.0 to send and receive e-mail; to read and post Usenet newsgroup messages; to gather files; and to explore a wide range of specialized Internet services. In the following chapters, we'll be exploring all aspects of this versatility using a hands-on approach, and you'll see for yourself that becoming a seasoned Internaut is easy and fun.

But first let's make sure your system is ready for the trip. The next chapter guides you through the process of getting connected to the Net if you're not already "wired," as well as installing and configuring Netscape Navigator 3.0. If you've already done all of this, you may just want to skim Chapter 2, "Getting Started" and then move ahead to Chapter 3, "A Quick Look Around," where the *real* fun begins!

Getting Started

After learning about some of the resources available on the Net, you're probably eager to get busy exploring this vast new electronic world. Thanks to Netscape Navigator 3.0, it's easy. But as with any journey, there are a few preparations to deal with first. In this chapter, we'll show you:

- How to make sure you have the necessary hardware and software.

- How to connect to the Internet.

- How to install Netscape Navigator 3.0 if you have the version of this book with CD-ROM.

- How to configure Netscape Navigator 3.0 so that it works the way you want it to.

TIP

If you're using Netscape Navigator Personal Edition 3.0, please follow the installation instructions that came with the software. The information below may be helpful as a reference, but Personal Edition includes special features for connecting and establishing an account with a PPP service provider.

Okay, first things first. What exactly do you need to run Netscape Navigator 3.0?

HARDWARE & SOFTWARE REQUIREMENTS

To run the Macintosh version of Netscape Navigator 3.0 including the Audio Playback plug-in, you need:

- Mac System 7.1 running on a 68020, with QuickTime 2.1 and Sound Manager 3.1, or

- Macintosh PPC with a PPC 601 (66MHz) running System 7.1.2, QuickTime 2.1 and Sound Manager 3.1. Users of System 7.5 software will want to install Apple's System 7.5.3 System Update 2.0 which includes the latest version of Open Transport 1.1.

- Minimum of 6MB of hard disk free space.

- At least 8MB of RAM, preferably much more (16MB would be a better operating minimum with the Power Mac and System 7.5).

- If you expect to install the Live3D plug-in version of Navigator 3.0, you will need the Macintosh PowerPC with at least 24MB of physical RAM (16MB for Navigator 3.0 and 8MB for System Software) and be operating with virtual memory turned on. The Live3D version requires a minimum of 10MB hard disk free space during installation. The PPC 604 Power Macintosh is preferred, although Live3D will work satisfactorily on a PPC 601 or PPC 603 system.

- A live connection to the Internet, either via your LAN or via a SLIP or PPP connection with an Internet access provider. If you're using SLIP or PPP, you also need:

  - A modem properly connected to your computer. The modem should be rated for data transmission speeds of at least 14,400 bits per second (bps), and 28,800 bps is strongly recommended.

  - An account with an Internet access provider. If you don't already have one, see the section later in this chapter called "Finding an Internet Access Provider."

■   Software for establishing your connection with your
     Internet access provider and for providing TCP/IP
     communications on your machine. (More about this in
     the section "Connecting to the Internet.")

CONNECTING TO THE INTERNET

Before you can use Netscape Navigator 3.0, you have to be connected to the Internet. There are several different types of Internet
connections. The simplest, from the point of view of the end user
of Netscape Navigator 3.0, is a *permanent LAN connection.*

PERMANENT LAN CONNECTIONS

These days businesses large and small use LANs, or local area
networks, to share files as well as devices such as printers. LANs
are a cost-effective way to coordinate tasks, and they eliminate the
need for multiple copies of business documents. And as a bonus,
many office LANs are wired directly into the Internet via a special
leased line, often a high-speed T1.

Hardwired connections like this really only make economic
sense when several individuals on a LAN need to access the
Internet simultaneously, or when an organization wants to make a
Telnet, FTP, or Web server available for access by remote Internet
users. At this point, leased lines are still too expensive for you to
hardwire your home. Besides, the Internet is so addicting that
round-the-clock access might be dangerous!

If your workplace already has Internet connectivity, you may be
able to fire up Netscape Navigator 3.0 and visit some great interactive game sites right away—on your break, of course. But if you
haven't accessed the Internet from work already, there may be a
few preliminary steps before you can go online. Your network
administrator may need to configure the TCP/IP software on your
local machine, or change some aspects of your network account.
The good news is that there's very little you have to do yourself.
Once you can connect to the Internet from your desk, you're ready
to travel anywhere in cyberspace with Netscape Navigator 3.0.

And if you plan to use Netscape Navigator 3.0 with a permanent LAN connection, you can probably skip the next few sections of this chapter and move ahead to "Internet Connectivity Software."

TIP

If you're on a LAN that supports TCP/IP, you don't necessarily *need a connection to the Internet. Netscape Navigator 3.0 can be used within your organization for accessing documents and sharing multimedia resources on your local file servers without ever connecting to the outside world. While this book emphasizes the Internet, most of the information also applies to the more specialized use of the product. Please see your network administrator for more information.*

But what about Internet access for the home, or for businesses that don't require a round-the-clock hardwired connection? That's where we get into MacSLIP and MacPPP.

SLIP & PPP CONNECTIONS TO THE NET

If you don't have to be linked to the Internet all the time, you can get what is known as a Serial Line Internet Protocol (SLIP) or Point-to-Point Protocol (PPP) account with an Internet access provider. These are dial-up accounts that give you the same full access to the Net as hardwired connections, but you are online only during the time your computer is actually linked by phone with your access provider.

Here's how it works: Whenever you want to be "live on the Net," you click an icon on the desktop or open the appropriate application from your Apple menu, and your computer places a modem call to the access provider. After the remote computer determines that you are in fact a valid customer, it connects you to the Internet, and you communicate using Netscape Navigator 3.0 or any other Internet software just as if you were wired in directly via a LAN. The information you send and receive is in the correct format for communicating over the Net. In addition, each packet of data is "wrapped" with extra information that allows it to be transmitted or received by modem instead of coaxial network cable. This extra envelope is the SLIP or PPP protocol. You need to use only one of them, whichever one your access provider supports.

Many access providers charge by the hour for SLIP or PPP connectivity, but your bill will be much, *much* lower than with a leased line connection, sometimes as low as $20 a month for unlimited connection time.

WHAT ABOUT ISDN?

Normal telephone lines are low-bandwidth analog lines; compared to digital lines, they can't handle large amounts of information very quickly. An ISDN line is a special kind of all-digital line that your phone company may be able to run to your house or office. There are some hefty installation fees, and then you're usually charged by how much you use the line. This fee is in addition to whatever hourly rates you pay your Internet access provider.

In order to use your ISDN line for Internet access, you need a few pieces of specialized equipment and an account with an access provider that supports ISDN connectivity. Unfortunately, you still need to understand some complex terminology before even ordering a line from your phone company. It is beyond the scope of this book to address these issues, and for most individual users ISDN is not yet a cost-effective option. If you want to investigate this connectivity method further, there's lots of information available on the Net itself.

FINDING AN INTERNET ACCESS PROVIDER

You might already have a SLIP or PPP account with an Internet access provider. For instance, if you have already installed the Personal Edition of Netscape Navigator 3.0 or a prior version, you may have already signed up with an access provider. But if you don't currently have a way to get on the Net, this section's for you!

These days there are hundreds of providers to choose from, and there's a good chance you can find one with a local access number. But you might not find the access provider of your dreams in the Yellow Pages, since it's not worth it for companies to list every local point-of-presence. But who needs the Yellow Pages anyway in this electronic age? Just find a friend who is already connected to the Internet and get him or her to point Netscape Navigator 3.0 or some other less cool Web browser to http://thelist.com. (Don't worry, this will all make sense after Chapter 3, "A Quick Look Around.") This document claims to include the most complete list of Internet access providers, conveniently arranged by geographic area. And if there isn't an access number in your area, you can always sign up with one of the larger providers that offer an 800 number service for a small extra fee.

Figure 2-1 shows a small portion of the access provider list, displayed in Netscape Navigator 3.0, of course.

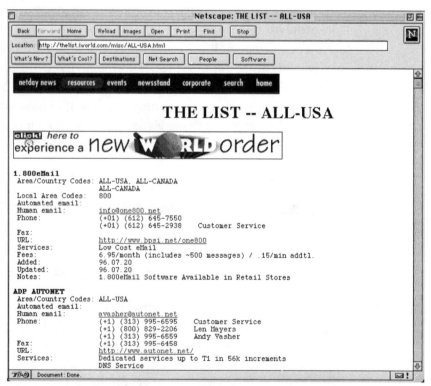

Figure 2-1: *THE LIST of Internet access providers.*

But with all these access providers out there, how do you choose one? Of course, you should call several providers and compare their charges. Just a year or two ago, pricing was all over the map. Luckily, increased competition has both lowered and leveled the pricing, but there can still be a lot of variation. For instance, many access providers offer a number of hours per month for a set fee, and after that charge on an hourly basis. You should ask how many hours are included in the base monthly charge as well as what the rates are for additional online time.

Besides cost, there are a number of other questions you should ask as you shop around for an Internet access provider:

- Do I get an Internet e-mail account at no extra charge? (The answer should be yes.)

- Do you support 28.8 kbps modems? (Even if you don't have a 28.8 kbps modem now, who knows when you might? The answer to this should be yes.)

- Do you have a network news server that includes a full range of Usenet newsgroups? (The answer should be yes, and there should be no extra charge for newsgroup access.)

- Do you have a Web server where I can put up my own Web pages? (This is a service you may not need. If you do, shop around carefully; extra charges for this vary from zero to hundreds of dollars!)

- Which do you provide, SLIP service or PPP service? PPP is preferable.

TIP

Open Transport 1.1, available with System 7.5.3 Update 2.0, can be used with MacPPP version 2.1.4 SD or later, available from Apple as part of the Apple Internet Connection Kit. Serial Line Interface Protocol (SLIP) and Point-to-Point (PPP) connectivity are provided through Link Access Modules (or mdevs) which, when installed on your system, are available in the "Connect Via:" pop-up menu in the TCP/IP control panel. Other supported Link Access Modules include

FreePPP 1.0.4 or later, InterPPP 1.2.9 or later, MacSLIP 3.0.2 or later, and VersaTerm SLIP 1.1.4 or later. For more complete information, check the Open Transport 1.1 Readme file included with your MacOS system software or available via FTP download from Apple Computer, Inc.

- Can you assign me a fixed IP address rather than dynamically assigning one each time I call in? (This is not essential unless you want to set your machine up as a server that can be accessed by the general public.)
- How do you provide technical support? (The answer should be that real-time support is available via a toll-free voice line, and same-day support is available via e-mail and fax.)

And of course if you're considering a small, local access provider, ask around to make sure they can adequately handle the current traffic, can grow to handle the traffic for years to come, and that they can generate enough revenue to stay in business. Once you've given everyone your e-mail address, it can be a real pain to switch providers.

TIP

Many of the large online information services such as America Online, CompuServe, and the Microsoft Network now provide Internet access via dial-up SLIP and PPP. You might want to check out their rates and the availability of access numbers in your area.

INTERNET CONNECTIVITY SOFTWARE

So far everything's been pretty simple and straightforward, right? Well, here's where it gets a bit complicated. Don't worry, the information in this section is the hairiest stuff in this book. If you get through it without scratching your head a time or two you are probably better prepared for this adventure than you suspected.

Unless you are already using Mac System 7.5, which include Apple's Open Transport, you will need a a TCP/IP Open Transport layer. What is a TCP/IP layer? When you type a message into an e-mail program, for instance, it has to be formatted for transmission over the Net; in addition, it has to have an address attached so that it gets to the right destination. Conversely, incoming messages must have the addressing information stripped off and have to be reconstituted into something you can read. This process of packaging and unpackaging Internet information is the task of the *Transmission Control Protocol/Internet Protocol* (TCP/IP) layer.

If you're directly connected to the Internet via a LAN (AppleTalk or Ethernet), that's all you'll need. But to establish an active account with a SLIP or PPP service provider, you also need software that dials an access number and packages TCP/IP packets so that they can be sent out via modem. Fortunately, most TCP/IP software packages also include a dialer and SLIP or PPP features.

TIP

As I mentioned before, Netscape Navigator Personal Edition 3.0 includes everything you need for establishing a PPP connection with an Internet access provider. If you have the Personal Edition, please see the instructions that came with it.

MacPPP is a Macintosh implementation of PPP, the Point-to-Point communications protocol which allows you to use TCP/IP applications over asynchronous serial lines. This means you can use Telnet, FTP, Gopher and WAIS client servers, and other services directly from your Macintosh over conventional voice-grade telephone lines. FreePPP is the "official" successor to the earlier MacPPP which was developed at, and is copyrighted by, the Merit Network, Inc. and the University of Michigan. (These products are shareware, and are therefore readily available.) MacPPP requires MacTCP 1.1 or higher, Macintosh systems 6.0.5 or higher, and a Hayes-compatible modem for dial-in connections. FreePPP currently requires Color QuickDraw, which limits its use to 68020 or higher processors, and also requires System 7.1 or later Macintosh system software.

To use PPP on an earlier Macintosh, you'll need three packages: MacTCP, which is Apple's control panel device that provides a standard network interface for TCP/IP applications; MacPPP or a similar package; and software that supports MacTCP. You must also be dialing into a terminal server which supports PPP. If you have System 7.5, make certain you install 7.5.3 Update 2.0, which includes the latest version (as of this writing) of Open Transport 1.1. According to the developers, Netscape Navigator 3.0 will not work reliably with versions of Open Transport earlier than 1.1!

The service provider you select can be (and should be) a source of comfort and technical support as you proceed down what seems to be a complex technical labyrinth! (Setting up my own Power Macintosh with a local network access provider was simply a matter of my loading an installation diskette they supplied, then following a short set of instructions, and finally making two brief telephone calls to technical support for good, quick answers to some pretty dumb questions!)

When you install separate connectivity software on your system for Internet access, there are several account-specific Internet addresses and other numbers you will need to enter. When you sign up with an Internet access provider, you are usually sent a data sheet that includes this configuration information. Now's the time to drag that piece of paper out and transfer the information into the handy little chart in Table 2-1.

By the way, if you pass this book on to somebody else, or if you keep it where it is accessible to people who are just dying for some free time on the Net, make sure *not* to include your passwords in the access information table!

Name of access provider:
PPP, SLIP, or CSLIP:
Local access number:
My user ID:
My account password:
My IP address, if any:
Subnet mask, if any:
Primary DNS address, if any:
Secondary DNS address, if any:
Address of mail server:
My e-mail account name:
My e-mail password:

Table 2-1: *Personal Internet access information.*

WHERE TO GET INTERNET CONNECTIVITY SOFTWARE FOR MACINTOSH

As I already mentioned, Macintosh System 7.5 already includes Open Transport, a more up-to-date version of MacTCP. But you may still need TCP-based connectivity software to make your system complete. Where do *you* get software for Internet access?

The answer is, it's all over the place! Here are a few of your options:

- Netscape sells a special version of Netscape Navigator 3.0 called the Personal Edition. This software operates exactly like the program included on the CD-ROM that accompanies the CD-ROM Edition of this book, but also includes TCP/IP software as well as a dialer and SLIP or PPP options. It even includes a special introductory offer from an access provider.

■ Ventana Communications Group, Inc., has released several excellent products, such as the Internet Membership Kit for Macintosh and the World Wide Web Kit for Macintosh, that include connectivity software and special offers from access providers.

■ Shareware connectivity products are generally available from large electronic bulletin board systems, colleges and universities, and online services such as AOL and CompuServe. MacPPP is available for anonymous FTP in the file /internet.tools/ppp/mac/macppp2.0.1.hqx on the nic.merit.edu (University of Michigan) host. Extensive documentation is also available from this shareware source. Sites where FreePPP can be found as of this writing include ftp://mirrors.aol.com/pub/info-mac/comm.tcp.conn/ and ftp://mirror.apple.com/mirrors/Info-Mac.Archive/comm/tcp/conn/.

■ MacSLIP is commercial software developed by Hyde Park Software. For availability information in the U.S., phone 1-800-531-5170.

■ MacPPP version 2.1.4 SD is available as part of the Apple Internet Connection Kit, available from Apple Computer, Inc.

INSTALLING A PPP CONNECTION

Obviously it's impossible to cover installing and configuring all these different pieces of software! But don't worry: all of the products just mentioned come with pretty good documentation, and armed with the chart you filled out above, you should do just fine. You should also rely on your access provider for technical support. Most access providers are familiar with a broad range of connectivity software.

If you are able to get to a Web site by some other means, take a close look at http://www.tfs.net/business/tbutler/pppstuff.html. There you will find everything you might want to know about PPP communications on the Macintosh, including some early reviews of Apple's Open Transport. Keep this site in mind, too, for later reference once you're up and running on the Web. Also, visit Apple at http://support.info.apple.com/.

Let's assume for a moment that you've obtained the software we discussed earlier, and you'd like to get a few tips about getting it installed and connected to the Net. Let's start from the beginning, keeping in mind that individual steps may vary depending upon your specific hardware and software configuration:

1. Make sure you have obtained stable versions of MacTCP or Open Transport 1.1 (earlier releases of Open Transport are not stable with Netscape Navigator 3.0), and MacPPP 2.1.4 SD or FreePPP 1.0.5. Use a clean copy of MacTCP. MacTCP Updater 2.0.6 will patch a clean copy from your unused master diskettes updating version 2.0.4 to 2.0.6. MacTCP Updater is free to licensed owners of MacTCP.

2. If you've already been using a version of MacTCP, go to your System folder and drag the MacTCP DNR file to the trash. Also, find MacTCP Prep and PPP Preferences in the Preferences folder, and drag them both to the trash. These files will be recreated for you automatically.

3. Drag your new PPP icon to the Extensions folder, and the ConfigPPP icon to the Control Panels folder, both of which should be in your System folder. Open the MacTCP control panel from the Apple menu, and configure it to use PPP by selecting the PPP icon and clicking on the More button. You should then see a dialog box which looks like Figure 2-2. Select Server in the Obtain Address section of the dialog box, mark C in the Class box of the IP Address (leave the rest alone), then complete the Domain Name Server Information. The first domain name server should be your access provider's host, with its IP address. Mark this one as the default position. Click on the OK button and restart your Mac.

4. If you're using Open Transport 1.1, configure your system with FreePPP. Open the TCP/IP Control Panel and select PPP as the interface to use. Turn on the button marked Manually, and type in 0.0.0.0 for the IP Address assuming

you will be assigned this number dynamically by your server. Subnet Mask and IP Router information will be filled in by the server. Then complete the Domain Name Server information. Click on the OK button and restart your Mac.

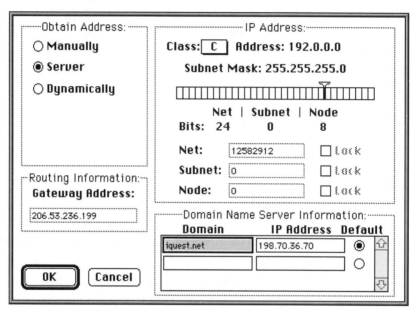

Figure 2-2: *Configuring MacTCP for your new PPP connection.*

Now let's move on to configuring MacPPP or FreePPP so we can connect to the outside world! The following steps assume you are working with FreePPP, the more recent of the two shareware applications.

1. Make sure you have PPP in your Extensions folder. From the Control Panels folder, open Config PPP. Set Port Name to Modem Port, set Idle Timeout (minutes) to None, Set Echo Interval (seconds) to Off, check the Hangup on Close and Quiet Mode boxes. Make sure Terminal Window is <u>not</u> checked. Your completed entries should look similar to Figure 2-3.

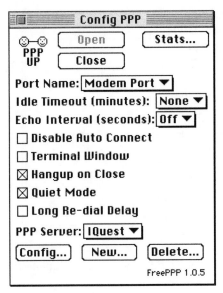

Figure 2-3: *Setting up FreePPP.*

2. Choose the New button, and type in the name of your
   server. Click OK, then click Config. You should see a dialog
   box which looks like Figure 2-4. Set Port Speed to 57,600
   for Global Village Teleport and US Robotics 28.8 bps
   modems. Set other 28.8 baud modems to 38,400 and 14.4
   baud modems to 19,200. Flow Control should probably be
   set to CTS only. Select Tone Dial, type in the access telephone number assigned you by your provider, and set the
   modem initialization string to whatever your modem
   manufacturer recommends. Modem connect timeout
   should be set at 90 seconds. Next, click on Connect Script
   and enter a login script.

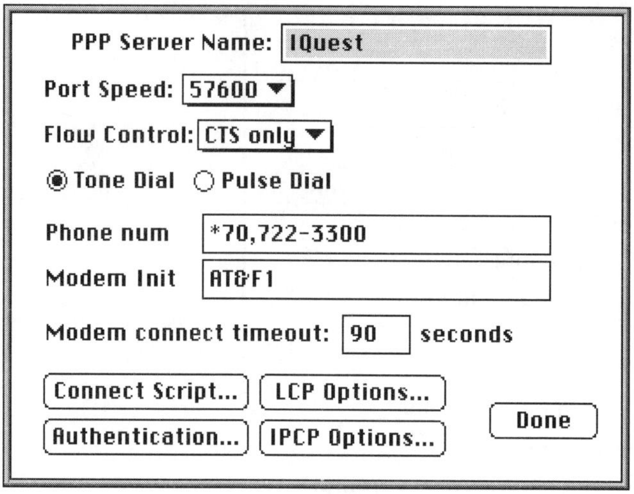

```
PPP Server Name: IQuest

Port Speed: 57600 ▼

Flow Control: CTS only ▼

◉ Tone Dial  ○ Pulse Dial

Phone num    *70,722-3300

Modem Init   AT&F1

Modem connect timeout: 90   seconds

[ Connect Script... ] [ LCP Options... ]
                                          [  Done  ]
[ Authentication... ] [ IPCP Options... ]
```

Figure 2-4: *Configuring MacTCP for your new PPP connection.*

3. Wait Timeout should be set for 30 or 40 seconds. Your login script should look similar to this:

					<CR>
(*)	Out	( )	Wait		[X]
( )	Out	(*)	Wait	gin:	[ ]
(*)	Out	( )	Wait	[your username]	[X]
( )	Out	(*)	Wait	word:	[ ]
(*)	Out	( )	Wait	[your password]	[X]
(*)	Out	( )	Wait		[ ]
(*)	Out	( )	Wait		[ ]
(*)	Out	( )	Wait		[ ]

4. Click on OK, and then on Authentication. If you enter your username and password here, you may let your Macintosh automatically connect you to your server whenever Netscape Navigator 3.0 launches. You may want, on the other hand, to leave these items blank, in which case you will need to enter your username and password each time. This is a security decision you have to make, depending upon whether it is likely or not that others may have indiscriminate access to your system. (I have set my system on "automatic pilot" because I work at home. Others might not be as comfortable as I am with this approach.)

5. Now go to the Control Panels, open Config PPP, make sure you have selected the correct PPP server, and click on Open. At this point, the Open button should be darkened and the words PPP DOWN should be displayed in the upper-left corner of the Config PPP dialog box. If not, make sure that all your fax extensions are turned off, that there is no other program using your modem, and the modem is not set at a speed higher than it's capability.

6. Click on the darkened Open button. The modem will dial out and make a connection. You may see various intervening messages on the screen, indicating what progress is being made. These messages will vary depending upon your access provider's creativity and ingenuity; Macintosh users are accustomed to seeing smiling faces. Therefore, once the connection has been made, the two faces in the upper-left corner of the dialog box will be smiling. So will you! To disconnect, be sure to click on Close.

7. Test your connection with something simple, that is, if you can wait to launch Netscape Navigator 3.0.

For more information about connecting your Mac to the Internet, see the Netscape Press online companion at http://www.netscapepress.com/. Once you have finished installing and configuring MacTCP and MacPPP on your system, your dial-in sessions will be handled automatically. You will simply click on the Open button on MacPPP's Config PPP Control Panel (Netscape Navigator 3.0 will do this for you) and your modem will dial and connect automatically.

Installing Netscape Navigator 3.0

This section is for those of you who have the version of the book with the CD-ROM. If you have already installed Netscape Navigator 3.0, you can skip this section. Or if you want to install Netscape Navigator 3.0 Personal Edition, or a copy of the software you have downloaded from the Internet, make sure to carefully follow the instructions included with the program. Remember, Readme files are our friends.

This is going to be a breeze! Let's get right down to business:

1. It is generally considered good practice to temporarily disable any virus detection software and non-essential Extensions or Control Panels prior to installing new, tested software on your Macintosh. Also, I suggest you set Virtual Memory to Off, at least until you've completed the installation and are running satisfactorily. Once you've done the required housekeeping, insert the CD you will find at the back of this book into your CD-ROM drive.

2. After the NetPress icon appears on your desktop, double-click on it. The NetPress window will open (see Figure 2-5).

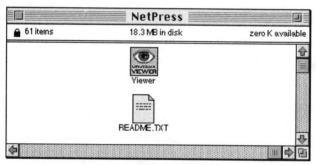

Figure 2-5: *The NetPress Window.*

3. You should view the README.TXT file to learn about the latest changes to the software contained on the Companion CD-ROM, and find out about any additional goodies which might accompany your purchase. Also, in case the software or the CD has changed slightly since this book went to print, you should follow any instructions that appear in the Readme file for installing Netscape Navigator 3.0. You can also click Help for further information.

4. After you have finished with the Readme file, double-click on the Viewer icon. The CD will launch, and the opening screen appears as shown in Figure 2-6.

Figure 2-6: *The highly animated opening screen.*

5. Click on Install Netscape. A new window appears (see Figure 2-7). If you want to continue with installation, click on the Continue button which appears near the bottom of the window.

Figure 2-7: *The introductory window for Netscape 3.0 Installer.*

6. The Netscape 3.0 Installer dialog box appears (see Figure 2-8). Choose Easy Install, which is the automatic default selection displayed in the upper-left corner of the Installer window. Navigator 3.0 will automatically look at your system to determine whether you have a 68000 configuration or the PowerPC, and will install the appropriate version of software. Navigator 3.0 will also place the plug-ins in the proper folders, which is a must! You also have the option of either accepting the default installation location or choosing another location (folder) on the same disk or another disk if your system is so configured. Ignore the button marked Select Folder. Installer will create a folder for you and place the appropriate software there, as well as in your System Folder and a Netscape Preferences folder, as required. For the time being, accept Installer's recommendation; if you make significant changes in your Macintosh system setup at a future time, you can rerun Installer to accommodate those changes.

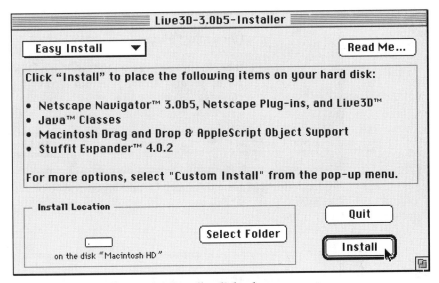

Figure 2-8: *The Netscape 3.0 Installer dialog box.*

7. Once you have determined what you want the installation
   location to be, click Install. A standard Macintosh dialog
   box with a slide bar appears (Figure 2-9) and shows installation and file copy routines in progress.

Figure 2-9: *The familiar look of progress being made on the Macintosh.*

8. Netscape asks whether you want to install the LiveAudio
   Plugin; go ahead, if you have been using QuickTime, but
   skipping this part of the installation is not critical at this
   time. If you're running on a smaller system, you might not
   be able to fully utilize the extensive audio capabilities
   available to you. (see Figures 2-10 and 2-11 for the two
   intermediate dialog boxes which appear before installation
   can continue).

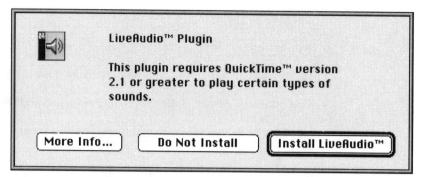

Figure 2-10: *Netscape 3.0 tending to some housekeeping chores involving LiveAudio.*

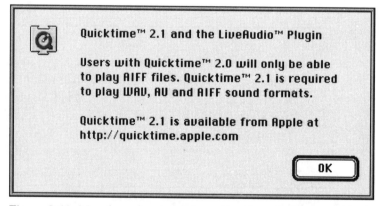

Figure 2-11: *More housekeeping information from the Netscape Navigator installation process.*

9. Once installation is complete, the program pauses and another dialog box appears as shown in Figure 2-12. Unless you want to make other installations, you should click on the Quit button. Netscape Installer has completed this portion of its work, and now it's time for the next sequence of steps to get you onto the Net!

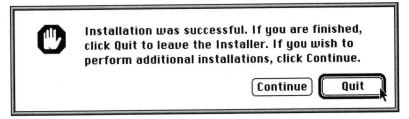

Figure 2-12: *The Netscape Installer shows that installation is complete.*

At this point in the installation process, Netscape Setup offers to take you to the Netscape Setup site, as shown in Figure 2-13. But let's not! Instead, let's pause for a moment to consider what's been accomplished and what more needs to be done. If you select the Continue Setup Later button, the installation program exits and the routine for Netscape Setup is stored in your System Folder as a Startup Item. You'll automatically have the opportunity to continue your installation the next time you restart your Mac!

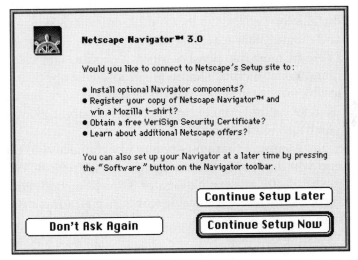

Figure 2-13: *The dialog box asking if you want to connect to the Netscape Setup site.*

Netscape 3.0 Installer has accomplished a lot. You are at the brink of an exciting adventure into Cyberspace. But before you click on that Continue Setup Now button, it might be a good idea to test your communications configuration using something a little less powerful. In order for you to get out onto the Net right away, a few things must be in order:

- You must currently be connected to the Internet via a direct connection (LAN) or a SLIP or PPP connection to your access provider, or

- Your Internet access software must be configured so that it dials your provider automatically when you launch an Internet application.

If you are not currently connected to the Internet and you do not have an automatic dialing feature installed, then you must click the Continue Setup Later button. If there's some question, check it out first before launching Netscape Navigator. A good procedure to follow is to check and double-check each step in the installation process, so that if problems occur your fault isolation and diagnostic troubleshooting process will be quick and certain. Even the most inexpensive modem products for sale in today's marketplace include shareware or low-cost application programs to link you to different dial-up facilities or services which could be used to assure your communications capabilities are okay before you begin working on the Net.

Let's assume that you are already connected to the Internet, and you decide to click on Continue Setup Now. What happens next is that Netscape Navigator 3.0 is launched, within a few seconds the Netscape Navigator Setup window appears, as shown in Figure 2-14.

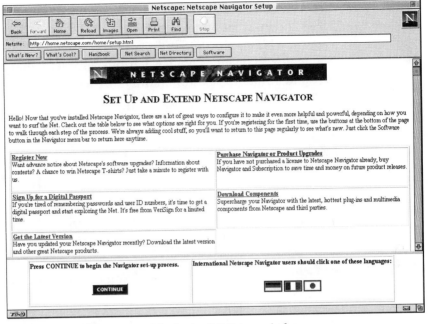

Figure 2-14: *The Netscape Navigator 3.0 Setup window.*

To register your copy of Navigator click Yes. After filling out a short questionnaire, you'll receive your registration number. All you have to do now is follow the instructions that appear. If you can't figure out how to move around at all in the program, you might skim the first few pages of Chapter 3, "A Quick Look Around." And if you get completely disoriented, don't worry: just click the Home button and join the rest of the class in the section called "Configuring Netscape Navigator 3.0."

TIP

By going through the Netscape online registration process, you will automatically receive what is known as a digital ID or digital certificate. This is a unique software key that Netscape Navigator 3.0 can use to identify you to secure Web servers. A digital ID will enable an online bank, for instance, to verify that you are really you—or at least that they're dealing with somebody who's sitting at your machine! For more information about Navigator 3.0's security features, see Chapter 10, "Commerce and Security."

Whether you click Continue Setup Now or Continue Setup Later, the installation program exits, and there is now a new Netscape Navigator folder on your desktop. It contains Netscape Navigator 3.0 itself as well as various supplementary programs and a Readme file, as shown in Figure 2-15.

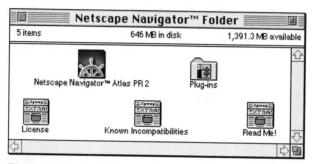

Figure 2-15: *The Netscape Navigator Folder created by Netscape Installer.*

Since only intelligent people buy my books, I'm not going to remind you how important it is to read the ReadMe! file right away. I won't even bother telling you that Readme files often contain crucial, last-minute information, information that can mean the difference between pleasant, trouble-free navigating and late-night wrestling matches with the software.

OK, on to configuring Netscape Navigator 3.0. Even if you worked through Netscape's own online setup instructions, you should still read the next section to check your configuration and gain a better understanding of some of the options.

Configuring Netscape Navigator 3.0

Once it's installed, Netscape Navigator 3.0 needs very little configuration. Most of the default options will work just fine for you, and there are only a few dialog boxes where you have to enter specific information in order to activate a particular feature.

Most of the configuration options are covered in detail in the appropriate chapters of this book, but for now let's take a quick look around in case you want to start customizing the program on your own. To look at the configuration options:

1. Make sure you're connected to the Internet.

2. Double-click the Netscape Navigator 3.0 icon to launch the program. The main window appears, and the Netscape home page starts loading, as shown in Figure 2-16.

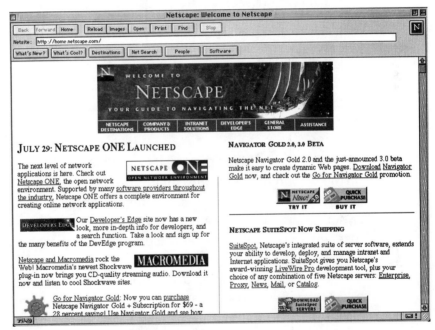

Figure 2-16: *The Netscape home page—Welcome to Netscape!*

That colorful Netscape page probably makes you eager to start exploring right away, but hold on—that's coming up in Chapter 3, "A Quick Look Around."

3. Pull down the Options menu as shown in Figure 2-17.

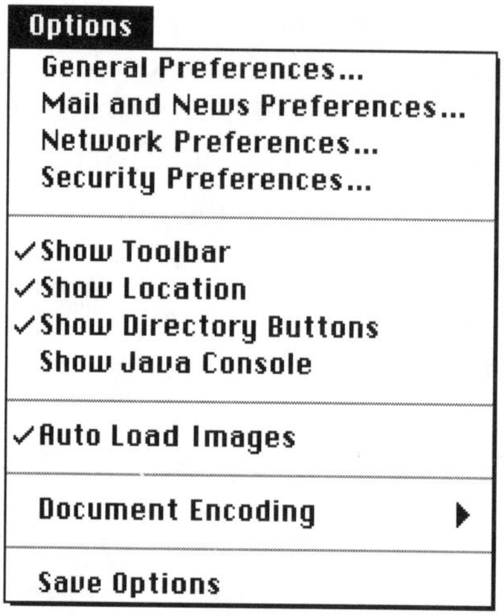

Options
General Preferences...
Mail and News Preferences...
Network Preferences...
Security Preferences...
✓ Show Toolbar
✓ Show Location
✓ Show Directory Buttons
Show Java Console
✓ Auto Load Images
Document Encoding ▶
Save Options

Figure 2-17: *The Options menu.*

ADJUSTING NAVIGATOR'S LOOK & FEEL

In the second section of the Options menu are several "checkmark" items, or toggles. When these items are checked, they are active; when unchecked, they are inactive. Most of them have to do with user interface objects that are displayed in the main Netscape Navigator 3.0 window. Later on, when you get more familiar with the program, you may not need all of the "window dressing." You can play around with these items to see what works best for the way you use the program. But for now leave them alone, or set them back to the default settings after trying them out. That way your screen will look pretty much like the illustrations in this book.

In the top section of the Options menu there are four items representing different areas of Netscape Navigator 3.0 that can be customized: General Preferences, Mail and News Preferences, Network Preferences, and Security Preferences. The Mail and

News settings are covered in Chapters 4, "Netscape Mail," and 5,"Newsgroups," respectively, and the Security settings are covered in Chapter 10, "Commerce and Security." We won't bother looking at those options right now, but let's glance at the General Preferences options so you get a sense of what kind of customization is possible in Netscape Navigator 3.0.

GENERAL PREFERENCES

To access the General Preferences, select General Preferences from the Options menu, shown earlier in Figure 2-17. The Preferences dialog box appears, with the Appearance tab selected as shown in Figure 2-18. If that tab isn't selected, click it now.

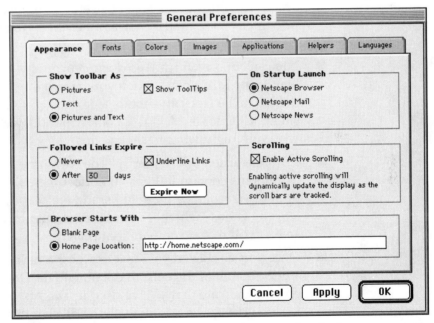

Figure 2-18: *The General Preferences dialog box, opened to the Appearance panel.*

Now we'll go very quickly through each of the tabs, pointing out where you can get more information on each one.

APPEARANCE

In the Appearance panel, you can make several choices that determine how Netscape Navigator 3.0 will look on your screen:

- You can choose whether the toolbar buttons will be displayed as Pictures, Text, or Pictures and Text. The default is Pictures and Text, but you can change this to one of the other options if you find the text annoying, or the pictures too busy. You may also turn Show ToolTips on or off; some folks like Apple's Balloon Help, and ToolTips provides similiarly annoying text messages which appear when the cursor stays over a toolbar button.

- You can choose to have Netscape Navigator 3.0 start with the Mail or News window displayed instead of the usual browser window. This may be useful if you use Navigator principally for e-mail or news rather than Web browsing (see Chapters 4 & 5).

- You can choose which Web document, if any, Netscape Navigator 3.0 displays when you launch the program. The default is the Netscape home page, located at the Netscape site. In Chapter 3, "A Quick Look Around," we'll talk about why you might want to change this.

- As you learned in Chapter 1, "The Net & the Web," Web documents contain links to other documents. You have to be able to recognize these links, and Netscape Navigator 3.0 lets you choose whether or not they should be underlined so that you recognize them more easily.

- Once you've clicked on a link to access a new document, or a new section of the current document, the link changes color to indicate that you've used it. The Appearance tab lets you choose how long the link will stay this new color. More about this in Chapter 3.

■ A new feature is the Enable Active Scrolling option. When enabled by checking the box, movement of the scroll bar thumb causes the content area of the active screen to scroll as you drag. When unchecked, movement of the scroll bar thumb causes the content area to scroll only after the mouse button is released. The default position is enabled. However, on slower computers, scrolling performance might improve when the setting is unchecked.

FONTS

The Fonts panel lets you associate incoming data with particular display fonts. In the United States, just about all the Web information you receive will be in the ISO-Latin-1 character set, and this character set will be displayed using the default Times New Roman and Courier New fonts. However, you can change these fonts if you want.

COLORS

The Colors panel lets you change the default colors for text and links that are displayed in Netscape Navigator 3.0. In addition, it lets you specify a new background color, or even a .GIF file for the display background. You can also decide here whether or not you want Netscape Navigator 3.0 always to use these colors rather than responding to the special color requests in Web documents. Figure 2-19 shows you the color settings available in the Colors panel.

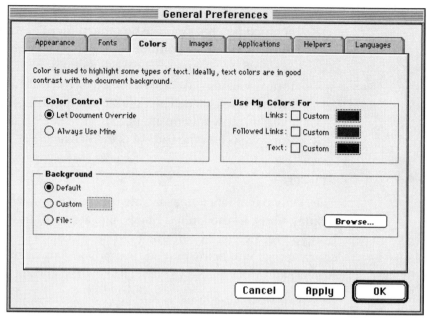

Figure 2-19: *The Colors panel in Netscape Navigator 3.0.*

IMAGES

The Images panel simply indicates when images are to be displayed. The default setting is the While Loading radio button, which will display images a little quicker. While Loading allows Navigator 3.0 to paint your screen as resources become available, rather than waiting until the entire document or page is loaded. We'll discuss these settings in Chapter 8, "Graphics, Sound & Video."

APPLICATIONS

To access Telnet resources, Netscape Navigator 3.0 can launch a separate application anywhere on your hard drive. This allows you the maximum flexibility in connecting to sites via Telnet or TN3270 (please see Chapter 7, "Gopher & Telnet," if you don't know what I'm talking about). The Applications panel lets you choose what applications to use. In addition, it lets you specify an external text viewer or editor to look at the source HTML code of Web documents you view, and you can even choose the work directory Netscape Navigator 3.0 uses to store temporary files.

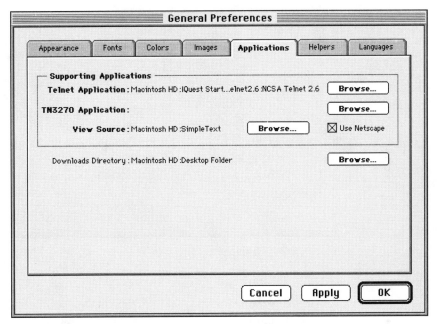

Figure 2-20: *The Applications panel.*

HELPERS

Helper applications are separate programs on your system that handle particular tasks for Netscape Navigator 3.0. For instance, a helper application might play a sound that's included in a Web document, or display a video clip. When Netscape Navigator 3.0 encounters particular kinds of files that are part of Web documents, it launches the appropriate helper applications. The Macintosh Helpers panel has been redesigned to simplify editing, adding, and deleting helper applications and plug-ins. You will read lots more about helper applications and this panel in chapters 7, 8, and 9.

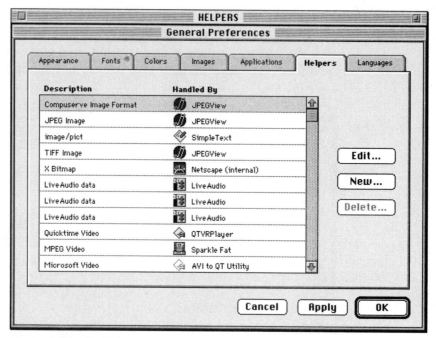

Figure 2-21: *The Helpers panel.*

LANGUAGE

The Language panel is self-explanatory: this is where you choose the language used by Netscape Navigator 3.0. Some of us are eagerly awaiting a Klingon radio button in this panel.

CACHE SETTINGS

Okay, bear with me for a few minutes, we're going to get a little bit technical. It won't hurt too much, and it's for your own good. (Do you ever *really* believe it when people tell you that?) If you're not too worried about performance right now, you can just skip the rest of this chapter and come back here later. But if you want to make sure Netscape Navigator 3.0 is operating as efficiently as possible—and this can be important when you're paying for Internet access on an hourly basis—read on.

A *cache* (pronounced "cash") is a reserve area on your computer that houses information downloaded from the Internet as you navigate. You can think of it as a temporary holding area that Netscape Navigator 3.0 uses to store data between the time it is downloaded and the time it is displayed. If your cache is large enough, it can store entire Web pages and even graphics. That way, when you return to a previously visited site, Netscape Navigator 3.0 doesn't have to download the information all over again; it can simply grab it from the cache.

There are actually two forms of cache: memory cache and hard disk cache. Memory (real RAM) holds text and graphics only as long as you run Netscape Navigator 3.0. The hard disk cache, on the other hand, is persistent: it holds information even after you exit the program. That way you can retrieve large documents quickly, without having to re-download them from the original site on the Net.

> ### TIP
>
> *The Netscape Navigator 3.0 Load Images command (available from the View menu or the Images button on the toolbar), displays the current document using information stored on your system in the cache. The Reload command, on the other hand, actually goes back to the original document on the Net, compares it to the current document on your system, and reloads the most current version. If you think that a document may have changed since the last time you visited it during the current session, you could use the Reload button to view the updated material.*

There are advantages and disadvantages in using high cache sizes for both types of caches. Even though memory (RAM) caches are much quicker than disk caches, devoting more RAM to this type of cache can slow down your computer's overall performance. On the other hand, higher disk cache settings eat up your hard disk space.

Follow these steps to change your settings for cache sizes:

1. Select Network Preferences from the Netscape Navigator
   3.0 Options menu. The Cache panel, shown in Figure 2-22,
   will automatically open and display the first of five Network Preferences panels.

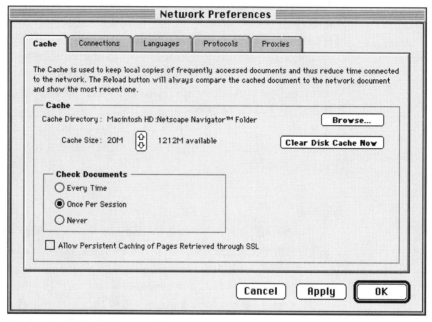

Figure 2-22: *The Cache panel.*

2. Set the amount of hard disk space that you want to reserve
   for a disk cache. This value is entered in the Cache Size
   field; its default setting is 10MB of hard disk space. In the
   example shown in Figure 2-22, the Cache Size has been
   adjusted up to 20MB, using the up arrow on the switch
   button. (We've still got 1.212 gigabytes left on the machine
   we're using to write this—as you can see from the notation
   1212M available.) On newer systems which come standard
   with 500MB and sometimes much larger hard drives,
   setting Cache Size at 20MB or more should be no problem!
   Too large a disk cache might, however, be slower than
   what time it might take to reload images. You'll have to

experiment (I tried 20MB, and turned Cache Size back down to 10MB when the larger cache seemed to slow down my Macintosh PPC.)

3. You may want to experiment with the amount of RAM you allocate to Netscape Navigator 3.0, using the Get Info command in the Finder menu (refer to Figure 2-23 for a reminder of how this information is presented on Macintosh systems). With Virtual Memory turned off, 16MB is the minimum recommended amount of RAM which should be allocated to a complete version of Navigator 3.0 with QuickTime plug-ins and Live3D. Without Live3D, you might get by with 10MB of physical RAM. Virtual Memory allows you to use about 3.2MB less for Navigator 3.0, which might make room for another application to be used concurrently. Less robust implementations of Navigator 3.0 will require less memory; once you've gained experience, you could try adding and subtracting different features and plug-ins to optimize performance.

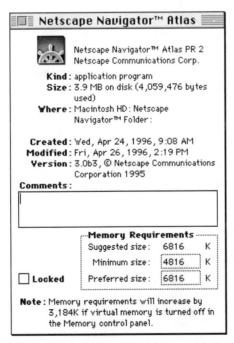

Figure 2-23: *Memory requirements information from Get Info, with Virtual Memory turned on.*

Experiment with Virtual Memory and memory requirements settings, and hard disk cache sizes, to determine the best performance options for your system. If you tend to use Netscape Navigator 3.0 without other applications running at the same time, such as a word processor or spreadsheet, you should set the memory allocation much higher to make Netscape Navigator 3.0 run quicker. In Finder, pull down the Apple menu and review the About This Macintosh information window. To set the memory allocation for Netscape Navigator 3.0 to a higher value, use Get Info from the Finder and reset the recommended and preferred memory settings. My experience is that you cannot allocate too much memory to Navigator 3.0!

4. You can change the directory or folder in which Netscape Navigator 3.0 stores the cached items to disk by selecting Browse (refer to Figure 2-22), which will automatically take you to the Macintosh File Menu shown in Figure 2-24. If you click on the Default button, Netscape Navigator 3.0 creates a directory called CACHE in the Netscape Navigator 3.0 folder. Unless you have specific reasons for changing it, this location should be fine.

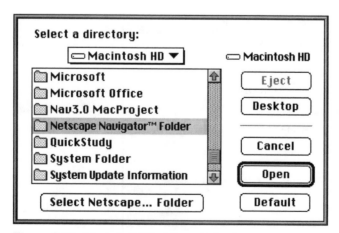

Figure 2-24: *Macintosh File Menu dialog box.*

5. To clear the current content from your disk cache, click on the Clear Disk Cache Now button on the Cache panel as shown in Figure 2-22. A confirmation box pops up, warning you that clearing the cache will remove all files located there. Click OK to confirm that you do; click Cancel if you change your mind.

WHY WOULD I WANT TO CLEAR A CACHE?

Depending on how much navigating you do or how often you visit a site, you may want to periodically clear a cache setting. Having a cache decreases the time it takes to access sites that you've recently visited, but it does increase the strain on your local computer. When your memory requirement is set to a very high value, the amount of memory devoted to Netscape Navigator 3.0 cannot be used by other resources. This slows down your machine when you run these other applications. You may experience an Out of Memory message, precluding you from concurrently using other desirable applications. Also, you may want to clear the cache if you've been online for several hours and you feel your machine responding sluggishly to Netscape Navigator 3.0. After you clear the cache, you should notice an improvement in your Mac's performance.

6. Click one of the radio buttons in the Check Documents section. If a document stored in cache has been revised, you'll want to see the revision instead of the old document. These buttons specify how Netscape Navigator 3.0 checks the Web for document revisions:

   ■ **Once Per Session.** Checks for page revisions only once during the time you start and quit Netscape Navigator 3.0. This is the default setting.

- **Every Time.** Checks for changes each time you request a Web document rather than relying on data stored in the cache. Because Netscape Navigator 3.0 is constantly checking the cached item against the Web page, you encounter a little performance degradation when you use this option.

- **Never.** Performs no verifications; a page available in cache is always brought from cache. Not a good selection if you want to see the latest-and-greatest offerings at a particular Web site.

7. You can ignore the Allow Persistent Caching of Pages Retrieved through SSL option. I'll cover that in Chapter 10.

8. Click OK to return to the main Netscape Navigator 3.0 window.

SETTING NETWORK CONNECTIONS

One way to speed up a connection to a site is to increase the number of connections to a specific server (a server is the computer that houses the Web page). With more than one connection to a server, Netscape Navigator 3.0 can bring in a page's text and multiple image files simultaneously. You can set this by clicking the Connections tab after selecting Network Preferences from the Options menu. By specifying a larger number of connections in the Number of Connections field (4 is the default), you are specifying more simultaneous connections. However, doing so can slow down the speed of each individual connection.

The other setting in this panel is the Network Buffer Size value. You can set the amount of data that your computer receives per transmission. The default is 8KB. Larger values may speed things up, but they may also allow so much data through that your computer becomes saturated. This means it may slow down instead of speeding up. Unless you really know what you are doing, you should leave this setting as it is.

When you're done looking through the Network Preferences tabs, simply click the Cancel button to return to the main Netscape Navigator 3.0 window. Now you can either exit the program or get busy exploring the Net. I know which I'd do!

Moving On

By now you know how to get on and off the Internet, and you have Netscape Navigator 3.0 installed on your computer. Netscape Navigator 3.0 is so easy to use that I'd be surprised if you have any trouble at all cruising around and discovering exciting new resources on the Net.

In the next chapter, you'll learn all the basics of using Netscape Navigator 3.0 effectively, and subsequent chapters will show you how to take advantage of some of the program's most powerful features. Before you know it, you'll be a seasoned Net explorer, cruising from newsgroups to file archives to hypermedia Web sites with a few easy clicks of the mouse.

A Quick Look Around

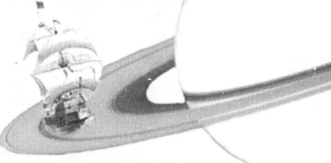

Now that you've installed Netscape Navigator 3.0 and configured it so that it works properly on your system, it's time to take a look around the Net. In this chapter, you'll learn some basics of the program and of Internet navigation. You'll learn:

- How to use the various controls in the program.

- How to move around a Web document, and how to get from one document to another.

- How to take advantage of exciting Web resources like Yahoo!, where you can easily search for specific topics and keywords on pages all around the world.

- How to use navigation aids such as the history list, bookmarks, and desktop shortcuts.

Netscape Navigator 3.0 is so simple to use that you can really master the program by trial and error. I taught my daughter how to use it by saying, "When you see some words that are underlined and in another color, click on them. That takes you to other places." After an hour she was whizzing around the Web like a seasoned veteran. Of course, she is 13 years old and learns this kind of stuff a lot faster than those of us who were born before desktop computers and Nintendo. By the end of this chapter, you may not quite be an adolescent Web-geek, but you'll know how to use the main features of Netscape Navigator 3.0 and how to find what you're looking for quickly and easily. Now let's get going!

THE NETSCAPE NAVIGATOR 3.0 WINDOW

We'll start by taking a closer look at the Netscape Navigator 3.0 main window:

1. Make sure you're connected to the Internet, either directly or through a SLIP or PPP connection with your access provider. If you are using MacPPP or Free PPP, Netscape Navigator 3.0 should launch your communications connections automatically when you start up the Netscape Navigator 3.0 application. You may want to put a Netscape Navigator 3.0 alias in your Start-up folder so that you launch automatically when you turn on your Macintosh. Memory availability and competing applications will determine whether this is a good idea. Check the About This Macintosh information display (see Figure 3-1) in the Apple menu with Finder selected to determine whether you've got the system capability to keep everything you need open concurrently.

   ■ If you launch Navigator 3.0, but see a message displayed that says a network connection cannot be found, click on OK, quit Netscape Navigator 3.0, and return to the Config PPP application in the Control Panels. Config PPP requires a hard close in order to properly reset your communications capability. You may need to turn your modem off momentarily to reset. If Netscape Navigator 3.0 does not launch your connection automatically, troubleshoot by starting up your connection using Config PPP only.

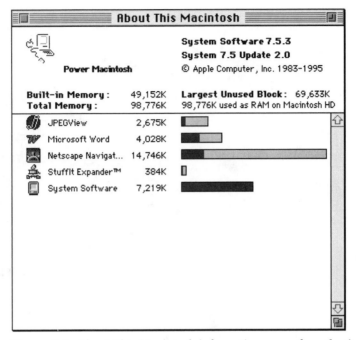

Figure 3-1: *About This Macintosh information screen from the Apple menu.*

2. Double-click the Netscape Navigator 3.0 icon to launch the program. The main window appears, and the Netscape home page starts loading as shown in Figure 3-2.

   ■ By default, Netscape Navigator 3.0 uses the Netscape home page as your personal home page (your *home page* is the document that loads automatically when you launch the program). Depending on the speed of your Internet connection and how busy the Netscape site is, this might take a few moments. Later in the chapter, you'll learn how you can select a different Web document as your home page in the sidebar "Changing Your Home Page."

   ■ If you configured Navigator 3.0 so that it requires a password, you will be asked to enter your password when you launch the program. For more about passwords, see Chapter 10.

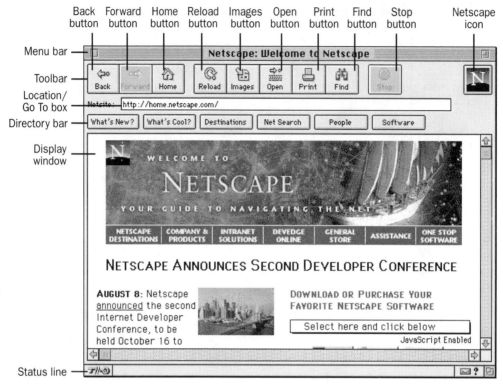

Figure 3-2: *The Netscape Navigator 3.0 window with the Netscape home page open.*

Let's identify each of the major components of the Netscape Navigator 3.0 window:

- **The menu bar**. Like other Macintosh programs, Netscape Navigator 3.0 arranges many of its user-accessible features in a menu bar across the top of the window. Some menu families like File and Edit are familiar and practically self-explanatory, while others are unique to an Internet application. We'll discuss the Bookmarks and Directory menu families in detail later in this chapter, in the "Bookmarks" section and in the "Directory Menu" sidebar. Take a moment to look around the menu bar items. As you pull down various menus, you will notice that many are similar to the toolbar and directory items in the Netscape Navigator 3.0 window. We'll save the review of the menu bar until a later section in this chapter.

■   **The toolbar**. Again, a toolbar is a familiar feature in many current Macintosh applications. You click each individual button to control a different program function. The toolbar is such an easy way to use the program that you may never have to resort to the menus.

You won't be tested on this since we're going to cover each button more thoroughly later on, but from left to right, the Netscape Navigator 3.0 buttons are:

  ■   **The Back and Forward buttons**. Pressing these buttons allows you to cycle through the documents you have already viewed. You can revisit these documents in reverse order (relative to the order in which you originally viewed them) by pressing the Back button, and then you can retrace your path using the Forward button.

  ■   **The Home button**. Pressing this button returns you to your home page.

  ■   **The Reload button**. Pressing this button reloads the currently displayed document into the Netscape Navigator 3.0 window.

  ■   **The Images button**. This button is useful if you've turned off the Auto Load Images option in the pull-down Options menu. With Auto Load Images off, Web pages are displayed without graphics. Instead, icons appear where the graphics normally would be loaded. When you press this button, Netscape Navigator 3.0 loads the images for the current page.

TIP

If you have a slow Internet connection, surf the Web in text-only mode (which is much, much faster than graphics mode) and load graphics only for those pages with images you'd like to see.

■ **The Open button**. Pressing this button pops up a dialog box that lets you type in a URL to open a new document, as shown in Figure 3-3. (If you don't know what I mean by a URL, please refer to Chapter 1.)

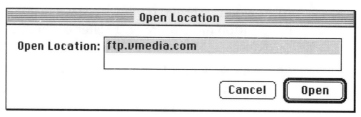

Figure 3-3: *The Open Location dialog box.*

■ **The Print button**. Pressing this button prints the currently displayed document.

■ **The Find button**. Pressing this button lets you search for a word or phrase in the currently displayed document.

■ **The Stop button**. When this button is red, Netscape Navigator 3.0 is loading a document into the window. Pressing this button stops the document from loading.

That's it for the toolbar. Now let's move on down to some of the other components of the main Netscape Navigator 3.0 window:

■ **The Location or Netsite box**. This text box has a morphing (changing) label that changes according to how you use it. When Netscape Navigator 3.0 displays a Web document (retrieved using the HTTP protocol) from Netscape's own site, the box is labeled Netsite. When Netscape Navigator 3.0 displays information retrieved from a non-Netscape server, the box is labeled Location. If you want to enter a URL manually, you may select the text box and delete some or all of the current address information. You can then either type or paste a new URL directly into this field (the label changes to Go To while you're typing the new URL). Press Return when you've finished entering the URL, and Netscape Navigator 3.0 jumps to that page.

TIP

*You can also use this capability by pulling down the Go menu in the menu bar to display a drop-down list of the sites you've recently visited. Select any site in the list to return to it. (**Note:** This list only shows pages whose URLs you have entered in the Location or Open boxes.)*

ENTERING URLs THE EASY WAY

You learned in Chapter 1, that a URL, or the address of a particular resource such as a Web page, includes three parts: the protocol used to retrieve the resource (such as HTTP, Gopher, or FTP), the name of the server where the information you want is located, and optionally a directory or filename. For instance, the URL for the Netscape home page is http://home.netscape.com, and the URL for one of its FTP sites is ftp://ftp.netscape.com. Both these examples include a protocol specification and a server name.

Most often you get to a site by clicking on a link within a Web page, but sometimes you need to type the URL itself into the Netsite or Location box. Wouldn't it be nice if you didn't always have to type that "http://" or "ftp://"?

Well, you don't! Netscape Navigator 3.0 has brains. You can leave off the protocol specification and the program will do its best to figure out what kind of resource you had in mind. For instance, if you type in *home.netscape.com* Navigator 3.0 knows you really mean *http://home.netscape.com*. If you type in *gopher.well.com* you are automatically transported to *gopher://gopher.well.com*. At the rate I type in URLs, after a year I'll be able to take a three week vacation with the time I've saved.

Throughout this book I'll tell you to type in complete URLs, including the protocol specification. I'm doing that so you get used to the format and to make very clear what kind of resource we're talking about. But after a while you might want to take advantage of this handy shortcut.

■ **The directory bar**. The directory bar is made up of buttons, much like the toolbar. But the directory buttons display only commands from the Directory menu. For example, clicking the What's New? button on the directory bar is the same as selecting the What's New? entry from the Directory menu—just a little more convenient. Both actions result in Netscape Navigator 3.0 displaying Netscape's own What's New? page, as shown in Figure 3-4.

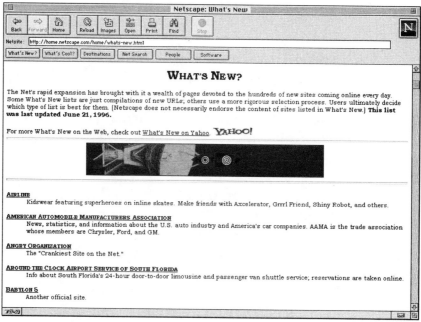

Figure 3-4: *The What's New? page.*

We'll be looking at each of the directory bar buttons more closely later, under "The Directory Buttons," but for now let's continue our overview of the Netscape Navigator 3.0 main window.

■ **The Netscape icon**. Although it's not really a control, the Netscape logo at the top right of the Netscape Navigator 3.0 window is very useful nonetheless. When this icon is animated with shooting stars, it indicates that the program is busy retrieving data from a Web site. When the icon is motionless, Navigator has received the entire document and is ready for your next action. ***Bonus:*** Clicking on the Netscape icon while you're connected to the Net will take you directly to Netscape's home page.

■ **The display window**. The display window is the most important area within Netscape Navigator 3.0. This is where Netscape Navigator 3.0 displays the formatted text, links, hotspots, form fields, graphics, and other items that make up a Web page. Some of these fields and controls are "static," like a standard paragraph of text, while others are "active" and actually perform a function. Some controls may be immediately obvious, like a button, while others may be hidden. For example, the Netscape page in Figure 3-5 includes a Welcome to Netscape graphic with hotspots. When you click on these hotspots, you are magically teleported to other Web pages, just as if you'd clicked on a text link. You'll learn more about these components of a Web page later in this chapter. For now, though, just remember that if your mouse cursor turns into a hand with a pointing finger, you can click there to do something or go somewhere else!

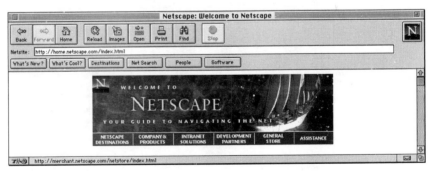

Figure 3-5: *A graphic menu with hotspots.*

TIP

Netscape Navigator 3.0 includes standard scroll bars along the right and bottom edges of the display window. If you resize the window (or if a Web page is longer than one screen length, which is usually the case), these controls let you scroll the display so that you can view the entire page. If you checked Active Scrolling in the Appearance panel as we stepped our way through General Preferences in Chapter 2, you will be able to scroll the material on a very long page as you move the scrolling thumb switch up and down, or back and forth, in the scroll bar. This feature really helps users who want to keep multiple applications open concurrently; using a word processing application alongside Netscape Navigator 3.0, for example, is practical even on systems with a single 13- or 14-inch display.

■ **The status line.** Navigator uses the very bottom line of the window, the line beneath the horizontal scroll bar, to display current status information. For example, if you're currently receiving a picture from a Web site, Netscape Navigator 3.0 fills in the status line with the name of the image file and a status bar that indicates the progress of the transfer. Or if you move your mouse pointer over a link, the status line shows its URL, as you can see in Figure 3-6.

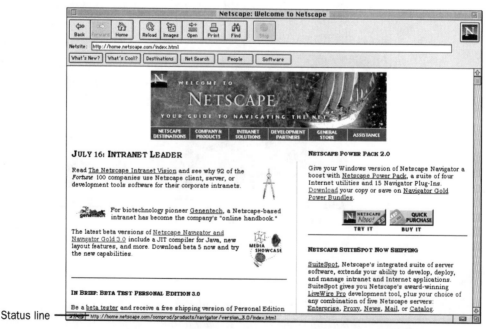

Figure 3-6: *The Netscape Navigator 3.0 status line showing the URL of a link.*

Note the small icon that looks like a broken key on the left side of the status line. This icon indicates whether or not your current session is using a special secure protocol for financial and business transactions. As you might guess, when the icon is "broken," the session is not secure. (Don't worry—you don't really need heavy-duty security for most of what you'll be doing on the Web.) You'll learn more about Netscape Navigator 3.0's security features in Chapter 10.

In addition, a small envelope icon at the far right of the status line links you to the Netscape Navigator 3.0 mail window. You simply click it to access your e-mail. If the icon has an exclamation point next to it, you have new mail. If it has a question mark next to it, Netscape Navigator 3.0 is configured so that it cannot automatically check your mail server for new messages. You'll learn more about e-mail in Chapter 4.

LOCAL AREA URLs

As I mentioned in Chapter 1, you don't even need the Internet to use Netscape Navigator 3.0 effectively. If you're on a local area network (LAN), you can use the program to access documents within your own organization. For instance, employees could call up the latest sales data, or view a fancy multimedia demonstration of a new product or service.

To access a document that is stored locally rather than at a remote site, press ⌘+X or select Open File from Netscape Navigator 3.0's File menu. A File Open dialog box pops up. Now you can simply choose the document you want. HTML documents appear with the Netscape logo, but you could also choose to view text or graphic files.

You can also access a locally stored document by clicking a link to it within another document. For instance, you may want to construct a home page that contains links to a variety of important files on your LAN. The URL for a locally stored file looks a little different from other URLs, and you should know how to construct one in case you ever need to enter one directly in the Location box.

➡

A local file URL starts with *file:*. After *file:*, there are *three* forward slashes rather than the usual two, the letter name of the local or network drive, a vertical bar (the pipe symbol...Shift+\), and the path to the file. Got all that? Here's an example, an HTML file called PRODUCT.HTM that's located in the Public directory on the Q drive of your LAN: file:///Q|/Public/PRODUCT.HTM.

Of course Netscape Navigator 3.0 supports all the same media on a LAN as it does on the Net. You can use the program to play sound files, run video clips, and even gather information from other employees using HTML forms (see "Forms on the Web" later in this chapter). And of course a document can contain a mix of links to Internet sites and to local files. This power and flexibility make Netscape Navigator 3.0 an excellent tool for disseminating enterprise-wide information.

Links & Hotspots

Let's continue our discussion of Web navigation with the most common active control found within Web pages: the *link*. A link is a special text string embedded within a document. It tells Netscape Navigator 3.0 to jump to another document or to a different place in the current document. Linked documents may be physically stored at the same site or another site halfway across the world. As I explained in Chapter 1, this is the essence of hypertext.

Links are considered "followed" once you click on them to display the new information. Netscape Navigator 3.0 changes the color of a followed link to indicate that you've used it before. This color coding can help you retrace your steps.

To use a link, simply move your mouse pointer over the link text and click. But how can you be sure you're on a link? It's really simple.

How Can I Tell I'm on a Link?

Netscape Navigator 3.0 provides a number of visual cues to indicate the presence of a link:

- By default, links that consist of text are underlined and appear in blue, while regular inactive text is not underlined and appears black. If you return to a page after using one of its links, the link now appears in purple to indicate that you've been there. You can always click the same link again; it does not become inactive once you've clicked it. The change in color is only a helpful reminder.

- As I mentioned earlier, if you rest your mouse cursor on a link, the status line changes to indicate the link's URL. No URL in the status line, no link!

- As I also mentioned earlier, your mouse cursor changes to a pointing hand when it rests on a link. Some linked connections may be displayed using graphics instead of text (we'll talk more about hotspots in a minute). Watch the cursor and the status line at the bottom of your active window!

Figure 3-7 shows a section of Netscape's own online Handbook that contains a number of links. The location of this useful feature has been changed from earlier versions of Netscape Navigator. It is now accessed using the Help or Guide menu; pull-down Help (the faintly colored yellow button with a question mark in the right corner of the menu bar), and the Netscape Navigator Handbook will become the active window on your screen.

TIP

Often the context of the text containing the link indicates what the link will do. For instance, "download PROGRAM.HQX now" and "jump to the index" are self-explanatory.

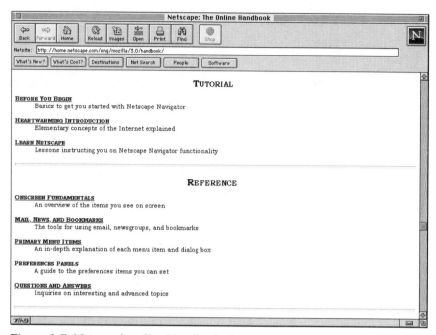

Figure 3-7: *Netscape's online Handbook, showing typical links to more detailed information.*

CHANGING WHAT LINKS LOOK LIKE

You can change the properties of link text from the Options menu. Pull down General Preferences from the Options menu to display the General Preferences dialog box. In the Colors panel, you can change the default colors for links you've used and those you haven't tried yet. In the Appearance panel you can specify whether links should be underlined or not. Here you can also set how many days it takes for a followed link to "expire" (expired links are returned to the default color, just as if you had never followed them). You can also cancel out all your current followed links and start over, by selecting the button Expire Now. Try it—there's a warning panel here that asks you if you really meant it! You can select No when asked.

USING HOTSPOTS

Hotspots are just like links, except they are embedded within graphical information rather than text. Like links, hotspots perform an action when you click them. You might click one to jump to another page, or to view an image or even play a piece of music. Sometimes hotspots are smaller "thumbnail" versions of full-size images that you can download, or they may be beautifully designed arrows pointing to the next in a series of linked documents. Many sites also use hotspots as "menu items" within larger images that serve as menu systems. In the Netscape home page, for instance, you can click on various areas within the same graphic to jump to different documents. Let's give this a try:

1. Make sure you can connect to the Internet.

2. Launch Netscape Navigator 3.0. (It's probably quicker to launch from an alias that you have placed in the Apple Menu folder.) The main window appears, and the Netscape home page starts loading, as shown earlier in Figure 3-2.

3. In the large graphic near the top of the page, click the General Store section. The General Store appears, as shown in Figure 3-8.

Congratulations! You just used a hotspot to get from the Netscape home page to the General Store. Traveling sure is simple in cyberspace.

> **TIP**
>
> *Usually clicking a link causes the text and graphics currently displayed in the Netscape navigator window to be replaced with new text and graphics. Sometimes, however, your current window will stay the same and an entire new window opens up to display the new information. The command to open a new window is part of the control information in the HTML file itself.*

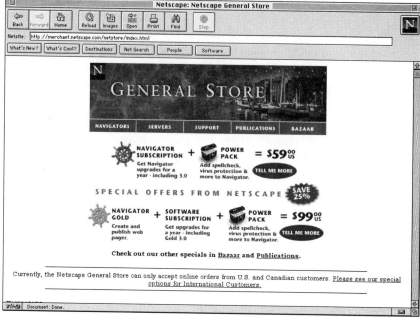

Figure 3-8: *The General Store.*

In this example, it was easy to find the hotspots in the graphic because they included text. But there are other ways to indicate hotspots as well. Sometimes they are displayed with a colored border, or the author of a Web page might refer to a hotspot in a line of text such as "Click the right arrow to move to the next page."

Now, let's try something just a little more complex, to demonstrate the power of links and hotspots and the flexibility of the tools and menus available to you with this powerful new software. Go back to the General Store hotspot we found on the Netscape home page, illustrated in Figure 3-2. Instead of clicking on General Store, move the cursor to that hotspot and hold the mouse button down as if you were getting ready to drag that hotspot to another location on the screen. What happens next is illustrated in Figure 3-9.

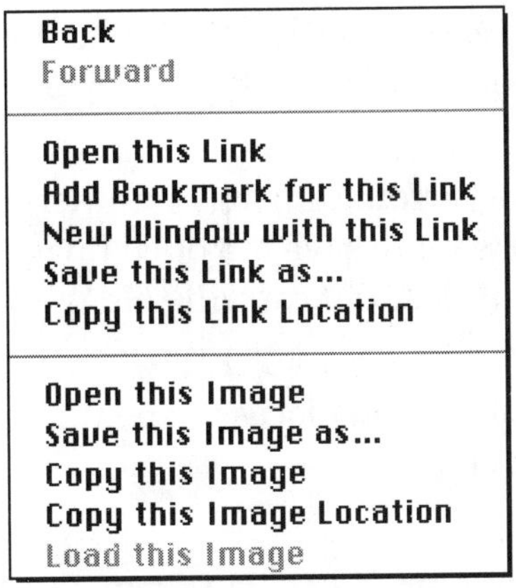

```
┌─────────────────────────────────────┐
│ Back                                │
│ Forward                             │
│                                     │
│ Open this Link                      │
│ Add Bookmark for this Link          │
│ New Window with this Link           │
│ Save this Link as...                │
│ Copy this Link Location             │
│                                     │
│ Open this Image                     │
│ Save this Image as...               │
│ Copy this Image                     │
│ Copy this Image Location            │
│ Load this Image                     │
└─────────────────────────────────────┘
```

Figure 3-9: *Some shortcuts to using hotspots and links!*

You can use the menu you find here to work with both the images themselves as well as the complete link, helping you develop highly customized and professionally appearing messages and documents with every little complexity! Let's briefly review each capability presented in this menu.

- By using the Back and Forward commands in the top portion of the pull-down menu, you can navigate without using the buttons on the toolbar or selections from the menu bar.

- Open this Link issues the same command as if you had clicked on the link to open the document.

- Add Bookmark for this Link lets you add the link to your Bookmarks folder without actually having to navigate to the target document.

- The New Window with this Link command creates a new Browser window for the target document.

- Save this Link as ... provides the same capability as any other Save as ... Macintosh command. The entire HTML file may be placed on your hard drive, a network disk, or a similar storage peripheral. (High capacity mobile storage devices are becoming more and more affordable for uses such as HTML and image storage.)

- Copy this Link Location copies the link to the clipboard, in a conventional copy-and-paste type of operation.

- Open this Image allows you to view the selected hotspot by itself, without the surrounding text or other graphics on the page. You might want to save the open image for use with another document, without carrying along the location data associated with it.

- Copy this Image Location places the textual URL of the image on the clipboard.

USING THE NETSCAPE NAVIGATOR 3.0 TOOLBAR

As I mentioned earlier, the Netscape Navigator 3.0 toolbar is a major portion of the program's control center. You can use these buttons like the forward and reverse gears of a car, moving back and forth through Web documents. You can also use them to print the contents of any page or to locate a specific word or phrase within the text of a page.

Of course, all these functions and a few more are also available from the menu bar, and many of these features can be invoked by the "power user" with corresponding shortcut keystrokes which are also shown in the menu bar.

In this section, I'll discuss the buttons you'll use the most as we navigate through Netscape's own Web site.

TIP

Note that pages on the Netscape Web site may change from time to time, so the screens and links we use may not agree exactly with what you see on your own screen as you read or review this material. However, you should still be able to follow the steps in a general fashion.

THE FORWARD & BACK BUTTONS

You've already seen how easy it is to get to a new document by clicking on a link or hotspot. But what if you need to return to a previously viewed page? Perhaps you forgot to download a file, or you suddenly decide to back up and follow a different information trail. This is where the first two buttons on the toolbar come into play. Back and Forward allow you to retrace your steps to a previous page or, if you've already backtracked, to jump forward to the last page you accessed.

To see how this works, follow these steps:

1. Make sure you are connected to the Internet. If Netscape Navigator 3.0 is not currently running, launch it.

2. In the Netscape home page, click the hotspot for the General Store.

   ■ If you're already at the General Store because you're a good student who followed the last set of directions, just stay there!

3. Now click the Back button. We're back where we started, at the Netscape home page. Guess what the Forward button does? Go ahead and click it now. As you probably guessed, the General Store page pops up once more.

4. Now click a new link or hotspot. It doesn't really matter which one. Once the new document appears, click the Back button twice. Yes, as you probably expected the Back button can lead sequentially back through all the pages you have visited. And of course Forward works the same way, in reverse.

MULTIPLE CONNECTIONS

You can display several Web documents at once with Netscape Navigator 3.0. Select New Web Browser from the File menu, or simply press ⌘- N. Another window appears, and you can use it, like the first window, to navigate to any site.

And why would you want to connect to more than one site at a time?

■ If you're researching a specific topic and you've found more than one page with pertinent information or links, it's a good idea to load each page in a separate window if you need to compare them.

■ Certain sites may be particularly slow, and opening an additional window allows you to continue exploring while you wait for the display of the first page to finish.

■ Extra-large files like .MOV or .AVI animations may take several minutes to download. With a second window, you can continue surfing while you wait.

It's important to remember that each window you load will use the original connection you've made to the Internet; opening too many windows will slow down the overall speed of *all* of them!

THE HOME BUTTON

You can click new links and dance around with the Forward and Back buttons as long as you want, but eventually you might get dizzy and long for home. To return to the Netscape home page:

1. Click the Home button.

That's it. (I love throwing in these one-step procedures.)

WHY DO I NEED A HOME PAGE, ANYWAY?

You may be asking, "Why do I need a home page, anyway?" There are several reasons:

■ A home page helps you stay oriented with a familiar starting point. Imagine what surfing would be like if you started without a home base—or, even worse, jumped to a random page every time you started the program!

■ Many seasoned Web surfers set their home pages to their favorite site, especially if the contents of the page change often. This way, you can check your favorite page each time you begin a Netscape Navigator 3.0 session. If you have your own personal Web page, for example, you might set it as your home page.

■ Some pages are especially designed to offer as much as possible for new Web surfers, making them ideal launching pads for Web exploration. For example, the Netscape home page offers links to the newest and most popular pages, Web search tools, and a wealth of exciting Internet resources—all from one screen.

As you can see, the Home button returns you directly to whatever home page you've selected with a single click of your mouse. And by the way, changing your home page is easy. To find out how, see the "Changing Your Home Page" sidebar.

CHANGING YOUR HOME PAGE

Why change your home page? First, a purely practical reason: if your current home page is particularly busy or it's operated on a slower connection, it may take 30 seconds or so to load the page! Delays like that can get quite tiring after a few sessions, so you'd probably want to select a faster site (or perhaps even use a page you've created on your local hard disk). If you're really interested in saving time, you can even set your home page as "blank," so there's no load time at all.

Additionally, your interests are likely to change. You can save valuable Internet connect time by constructing a customized home page and including in it the sites you access the most. (To learn how to do this, see Chapter 11, "Your Personal Workspace & Web Page.")

To change your home page, follow these steps:

1. Select General Preferences from the Options menu.

2. Select the Appearance tab.

3. Click the Home Page Location radio button and type in the URL of your new home page. Make sure you spell the address correctly! If you've saved or created a page on your local hard drive, you can enter the URL for the file instead of a remote site.

4. Click OK, then make sure to select Save Options from the Options menu.

THE PRINT BUTTON

Okay, so you've found the Secret to Life's Eternal Mystery on a particular Web page, and you'd like to save it for future reference. You could highlight the text with your mouse and copy the text to the scrapbook, but why not print out the whole thing? That way you can keep a hard copy of all of the contents of the page, including the images.

To print the contents of a page, click the Print button. Navigator takes you to the standard options that you can access from within the dialog box for your specific printer configuration. To change the appearance of printed documents, select Page Setup from the pull-down File menu.

You can also display a preview image of the output before you print it by selecting the Print Preview option from the File menu or the Print dialog box, depending upon your printer's configuration. Figure 3-10 shows a print preview of the Netscape home page.

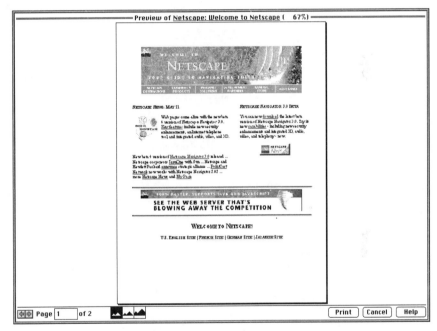

Figure 3-10: *Print preview of the Netscape home page.*

THE FIND BUTTON

From time to time you'll encounter huge documents that are crowded with text and links. Scrolling slowly through a mountain of text, line by line, is one method of locating that link you remember, but Netscape Navigator 3.0 makes it much easier with the Find command.

Let's look for a specific string of text in Netscape's own Handbook.

1. Make sure you are connected to the Internet. Launch Netscape Navigator 3.0 unless, of course, you're connected and using the application already.

2. From the Help or Guide menu, select Handbook. Netscape's online Handbook appears, as shown in Figure 3-11.

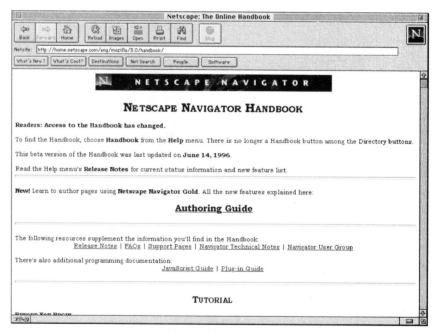

Figure 3-11: *The Netscape Navigator Handbook.*

3. Click the Find button on the toolbar, or select it from the pull-down Edit menu on the Menu bar. Netscape Navigator 3.0 displays the Find dialog box, as shown in Figure 3-12.

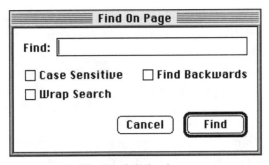

Figure 3-12: *The Find dialog box.*

4. For the purposes of this tutorial, type the word **Mail** in the
   Find field and click the Find button. In a flash, Netscape
   Navigator 3.0 finds a mention of Mail, highlights it, and
   displays the surrounding section of the document as
   shown in Figure 3-13.

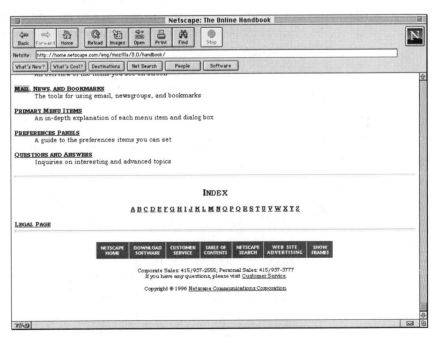

Figure 3-13: *The results of a successful Find command.*

■ If you need a case-sensitive search, enable the Case Sensitive option; Netscape Navigator 3.0 will display only those instances in which the capitalization matches your entry. You can specify in which direction the program should search—check the Find Backwards box to search upward through the document. The search begins at the current cursor position. The Wrap Search box will permit you to search for phrases which wrap around the end of one line of text and the beginning of the next.

5. To search for more occurrences of the same string, click the Find button again, use Find Again from the Edit menu in the menu bar, or type ⌘-**G**.

THE STOP BUTTON

Our final stop on the Netscape Navigator 3.0 toolbar is the Stop button. If you need to abort the transfer of any data to or from Navigator, click this button. You might not need the Stop button often, but when you do it'll make the difference between continuing your session or waiting for what seems like a lifetime for the transfer attempt to finally time out.

Why do some pages seem to take forever to load? Possible reasons for a long wait can include:

■ **Heavy usage on the Web site you're calling**. Try calling during low-traffic hours—late at night or early in the morning.

■ **Heavy usage on the system that provides your Internet connection**. Check with your access provider to see when the system is being used the least. Remember that the server where a particular page is located may be in another part of the world, so you may have to make allowances for time differences.

■ **Extra-large graphics or files you're receiving**. (Remember, you can always keep track of where you are in the transfer process by watching the progress bar that appears in the Navigator status line).

■ **A slow data pipeline**. In plain English, this means that some sites are connected to the Web by leased modem lines or older networks, and these slower connections can be bottlenecks.

TIP

If Navigator is attempting to receive a Web page or a file and the transfer seems "stuck," you can often retrieve the data successfully by aborting the current transfer with the Stop button and immediately trying the same link again.

Here's a good rule of thumb: the best time to surf the Net is when you really should be sleeping.

So far we've looked at Web pages that simply present information. But Netscape Navigator 3.0 supports more interactive uses of the Internet as well. In the next section, we'll look at a different kind of Web page, the fill-out form.

RELOADING VERSUS REFRESHING

I haven't talked much about the Reload button because it's pretty obvious: it simply goes out on the Net and reloads the Web document that's currently displayed. This can be useful if you want the latest information from a site that changes daily, for instance. But since reloading means reconnecting with the remote site, it can also be slow, especially when the Net is particularly busy. If you want to redisplay a page in Netscape Navigator 3.0 but don't particularly care if it's the very latest version, you can use the Load Images (⌘-I) command that's located in the View menu, or the Images button on the toolbar. This command loads the latest version of the URL that has been saved to the program's cache on your hard drive.

FORMS ON THE WEB

"Please fill in your name, address, and phone number." You've been doing it your whole life on paper, and now you can do it electronically too.

Forms are scattered all over the Web. Some let you fill in a search word and then find the word for you in a collection of documents; some let you buy a CD or new software product; some even engage you in a real-time conversation. Whatever their purpose, World Wide Web forms share a common look and feel when displayed in Netscape Navigator 3.0. Here's an example:

1. Make sure you are connected to the Internet. Launch Netscape Navigator 3.0 unless, of course, you're connected and using the application already.

2. Click the Open button. The Open Location dialog box appears.

   ■ Yes, you could simply type the new URL in the Netsite box. It's a good idea, though, to try the various ways to accomplish a particular task in Netscape Navigator 3.0 so you can see which feels easiest to you.

3. In the Open Location field, type **http://hoohoo.ncsa.uiuc. edu/archie.html** and click Open. The Archie request form appears, as shown in Figure 3-14.

TIP

Remember, you don't need to type in entire URLs. Typing **hoohoo.ncsa.uiuc.edu/archie.html** *will do the trick.*

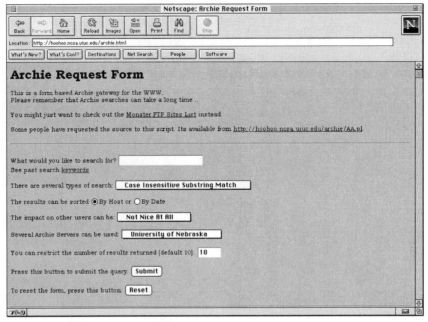

Figure 3-14: *The Archie Request Form.*

Archie is an Internet service that's been around much longer than the Web. It is a tool for finding files at FTP sites (see Chapter 6, "Getting Files via FTP"). But until the Web came along and provided convenient fill-out forms like this one, Archie was much more difficult to use.

Take a few minutes to scroll through this page and examine its various forms elements. There are boxes you can type text into, drop-down lists, and radio buttons. There is also a Submit button that lets you send your request once you have completed filling in the information. If you want, type something in the What would you like to search for? box and then click the Submit button. Let's say you typed the word **Netscape**, set the Archie server drop-down menu to Rutgers University, and left all the other fields alone. In a few seconds you'd be presented with something like Figure 3-15.

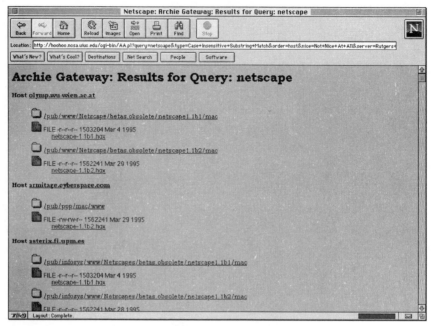

Figure 3-15: *The results of an Archie search.*

As the commercial uses of the Internet become more prominent, we'll see more and more forms for actual transactions. Already you can buy all kinds of products directly over the Net, and the Web's forms interface makes it easy. By the way, Netscape has been a leader in Internet security, and Netscape Navigator 3.0 indicates when a form is not secure by displaying the following text:

```
Any information you submit is insecure and could be observed
by a third party while in transit. If you are submitting
passwords, credit card numbers, or other information you
would like to keep private, it would be safer for you to
cancel the submission.
```

This may sound a bit frightening, but security is typically not a problem with the vast majority of forms you'll fill out online. As a rule, simply take the same precautions as you would if someone were asking similar questions over the telephone. If you feel uncomfortable providing a particular piece of private information, you'll probably want to follow Navigator's recommendation and cancel the form without submitting it. Chapter 10, "Commerce & Security," discusses security issues in more detail.

As more and more companies start collecting data and even selling products via the Internet, online forms may become the bread-and-butter interface on the Web. But fortunately the Web is not all bread and butter, it's champagne and Jell-O, too. Let's take a look at something a bit more fun than forms: *frames*.

UNDERSTANDING FRAMES

One of the coolest features of Netscape Navigator 3.0 is its support for frames. Frames are distinct areas within the Netscape Navigator 3.0 display area. Special HTML commands in a Web document tell the program to partition the display. Each frame is a stand-alone environment that recognizes mouse clicks, has its own scroll bars, and can include all the features of any Web page. Each frame has its own distinct URL. In short, each frame is actually a window displaying its own Web page. Netscape Navigator 3.0 can actually "freeze" one of the frames so that it stays onscreen all the time while you interact with the links and hotspots in another frame. You might see logos, advertisements, or tables of contents handled in this fashion.

Let's take a look at an example of frames, as shown in Figure 3-16. This figure is the Netscape Web site at http://home. netscape.com/comprod/upgrades/. You may have seen this page already if you elected to complete the online registration process way back when you were installing the software.

TIP

Because each frame is its own entity, make sure you select the appropriate frame (by clicking) when you decide to print something. Only the contents of the selected frame, and not the entire display window, print. In addition, you can reload the contents of individual frames by selecting Reload Frame from the View menu, and you can even e-mail the contents of a frame by selecting Mail Frame from the File menu.

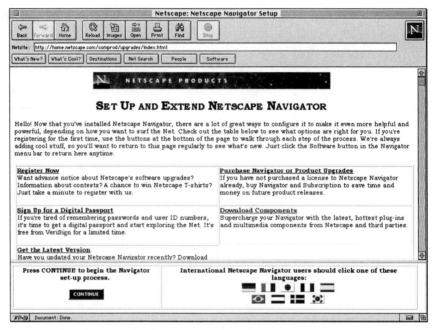

Figure 3-16: *An example of a Web page with frames.*

The way developers use frames makes Web sites very flexible and dynamic for the user. At this Netscape site, notice how each of the two frames is used differently. The top frame displays information and instructions, while the bottom frame solicits user input. Also, notice how each frame has its own scroll bars.

Other sites use frames to display different types of elements. One frame, for instance, may contain text, while another contains graphics. As you click and read through the text, the graphics can change or rotate based on the text displayed. Frames are also used with multimedia or 3D objects. One pane may contain instructions or a story about how to navigate a VRML world with WebFX, while the other contains the actual VRML objects. (What, you don't know what VRML and WebFX are? Please turn to Chapter 9, "Power Navigator 3.0.")

> **TIP**
>
> *You can go backward and forward in frames just as you do in the browser window as a whole. To go back to the information previously displayed in a frame, select that frame (by clicking in it) and click the Back button. To go forward, select the frame and click the Forward button.*

By now you're well on your way to gathering a wide variety of information from the Web. In the next few sections, we'll look at some ways of organizing all this information.

THE HISTORY LIST & BOOKMARKS

As you travel around the World Wide Web, you'll often find yourself jumping back to the same pages over and over again. From time to time you may also need a specific URL that you visited two or three sessions ago. And you're certain to find a number of Web pages that become your favorites, so you'll want to visit them often.

Netscape Navigator 3.0 provides several methods for keeping track of where you are on the Web—and where you've been. In this section, we'll discuss the two important features that help you maintain your own Web road map: the history list, which keeps track of where you've been in the current session, and bookmarks, which are permanent pointers to your favorite Web pages.

USING THE HISTORY LIST

The history list is a collection of entries automatically maintained by Netscape Navigator 3.0. Each entry represents a single site you have visited in the current session. Each time you load a new Web page, the URL for that site is saved in your history list. This makes the history list an excellent tool for jumping among pages while you check references.

The history list (shown in Figure 3-17), available from the pull-down menu bar Window file, includes only URLs you've entered in the Netsite/Location box itself or entered by using the Open button; it does not include any sites you've visited by clicking on a link. From the History dialog box, you may select a specific URL and either double-click on it or click on the Go To button, to immediately jump to that site. The other methods of accessing your online history, described later in this chapter, show *all* the sites you've visited.

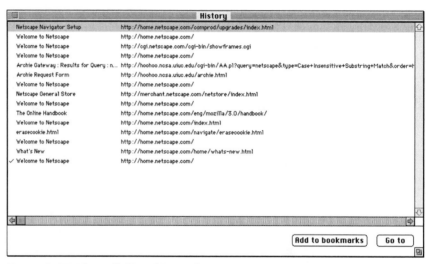

Figure 3-17: *The pull-down history list.*

You can also return to a previously viewed page directly from Netscape Navigator 3.0's Go menu. Simply select Go. You will see the history list at the bottom of the pull-down menu, as shown in Figure 3-18. Once again, you can simply select one of the entries to jump to it immediately. Note that the checkmarked item is the current active window. Other entries may be selected with the cursor, or by using the indicated keyboard combination.

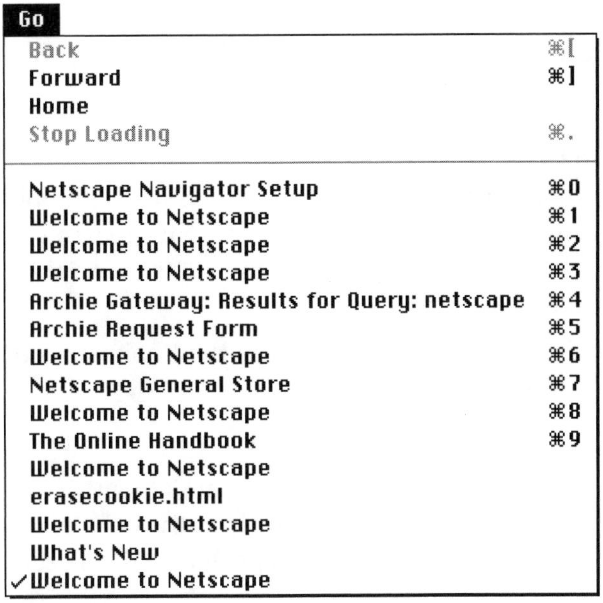

```
Go
  Back                                         ⌘[
  Forward                                      ⌘]
  Home
  Stop Loading                                 ⌘.
  ─────────────────────────────────────────────────
  Netscape Navigator Setup                     ⌘0
  Welcome to Netscape                          ⌘1
  Welcome to Netscape                          ⌘2
  Welcome to Netscape                          ⌘3
  Archie Gateway: Results for Query: netscape  ⌘4
  Archie Request Form                          ⌘5
  Welcome to Netscape                          ⌘6
  Netscape General Store                       ⌘7
  Welcome to Netscape                          ⌘8
  The Online Handbook                          ⌘9
  Welcome to Netscape
  erasecookie.html
  Welcome to Netscape
  What's New
✓ Welcome to Netscape
```

Figure 3-18: *The pull-down Go menu, showing your history list. See the command keys next to each entry? Navigator assigns a key to each of your last 10 Web stops, providing a shortcut back to recent pages.*

To add a history entry to your bookmarks, select the site you wish to add, then click the Add to bookmarks button. (We'll cover bookmarks in the next section.)

TIP

Remember, your history list is erased when you finish your session. That's why bookmarks are important.

BOOKMARKS

Now that you're familiar with the history list, you may be saying to yourself, "Well, that's great for a single session, but what about documents that I want to return to at some later date?" Luckily you don't have to resort to paper and pencil or try to maintain a text file of your favorite sites—Netscape Navigator 3.0 provides you with bookmarks, which are saved permanently in your own

"Web page directory." You can also create a simple Web page of your own that includes your favorite sites; we'll discuss this in Chapter 9, "Power Navigator 3.0."

ADDING & USING BOOKMARKS

The two actions you'll perform most often with bookmarks are (1) adding them and (2) using them to jump to a stored URL. To add a bookmark for the document that's currently displayed in Netscape Navigator 3.0:

■ Select Add Bookmark from the Bookmarks menu, or simply press ⌘+D.

Using bookmarks to jump to a document is just as easy:

■ Select the pull-down Bookmarks menu, then select one of the bookmarks that appears at the bottom (see Figure 3-19). You are immediately teleported to the selected URL.

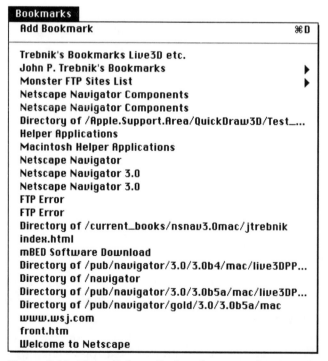

Figure 3-19: *The pull-down Bookmarks menu, showing a long list of bookmarks at the bottom.*

As with the history list, Netscape Navigator 3.0 provides a fuller, alternative interface to your bookmarks: the Bookmarks window.

TIP

You can also add a bookmark for a link within a document by holding down the mouse button while the cursor is on the link you wish to add, revealing a pull-down menu from which you may then select the command Add Bookmark for this link.

THE BOOKMARKS WINDOW

Now that you know how to use bookmarks at the simplest level, let's advance a bit. Just as history entries can be displayed in the History dialog box, you can also display a bookmarks list that offers a lot more functionality than the Bookmarks menu. To open the Bookmarks window, select Bookmarks from the pull-down Windows menu, or simply press ⌘+B. The Bookmarks window appears, as shown in Figure 3-20.

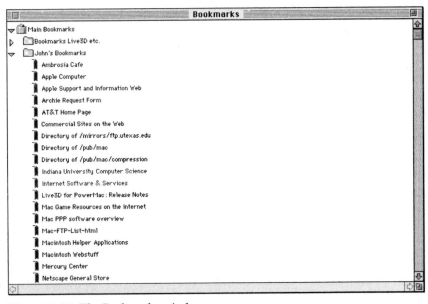

Figure 3-20: *The Bookmarks window.*

- Depending on what sites you've already added to your bookmarks list, your window may look different from mine.

- The top-level bookmark folder may include your own name instead of simply reading "Main Bookmarks" or "Personal Bookmarks."

As you can see, Netscape Navigator 3.0 displays the contents of the current bookmark file in a tree format, with entries appearing under the folder icon. You'll notice that the default bookmark file, Main Bookmarks, contains a single entry, Welcome to Netscape. The Bookmarks window has its own menu bar, which we'll refer to as we explain the other Bookmark functions. But to jump to the document represented by a bookmark entry you don't even need the menu. Simply double-click the entry itself.

TIP

Netscape Navigator 3.0 lets you use more than one bookmark file and also makes it easy to switch between files. From the File menu in the Bookmarks window, you can choose Open Bookmark File ... to select a new file, or Save As ... to save the current file under a new name.

ORGANIZING YOUR BOOKMARKS

If you're familiar with Macintosh file and folder structures, you'll have no problem organizing your bookmarks any way you like. For example, let's say you'd like to categorize your bookmarks by subject matter, with each subject represented by its own folder. For the purposes of this exercise, we'll add a new folder called Computers under the existing Main Bookmarks folder.

First, to create a new bookmark folder:

1. Highlight the existing folder under which the new folder should be created. In this case, the existing folder is Main Bookmarks.

2. Choose Insert Folder from the Item menu. Netscape Navigator 3.0 displays the New Folder dialog box shown in Figure 3-21.

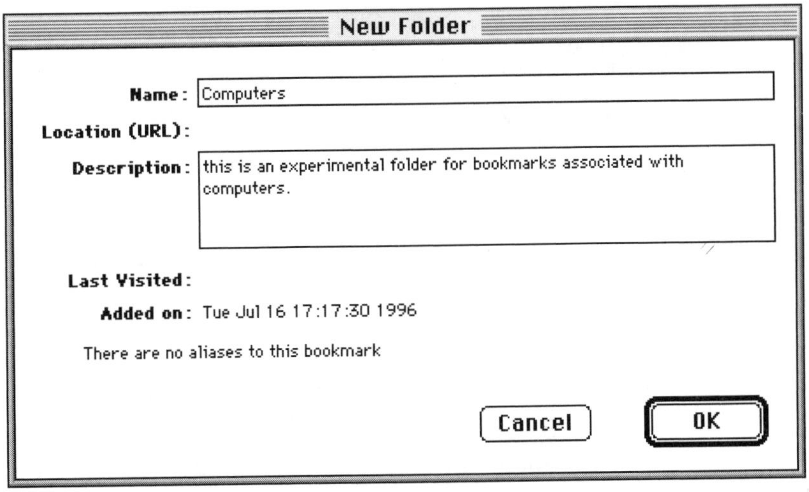

```
┌─────────────────────────────────────────────────────────────┐
│ ══════════════════════════ New Folder ═══════════════════════ │
│                                                               │
│        Name : │Computers                                    │ │
│  Location (URL):                                              │
│    Description : │this is an experimental folder for bookmarks associated with │
│                  │computers.                                  │
│                  │                                            │
│                  │                                            │
│                  │                                            │
│                                                               │
│    Last Visited :                                             │
│      Added on : Tue Jul 16 17:17:30 1996                      │
│                                                               │
│    There are no aliases to this bookmark                      │
│                                                               │
│                          ┌──────────┐   ┌──────────────┐      │
│                          │ Cancel   │   │     OK       │      │
│                          └──────────┘   └──────────────┘      │
└─────────────────────────────────────────────────────────────┘
```

Figure 3-21: *The New Folder dialog box.*

3. Type **Computers** in the Name field. If you like, you can add a simple text description that will display when you edit the folder.

4. Click OK to save the folder.

Now that you've added the Computers folder, you can either create new bookmark entries within it, or move existing entries into it.

To create a new bookmark:

1. Highlight the folder under which the new entry should be created. In this case, we'll select Computers.

2. Select Insert Bookmark from the Item menu. Netscape Navigator 3.0 displays the New Bookmark dialog box.

3. Type the name for your new bookmark in the Name field. As an example, let's use **A nifty Computer URL**.

4. Type the URL into the Location (URL) field. Make sure you type the complete address correctly!

5. Click OK to save the entry. Your Bookmarks window should now look something like Figure 3-22.

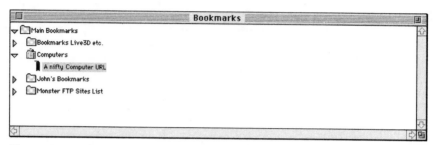

Figure 3-22: *The Bookmarks window with new entry.*

It's even easier to move an existing bookmark into a folder. Select and drag the entry icon (which looks like a sheet of paper with the edge folded down) and drop it on top of the desired folder. Notice that your cursor changes appearance to indicate you're dragging the entry to a new spot. The entry will now appear as a sub-branch under the folder.

When you add entries under a folder, Netscape Navigator 3.0 also displays the entries and folder hierarchy as part of the Book-marks menu. Folders with entries in them appear with arrows on the right side of the menu; when you select the folder, the folder name expands to show the bookmark entries within.

If you'd like to separate your entries or folders on the Book-marks menu, highlight the name in the Bookmarks window and select Insert Separator from the Bookmarks dialog box Item menu. When you return to the Bookmarks menu, you'll see a line sepa-rating that entry or folder from the others on the menu.

TIP

Once you've expanded your entries within several folders, it may be harder to find a particular entry. Of course, you can use the Find command in the Bookmarks window, but it also helps to close folders you're not using. Closing a folder hides all the bookmark entries under it. To close a folder, double-click its icon; to expand it and display the entries it contains, double-click its icon again.

ADDING BOOKMARKS

You already know how to add Bookmarks, you say. Keying ⌘+D or selecting Add Bookmark from the Bookmarks menu certainly *does* add a bookmark, but it always puts new bookmarks in the same place. Suppose you want more control over where a bookmark ends up? That's where the Link feature of Netscape Navigator 3.0 comes in handy.

To add the currently displayed URL to the Bookmarks file using the Link feature:

1. Open the Bookmarks window by keying ⌘+B.

2. Select the current URL by highlighting it in the Location/ Netsite box. You can copy and paste the URL into any folder that appears in the Bookmarks window.

3. You may also add a bookmark for any URL in the current document by moving the cursor to it, holding down the mouse button, and selecting the command *Add Bookmark for this link*. The URL will be added to your New Bookmarks folder.

You can start right out by putting bookmarks in the proper folders instead of having to clean up later.

CHANGING WHERE NEW BOOKMARKS GET ADDED

There is another way to stay organized. You can configure Netscape Navigator 3.0 so that new bookmarks are always placed in a folder you specify. By default, when you key ⌘+D the new Bookmark is added to the end of the top-level Bookmark folder. But let's say you want all new bookmarks to go into a subfolder called New. Here's how you do it:

1. In the Bookmarks window, select the folder you want to use for all bookmarks added using ⌘+D or the Add Bookmark command.

2. With that folder highlighted, select Set to New Bookmarks Folder from the Item menu. A book icon appears on top of the file icon for that folder.

There can be only one New Bookmarks folder at a time, at least within the same Bookmarks file. If you want to change it, simply select a different folder and repeat step 2. Remember, you can always return the program to its default mode of operation by selecting the top-level folder as the default New Bookmarks folder.

CUSTOMIZING THE BOOKMARKS MENU DISPLAY

As you collect dozens or even hundreds of bookmarks, all neatly categorized within their folders, the Bookmarks menu starts looking pretty long. You probably don't need to see all these bookmarks every time you run the program, so why not limit what's displayed in the menu? Netscape Navigator 3.0 makes this easy:

1. In the Bookmarks window, select the folder that you want to have displayed on the Bookmarks menu.
2. With the folder highlighted, select Set to Bookmark Menu Folder from the Item menu.

Now only the items in that folder will appear in the Bookmarks menu. You can always change back to the program's default display of all bookmarks by selecting the top-level folder and repeating step 2.

CHECKING FOR WHAT'S NEW?

Let's suppose it's been a week or two since you last surfed the Web (after all, there is more to life than the Internet), and you'd like to catch up on any changes to your favorite bookmarked Web sites. Unfortunately, you have dozens of sites, and not enough time to check all of them for updated information.

Netscape Navigator 3.0's advanced What's New? feature takes all the hassle out of keeping up-to-date with some or all of the sites you've added to your bookmark files. To check for updated Web pages in a bookmark file, follow these steps:

1. If you want to scan a selected group of sites, highlight them with your mouse.
2. Choose What's New? from the File menu. Netscape Navigator 3.0 displays the What's New? dialog box shown in Figure 3-23.

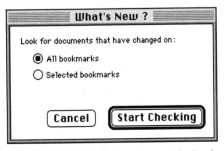

Figure 3-23: *The What's New? dialog box.*

3. To check all documents for updated information, choose All bookmarks. To check only the sites currently selected in the Bookmarks window, click on Selected bookmarks.

4. Click Start Checking to begin the scanning process.

Netscape Navigator 3.0 will report the sites where any information has been updated or changed as shown in Figure 3-24.

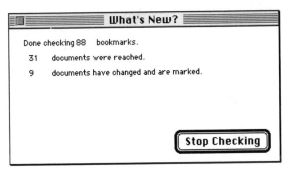

Figure 3-24: *The What's New? dialog box shows where information has been updated.*

IMPORTING & EXPORTING BOOKMARKS

As you build your collection of bookmarks, you may want to share your favorite Web sites with others. In fact, many Web surfers keep a "favorite sites" file or "hotlist" in HTML format that they can share with others through Internet mail. Netscape Navigator 3.0 makes it simple to import a bookmark file (bring new entries from some other HTML file into your bookmark file) or export your entries (create an HTML hotlist that others can use).

Remember, an HTML file is simply a text document that contains links to other Web documents. HTML documents are standardized so that all Web browsers can interpret them correctly. That's why importing and exporting allow you to trade files with any Web user, whether or not they have Netscape Navigator 3.0.

From the Netscape Navigator 3.0 window, follow these steps to *import* a bookmark file:

1. Select Bookmarks from the pull-down Window menu. The Bookmarks window appears, as shown earlier in Figure 3-19.

2. From the Bookmarks window pull-down File menu, select Import Bookmarks. Netscape Navigator 3.0 displays a standard Macintosh File Open dialog box, as shown in Figure 3-25.

Figure 3-25: *The File Open dialog box.*

3. Navigate to the directory where the HTML file to be imported is stored and then double-click on the file you want to import.

From the Navigator display window, follow these steps to *export* a bookmark file:

1. Select Bookmarks from the pull-down Window menu. The Bookmarks window appears, as shown earlier in Figure 3-19.

2. Select the bookmark file you want to export.

3. From the pull-down File menu, select the Save As command. Netscape Navigator 3.0 displays the standard Macintosh File Save dialog box, as shown in Figure 3-26.

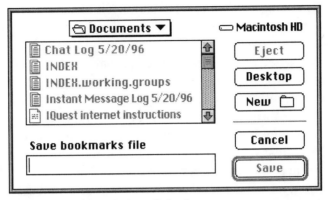

Figure 3-26: *The File Save dialog box.*

4. Save the file in any folder or location and under any name you want.

Now that you're familiar with some of the program's main features, let's take a quick look at the information Netscape makes available to you with a single mouse click.

THE DIRECTORY BUTTONS

Already you know how to use many of Netscape Navigator 3.0's main features, and you're probably pretty used to leaping from link to link across the vast stretches of the Internet. One of the great things about Netscape Navigator 3.0 is that it not only provides the tools for getting places, it actually has some of the best Web links built right in. The Directory buttons serve as quick and easy shortcuts to some of the most important Internet resources. We'll also pop in on one of the most popular and well-known sites on the Web: the Yahoo! Web page search site.

THE WHAT'S NEW? BUTTON

Let's face it: the World Wide Web is an immense world within cyberspace, and it's getting bigger every day. Even the mass-market magazines and television news shows are listing Web sites these days, and your Net-surfing friends will certainly send you their share of cool URLs.

But where do you go for the very latest sites? Wouldn't it be nice to check a single page for the "best of the newest" sites that have recently opened?

That's the idea behind the first button on the Directory bar, What's New?. This button brings up a page that acts as a doorway to the latest sites on the Web, and it's one of the most popular starting points for owners of Netscape Navigator 3.0. In this section, let's check the What's New? page and jump to a new site. Follow these steps:

1. If Netscape Navigator 3.0 is not currently running, go to Recent Applications in the pull-down Apple menu, and launch the application. (I assume you've set your system up for this? If not, use the alias you installed in the Apple menu instead. Aren't these Macs great?)

2.
   Click the What's New? button on the Directory bar. Netscape's What's New? page appears, as shown in Figure 3-27.

TIP

You can click the Directory buttons no matter where you are on the Net. You don't have to be displaying documents from the Netscape site for these buttons to work.

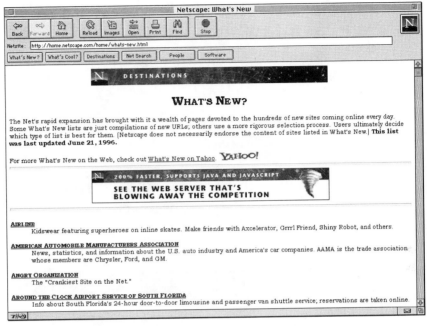

Figure 3-27: *The What's New? page.*

3. Scroll down until you see the links to new sites, along with their descriptions. To jump to one of these new pages, simply click its link.

4. To return to the What's New? page, simply click the What's New? button again.

THE WHAT'S COOL? BUTTON

The What's Cool? button has a similar function to the What's New? button. It brings up a page full of links to documents that may not be brand new, but which:

■ Are especially well designed or colorful.

■ Have unique resources, like extensive image libraries or databases.

- Offer animation or unusual Web applications.
- Have proven particularly popular with Web surfers.

Figure 3-28 shows what was on the What's Cool? page when this book went to press.

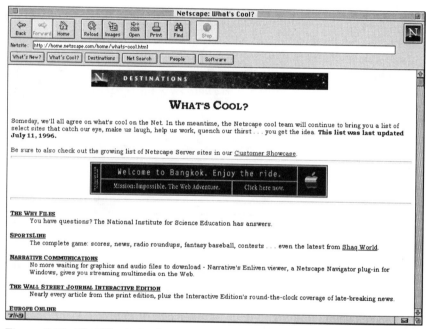

Figure 3-28: *The What's Cool? page.*

THE NET SEARCH BUTTON

As we mentioned earlier, the sheer size of the World Wide Web makes it extremely difficult to locate a particular piece of information or a specific Web page by simply fishing for the right URL. For this reason, topical search engines have been around for as long as the Web itself.

Search engines usually look through an index of documents for a query string that you specify. Some search tools also allow you to add logical operators like "either," "and," and "or" so that you can perform more sophisticated searches.

Netscape Navigator 3.0 provides you with links to all the search engines you're likely to need. Clicking the Net Search button brings up the Net Search page, shown in Figure 3-29.

Figure 3-29: *The Net Search page.*

You can access a variety of search engines such as Infoseek, Lycos, Magellan, Excite, and Yahoo! by clicking their respective buttons near the top of the page. To access other utilities, scroll down to the list of links.

Now let's search for a specific topic using Infoseek:

1. Select one of the domains beneath the search field. For instance, if you just want to search Web pages, select the World Wide Web domain.

2. Enter the string **batman** in the search field and then click the Search button. Your screen should look like Figure 3-30. Then, Infoseek returns the search results shown in Figure 3-31.

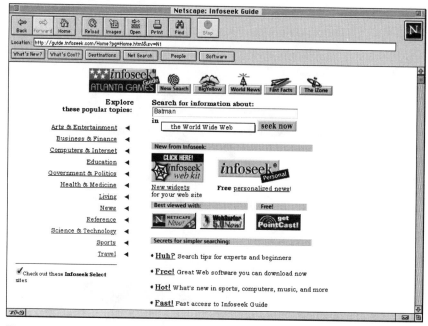

Figure 3-30: *Using the search screen is just a matter of keying in your search parameters.*

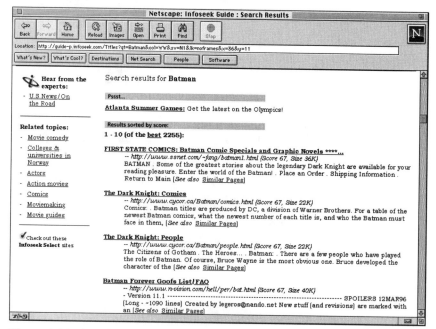

Figure 3-31: *Search results from an Infoseek query.*

3. To jump directly to one of the pages, simply click on the corresponding link.

A Net search is not guaranteed to locate every site on a particular topic, but if you're hunting for reference material or just surfing because you're interested in the subject, you'll find more than enough sites to keep you busy. Here's where you can jump on to undoubtedly the best (and most famous) directory, the Yahoo! Web Guide.

SEARCHING THE EASY WAY

I'm about to tell you about one of the coolest new features in Netscape Navigator 3.0, so pay close attention. This little tip will save you so much time and trouble that you're sure to respond with thank you notes, flowers, and cash donations (make checks payable to Phil James and include your social security number and daytime phone).

Here's the deal: you don't even need to bother with the Net Search button. If you type something in the Netsite/Location box that doesn't look like a valid URL, Netscape Navigator 3.0 assumes you're trying to initiate a search. For instance, if you **type netscape.com** into the box and press Return, Navigator will try to connect you to Netscape's home page. But if you type **Batman and Robin** instead, Navigator will automatically use one of the search engines to search for the words "Batman and Robin" throughout the Web! Figure 3-32 show just how easy it is to find a needle in a Webstack!

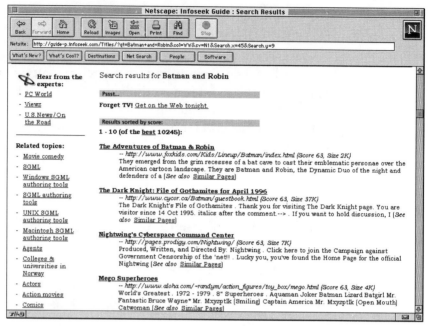

Figure 3-32: *Results from a search the easy way!*

THE DESTINATIONS BUTTON

Next, we arrive at the Destinations button. Here we're dealing with places rather than people. Sites are grouped into sections like "Art," "Science," "Computers," "Business," and so on. In this way, this directory is more akin to a tourist's guidebook, and it appeals more to those who like a broad range of sites rather than the focus provided by a search engine. This feature has replaced the Internet Directory button found in previous versions of Netscape Navigator.

Throughout the Web you'll find many pages featuring specialized directories covering only music, for example, or only films. Figure 3-33 shows a page for sports enthusiasts. As you become more experienced in surfing the Web, you'll encounter directory sites that literally provide hours of exploration before you've exhausted their resources.

Figure 3-33: *Some opportunities for sports enthusiasts found by using the Destinations button!*

THE PEOPLE BUTTON

Being a member of the Internet community provides access to millions of people from around the globe. Here are a few tools available to help find an e-mail address, organization name, or domain name. This feature has replaced the Internet White Pages found in earlier releases of Netscape Navigator. And Netscape is committed to adding new directories and search tools to these pages as they become available.

Figure 3-34 shows some of the "white pages" resources that are available through use of the People button.

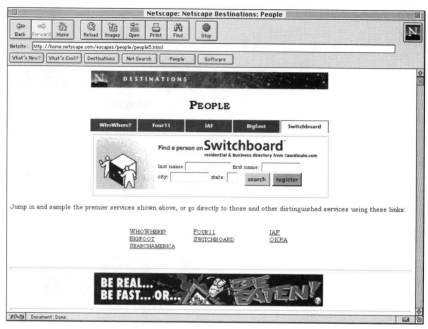

Figure 3-34: *How to connect with people on the Net!*

THE SOFTWARE BUTTON

Finally, let's take a look at the last Directory button. Click the Software button to display the Netscape Navigator Upgrade page, which contains all the details on purchasing and upgrading Netscape software. The Upgrade page provides information on the Netscape Navigator Subscription Program and the latest-released versions of Navigator for different computers. Of course, you'll also find a number of convenient links for downloading demonstration software.

Just think of the Software Button as your Netscape software catalog, complete with the option to purchase products online.

EXPLORING YAHOO!

For a taste of the limitless expanse of information available on the Web today, there's no better site to begin with than Yahoo!. This Web guide started as a hobby project by Stanford University students David Filo and Jerry Yang in April 1994. Since then, Yahoo! has mushroomed into a profitable business that's become a career, but Filo and Yang still offer their original service free of charge to everyone, and the site has become the home page for uncounted Web surfers.

What are we waiting for? Let's start exploring! To access Yahoo!:

1. Launch Netscape Navigator 3.0. Make sure you are connected to the Internet. (By now, this should be second nature to you!)

2. Click the Net Search button.

   ■ Netscape has provided convenient links to each of the major subjects on the Yahoo! page, so you don't even really need to load the Yahoo! top-level page itself. But just so you can see what Yahoo! looks like, let's do this the slightly slower way.

3. Click the link Yahoo! Directory. Netscape Navigator 3.0 displays the Yahoo! top page, as shown in Figure 3-35.

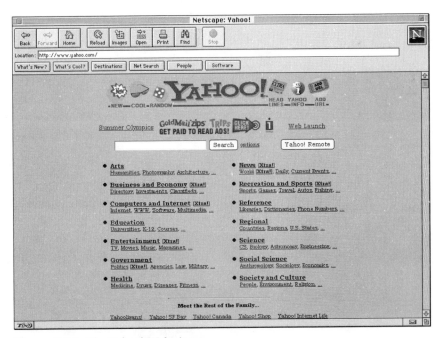

Figure 3-35: *The Yahoo! Web site.*

You can see that each section in the guide is actually a link. In fact, each section is further broken down into subsections, and these subsections are links as well. If you don't see the subsection you're looking for, click on the ellipsis (...) link to display more.

Like the Net Search page, Yahoo! also provides its own search engine. You can specify keywords, URLs, or simple text strings as search targets. Click the Options link to learn more about the Boolean search operators available.

Yahoo! also offers these other features through the hotspots that surround the title graphic:

- **Headlines.** The latest news from the Yahoo! newswire.

- **New.** A listing of the latest sites added to the guide.

- **Cool.** Those sites that are especially unusual or inventive.

- **Random.** If you're looking for something new and unexpected, or if you just like to waste time, click the **Random** hotspot to display a site selected totally at random from the Yahoo! guide.

- **Yahoo Info.** Like most Web pages, the Yahoo! site provides an Internet e-mail link so that you can leave electronic mail for the administrators.

It's a good idea to check the Yahoo! site at least once per session, since it's constantly changing and new pages are added every day. This site is probably the best indication of the enormous popularity and constant expansion of the World Wide Web, so make sure you add it to your bookmark file the first time you visit.

TIP

Navigator 3.0's Help menu offers more than technical assistance. Not only can you access release notes for the product and Netscape's own online Handbook, you can even learn more about security and about creating your own Web documents. If you're struggling with a technical problem or just want to learn more about the Web, make sure to check out the Help menu.

THE DIRECTORY MENU

The Netscape Navigator 3.0 Directory pull-down menu contains all of the same commands available using the Directory buttons, but it also offers other resources of interest to new users:

- **Netscape Galleria.** The Netscape Galleria is a collection of links to Web servers running Netscape's server software, including the Commerce Server package for secure online financial transactions. Some of these sites are commercial; others focus on educational and scientific content. If you're interested in running a Web server, this page offers a great chance to sample what other individuals and companies have done.

- **About the Internet.** This menu item is provided for those who would like additional information about the Internet itself. The links on this page jump to other pages that provide both basic concepts and technical details on every aspect of the Internet and the World Wide Web, including the history of the Internet and current demographic statistics.

MOVING ON

In this chapter, you learned the basics of surfing the World Wide Web, as well as how to operate the major features of Netscape Navigator 3.0. You now know how to search for a particular site, as well as where you can find the newest and coolest pages on the Web.

In the next chapter, we get serious about Netscape Mail. You'll learn how to compose electronic mail to others, read mail they've sent to you, and reply to mail messages. We'll discuss features that Netscape Navigator 3.0 provides for electronic mail power-users as well, including mailing lists and message forwarding.

4

Netscape Mail

Netscape isn't content with just making the world's best Web browser. In Netscape Navigator 3.0, Netscape has created a multi-purpose software product that can do much more than just display Web documents.

The most basic of all Internet tools is electronic mail, or e-mail. E-mail is the most widely used software tool of any kind, and Netscape Navigator 3.0 provides a separate interface just to handle this messaging service. In this chapter, we'll show you how to use the Netscape Navigator 3.0 e-mail window to send, receive, read, and store e-mail. This window, shown in Figure 4-1, is accessed by selecting Netscape Mail from Navigator's pull-down Window menu.

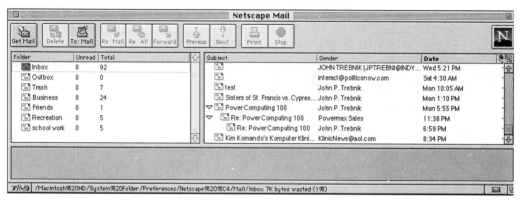

Figure 4-1: *The Netscape Mail window.*

Before we get into that, however, let's begin with a few words about e-mail itself.

WHAT IS E-MAIL & HOW DOES IT WORK?

E-mail, as you probably know, is the electronic messaging service of the Net. When you send a message to a friend via e-mail, that message travels from your machine over the Internet until it arrives at your friend's machine, or to a special electronic post office on a machine he or she can access. The message is then kept there until your friend retrieves it and reads it.

How does the Internet know how to get a piece of e-mail from your machine to your friend's post office account? It works just about like regular old-fashioned snail mail: all the necessary delivery information is contained in your friend's e-mail address.

When you write a piece of e-mail, it's essential to get the address right. No friendly Mr. Postman is going to figure out that you really meant the house down the block from the address you indicated. Every character counts. If there is a mistake in the address you enter—even one wrong letter—the mail will simply be returned to you as undeliverable.

The standard form for an Internet address is *user@domain*. This address is in two parts, separated by an @ sign (press Shift+2 on your keyboard). The part before the @ is the username, and the part after the @ is the domain name—the name of the machine where that user has an e-mail account. It is important that e-mail addresses not have any spaces in them.

Usernames are how users are identified by their Internet access providers. For instance, the username part of Count Dracula's e-mail address, dracula@transylvania.com, is *dracula*. Domain names are the names of the machines themselves. The domain name in the address, *transylvania.com*, identifies the name of a machine, transylvania. The *.com* at the end of the domain name means it is a commercial service. There are also *.gov* services, which are governmental institutions; *.edu* services, which are at educational institutions; and so on. We touched on some of this in Chapter 1, "The Net & the Web." Sometimes addresses will end with information about a country or network instead of a type of service. For example, addresses ending in .ca are in Canada, and addresses ending in .uk are in the United Kingdom.

WHAT'S MY E-MAIL ADDRESS?

Your e-mail address is your identity in the online world; you were probably given your e-mail address by the people who provide you with Internet access. If you are on an office LAN, your Internet e-mail address may be your network login name followed by an @ sign and the domain name of your company. Then again, it may not—you really need to check with your LAN administrator.

If you get on the Net using a SLIP or PPP account, you can usually figure out your e-mail address. If your login name is *frank* and your Internet access provider is *graveyard.com*, then your e-mail address is probably frank@graveyard.com. If this isn't correct, then you will have to call your access provider to figure out what your address is.

TIP

If your Internet access provider doesn't provide you with an e-mail account, you should seriously consider switching access providers!

EXCHANGING MESSAGES WITH ONLINE SERVICES

What if you have friends who are not connected directly to the Internet via a LAN or a SLIP or PPP account, but are users of some online service such as America Online (AOL) or CompuServe? Can you exchange e-mail messages with them?

Sure! Users of CompuServe, MCI Mail, AT&T Mail, Prodigy, and AOL can send you e-mail using your regular Internet address. Typically, the procedure is no more complex than sending a message to another user of the service. You can also send e-mail to a user on any of these services, using Netscape Navigator 3.0 in the same way you would when communicating with another individual on the Net. The only difference is the addressing. If an online service user gives you his or her ID, you have to know how to turn it into a valid Internet address so that any message you send can be delivered. The method for translating addresses varies from service to service.

COMPUSERVE

User IDs on CompuServe take the form of two numbers separated by a comma, as in 71234,5678. To send e-mail to a CompuServe subscriber, you address it to that ID number at (@) the domain compuserve.com. The only trick is that the comma must be replaced by a period. Thus the Internet e-mail address for the user whose ID is 71234,5678 would be:

```
71234.5678@compuserve.com
```

That's all there is to it; you send the message just like any other e-mail.

MCI MAIL

MCI Mail users really have three IDs: a number; a "handle," or abbreviated name; and a normal full name. For instance, the user Jake Barns might have the following set of IDs:

```
123-4567
jbarns
Jake Barns
```

To send e-mail to Jake, you could use any of the following
Internet e-mail addresses:

```
1234567@mcimail.com
jbarns@mcimail.com
jake_barns@mcimail.com
```

Please note that in the user number, you drop the hyphen, and
in the full name you have to add an underscore (_) character
between the first and last names.

AMERICA ONLINE

All you need to know is the AOL user's "screen name"; you then
just add the at sign (@) and the domain aol.com. A valid Internet
e-mail address for an AOL user might be, for instance:

```
aoluser@aol.com
```

Note that even if the AOL user has a space in his or her AOL
name—John Doe, for instance—you can ignore that space and
simply address your e-mail to johndoe@aol.com.

PRODIGY

This is just like America Online. You send e-mail to a particular
user ID at prodigy.com. Here's an example:

```
abc123@prodigy.com
```

AT&T MAIL

As with AOL and Prodigy, each AT&T Mail user has a unique
username. To address a message, you simply append @attmail.com
to the username. A valid address might be as follows:

```
msmuffet@attmail.com
```

CONFIGURING NETSCAPE NAVIGATOR 3.0 MAIL

Now that you know about e-mail addresses, you are ready to configure the Netscape Navigator 3.0 Mail window for your personal use. Let's start by configuring what the window looks like.

TIP

If you're eager to start communicating with the world and don't want to slog through all the setup options right now, just skip ahead to the Servers and Identity tabs. Those are the only ones that absolutely must be filled out in order for Netscape Mail to work properly. You can always come back and modify the settings in the other tabs later.

THE APPEARANCE TAB

1. With Netscape Navigator 3.0 loaded, select Mail and News Preferences from the Options menu. The Mail & News Preferences dialog box appears, with the Appearance tab selected as shown in Figure 4-2.

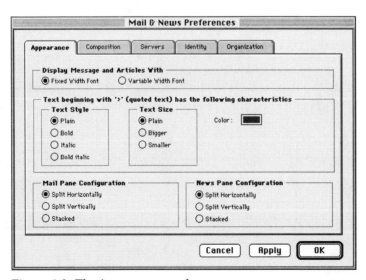

Figure 4-2: *The Appearance panel.*

- If the Appearance tab isn't automatically selected when you choose Mail and News Preferences from the Options menu, select it now.

2. Select whether you want messages to be displayed in a fixed-width font or a variable-width font by clicking the respective option button. You might want to try it both ways.

3. Select how you want *quoted text* to appear by selecting a style and a size option button.

WHAT IS QUOTED TEXT?

One of the great advantages of e-mail over snail mail is that without any retyping it allows you to include the text of previous messages you have received. For instance, in responding to a message you may wish to include sections of the original text as part of your reply, or you may want to forward the message to another recipient. Using text you've received is called quoting.

The Internet convention for quoted text is to precede each quoted line with the greater than symbol (>). You will sometimes see messages in which somebody includes quoted text that has already been quoted by somebody else—in that case each line is preceded by two greater than symbols. In Netscape Mail, you can make quoted text stand out even more by selecting among the font options in the Appearance panel.

One other important note on quoted text that is preceded by the (>) character: the lines are sent "as is," without wrapping at 72 characters like other text you enter into the Message composition window. This is because it is essential that each line always begins with the special character. The lines of quoted text may appear to be wrapped on your screen if you've resized your window, but when the recipient gets the quoted text it will look right.

In Netscape Mail, you can make quoted text stand out even more by selecting among the font options available from the General Preferences menu. Those of us with trifocals tend to need a little larger screen font!

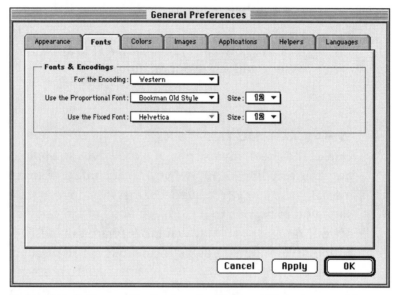

Figure 4-3: *Setting up the fixed- and variable-width fonts you wish to use.*

4. In the Mail Pane Configuration section of the Appearance tab, select how you want your Mail and News windows to look. The default, shown in Figure 4-2, is Split Horizontally. In this layout, the pane that contains the contents of a selected e-mail message is below the two other panes, one that lists your e-mail folders and another that lists the messages within that folder.

   ■ If you want to align the message content pane to the right of the two split panes, choose Split Vertically.

   ■ If you want to stack all three panes one on top of each other, with the content pane at the bottom, select Stacked.

TIP

In most cases the default window layout is the most convenient. You can always change it later, after you've become more familiar with the various e-mail features.

And now, on to the Composition tab.

THE COMPOSITION TAB

This tab lets you set various options such as an e-mail address or a file to copy all of your outgoing messages to. (Refer to Figure 4-4.) This can be useful if you want to save a paper trail (or rather a byte trail) of your correspondence. There are two convenient Browse buttons for you to use to select alternative folders should the default selections be inappropriate or inconvenient for you. For the time being, leave these settings in the default position. If reviewing your mail offline with another application is desirable later, you might was to set up different folders using this panel. There are two other options in the Composition tab that might need some explaining:

- **Send and Post.** This option lets you choose among two standard protocols for attaching files to your mail messages. Please refer to the sidebar, "Making Sure Your Attached Files Arrive Safely."

- **Automatically quote original message when replying**. If this is checked, Netscape Mail automatically includes the original message as part of your reply to that message. Each line of the quoted message is preceded by the greater than symbol (>).

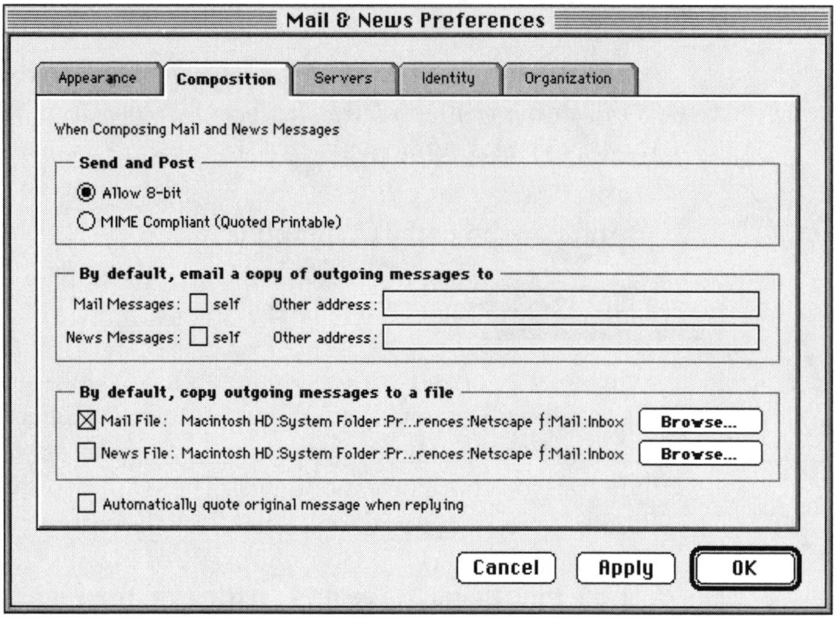

Figure 4-4: *Setting up your composition and retrieval options.*

Now the two most important tabs, the ones where you tell Netscape Mail who you are and actually how to send and retrieve your messages.

THE SERVERS TAB

In the Servers tab, there are two pieces of information Netscape Navigator 3.0 needs: your SMTP (Simple Mail Transport Protocol—aren't you glad you asked?) address, and your POP3 (Post Office Protocol) address. These are the network addresses the program uses to send and receive your e-mail. If you don't know what these addresses are for your Internet access provider, you still can probably figure them out.

SMTP & POP3

Like all Internet programs, Netscape Navigator 3.0 relies on established protocols to send and receive data. As explained earlier in this book, protocols are simply conventions that allow one piece of software to exchange data with another. For instance, a client program might expect a particular kind of acknowledgment after it sends a packet of data. Both sender and receiver need to play by the same rules.

Internet mail programs use SMTP (Simple Mail Transport Protocol) to *send* messages. The client, Netscape Navigator 3.0, first establishes a connection with the remote SMTP server, the machine that acts as host for the recipient's e-mail account. Once the link is established, Netscape Navigator 3.0 sends the recipient's name. If the server can accept mail for that user, it responds with an OK. If there are several intended recipients, this negotiation continues for each of them. Finally Netscape Navigator 3.0 sends the actual body of the e-mail message.

To *retrieve* messages from your e-mail server, Netscape Navigator 3.0 uses a very different protocol, called POP3 (Post Office Protocol, version 3). I won't go into the details of POP3 because they're somewhat complex, but it's important to make sure that your e-mail account is on a server that supports this protocol (most do).

OK, let's do this:

1. Enter the domain name for your Internet access provider in the Outgoing Mail (SMTP) Server field. Count Dracula would enter **transylvania.com**.

2. Now enter the domain name for your Internet access provider in the Incoming Mail (POP) Server field. Once again, Count Dracula would enter **transylvania.com**, as shown in Figure 4-5.

3. Enter your username in the POP User ID field. Count Dracula would enter **dracula**, as shown in Figure 4-5.

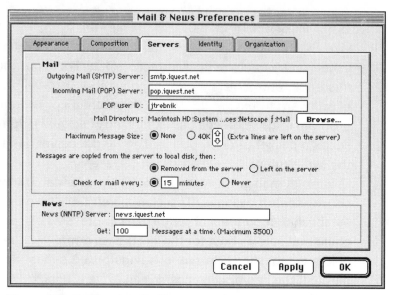

Figure 4-5: *Configuring the Servers panel.*

4. Unless you want to limit the size of messages you receive, leave the None radio button selected in the Maximum Message Size area. If you decide to limit the size, the value you enter is the maximum number of lines.

5. Select the Removed from the server radio button if you want all messages deleted from your post office account when you retrieve your mail. If you want your messages to remain on the server so that you can download them again later, select the Left on the server radio button.

   ■ If you decide to leave retrieved messages on your post office server, you may receive the same messages over and over when Netscape Navigator 3.0 gets new mail.

6. In the check for mail every area, tell Netscape Navigator 3.0 how often you want the program to log on to your post office server to collect any new messages.

   ■ If you click the Never radio button, you will have to click the Get Mail button in the Netscape Mail window every time you want to check for messages.

You can ignore the News options, which I cover in the next chapter. For now, move on to the Identity tab, as shown in Figure 4-6.

THE IDENTITY TAB

Here it is:

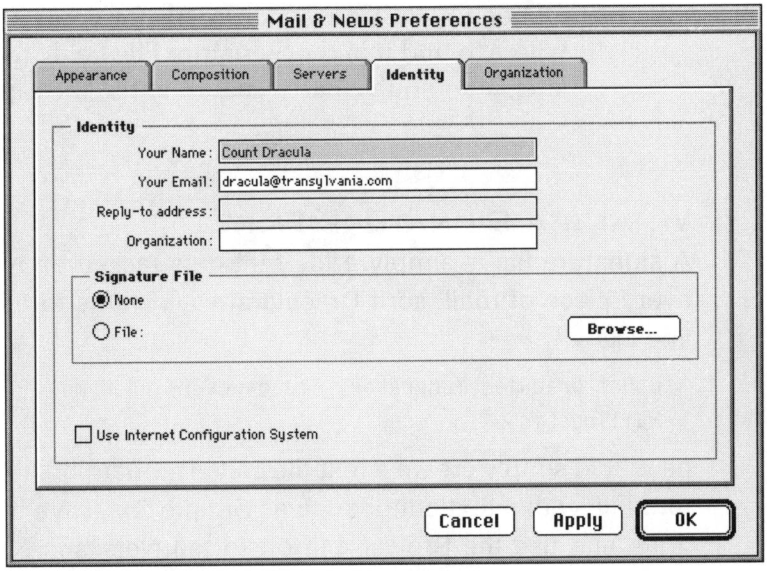

Figure 4-6: *The Identity tab.*

This is where you enter the information that will appear on all of your outgoing mail. To configure your identity preferences:

1. Type your name into the Your Name field. Dracula would enter **Count Dracula**.

2. Type your e-mail address into the Your Email field. Dracula would enter **dracula@transylvania.com**.

3. Optionally, enter an alternate e-mail address in the Reply-to address field. This is the address others will use when replying to your messages. It isn't likely you'll need to do this. You would only use Reply-to address if, for instance, you wanted to send mail out from Netscape Navigator 3.0 using a commercial access provider, but you wanted to get replies on another account, such as an account you have through school.

4. Optionally, enter the name of an organization or affiliation in the Organization field. This simply adds an identifying tag to your mail. Think of it as a kind of electronic letterhead, there if you want it but not really necessary.

5. Optionally, create a signature file for yourself and specify where to find it in the Signature File field. You can do this later, after you've had a chance to use the capability.

WHAT'S A SIGNATURE FILE?

A signature file is simply a file that gets tacked on to the end of every piece of mail, so if Dracula always wants to add a closing line like

```
Count Dracula, Moderator, Bloodsuckers Anonymous
Mailing List
```

he would simply create a text file called something like My Signature File with a text editor such as SimpleText, save it on his hard drive and use the Browse button to tell Netscape Navigator 3.0 where to find it. Like Organization, a signature file (often called a ".sig" on the Net) can be used to include more information in your mail, but isn't necessary. If you do include a signature file, make sure it is short (no more than four lines long) and pertinent (long and/or pointless .sig files tend to attract flames for wasting bandwidth).

Your completed Identity panel will look something like Figure 4-7.

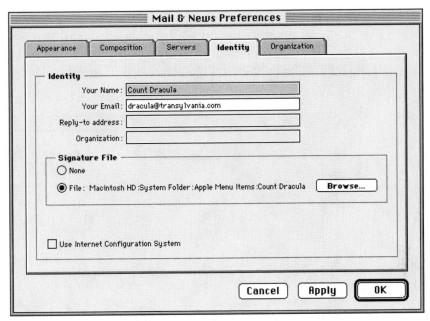

Figure 4-7: *A configured Identity panel.*

One more tab to go!

THE ORGANIZATION TAB

The Organization panel, shown in Figure 4-8, offers several options:

- **Password option**. When you open the Netscape Mail window, a dialog box asks you for your password for your POP3 server. You can avoid this message by checking the Remember Mail Password check box.

- **Threading options**. You can choose whether or not to *thread* e-mail messages. Threading is simply a means of organizing messages whereby all replies (and replies to replies) are kept together with the original message, creating a sort of automatic "file" of the related correspondence. Threading is almost essential for Usenet News (see the next chapter), but it can be pretty convenient for regular e-mail as well.

■ **Sorting options**. In the Organization panel you can choose whether to sort your incoming e-mail messages by the date you received them, by who sent them, by message number, or by subject. The default is to sort them by date received.

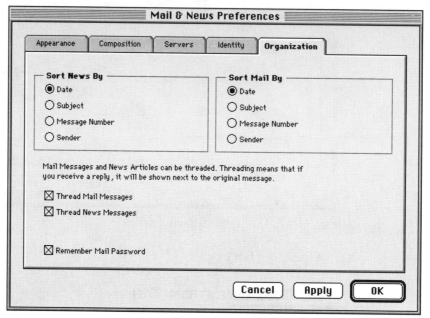

Figure 4-8: *The Organization panel.*

Click OK to leave the Mail & News Preferences dialog box and save your changes.

TIP

You can change the fonts Netscape Navigator 3.0 uses to display messages by selecting the Fonts tab under the Appearance panel from within the General Preferences dialog box. If you don't like the default fonts, you might want to experiment a bit.

SPLITTING AND RESIZING MAIL FRAMES

Before we move into sending and receiving e-mail, take another look at Figure 4-1. Netscape has provided a resizing tool very familiar to Macintosh users, whereby the individual frames in the window can be adjusted for easier viewing and better organization of your material. If you move the cursor (arrow) to one of the narrow areas between the different frames in the window, the arrow turns into a familiar resizing tool with a small arrow pointing in each direction. Adjust each frame just as if you were using a spreadsheet program. Here are three different ways (see Figures 4-9, 4-10, and 4-11) you might view your mail, all of which I achieved by resizing the initial window shown in Figure 4-1:

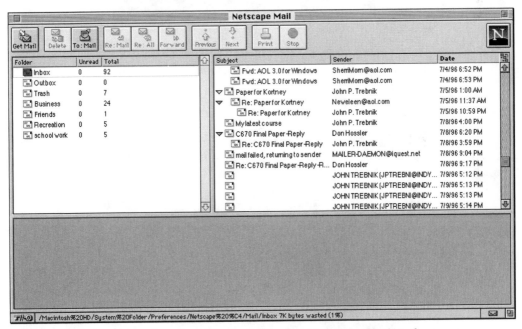

Figure 4-9: *Mail window opened with large viewing area devoted to the list of messages.*

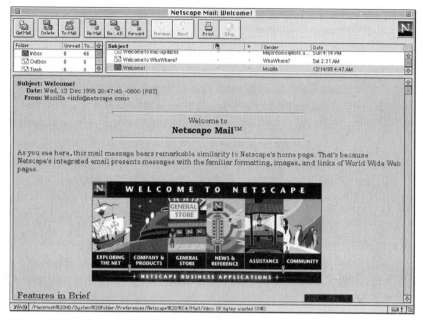

Figure 4-10: *Here's the Mail window accompanying Netscape's welcoming message.*

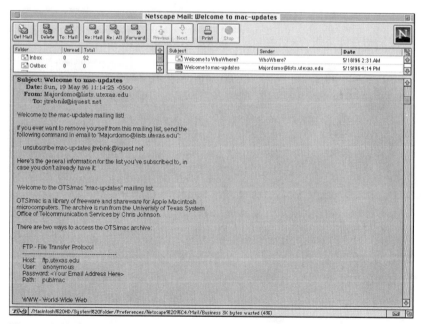

Figure 4-11: *Using maximum viewing area to read textual contents.*

A major improvement in Netscape Navigator 3.0 over previous versions is that on incoming messages you will always see the title "Sender" above the column that shows the name of the sender of the mail message. In the Outbox and Sent Mail folders, you'll see the title "Recipient" instead of sender, and the column shows the e-mail address of the mail recipient (see Figure 4-12).

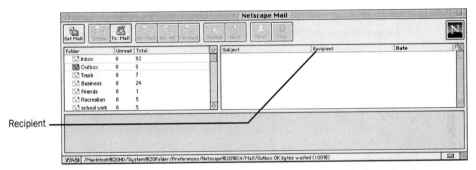

Figure 4-12: *Clicking on the Outbox will change the title from Sender to Recipient*

The sequence in which messages are displayed can also be changed by clicking on the primary field you wish to use to view them. Click on Subject, for example, and the title will change to "Subject" as messages are re-organized and represented to you. Click on Sender, and Netscape Mail will reorganize your messages in alphabetical sequence according to "Sender."

When viewing either the Netscape Mail or the Netscape News window, the pull-down Options menu offers a hierarchical item called Show Headers. This new menu item can be used to control the number of header information fields displayed when viewing messages. All displays are possible header fields. Normal displays the primary address fields, while Brief displays only subject and recipient fields. Set the option that suits you best!

SENDING & RECEIVING E-MAIL

Once you have configured your preferences, you are ready to send yourself a message. That might seem at first like an odd thing to do, but it's the best way to try out both sending and receiving e-mail. Let's get started.

SENDING AN E-MAIL MESSAGE

While you are still in Netscape Navigator 3.0 and connected to the Internet, select New Mail Message from the File menu or simply press ⌘+M. If you are already in the Netscape Mail window, click the To:Mail button. Whichever method you use, the Message Composition window appears, as shown in Figure 4-13.

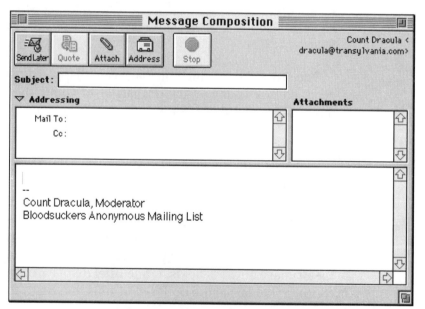

Figure 4-13: *The Message Composition window.*

As you can see, this window is divided into two parts. The top part contains the header information about the message, the text that will appear at the very beginning of the message when it is received. The bottom part is the pane where you type in your actual message.

Each of the headers in the top pane has a specific function:

- **Subject.** The Subject header is whatever you want it to be—it tells the recipient what your letter is about. Try to keep your Subject lines short and informative.

- **Addressing.** The Mail To field is where you enter the e-mail address of your recipient. If you want to send the same piece of mail to more than one person, just enter all their addresses in the Mail To field, separating each address with a comma.

- The Cc field works like carbon copies in the old-fashioned world of paper and typewriter—a copy of your message is sent to everyone listed on the Cc line. Typically, the message is sent to these recipients for their information, and they don't need to reply. Note that the designated recipient or recipients of the mail will see who has been Cc'ed.

TIP

Click the Mail To, Cc, or Address button to select addresses from your Address Book. You can read about setting up your Address Book later, in the section called, unsurprisingly, "The Address Book."

- **Attachments.** Netscape Navigator 3.0 allows you to attach other files stored on your computer to your mail, so that when you send the mail, a copy of that file travels along with the mail. You can also send URLs, links to files that aren't even on your machine but that will appear in your recipient's Mail window! We'll talk more about this in the section "Attaching Files to Messages."

There are other header lines you can add to your e-mail—Reply To, Newsgroups, Followups To, From and Bcc lines—which you add by selecting them under View in the menu (or, if you want to see everything, just select Show All).

- **Reply To.** The Reply To line is where you can put the e-mail address of another account where you want responses sent. You set this information up earlier, when you were using the Mail and News Preferences panels.

- **Bcc.** Bcc, for *Blind Cc,* is used when you want to send a copy of a letter to someone but do not want that person's name to appear in the Cc line. The recipient or recipients of the mail who are listed on the Mail To and Cc lines will not know who has been Bcc'ed.

- **Newsgroups.** In this field, you can list the names of any Usenet newsgroups you'd like your epistle posted to. Select Newsgroups from the View menu. You will learn more about Usenet newsgroups in Chapter 5, "Newsgroups

- **Followups To.** This field is also for use with Usenet news- groups. For more information, please see "Replying to an Article" in Chapter 5.

To write a test letter to yourself, you really only need to fill in a couple of these fields:

1. Fill in the Mail To field with your own e-mail address.

2. Fill in the Subject field with a subject like **Letter from me**.

3. Write yourself a message in the pane below the headers, just as you would type new text into a word processor document. In the end, you should have a message that looks something like the one in Figure 4-14.

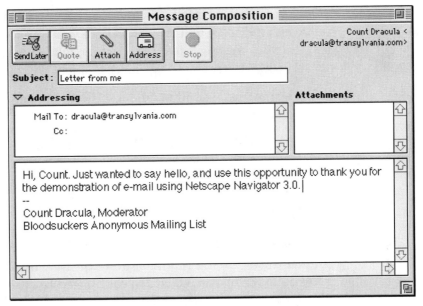

Figure 4-14: *A test letter to yourself.*

TIP

As you write, your lines wrap when you reach the right edge of the editing area. But when your recipient receives your message, the lines are not wrapped the same way you see them in the Message Composition window. Instead, they always wrap at 72 characters. This assures that even if you work in a very large or very small window, your messages will always be the same width and look right to your recipients. If you don't like this and instead want your messages to appear to your recipients exactly as they appear to you while you're writing them, uncheck Wrap Long Lines from the pull-down View menu of the Message Composition window.

Just above and to the left edge of the Addressing pane is a three-cornered arrow just like the arrows used to expand or collapse the contents of folders in the Macintosh hierarchical file structure. Click the arrow to point it rightward, and you make more space in which to compose your message as the Addressing pane collapses. Once you've completed your message, you can once more expand the Addressing pane to be sure you have completed that information correctly!

Once you have the Mail To and Subject fields filled out and you've entered some text in the text pane, you are ready to actually send your message.

1. Make sure you are still connected to the Internet.

2. While you are still in the Message Composition window, click the Send button in the toolbar.

If everything is set correctly, Netscape Navigator 3.0 will contact your Internet access provider and send the message. If it can't send the message properly, make sure that your Internet connection is really open, and check the name of the SMTP and POP servers in the Servers tab, shown earlier in Figure 4-5. If all of this is correct and you still can't send a message, you may need to contact your Internet access provider to make sure you have the right names for the machines handling the mail on your system.

Netscape Navigator 3.0 is also configured to save a copy of your outgoing messages in a folder called "Send." If you don't want a copy of these messages, you can delete them, which you will learn how to do later in this chapter under "Organizing Your Mail Folders."

MAILTO: TAGS

Besides calling up the Message Composition window, Netscape Navigator 3.0 offers another way to send mail. Web pages can include special HTML tags called MAILTO: tags. They look just like ordinary links, although often they appear in italics. When you click one of these, Netscape Navigator 3.0 pops up the Message Composition window, allowing you to send a message to the recipient indicated in the Mail To tag.

MAILTO: tags provide a convenient way to solicit feedback or comments in a Web document.

RETRIEVING E-MAIL

Now that you have sent yourself a message, you can go ahead and retrieve it from your post office server:

1. You should still be connected to the Internet. Back in the Netscape Navigator 3.0 main window, click the small envelope icon at the bottom right corner. You will immediately be asked for a password.

TIP

You will not be asked for a password if you checked the Remember Mail Password check box in the Organization tab of Mail & News Preferences.

2. In the Password Entry dialog box, enter your e-mail password. If you're connecting to the Internet via SLIP or PPP, this is probably the same password you use to connect to your Internet access provider.

   Once you enter your password, Netscape Navigator 3.0 logs you in to your post office account to retrieve your mail.

   ■ If you have configured Netscape Navigator 3.0 so that it does not retrieve mail automatically, you need to click the Get Mail button in order to get your waiting message.

If this is the first mail message you have sent, your test message is the only one that will be retrieved (if you don't see your test message in the mail window, press the Get Mail button to check once more). But if you are already using the e-mail address you filled in earlier in Mail & News Preferences, Netscape Navigator 3.0 will get the rest of your e-mail stored at that address as well.

TIP

The mail icon at the bottom right of the Navigator 3.0 window is the easiest way to access Netscape Mail. Simply click on it. If there is a question mark next to the Mail icon, Navigator 3.0 cannot automatically check your mail server for new messages, probably because you've told it not to when you set up the default commands in the Servers tab under the Mail & News Preferences panel. Once Netscape Navigator 3.0 retrieves any e-mail from your post office server, it puts an exclamation point next to the envelope icon in the main browser window. That way you know immediately when new mail has arrived, even if you are not in the Netscape Mail window.

Let's assume that the test message was the first piece of e-mail you have ever received—other than the Welcome message that from Netscape's "Mozilla." Once Netscape Navigator 3.0 retrieves the new message, your mail window will look pretty much like the one in Figure 4-15.

As you can see, this window is divided into three panes—Folder in the upper left, Message in the upper right, and the main reading window below. Each of these panes has information sorted in columns. In the Folder pane, you will see an Inbox, where incoming mail is stored, with a list of Unread and Total messages. (If the test message is the only mail you have, both Unread and Total will read "1.")

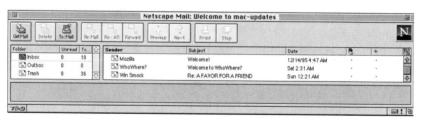

Figure 4-15: *Mail window after retrieving a new e-mail message.*

You can change the layout of the three panes in the Netscape Mail window. See the section on the Appearance panel.

You can move from folder to folder simply by clicking on each icon. For now, return to the Inbox folder. The Message pane shows you several things:

- The Subject line of the incoming mail.

- Whether you have marked the messages (a method of flagging important mail). Marked messages are indicated with a red flag.

- Whether you have read the message yet. Unread messages are flagged with a green diamond that may look like a dot if your eyes are like mine.

- The Sender line.

- The date of the message.

The width of each of these columns is adjustable. To change the size of the columns:

1. Position your mouse over the border of the column until it displays a pair of arrows pointing left and right.

2. Now click and drag the border of the column to the left or right, depending on which column you want to widen.

You can even switch the order of any of the columns in the Message and Folder panes. Simply drag the header button (the button at the top of the column with the word Sender, Subject, Date, etc. on it) right or left to its new location. For instance, you might want to drag the Date column to the far left in the Message window.

The borders between the panes operate exactly the same way, and you will probably want to shrink the size of the Folder pane to the left so that you can have more room to expand the From and Subject headers of your e-mail in the Message pane, as shown in Figure 4-16.

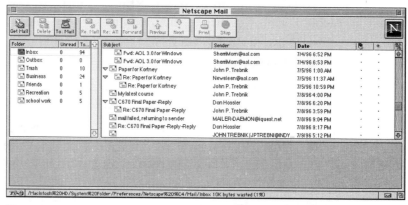

Figure 4-16: *A window configured to give more room to the Message pane, where information about the mail (like Sender and Subject) is displayed.*

TIP

To flag a message you've received, simply select it and click the dot in the flag column. You might want to flag messages that really need to be answered, thus differentiating them from those that are merely informational. Once you have replied to a message, you can unflag it by clicking in the flag column again.

Now let's actually read a message:

1. If your Inbox folder is not currently open, open the Inbox Icon by clicking it in the Folder pane. The headers of your messages appear in the Messages pane.

2. Click the Subject line of the mail you want to read. The message itself is now displayed in the lower window for reading, as in Figure 4-17.

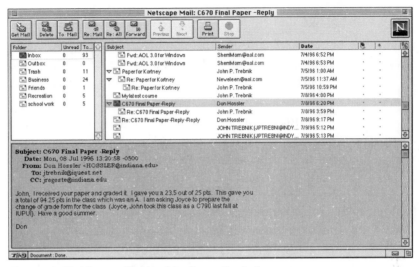

Figure 4-17: *New mail opened in the mail window.*

Maybe you should be polite and send a reply. Replying to e-mail is the last of the basic messaging functions.

REPLYING TO E-MAIL

Replying to a piece of e-mail differs from sending new mail in several important ways. First of all, when you reply, Netscape Navigator 3.0 fills in the Mail To field automatically, since the intended recipient is simply the sender of the original message. The program also fills in the Subject field with "Re:" and the subject of the mail you are replying to.

There is another important difference: the program lets you use a special quote feature to include the text of the e-mail you are responding to right in the body of your reply.

Let's try it:

1. In the Mail window, select a received message and click the Re:Mail button.

2. When the Message Composition window opens, the text of the letter to which you are replying appears in the bottom pane. You will notice that every line begins with a ">"—this is the Internet standard for indicating quoted material.

TIP

The text of the original message does not appear in your reply if you unchecked "Automatically quote original message when replying" in the Composition panel of Mail & News Preferences.

At this point, you can add whatever text you like below the quoted text. You can also add other people to the mail To or CC fields if you like. If the message you have quoted is long, or if you want to respond to only one or two sentences of a letter, it is considered polite to delete the portions not relevant to your reply, although it is bad etiquette to delete or alter quoted text without indicating removals by inserting [...] or **(snip)** or some other indication that you edited the quoted material.

Once you've completed your reply, sending it is just like sending a new message: simply click the Send button.

REPLY TO ALL & FORWARD

There are two other ways to reply to a letter—Re:All and Forward. The ordinary Re:Mail function just grabs the e-mail addresses of everyone in the From field, but it ignores everyone in the Cc field. Re:All will send your reply out to everyone in both the From and Cc fields. This is a good way to have a kind of group conversation via e-mail, since Re:All allows you to address the same group of people the sender of the letter addressed originally.

To select the Re:All option when you are reading a message, simply click the Re:All button on the toolbar.

E-MAIL ETIQUETTE

■ Keep in mind that e-mail can be saved, and you can find that what you write in haste can come back to haunt you. Every piece of e-mail is potentially permanent, so before you say something in e-mail, make sure you really mean it because you may see it again later.

➡

■ Don't assume that the person getting your mail can always understand what you meant when you wrote it. E-mail can be very impersonal. We instinctively understand the difference between a bill, a business letter, and a post card when they arrive in our mail box, but all e-mail looks the same. Without this context, it is easy to misinterpret and to be misinterpreted, so write carefully. If someone has written a message that upsets you, don't rule out the possibility that he or she didn't mean it the way you took it.

■ Don't send abusive mail. This advice seems obvious, but the line can sometimes be hard to draw. What seems like a straightforward comment to you may be read as an insult by someone else. There is one Golden Rule: if someone complains about mail you are sending them, stop.

■ Reread your message before you send it. It is so easy to dash off a thoughtless message; the only defense is to reread everything you write before sending it. That goes double if you are angry when writing, in which case it is best to save the message and reread it later before deciding whether or not to send it. Once you send a message, there is no way to retract it.

You use Forward when you want to send a letter along to someone other than the people listed in the From or CC fields. Forward is similar to Re:Mail, with a couple of differences. The Subject line is filled in with the subject line of the letter labeled Fwd instead of Re (with the entire field enclosed in square brackets), and the Mail To field is not filled in. To select the Forward button when you are reading a message, simply click the Forward button in the toolbar.

The message being forwarded is automatically included as an attachment to the mail rather than as text in your actual message. Clicking the Quote button will include the text of the forwarded letter, bracketed by >'s, but if you use this feature to annotate the forwarded letter, remember to delete the attachment so that you don't send two copies of the same letter.

THE ADDRESS BOOK

Now that you know how to send and retrieve e-mail messages, you're ready to start communicating with anybody who has an Internet e-mail address. Chances are that you already know dozens or even hundreds of individuals and businesses with e-mail accounts, but how do you remember all these addresses?

E-mail addresses are a little easier than phone numbers because they often include part of a name or some other meaningful information, but as the Net grows and names get used up, e-mail addresses will become more and more devoid of any real-world significance. I suspect that some day they'll be like license plates, and you'll have to pay extra for a meaningful one!

Of course, you can jot e-mail addresses in a paper address book, but that's pretty old-fashioned for a Net geek like you. Fortunately, Netscape Navigator 3.0 provides an electronic address book for storing frequently used e-mail addresses.

The Address Book has two options—it allows you to enter single addresses and groups of addresses. To use the Address Book:

1. Select Address book from the Netscape Navigator 3.0's pull-down Window menu. A window like the one in Figure 4-18 pops up.

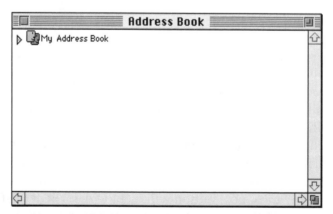

Figure 4-18: *The Address Book.*

■ Similar to the way in which other Macintosh hierarchical displays work, clicking the arrow to the left of a
folder so that it points downward, expands it to show
all the entries the folder contains. Clicking the arrow
sign so that it points to the right collapses the item.

2. To add a new user, select Add User from the pull-down Item
menu. A dialog box like the one in Figure 4-19 appears.

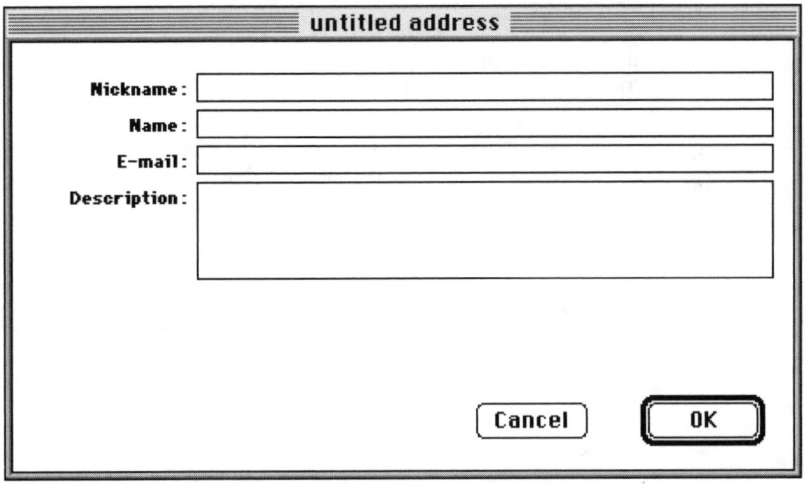

```
═════════════════════ untitled address ═════════════════════

     Nickname: [                                              ]
         Name: [                                              ]
       E-mail: [                                              ]
  Description: [                                              ]
               [                                              ]
               [                                              ]


                                    ( Cancel )   (   OK   )
```

Figure 4-19: *Add User dialog box.*

3. Fill in the Nickname field. It doesn't matter what you enter
as long as it's easy for you to remember and to associate
with this entry. The nickname is your way of remembering
who the recipient is.

4. Fill in the Name field with an actual name.

5. Fill in the E-mail field with a complete e-mail address for
the new entry.

6. Optionally, fill in the Description field. This field is just for
your reference.

7. Click OK. You are returned to the Address Book window,
and the new entry appears under your top-level folder,
with a little "person" icon next to it.

Let's say you entered your own address in the Address Book with the nickname **me**. Now, when you go to write a new piece of mail, you only need to type **me** in the Mail To field; Netscape Navigator 3.0 will fill in the real information automatically. This means that you can reduce e-mail addresses to a few easy-to-remember keystrokes. Why type in **president@whitehouse.gov** when you can simply enter **bill**? (Or **bob**, or **ross**, or whatever.)

You can also add lists of recipients to the Address Book. That way, a single nickname can represent as many addresses as you want. For instance, you could create an Address Book entry called Candidates that let you automatically send the same message to Bill, Bob, and Ross. To create a list:

1. In the Address Book window, select Add List from the Item menu. A dialog box like the one in Figure 4-20 appears.

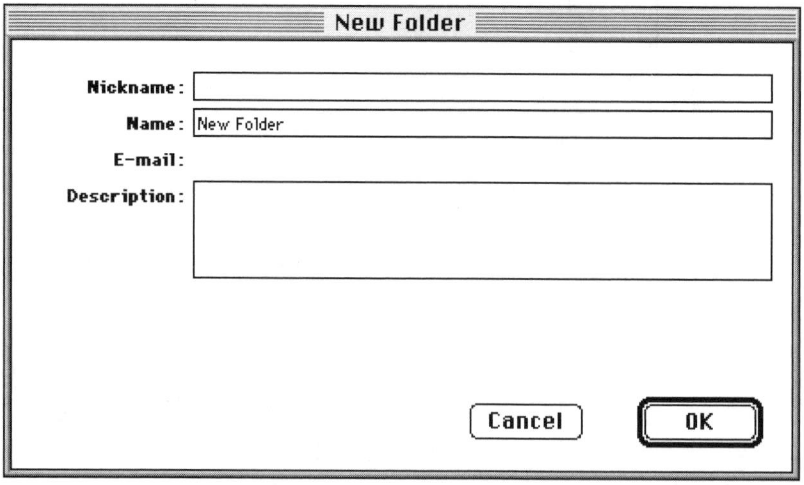

Figure 4-20: *Add List dialog box.*

2. Fill in the Nickname field with an easy-to-type nickname.

3. Fill in the Name field with the name of your list, for instance, Candidates.

4. Optionally, fill in the Description field. This field is just for your reference.

5. Click OK.

6. Back in the Address Book window, drag the names of people you want included into the new list from the main address book. You will get a new folder in your address book with all these names in it, like the one shown in Figure 4-21.

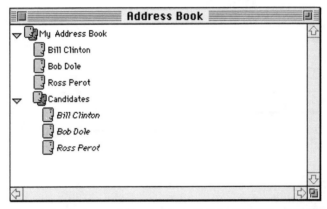

Figure 4-21: *A new folder (address list) in the Address Book window.*

7. Now, double-click on the Candidates folder icon. You are taken to a composition screen in which the addresses have already been selected as your candidates list. You can write your message, and it will be sent to each individual on the candidates list you have prepared.

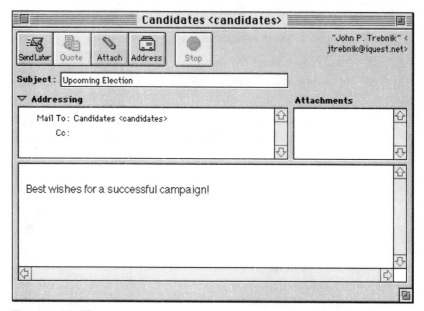

Figure 4-22: *The message composition screen where you can complete your work.*

TIP

You can also add entries to a list by selecting the folder and then clicking Add User in the Item menu.

MULTIMEDIA MAIL

Netscape Navigator 3.0 is really a multimedia program, and as you might guess, it can handle more than just plain text in e-mail. It can also display HTML formatting and GIF or JPEG images in the e-mail window, just as it can in the main Web browser window. You can see this in the piece of welcome mail included by Netscape in every browser, part of which is shown in Figure 4-23.

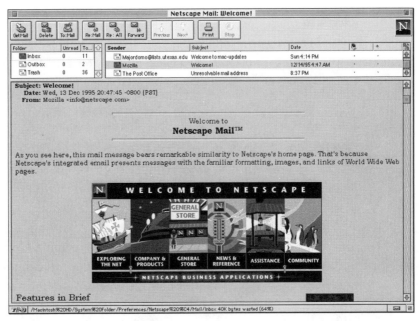

Figure 4-23: *An e-mail message with HTML formatting and a GIF image.*

When you send someone a piece of mail with HTML tags in it, Netscape Navigator 3.0 interprets these tags just as it would if they were in a Web page. This is how the message in Figure 4-22 is able to have text in boldface and italics. Although a course in HTML is beyond the scope of this chapter, if you know HTML and you are sending mail to someone else who uses Netscape, you can format the text, include inline images, and even add links to your mail. In fact, Netscape Navigator 3.0 is so good at handling HTML that if someone mentions a URL in a piece of mail, the program will recognize it as a URL and turn it into a link automatically! Just click on it, and you are transported to the site mentioned in the message.

In addition, when you send someone a GIF or JPEG image via e-mail, Netscape Navigator 3.0 opens it directly in the mail window, displaying the image for the recipient. This means you can now mail images directly to other Netscape Navigator 3.0 users. All of this allows you to create truly multimedia mail.

TIP

To learn a little bit about how to use HTML tags, see the section "Rolling Your Own Web Page" in Chapter 11, "Your Personal Workspace & Web Page."

FINDING PEOPLE ON THE NET

Suppose you want to find somebody's e-mail address. You can just go to the Internet "phone book" and look it up, right? Unfortunately the answer is, "No, not yet."

The Internet's greatest advantage as a communications tool is that it is decentralized, which allows small organizations and even individuals to take care of setting up their own Internet connection with little need to consult a central authority. The greatest disadvantage of this method is that it is, well, a little too decentralized to allow for anything like a net-wide "phone book." Instead there are several partial systems for looking people up, many of them good, but none of them perfect. Netscape in its wisdom has provided page of specialized services for finding people, accessible as a Web page from Netscape Navigator 3.0's pull-down Directory menu, or by simply clicking the People button in the browser window. Figure 4-24 shows what it looks like:

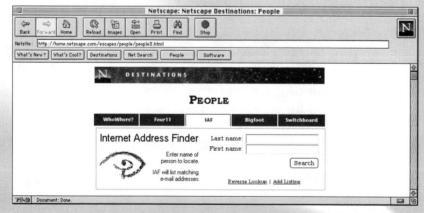

Figure 4-24: *Netscape's "People" page with Internet Address Finder selected.*

This page gives you access to a variety of different search services. To select a particular search tool, simply click the appropriate button. Be warned that many of the systems have arcane interfaces, but with a little practice you can extract useful information from them. The services offered on this page may change from time to time.

ATTACHING FILES TO MESSAGES

Besides including HTML tags and inline images in messages, you can also include entire HTML files or attach any kind of file, whether it's text or binary. There are no restrictions on the type of material you can include with your message. You can send spreadsheets, graphics, sounds, word processor files, programs, you name it. You can even attach files that are not on your own computer by sending the URLs for the files as attachments to your message!

To attach a file to an e-mail message:

1. Follow all the steps outlined earlier for creating a new e-mail message.

2. Before sending the message, click the Attachments button in the Message Composition window. The Attachments dialog box appears, as shown in Figure 4-25.

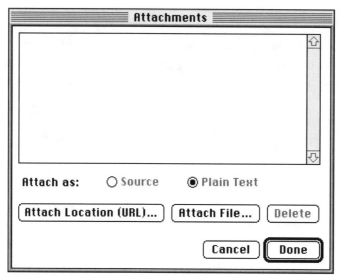

Figure 4-25: *The Attachments dialog box.*

3. Click either the Attach File button or the Attach Location (URL) button to send a file with your message or to include a link to a file that is on a remote computer.

   ■ Any kind of file can be attached to your mail. But if you are sending an HTML file, you can choose to send it as is (with its HTML formatting) or as plain text, without any special formatting. Select either the Source or the Plain Text radio button.

4. Once you have selected a file or typed in a URL (see Figure 4-26), click OK to return to the Attachments dialog box.

Figure 4-26: *The Attach Location dialog box.*

TIP

You can add as many files as you want to the attachment list before you close it.

5. Click OK to attach the file(s) and return to the Message Composition window.

6. Send the message, including any attachment, by clicking the Send button.

MAKING SURE YOUR ATTACHED FILES ARRIVE SAFELY

Internet e-mail is a system designed primarily for exchanging text messages, and attached files require special handling by Internet software. Netscape Navigator 3.0's default settings will work fine in most cases, but if somebody complains that a binary file you attached to a message was corrupt or wouldn't run, here's what to do:

1. Select Mail & News Preferences from the Options menu in the main window.

2. Select the Composition tab.

3. Click the MIME Compliant (Quoted Printable) radio button.

This makes Netscape Navigator 3.0 use an alternate method of encoding when it sends attached binary files.

DEALING WITH ATTACHED FILES YOU RECEIVE

Not only does Netscape Navigator 3.0 let you attach all kinds of files to e-mail messages, it also includes special options for dealing with attached files that you receive. For instance, as I mentioned before, when you receive an image file, it is automatically displayed as an image.

But Netscape Navigator 3.0 cannot automatically handle every type of file you might receive. Obviously there are thousands of different file formats, and new ones come along every day. Although Netscape Navigator 3.0 can't possibly know about all these different file types, it includes a facility for using special *helper applications* to handle them. For example, if you receive a Microsoft Word document attached to an e-mail message, Netscape Navigator 3.0 will automatically launch Word, if it's available on your system.

If you're an advanced user, you can customize the way Netscape Navigator 3.0 associates particular types of files with different helper applications, but that topic is beyond the scope of this chapter. For a full discussion of helper applications, turn to the section "Helper Applications" in Chapter 6, "Getting Files via FTP." All of the information there applies to e-mail as well as FTP.

ORGANIZING YOUR MAIL FOLDERS

Once you start receiving lots of e-mail, your Inbox folder can get pretty crowded. Luckily, Netscape Navigator 3.0 lets you create new folders in addition to the Inbox. It also lets you move messages around from folder to folder. Maybe you want to distinguish between personal mail and business correspondence. You can create new folders called "Friends" and "Business" to help you keep them separate.

To create a new folder:

1. In the Netscape Mail window, select the New Folder option from the pull-down File menu. The New Folder dialog box appears, as shown in Figure 4-27.

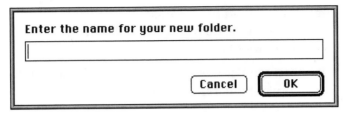

Figure 4-27: *New Folder dialog box.*

2. Enter a name such as **new folder** in the dialog box and press Return. Add some more if you wish. We've added folders for **Business** and **Recreation**.

The folders you just created will appear in the Folder pane alongside the Inbox folder, as shown in Figure 4-28.

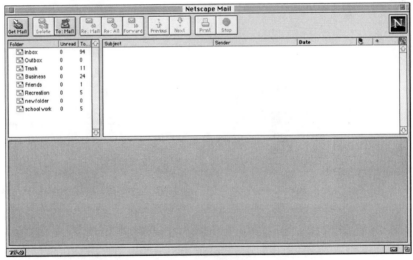

Figure 4-28: *New folders in the Folder pane. Now we can get organized!*

Once you have created a new folder, you can move mail into it to organize your e-mail in the same way you organize files on your desktop into folders. There are several ways to move e-mail around:

■ You can move a piece of mail into a folder by dragging and dropping the letter icon from the Message pane into the folder icon in the Folder pane (see Figure 4-29).

- You can use the command Move from the pull-down Message menu to move a selected letter or letters to another folder.

- You can use Copy to copy selected mail while leaving a copy where it is as well.

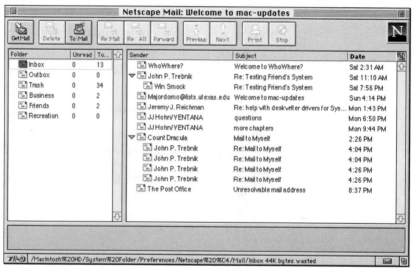

Figure 4-29: *Using the familiar drag-and-drop technique to reorganize your mail!*

What about removing e-mail you don't want to keep around any more? That's even easier!

1. Select one or more pieces of mail by clicking them.

2. Click the Delete button on the toolbar.

When you do this, a folder called Trash is created in the Folder pane. The Trash folder allows you to remove messages without making them unrecoverable. There are two ways to empty the Trash folder so that the e-mail in it is truly deleted.

1. Click the Trash folder in the Folder pane. You should now see a list of messages to be trashed.

2. Select all the messages you want to delete.

3. Click Delete on the toolbar.

TIP

If you don't need to look at the mail in the Trash folder before deleting it, select Empty Trash Folder from the pull-down File menu. Now it's really gone

SORTING E-MAIL MESSAGES
WITHIN FOLDERS

Folder provides a convenient way to sort mail into broad categories, but you still need ways to sort different pieces of mail within a folder. The Message pane provides several ways to do this:

- By default, mail in a folder is sorted in chronological order, with the earliest mail at the top of the folder and the latest mail at the bottom. To sort alphabetically by subject, click on the Subject bar at the top of the Message pane, as shown in Figure 4-30. Note that the program ignores any "Re:"s when sorting by subject.

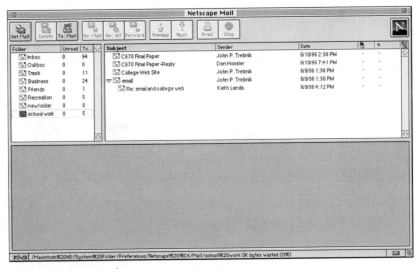

Figure 4-30: *Mail sorted by subject.*

- You can also sort by sender name, as shown in Figure 4-31. To do this, simply click the Sender bar.

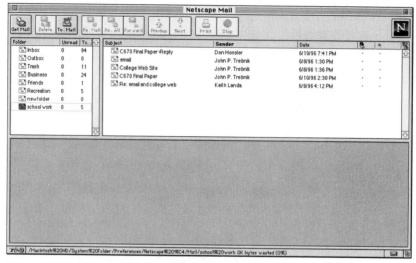

Figure 4-31: *The same Mail sorted by sender.*

Clicking Sender sorts your messages in alphabetical order by the first character in the From line, whether it is a first name or a last name. This can make your message list confusing.

- You can reverse any of these sorting tools by selecting Ascending in the Sort menu under View (see Figure 4-32). This makes date sorting run from most recent to earliest, and alphabetical sorting run from Z to A.

Messages can also be sorted by Subject, Date, Sender, or by thread (shared subject field).

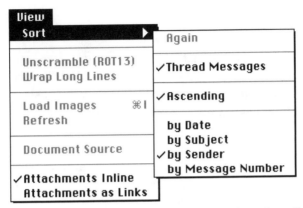

Figure 4-32: *Sort options available to you from the pull-down View menu.*

■ Selecting Thread Messages from the Sort menu (under the pull-down View menu) selects all messages in the same folder that are grouped together by a shared Subject line, such as an original letter and a number of replies to it.

CHANGING THE DEFAULT SORTING OPTIONS

There are two mail sorting options that you can access by selecting Mail & News Preferences from the Options menu and then choosing the Organization tab. You can sort your mail by *threading*, which means that all messages with a shared subject line will be grouped together automatically. You may also deselect threading from the pull-down View menu. You can also change the default sorting Netscape Navigator 3.0 provides when you open the Mail window. As you've seen, sorting by date is the default, but you can change the default to sorting by subject, by sender's name, or by message number.

MAILING LISTS

Internet e-mail is not just for exchanging private messages. It can also be used for gigantic group conversations among Internet users via an Internet service known as *mailing lists*.

A mailing list is simply a list of the e-mail addresses of everyone who wants to send and receive mail about a certain topic. There are mailing lists for discussing bonsai trees, rap music, adoption, cars, computer software, folk dancing, and on and on. There are thousands of lists, with new ones being created every week.

Adding your e-mail address to a mailing list is a way of joining these conversations. This is called *subscribing*, and removing your e-mail address from such a list is called *unsubscribing*. Once you've subscribed to a list, any mail you send to the list address gets sent back out to all the other e-mail addresses included on the list, and any mail from any of the other subscribers also gets sent to you.

When you subscribe to a mailing list, you immediately begin receiving mail from the other subscribers. If, after reading what other people on the list are talking about for a few days, you have something to add, you send mail back to the list address, and everyone else on the list sees your message.

So how do you find out what mailing lists are out there, and how to subscribe to them? The closest thing the Net has to an official list is Stephanie da Silva's list of *Publicly Accessible Mailing Lists*, originally created by Chuq Von Rospach. This list is an impressive compendium of mailing lists with a name, a short description, and information on how to subscribe for each one. The list itself is currently in 22 parts, arranged alphabetically and stored on a machine at MIT.

How do you retrieve this list of lists? Simple, you use Netscape Mail:

1. From the main Netscape Navigator 3.0 window, select New Mail Message from the File menu (or simply press ⌘+M). The Message Composition window appears.

2. Enter **mail-server@rtfm.mit.edu** in the Mail To field.

3. Enter **Mailing Lists** in the Subject field. (Do this for your own information. The MIT mail-server doesn't care what's in the Subject field. You must enter something in the Subject field, however, in order to complete your message for transmission.)

4. Type only one line in the body of the message:

   ```
   send pub/usenet/news.answers/mail/mailing-lists/part01
   ```

Your completed message should look like the one in Figure 4-33.

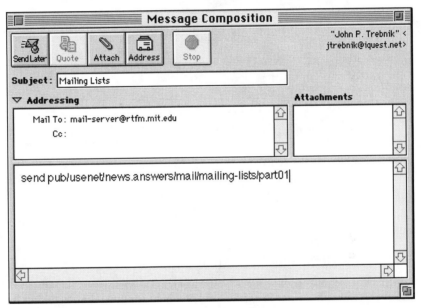

Figure 4-33: *Mail ready to go to the MIT mail server.*

This message instructs the MIT mail server, a kind of electronic file clerk, to send you Part 1 of the list. The list is large, and Part 1 shows you the names of all the mailing lists described in the other 21 parts, so take a look and make sure it's something you're interested in.

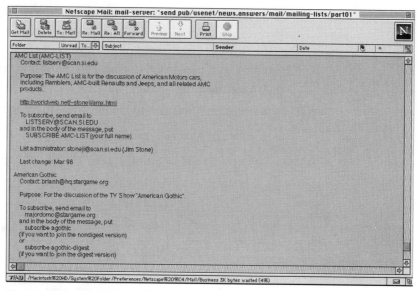

Figure 4-34: *A sample mailing list entry from Part 1 of the list of Publicly Accessible Mailing Lists.*

If there are mailing lists you'd like to subscribe to, send another piece of mail to mail-server@rtfm.mit.edu with just this line:

```
send  pub/usenet/news.answers/mail/mailing-lists/
part*
```

The asterisk there instead of an actual number means "Send me all the files." You should then receive 22 pieces of mail, containing the whole file cut into parts, with all the information you need to subscribe to mailing lists.

USING MAILING LISTS

There are a few differences between sending and receiving mail from a mailing list and sending and receiving personal mail, because mailing lists are a public forum. When you send a message to a mailing list, you don't even know how many people are reading it, much less who all of them are. This changes the way people read and write e-mail. Mailing lists are famous for long-running, voluminous, and often quite heated exchanges of e-mail, and because they are public forums, there are different rules of conduct there.

MAILING LIST ETIQUETTE

■ **Read before you write**. This is Rule #1. Before you send e-mail to a mailing list, remember that you are writing for a particular audience, and make sure that what you have to say is relevant. The rule of thumb when dealing with mailing lists is to read what other people are saying for a about a week before sending any mail yourself, to make sure that any questions or comments you might have are pertinent. (Reading a list without posting is called *lurking*.)

■ **Don't waste people's time**. This advice seems self-evident, but you will often see people posting mail that adds nothing to the discussion. Don't jump into a conversation just to tell everyone you agree with what someone else has said. If you are quoting another person's message, only quote what is relevant to your point. Nothing wastes people's time more than scrolling through screen after screen of a message they have already read once, only to read "I think you are completely correct" at the end.

■ **Use private e-mail when appropriate**. When you read something posted to a mailing list, you have a choice between replying to the writer in private or sending your reply to the entire list. If you merely want to say you agree, or ask where you can get a copy of something mentioned in the post, send e-mail to the writer instead of to the list.

■ **Use the Subject line carefully**. As with private e-mail, the Subject line is the first thing anyone sees in mail from you, and it tells people whether they are interested in what you have to say. Use the Subject line to describe, as succinctly as possible, the contents of your mail.

■ **Use unsubscribe procedures correctly**. If you are no longer interested in a particular mailing list, use the proper procedure for unsubscribing. When you signed up for the list, you were probably sent a message that included thorough instructions for both temporarily and permanently removing yourself from the list. Now's the time to follow those instructions! In most cases, you send an unsubscribe command to an address that's different from the one where you send regular messages. The whole world really doesn't care to know that you've decided to quit the list; your incorrectly communicated message may have to be manually deleted by hundreds or thousands of other lists subscribers.

One of the main differences between mailing list mail and personal mail is that when you want to reply to a message, you have a choice between replying only to the author of the article or sending the reply out to the whole list. If you have something to add to the debate, you should send your mail to the list, but if you just want to say that you agree with what someone has said, send it to the author only. The best way to tell what's appropriate is to read what other people are posting to the list to see what kinds of things are being discussed in public.

When replying to something you have read on a mailing list, make sure to examine the Mail To field of your outgoing mail. Different mailing lists handle the return address differently. On some lists, when you use the Reply function, the Mail To field is set up assuming that you want to send mail out to the whole mailing list, while on others it is set up assuming that you want to reply only to the author of the original post. If you want to reply to the whole group, you would select Reply to All.

> **TIP**
>
> *Checking the Mail To line of your mail before you reply will prevent you from sending mail you meant to be private to everyone on the list or from sending mail you meant to be public only to one other person.*

One concept that you will sometimes hear discussed on mailing lists is the *signal-to-noise ratio*. This is an engineering term that has been pressed into service to describe the percentage of messages sent to any given mailing list that are useful or interesting. Lists where there is generally an engaged and articulate discussion going on are said to have a high signal-to-noise ratio, while lists where the subscribers are posting messages needlessly are said to have a low signal-to-noise ratio. Good mailing list etiquette helps create a high signal-to-noise ratio.

MOVING ON

In this chapter, you've learned about using Netscape Navigator 3.0 to exchange e-mail with other Internet users, and you've worked with some of the program's powerful messaging features. In the next chapter, you'll learn another way to communicate with others on the Net: Usenet News. Like e-mail, News is a way of sending and receiving messages, but where mail is usually private, News provides a public forum. Netscape Navigator 3.0 also includes a separate interface, similar to the Netscape Mail window, just for handling News.

5

Newsgroups

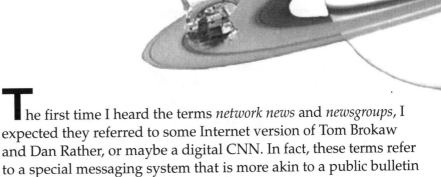

The first time I heard the terms *network news* and *newsgroups*, I expected they referred to some Internet version of Tom Brokaw and Dan Rather, or maybe a digital CNN. In fact, these terms refer to a special messaging system that is more akin to a public bulletin board at the local library or the grocery store.

It turns out that Netscape Navigator 3.0 is not only the best World Wide Web browser around but is also a top-notch *news reader*—a program that enables you to access and participate in newsgroups. After reading this chapter, you'll be able to read and respond to newsgroup articles and begin your own discussions. This chapter introduces you to *Usenet* (the "official" name for network news and newsgroups) and explains how to use Netscape Navigator 3.0 to get all the "news" that is fit to "print"— as well as some that might make Tom and Dan and maybe even Ted Turner blush!

INTRODUCTION TO USENET

Before we look at how to use Netscape as a news reader, let's take a quick look at Usenet itself.

WHAT IS IT & HOW DOES IT WORK?

Usenet (also known as Netnews) was originally developed for UNIX systems in 1979. It has become a worldwide network of thousands of Usenet sites, known as *news hosts* or *news servers*, running many operating systems (such as Mac OS, UNIX, MS-DOS, and Windows NT) on various types of computers. Millions of people share messages electronically over these Usenet sites. The messages are sent from news server to news server using UNIX-to-UNIX Copy Protocol (UUCP).

People post their Usenet messages or articles to categories known as newsgroups instead of to individuals (as would be the case with e-mail). A newsgroup is a great place to exchange ideas, ask questions, or discuss opinions and experiences. It's the place to learn what both your neighbor next door and someone in Moscow you've never met think about almost any subject imaginable. Everyone who subscribes to a newsgroup can read and respond to the articles posted there. Popular newsgroup categories include computers (of course), business, biology, recreation, science, social issues, miscellaneous, and alternative discussions.

Individual discussions posted to a particular newsgroup are known as *threads*. I post a message. You post a response. Someone else responds to your response. And so it goes. Generally speaking, all threads posted to a particular newsgroup share a common theme: music, cars, sports, electronics, bizarre sexual practices, and so on.

Most newsgroups are *unmoderated*, which means subscribers may post directly to the newsgroup. In *moderated* newsgroups, on the other hand, a moderator screens the messages and posts only messages deemed of interest to other subscribers.

Usenet servers don't have to be connected to the Internet; many are not. But because thousands of Usenet sites do have access to the Internet, the Internet has become the most commonly used electronic postal route for network news. The total number of distinct newsgroups on the Internet is in the thousands and growing daily. Consequently, millions of people who may have started using the Internet to gain access to the World Wide Web or to the Internet's electronic mail find that they can participate in Usenet newsgroups as well, provided they have the right client software. News servers on the Internet use Network News Transfer Protocol (NNTP) to communicate with client software. Luckily for you, Netscape Navigator 3.0 knows NNTP.

Before you can use Netscape Navigator 3.0 to access newsgroups, you must do two things:

1. **Obtain access to a news server**. Generally speaking, most Internet service providers (ISPs) run news servers. If you haven't already done so, ask your ISP for the name of the news server to which you have access (the name will be something like *news.myisp.com*). Later in this chapter (in the "Configuring Netscape News" section), you'll learn how to configure Netscape Navigator 3.0 to access this news server.

2. **Subscribe to one or more newsgroups**. Subscribing to a newsgroup is nothing more than adding it to the list of newsgroups you want your news reader software (Netscape Navigator 3.0 in this case) to check each time you go online. Follow the procedures described in this chapter (in the "Subscribing to & Unsubscribing from Newsgroups" section) to subscribe to newsgroups.

HOW MANY NEWSGROUPS CAN I GET?

How many angels can dance on the head of a pin? Nobody knows, and the same is true regarding the total number of newsgroups available at any time via the Internet. To impose some order on the basically anarchic structure of Usenet, newsgroups have a fairly strict hierarchical naming convention. Newsgroup names look similar to Internet addresses, and are a series of words or abbreviations separated by dots:

```
rec.arts.movies.reviews
```

The first word in the name denotes the major category to which the newsgroup belongs. A few of the major, hierarchical categories of Usenet newsgroups are:

- **alt.** *Alternative* newsgroups contain articles that are often very interesting, but can be on the controversial side, if not downright disgusting. Reader beware! This major category alone accounts for thousands of Usenet newsgroups.

- **comp.** *Computer* newsgroups discuss computer-related issues.

- **misc.** The *miscellaneous* newsgroups category (as you no doubt have guessed) is a catch-all category for discussions that don't fit into one of the other categories.

- **news.** The *news* category is for newsgroups discussing Usenet network news itself. These newsgroups are a great source of information about Usenet.

- **rec.** *Recreation* newsgroups discuss recreation, sports, and the arts.

- **sci.** *Science* newsgroups cover scientific topics.

- **soc.** *Social* newsgroups focus on issues of perceived social importance.

- **talk.** If you like good arguments, *talk* newsgroups are the place for you.

Newsgroups in these categories are usually distributed world-wide. Originally, Usenet consisted only of the newsgroups comp, news, rec, sci, soc, talk, and misc. All other newsgroups were referred to as *alternative* newsgroups. The term Usenet is now more commonly used to refer to the collection of all newsgroups

Other major categories that may be distributed throughout the world include bionet (biology newsgroups), biz (business newsgroups), and vmsnet (discussions about the VMS computer operating system). Many other major categories of newsworthy topics are usually distributed around the world as well. Geographical, organizational, and commercial newsgroups are usually distributed only within their area of interest.

Newsgroups in the *bit* major category are actually an alternative distribution method for Bitnet LISTSERV mailing lists. Conversely, many newsgroups also distribute articles via mailing lists to users who don't have access to a news server. In effect, the pertinent messages are mailed to the user's electronic mail box, enabling the user to get network news via a simple dial-up Internet e-mail account.

Because of the sheer volume of Usenet traffic, and due to the timely nature of much of newsgroup content, most newsgroups put a limit on the number of days an article will be available for reading. Past the time limit, an article is said to have expired and is removed from the newsgroup. The time limit varies from newsgroup to newsgroup, but many long-standing newsgroups keep archives of expired articles.

Do you have access to all the newsgroups on the Internet? Maybe, maybe not, depending on your news server. Later in this chapter, we'll see how to get a list of all the newsgroups available through your server.

The best way to gain an understanding of Usenet news is to browse through several newsgroups, reading the messages but not responding. This practice is affectionately known as *lurking.* In this case, lurking for a while makes a lot of sense. Before you know it, you'll feel compelled to jump in there and participate in the conversation.

CONFIGURING NETSCAPE NEWS

Even though you're probably anxious to try your hand at network news, there's still a little bit of housekeeping we need to take care of. Before Netscape Navigator 3.0 can access news, you have to give it the name of your news server. While you're at it, you may also want to configure the way news is displayed.

SPECIFYING YOUR NETWORK NEWS SERVER

Because Usenet is a network of news servers, you need access to one or more of these servers in order to participate in network news. The server uses the NNTP protocol to communicate with Netscape Navigator 3.0's news reader. The server keeps track of which articles have been posted to which newsgroups. Netscape Navigator 3.0 keeps track of the newsgroups in which you are interested as well as the articles you have read.

To specify a news server:

1. Launch Netscape Navigator 3.0. The main window appears. If you are connected to the Internet, the Netscape home page starts loading as shown in Figure 5-1.

   ■ You don't need to be online to configure Netscape News. If you're not connected to the Internet, simply click the Stop button in the main Netscape window so that the program will stop trying to load the Netscape home page.

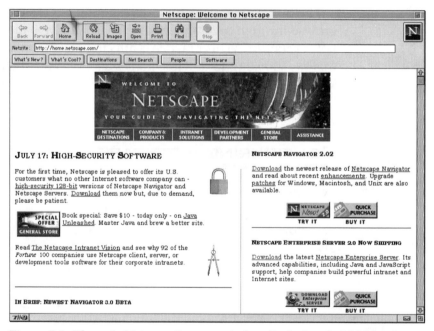

Figure 5-1: *The main Netscape Browser window displaying the Netscape home page.*

TIP

By default, Netscape Navigator 3.0 starts in the Browser window and attempts to load the Netscape home page. This behavior can be changed to (1) start in either Netscape Mail or Netscape News and (2) load a blank page rather than the home page. To display the screen where you can make these changes, select General Preferences from the pull-down Options menu and click the Appearance tab.

2. In the Netscape Navigator 3.0 main window, choose Mail and News Preferences from the Options menu. Netscape displays the Preferences dialog box, as shown in Figure 5-2. The tab last accessed will be displayed.

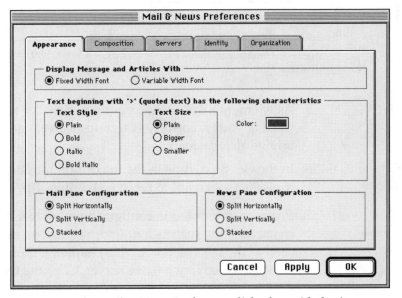

Figure 5-2: *The Mail & News Preferences dialog box with the Appearance tab selected.*

3. Click the Servers tab, as shown in Figure 5-3.

4. In the text box labeled News (NNTP) Server, type the name of the news server you will be using. If you don't know this address, obtain it from your ISP or from your system administrator (if you are configuring Netscape News on your computer at work).

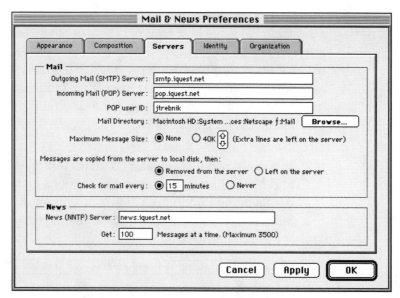

Figure 5-3: *The Mail & News Preferences dialog box with the Servers tab displayed.*

5. As we mentioned earlier, your news reader software keeps track of your favorite newsgroups as well as the articles you've already read.

6. In the Get field, type in the maximum number of new messages you want to receive at a time. Tip: 100 is plenty!

7. If you are interested in configuring other Netscape News characteristics, such as font width or sort sequences, proceed to the next section in this chapter. Otherwise, you are finished specifying a news server. Click the OK button in the Mail & News Preferences dialog box to confirm any changes you made and return to the main Netscape Navigator 3.0 window.

TIP

Although most people have access to only one news server, you may have access to multiple news servers. To open a news server other than the one listed in the Servers panel of the Mail & News Preferences dialog box, choose Open News Host from the News window's File menu and specify the server's name.

You are now ready to take a look at network news. You might want to skim through the sections that describe how to configure Netscape News, but you probably don't need to change the default settings. Then proceed to the "Subscribing to & Unsubscribing From Newsgroups" section to try out your first newsgroup.

CONFIGURING THE WAY YOUR NEWS IS DISPLAYED

One of the most obvious improvements in personal computers over the past 10 years has been the advent of *graphical user interfaces* (GUIs). A hallmark of GUIs is the capability to display text in multiple typefaces (fonts). Later versions of Windows and all versions of the Mac operating system are capable of displaying fonts in which each character has a unique width (*variable width,* also known as *proportional spacing*), rather than all characters having the same width (*fixed width,* also known as *monospacing*). You are used to seeing proportional spacing in most printed material, such as books, magazines, and newspapers.

Netscape Navigator 3.0 gives you the option of displaying newsgroup messages in either variable-width or fixed-width spacing. Usenet was developed several years before the PC was introduced and almost 10 years before proportional spacing was introduced to PC users in Windows. If you are a purist and would prefer to view newsgroup articles in their "natural" state— fixed-width spacing—you have that option with Navigator.

Since news articles are often a continuation of an ongoing discussion (that is, another article in the same thread), articles often include quoted portions of earlier articles in the same discussion. News reader programs typically denote quoted sections of text by placing an angle bracket (>) at the left margin. Netscape Navigator 3.0 enables you to control the font style and size of these quoted sections as well.

Since electronic mail messages and network news messages are closely related in purpose, Netscape's Mail window and News window are very similar. When you configure the appearance of your network news, you are also configuring the appearance of your e-mail.

To set how Netscape Navigator 3.0 displays news and e-mail:

1. Select Mail & News Preferences from the pull-down Options menu. Select the Appearance tab.

2. If you want text displayed in a fixed-width font (the default option), click the Fixed Width Font option button. If you prefer variable-width spacing, click the Variable Width Font option button. (*Note:* You can select the font itself using the Fonts panel in the General Preferences dialog box.)

3. Choose from among the following options to determine how Netscape News will display quoted text in e-mail messages and news articles:

   ■ Plain

   ■ **Bold**

   ■ *Italic*

   ■ ***Bold Italic***

4. Select one of the following options to determine the size of quoted text:

   ■ Plain

   ■ Bigger

   ■ Smaller

5. Click on the Color button to reveal the color selection panel appropriate for your Macintosh configuration. The color you select here will determine the color in which quoted text is displayed in e-mail and news articles.

6. In the News Pane Configuration section of the Appearance panel, select how you want your News window to look. The default is Split Horizontally. In this layout, the pane that contains the contents of a selected article is below the two other panes, one that lists your subscribed news-groups and another that lists the messages within that folder.

   ■ If you want to align the message content pane to the right of the two split panes, choose Split Vertically.

■ If you want to stack all three panes one on top of each other, with the content pane at the bottom, select Stacked.

TIP

In most cases the default window layout is the most convenient. You can always change it later, after you've become more familiar with the various News features.

7. Click OK to save your changes. (Apply will permit you to see your changes immediately without closing the panel. This command may be useful if you are toggling between your Mail window and the Appearance panel.)

STORING NEWS

As you have learned, e-mail messages and network news articles are closely related. Navigator's facilities for the two types of messages are nearly identical. However, one significant difference between e-mail and news is in where incoming messages are stored. While you have the option to store e-mail messages on the server or on your local hard disk, incoming news articles always reside on the server. The news reader displays them to your screen during an online session, but doesn't keep a copy on your hard disk. If you like, you can save an article using the Save As option from the pull-down File menu, but Navigator does not do so automatically.

Even though Netscape Navigator 3.0 doesn't automatically keep a copy of news articles that you have read, you may want to have Netscape Navigator 3.0 automatically save a copy of all articles that you post to a newsgroup. You can choose to e-mail a copy to yourself, to add the article to a running text file, or both.

To change how Navigator handles copies of outgoing news articles:

1. Choose Mail & News Preferences from the Options menu. Netscape Navigator 3.0 displays the Mail & News Preferences dialog box.

2. Click the Composition tab to display the dialog shown in Figure 5-4.

3. To have a copy of each outgoing news article sent to a particular e-mail address, type the address in the News Messages text box. (Of course, you could click in the *Self* check box, and Netscape Navigator would send each outgoing news article to your own e-mail address.)

4. To have the contents of each outgoing article copied to a specific text file stored on your computer, click the Browse button to display a standard Macintosh dialog box which will permit you to explore the hierarchical file structure on your Desktop and select an appropriate folder. Each news article you send will be added to the end of the folder you selected.

5. Click the OK button to save your changes and return to the Netscape window.

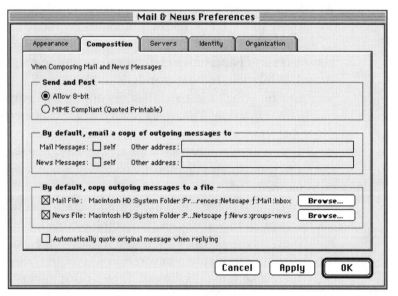

Figure 5-4: *The Mail & News Preferences dialog box with the Composition panel selected.*

CONFIGURING THREADING & SORTING

As you may recall, a series of news articles on the same topic is called a thread. Usually the articles in a thread make sense only if they are read together in chronological order. Netscape Navigator 3.0 makes it very easy to see the relationship between related articles and to follow the thread of the discussion. But this threading feature is an option, and in order to use it, you must first turn it on.

Netscape Navigator 3.0 also enables you to choose how you want messages sorted: by date, by subject, by message number, or by sender. You can configure the threading feature and the sort order from the same configuration window.

To activate the newsgroup threading feature and select a sorting order:

1. Choose Mail and News Preferences from the pull-down Options menu. Netscape displays the Mail & News Preferences dialog box.

2. Click the Organization tab to display the panel shown in Figure 5-5.

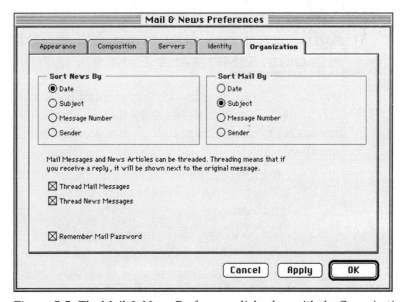

Figure 5-5: *The Mail & News Preferences dialog box with the Organization panel selected.*

3. Click the Thread News Messages check box to have articles in the same thread listed together, in chronological order. If you don't activate this option, Netscape Navigator 3.0's news reader will list newsgroup articles in the order received.

   ■ As an alternative way to toggle the threading feature, select the Sort option from the pull-down View menu and then choose Thread Messages.

4. You can also specify how articles will be sorted by choosing the Date, Subject, Message Number, or Sender option button. If you have chosen the Thread News Messages check box, you probably should sort messages by subject, at least for starters. You can change the sort order later if you like. If you choose to sort articles by date, by sender, or by message number you will still see the articles in each thread grouped together on the screen, but the order in which the threads appear (as well as the order of the articles within each thread) will be by date, sender, or message number, as you specified.

5. Click the OK button to save the changes you have made and return to the Netscape Main window.

ARRANGING THE NEWSGROUP LIST, MESSAGE HEADING & MESSAGE PANES

You can also configure the arrangement of Netscape Navigator 3.0's News window. Before we do that, however, let's go online so that we'll have something to look at as we arrange the parts of the window:

1. Launch Netscape Navigator 3.0. The main Netscape (Web Browser) window appears, and the Netscape home page starts loading.

2. Select Netscape News from the pull-down Window menu to display the main Netscape News window, shown in Figure 5-6.

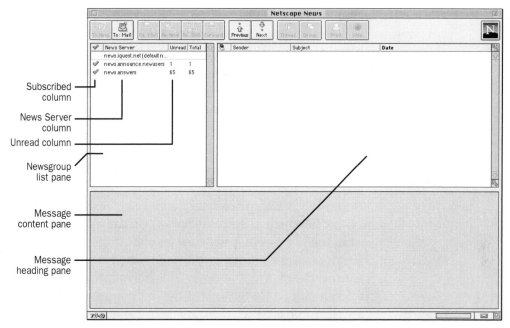

Figure 5-6: *The main Netscape News window.*

The main News window is divided into three panels: the *newsgroup list pane* in the upper left portion of the window; the *message heading pane* at upper right; and the *message content pane* across the bottom. This screen is almost identical to the Mail window that you learned about in Chapter 4, "Netscape Mail." You can control the size of each pane by placing the cursor (arrow) on a panel border and dragging the split window cursor in the appropriate direction. (We did this when we were changing the configuration of the Netscape Mail window panes.)

TIP

Remember, you can change the layout of these three panes in the Appearance panel of Mail & News Preferences.

ARRANGING THE NEWSGROUP LIST PANE

Obviously, the *newsgroup list pane* lists newsgroups. The first time you use Netscape News, the program lists your news server in the News Server column of the newsgroup list pane and lists three newsgroups intended to provide helpful information to new users of Usenet network news: *news.announce.newusers*, *news.newusers*, and *news.answers*.

The newsgroup list pane has four columns:

- **News Server**. This column lists one or more news servers. By default, it lists the news server you specified when you configured Netscape News. If you know of other news servers to which you have access, you can add them to this list in the Newsgroup window by selecting Open News Host from the File menu and typing the news server's name in the dialog that opens. Each available news server is denoted by a folder icon at the left margin of the newsgroup list pane.

- **Subscribed**. The Subscribed column (the one with the checkmark at the top) contains an icon that resembles a checkmark if you are subscribed to a newsgroup.

- **Unread**. This column contains a number in each row that indicates the number of articles in the respective newsgroup that you have yet to read.

- **Total**. This column indicates the total number of articles in the newsgroup.

You can control the width of each column by placing the mouse pointer on the right or left border of the column heading and dragging it in the appropriate direction.

TIP

You can even switch the order of any of the columns in the newsgroup list and message heading panes. Simply drag the header button right or left to its new location. For instance, you might want to drag the Total column to the far left in the newsgroup list pane.

ARRANGING THE MESSAGE HEADING PANE

So that we can examine the message headings and message panes of the window, let's display a message from the *news.answers* newsgroup:

1. In the newsgroup list pane, click the *news.answers* newsgroup icon. In the message heading pane, Netscape News displays a message heading for each article currently found in this newsgroup. Figure 5-7 shows several message headings.

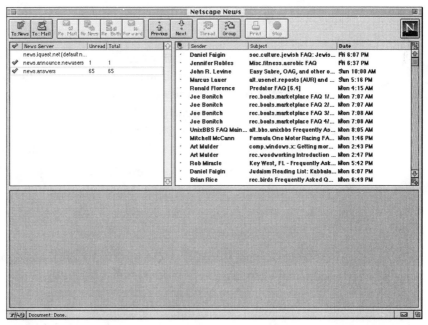

Figure 5-7: *The Netscape News window with the news.answers newsgroup selected.*

2. In the message heading pane, click one of the messages. Netscape News displays the selected article in the message content pane.

The message heading pane provides information about each article that may be helpful when you're trying to determine which article to read. This information is displayed in five columns:

- **Sender**. This column lists the name of the individual who posted the article to the newsgroup.

- **Flagged**. The flagged column contains a flag icon if you have *flagged* the article using the Flag Message option in the message pane. This feature is discussed in "Flagging Articles To Be Read Later" later in this chapter.

- **Read**. The Read column contains a green diamond if you haven't yet read the article.

- **Subject**. This column lists the subject of the article. The subject of each article was assigned by the article's author.

- **Date**. This column lists the date and time the article was posted to the newsgroup.

You can control the width of each column by placing the mouse pointer on the right or left border of the column heading and dragging the border in the appropriate direction.

You have learned already that you can establish a default sort order for articles in the message heading pane. You can also instantly sort the list again using either of two methods:

- Choose Sort from the View menu and click by Date, by Subject, by Sender, or by Message Number; or

- In the message heading pane, click the Sender, Subject, or Date column heading.

Navigator uses bold face type for the descriptive heading of the column by which articles are currently sorted.

By default, the message headings are sorted in descending order. To sort in ascending order, choose Sort from the View menu and click the Ascending option. To toggle off this option, returning to descending order, repeat the same step.

ARRANGING THE MESSAGE CONTENT PANE

The message content pane displays *header* information at the top of each article. By default, the message content pane lists the article's Subject, Date, From, Organization, Newsgroups, and References header information (see Figure 5-8).

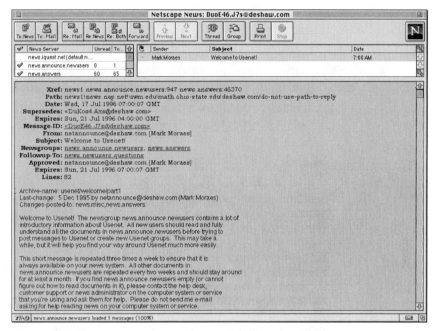

Figure 5-8: *The News window with an article from the news.announce.newusers newsgroup selected.*

To display additional header information, select the Show All Headers option on the Options menu (see Figure 5-9).

You can control the size of the message content pane by placing the mouse pointer on one of its borders and dragging the border in the appropriate direction.

DETERMINING WHICH NEWSGROUPS & ARTICLES WILL DISPLAY

Since there are literally thousands of newsgroups and hundreds of thousands of news articles, there obviously must be ways for you to filter newsgroups and news articles and list a select few for your consideration. We have already discussed briefly the concept of subscribing to newsgroups, and we'll cover the procedure of subscribing to newsgroups in one of the next sections in this chapter. Netscape Navigator 3.0's Options menu also provides several other ways to help you keep the volume of news articles listed on your screen to a manageable level.

Use the following options on the News window's pull-down Options menu (shown in Figure 5-9) to control which newsgroups and articles (messages) are listed on your screen (note that checkmarks indicate menu options that are currently active).

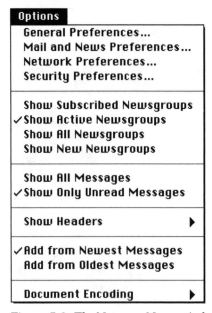

Figure 5-9: *The Netscape News window's pull-down Options menu.*

- **Show Subscribed Newsgroups**. This option causes Netscape News to list only newsgroups to which you have subscribed. With this option checked, Netscape News lists all subscribed newsgroups, even if they contain no unread articles.

- **Show Active Newsgroups**. This option lists only subscribed newsgroups that contain articles you have yet to read. This option is active by default.

- **Show All Newsgroups**. This option lists all the news-groups currently available through your news server. We'll try this option out later in the chapter so that you can subscribe to a few more newsgroups. Be aware, however, that choosing this option causes Netscape Navigator 3.0 to download to your disk a file that may take a few minutes to retrieve.

- **Show New Newsgroups**. Choose this option when you want to list all newsgroups available through your news server that have been added since you last connected to the server.

- **Show All Messages**. This option causes Netscape News to list the message headings of all messages found in the selected newsgroup.

- **Show Only Unread Messages**. This option, active by default, lists in the message heading pane only unread messages from the selected newsgroup.

- **Show Headers**. This option lets you choose how much or how little information you want to appear at the beginning of each article. You can select Brief to show minimal infor-mation, or All to show very complex header information. My recommendation is to use Normal. For more informa-tion about headers, see the section called "Reading an Article."

- **Add From Newest Messages.** This option, active by de-fault, tells Netscape News to display the newest message headings from the current newsgroup first.

- **Add From Oldest Messages.** This option causes the oldest message headings to be listed first.

TIP

You can change the language Newscape Navigator 3.0 expects articles to be in, by selecting Document Encoding from the Options menu, and then clicking a new language. This will let you properly display articles that use other character sets.

SUBSCRIBING TO & UNSUBSCRIBING FROM NEWSGROUPS

The concept of subscribing to network newsgroups is a bit of a misnomer. You don't really subscribe to newsgroups as you might subscribe to a magazine. If your news server has access to a particular newsgroup, then so do you. In the Usenet context, subscribing to a newsgroup simply involves instructing your news reader—Netscape News, in this case—to list articles from that newsgroup in the News window.

DEFAULT NEWSGROUPS

The first time you use Netscape News, the program lists your news server in the News Server column of the newsgroup list pane and lists three newsgroups: *news.announce.newusers*, *news.newusers.questions*, and *news.answers* assuming of course that these newsgroups are available through your news server. These newsgroups are specifically intended to provide helpful information to new users of Usenet network news.

Notice that a checkmark in a newsgroup's Subscribed column indicates that you're subscribed to that newsgroup.

GETTING A LIST OF ALL NEWSGROUPS

Before you can subscribe to a newsgroup, you have to instruct Netscape News to display a list of all newsgroups available through your news server. To do so:

1. Launch Netscape Navigator 3.0. The main Netscape (Web Browser) window appears, and the Netscape home page starts loading.

2. Select Netscape News from the pull-down Window menu to display the main Netscape News window, shown in Figure 5-6.

3. Select Show All Newsgroups from the Options menu.

4. Netscape Navigator 3.0 then retrieves from your news server a complete list of all newsgroups available via the server and displays this list in the newsgroup list pane of the News window, as shown in Figure 5-10.

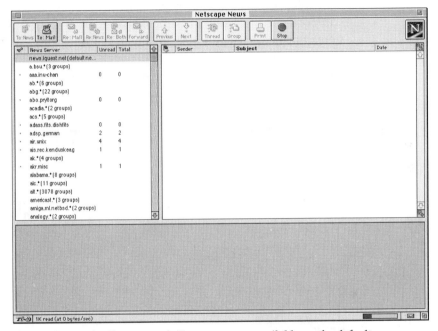

Figure 5-10: *The first page of all newsgroups available on the default news server.*

Notice that Netscape News doesn't immediately show every available newsgroup in the newsgroup list pane. The list groups all newsgroups in folders by category. The first page of the list shown in Figure 5-10, for example, shows two categories of newsgroups: a.bsu.* and ab.*. The plus sign in the subscription column (the one with the checkmark in the header) to the left of these folders indicates that each contains newsgroups that are not displayed. The number in parentheses (to the right of the folder's name) tells how many newsgroups there are in the folder.

Many newsgroups no longer contain active articles. When a newsgroup does contain active articles, Netscape News shows the number of unread articles and the total number of articles in this newsgroup in the Unread and Total columns, respectively.

To see a list of newsgroups in a category, scroll to the category and double-click on the name of the category. Netscape News opens the folder and lists the newsgroups in the category. The major category may contain subcategories. In that case, Netscape News groups the subcategories into folders. Figure 5-11, for example, lists newsgroups in the news* major category. This category contains several subcategories including news.answers*, news.announce.questions*, and news.announce.newusers*.

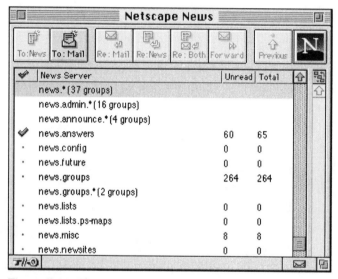

Figure 5-11: *The news* category of newsgroups as listed in the newsgroup list pane of the Netscape News window.*

FINDING OUT ABOUT NEW NEWSGROUPS

If you completed the procedure described in the preceding section, you have discovered just how long it can take to display a complete list of all available newsgroups. Unless you enjoy watching grass grow, you probably don't want to download this list very often. But you probably do want to periodically find out about any new newsgroups that may have formed since the last time you checked. Here's how:

1. Launch Netscape Navigator 3.0. The main Netscape (browser) window appears, and the Netscape home page starts loading.

2. Select Netscape News from the Window menu to display the main Netscape News window.

3. Select Show New Newsgroups from the Options menu. Netscape News displays a message box, shown in Figure 5-12, telling you the number of newsgroups that have been added since you last checked. Netscape News adds the new newsgroups to the end of the list of subscribed newsgroups in the newsgroup list pane of the News window. By clicking on the dot in the column with the checkmark (the "subscribed" column), you can turn on one of these new newsgroups to see whether it has useful information for you.

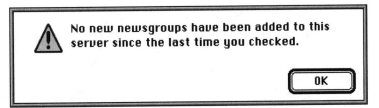

Figure 5-12: *A message about new newsgroups.*

SUBSCRIBING FROM THE LIST

Once you have displayed a list of available newsgroups, it is very easy to subscribe to one. To subscribe, click the newsgroup's check box in the Subscribed column. Netscape News adds a subscribed (checkmark) icon to the check box.

Each time you open Netscape News, the program asks your news server to determine whether each of your subscribed newsgroups contains articles you haven't read. By default, Netscape News lists in the newsgroup list pane all subscribed newsgroups that contain unread articles. If you choose the Show Subscribed Newsgroups option from the Options menu, Netscape News will always list all newsgroups to which you have subscribed.

If you decide later that you're no longer interested in a particular newsgroup, just click the newsgroup's Sub column again to remove the subscribed icon. Netscape News will no longer list this newsgroup in the newsgroup list pane of the Netscape News window.

READING NEWS

Assuming that you have completed the steps described earlier in this chapter to configure Netscape News and to subscribe to newsgroups, you are ready to start reading news.

CHOOSING A GROUP

As you know, all network news articles are found in Usenet newsgroups, so before you can read the news, you need to choose a newsgroup. Follow these steps:

1. Launch Netscape Navigator 3.0. The main Netscape (browser) window appears, and the Netscape home page starts loading.

2. Select Netscape News from the Window menu to display the main Netscape News window. By default, the Netscape News window lists all subscribed newsgroups that contain active articles, as shown in Figure 5-13.

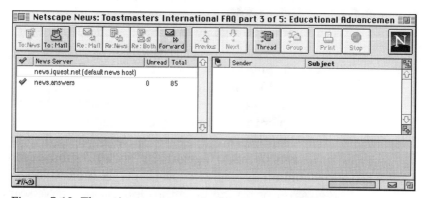

Figure 5-13: *The active newsgroups in the newsgroups list pane of the Netscape News window.*

3. Click one of the groups listed in the newsgroup list pane. Netscape News populates the message heading pane with the headings of all active articles in that group. In Figure 5-14, articles from the *news.answers* newsgroup are listed in the message heading pane. (***Note:*** The message heading pane in Figure 5-14 is threaded and sorted by subject.) The Subject line for messages that have not yet been read is in boldface font, while the articles that have already been read are shown in plain font.

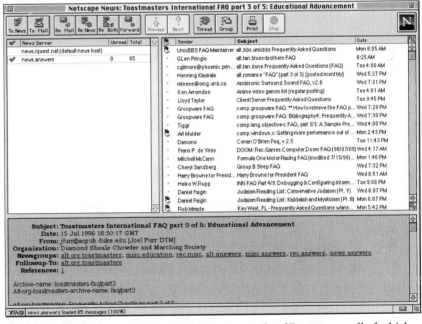

Figure 5-14: *The news.answers newsgroup contains 85 messages, all of which have already been read*

READING AN ARTICLE

After all the effort you've expended to configure Netscape News, list available newsgroups, and subscribe to newsgroups, actually reading an article is so easy that it's almost a letdown. To display the contents of an article, simply click the article's heading in the message heading pane. Netscape News displays the article's contents in the message content pane. The message content pane in Figure 5-15 shows the header information of an article from *news.groups*. Use your mouse and the vertical scroll bar or use tab to select the message content pane and the cursor keys to scroll the article into view.

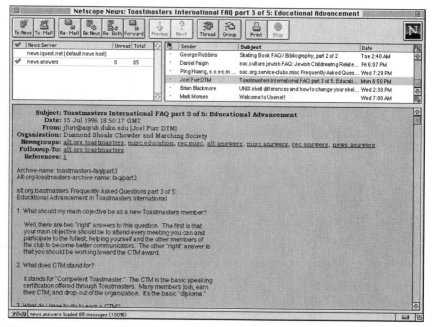

Figure 5-15: *An article from the news.groups newsgroup.*

By default, Netscape News displays the following article header information at the top of the News window message content pane:

- **Subject**. Briefly describes the subject matter of the article. All articles in a thread have the same subject.

- **Date**. Gives the date the article was posted to the newsgroup.

- **From**. Provides the return e-mail address of the article's author.

- **Reply-To**. Provides an address, if one was specified by the sender, that is used for responding directly to the message. The toolbar also contains a convenient *Reply to* command button.

- **Organization**. Identifies the author's organization (if any).

- **Newsgroups**. Lists hyperlinks to all the newsgroups to which the article was posted. You can go directly to a newsgroup by clicking on the newsgroup name.

- **References**. Identifies as hyperlinks other messages earlier in a thread: the numeral *1* denotes the original message in the thread; the numeral *2* denotes the second message; and so on. You can go directly to the referenced message by clicking on the numeral.

TIP

If you don't want to be bothered with all these headers every time you view a message, select Brief from the Show Headers submenu under pull-down Options in the Netscape News main menu bar. Instead of the usual headers, you'll see a single line that includes the Subject, From, and Date information. If, on the other hand, you want to see even more header information, select All from the same submenu. Some of the supplemental information may be useful in debugging a technical problem or in discovering the true source of a message.

When you display an article, Netscape News cancels the bolded font from the Subject column to indicate that you have read the article. If you want the article still to be marked as *unread*, highlight the article by clicking on it in the message heading pane, then select Mark as Unread from the pull-down Message menu . (Refer to Fig. 5-16)

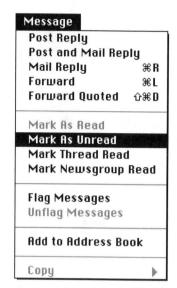

Figure 5-16: *The pull-down Message menu.*

TIP

You can get another group of messages by selecting Get More Messages from the File menu in the Netscape News window.

USENET PICTURES

One of the more popular pastimes unique to the Internet is the trading of digital pictures of all kinds—pictures of animals, cartoons, heavenly bodies of various sorts, you name it. While digital pictures can be made available on FTP sites or attached to electronic mail, Usenet has become a widely used method of sharing favorite electronic images. Most such files are posted in the newsgroups that have names beginning with *alt.binaries.pictures*.

Many image files on the Internet, including most images displayed on the World Wide Web, are stored as Graphics Interchange Format (GIF) files. The GIF standard was originally designed for use on CompuServe. GIF files can be displayed by Netscape Navigator 3.0 as inline images within a page of text and perhaps other pictures. Or a hyperlink could point to a GIF file that would display in a window by itself when you click the hyperlink.

Because of its high resolution and the relatively high data compression, the Joint Photographic Experts Group (JPEG) file format is the current favorite for storing digital pictures for transmission over the Internet.

If a network news article contains either a GIF file or a JPEG file, Netscape Navigator 3.0 will display the image, along with the rest of the article, in the message content pane.

You can even save the images to disk in a viewable form. Simply hold down the mouse button when the cursor is positioned on the graphic and select "Save Image as..." from the context menu that appears.

FOLLOWING A THREAD

By choosing to thread newsgroup headings (see the "Configuring Threading & Sorting" section earlier in this chapter), you can quickly read an entire series of related articles from beginning to end. Each subsequent article in a thread is listed, indented, in the message heading pane and just below the article to which it replies. Figure 5-17 shows a series of threaded messages from the *news.answers* newsgroup. To read the next article in the discussion, simply select the next article listed in the message heading pane. To read the preceding message in the thread, display the preceding message in the list.

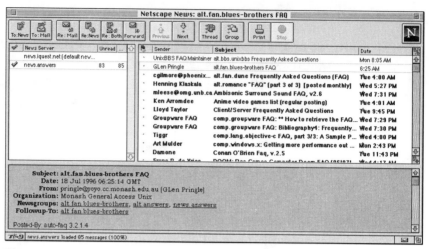

Figure 5-17: *A series of threaded messages.*

At times, it may be convenient to maximize the size of the message content pane in order to more easily read news articles. Since the message heading pane wouldn't be visible, Netscape News provides a couple of ways to move from one article to the next and back without displaying the message heading pane. When the threading feature is active, these navigation shortcuts move between articles in the same thread.

To read the next article, as it would appear in the message heading pane, either:

- Click the Next button in the toolbar; or
- Select Next Message from the pull-down Go menu.

To read the next unread article, either:

- Click the Next button in the toolbar; or
- Select Next Unread from the pull-down Go menu.

To read the preceding message in the message heading pane:

- Select Previous Message from the pull-down Go menu.

To read the preceding unread article, either:

- Click the Previous button in the toolbar; or,
- Select Previous Unread from the pull-down Go menu.

TIP

You can also move through unread messages quickly by using the shift-command-up arrow or shift-command-down arrow combinations of key strokes. In a similar manner, you can move up or down the list of all messages (read and unread) by using command-down or command-up arrows.

As mentioned in the preceding section, you can also use the References field in the message header itself to move to previous articles in the current thread. Clicking a reference number displays an earlier article in the thread in the News window.

FLAGGING ARTICLES TO BE READ LATE

Often it is convenient to attempt to identify articles of interest from the article headings. As you scroll through the headings list, flag articles that you want to read later by clicking the articles' Mark column (see Fig. 5-18). When all the articles you want to read are flagged, you can use the Next Flagged, Previous Flagged, and First Flagged options on the pull-down Go menu to move between flagged messages.

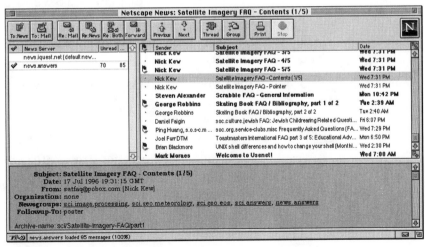

Figure 5-18: *A series of flagged messages.*

Marking Articles Read

A particular newsgroup may contain a thread that you're just not interest in. So that you can avoid seeing the article headers in the future, Netscape Navigator 3.0 lets you "pretend" you've already read them. To mark a thread as already read, simply select the top article in the thread and then click the Thread button in the toolbar.

You can also mark an entire newsgroup as read. Just select that group and click the Group button in the toolbar. (The same results can also be accomplished from the pull-down Message menu if you prefer.)

Saving Articles

From time to time as you are perusing the thousands of network news articles available on the Internet, you undoubtedly will want to save an article or two for future reference.

To save an article to a disk file:

1. With the article displayed, select Save As from the File menu. Netscape News displays the Save Message As dialog box.

2. Type a filename for the new file in the Save Message As text box.

3. Click the OK button. Netscape News saves the file to disk.

Tip

You can save multiple messages at one time by selecting them from the message list and then selecting Save Message As from the File menu.

PRINTING ARTICLES

Printing a Usenet article is just as easy as saving a copy. To print an article:

1. Make sure your printer has paper and other necessary supplies, is turned on, and is properly connected to your computer.

2. Click the Printer button on the toolbar. Netscape News displays the Print dialog box.

3. Make sure the printer settings are correct, and click the OK button. Netscape News sends the article to your printer.

OFFENSIVE MATERIAL

Unless you've been living on a mountaintop in Tibet, you are certainly aware of the Internet's reputation as a place where children (and adults, too, for that matter) can be exposed to offensive material. Most of the offensive material spoken of in the lurid headlines is found on Usenet. Network news is the First Amendment in action, at its best and at its worst. The same network that brings you uplifting information about health, religion, art, and education also can bring you (and your children) explicit sexually-oriented conversations and graphic erotica.

Fortunately, objectionable material tends to be found on a finite list of Internet sites. Several commercial software products are available that enable parents to in effect *block* these objectionable Internet sites. The best-known brand of child protection software is SurfWatch. SurfWatch is a subscription-based product, updated monthly, and is available in most major software outlets. Each month, the makers of SurfWatch scour the Internet for new sites that some parents may find objectionable and add these sites to the list of blocked Internet resources. The new blocked list is then encrypted and sent out to parents for installation to their SurfWatch-protected computer.

Make certain you have the latest version of SurfWatch, however. Version 1.2V6 and earlier versions have been found to be incompatible with Netscape Navigator 3.0. For more information, navigate to the URL http://www.surfwatch.com.

WRITING NEWS

You learned earlier in this chapter that lurking on Usenet newsgroups is considered acceptable behavior, but Usenet is fundamentally a collaborative medium of communication, a virtual community of sorts. When you get the urge to become an active member of this community, Netscape News is ready to assist you.

REPLYING TO AN ARTICLE

The easiest way to begin to participate in newsgroups is to reply to, or follow up on, an existing article. You don't have to worry about how to break the ice or what to type into the various header fields. Just join in the conversation. There are, however, several ways to reply: in public with a posted article; via e-mail directly to the author of the article to which you are replying; or both publicly and via e-mail.

IN PUBLIC

To reply to a news article publicly with a news article of your own:

1. While connected to the Internet, and with the original article displayed in the News window's message content pane, either click the Re:News button in the toolbar (the one with the newspaper-clipping-and-arrow icon on it), or choose Post Reply from the pull-down Message menu. Netscape News displays the Compose window.

For example, suppose you are displaying the article shown in Figure 5-19.

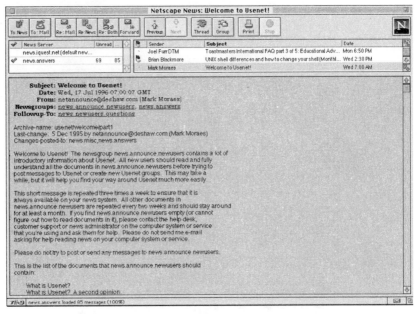

Figure 5-19: *The news article to which you are going to reply.*

When you click the Re:News button in the toolbar, Netscape News displays the Compose window shown in Figure 5-20. Notice that the Subject and Newsgroup fields in the Compose window are already filled in. Netscape News repeated the subject of the original article and will post your new article to the newsgroup specified by the Followup To field in the original article—the *news.newusers.questions* newsgroup.

In Figure 5-20, you see what a Reply window looks like if you have checked "Automatically quote original message when replying" in the Composition panel of the Mail & News Preferences menu. This may be a convenient setting if you often include extensive quotations from articles to which you are responding. This setting will provide you with an accurate quotation from which you might then snip or cut away to make your entire message more succinct.

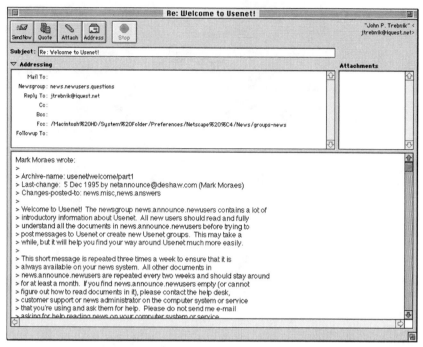

Figure 5-20: *The Compose window.*

2. Type your article and either click the Send button on the toolbar or select Send Now from the File menu, or press ⌘+Enter. Netscape News sends your article to your news server, which takes care of posting the article to the appropriate newsgroup. Netscape News then returns you to the News window. For example, after reading the article in Figure 5-19, you might have a question about newsgroups. Type your message in the Compose window and post it to the *news.newusers.questions* newsgroup. You can then check back later in that newsgroup to see if anyone responded to your question.

From the pull-down View menu, you may select (or choose Show All) the header fields you want to automatically display:

- **Cc**. Use this field to address a copy of your message to an e-mail address. If you have filled in an e-mail address in the News Messages field in the Composition tab of the News & Mail Preferences dialog box, that address will appear here.

- **Newsgroups**. By default, this field contains the name of the same newsgroup to which the original article was posted, unless the header of the original article lists a different newsgroup in the Followup To field.

- **Subject**. This field contains the subject of the thread.

- **Attachments**. If you attach a file to your article, the name of the attached file appears in the Attachments display panel.

- **From**. By default, this field contains your name and return e-mail address, as entered in the Identity tab of the News & Mail Preferences dialog box.

- **Reply To**. Use this field if you want e-mail replies to your article to be sent to an e-mail address other than your standard From address.

- **Mail To**. Use this field to send the article to an e-mail address.

- **Mail Bcc**. Use this field to e-mail a blind copy. This field will not appear in the header of the message actually transmitted to the other recipients of the article/message.

- **Followup To**. Use this field to specify the newsgroup to which follow-up articles should be posted. If you leave this field blank, follow-ups will be posted to the newsgroup to which your article is posted.

VIA E-MAIL TO THE AUTHOR

If you would rather not post a follow-up to an article publicly—because what you have to say may not be of general interest, because your comments are of a personal nature, because you are shy, or for whatever reason—you can send an e-mail message instead to the author of the article.

To reply via e-mail:

1. While connected to the Internet, and with the original article displayed in the News window's message content pane, either click the Re:Mail button in the toolbar (the one with the icon of an envelope and an arrow), or choose Mail Reply from the Message menu (or press ⌘+R). Netscape News displays the Compose window.

2. Type your message and either click the Send button on the toolbar or select Send Now from the File menu, or press ⌘+Enter. Netscape News sends your message as e-mail to the author of the article to which you are replying. Netscape News then returns you to the News window.

> **TIP**
>
> *You can very conveniently add an author's e-mail address to your address book as you are reading a specific message, by simply selecting Add to Address Book from the pull-down Message menu. For more information on the Address Book, see Chapter 4, "Netscape Mail."*

BOTH IN PUBLIC & TO THE AUTHOR

Occasionally, you may want to post an article in reply to an existing article and also send a copy to the article's author. To do so:

1. While connected to the Internet, and with the original article displayed in the Netscape News window's message content pane, either click the Re:Both button in the toolbar (the one with the icons of both a newspaper *and* an envelope with an arrow), or choose Post and Mail Reply from the Message menu. Netscape News displays the Compose window.

2. Type your article and either click the Send button on the toolbar or select Send Now from the File menu, or press ⌘+Enter. Netscape News sends your article to your news server, which takes care of posting the article to the appropriate newsgroup. Netscape News also sends your message as e-mail to the author of the article to which you are replying. Netscape News then returns you to the News window.

TIP

Just as with regular e-mail, you can also forward newsgroup posts to other recipients. Simply click the Forward button in the Netscape News window.

POSTING A NEW ARTICLE

Starting your own thread in a newsgroup is really just as easy as replying to an existing article. You just have to come up with the subject line.

To post a new article:

1. While connected to the Internet, and while browsing in the newsgroup to which you want to post your article, either click the To:News button in the toolbar, or choose New News Message from the File menu. Netscape News displays the Compose window.

2. Netscape News automatically enters the name of the current newsgroup into the Newsgroups field. You can change the newsgroup and/or add other newsgroups as destinations for the article.

3. Type a subject for your article in the subject line. Try to be concise, but make your subject line descriptive. Remember that everyone else browsing the newsgroup will decide whether or not to read your article based on the subject line.

4. Type your article and either click the Send button on the toolbar or select Send Now from the File menu (or press ⌘+Enter). Netscape News sends your article to your news server, which takes care of posting the article to the appropriate newsgroup.

INCLUDING ATTACHMENTS IN YOUR ARTICLES

You too can distribute GIF and JPEG graphics via network news! It's easy to attached graphics or other bvinary files to articles you post. With netscape navigator 3.0 you can even attach files that are not on your own computer by sending the URLs for the files as attachments to your message.

To attach a file to a newsgroup article:

1. Follow all the steps outlined earlier for creating a new article.

2. Before sending your article, click the Attach button in the Message Composition window. The Attachments dialog box appears.

3. Click either the Attach File button or the Attach Location (URL) button to send a file with your message, or to include a link to a file that is stored on a remote computer.

   ■ Any kind of file can be attached to your mail. But if you are sending an HTML file, you can choose to send it as is (with its HTML formatting) or as plain text, without any speciual formatting. Select either the Source or Plain Text radio button from the Attach As section of the dialog box.

4. Once you've selected a file or typed in a URL, click Open or OK to return to the Attachment dialog box. You should see an icon which represents the type of file(s) you are attaching, along with the name(s) of that file(s).

5. Click Done to attach the file and return to the Message Composition window. In the Attachments pane you will again see the icon and name of the file you have attached to your message.

6. Send the message, including any attachments, by clicking the Send Now button at the top of the Message Composition window.

USENET ETIQUETTE

Even though your contact with Usenet is through your computer, the Usenet itself is really a VERY LARGE community of people. Always keep that fact in mind when you are reading and posting articles. Following is a summary of the article "A Primer on How to Work With the Usenet Community Newsgroups," which is periodically posted to the *news.announce.newusers* newsgroup. I highly recommend you read the full article as well.

"Never forget that the person on the other side is human. Don't blame system admins for their users' behavior. Never assume that a person is speaking for their organization. Be careful what you say about others. Be brief. Your postings reflect upon you; be proud of them. Use descriptive titles [subjects]. Think about your audience. Be careful with humor and sarcasm. Only post a message once. Please rotate [rot13] material with questionable content. Summarize what you are following up. Use mail, don't post a follow-up. Read all followups and don't repeat what has already been said. Double-check followup newsgroups and distributions. Be careful about copyrights and licenses. Cite appropriate references. When summarizing, summarize. Mark or rotate [rot13] answers or spoilers. Spelling flames (i.e., criticism about misspellings) are considered harmful. Don't overdo signatures. Limit line length and avoid control characters. Please do not use Usenet as a resource for homework assignments. Please do not use Usenet as an advertising medium. Avoid posting to multiple newsgroups."

MOVING ON

After reading this chapter and trying your hand at network news, you should now feel like a full citizen of Usenet. You have learned how to subscribe to newsgroups and are now able to read and respond to newsgroup articles and begin your own discussions. Move on next to Chapter 6, "Getting Files via FTP," to learn how easy it is to find and download from the Internet *tons* of useful software using FTP (File Transfer Protocol).

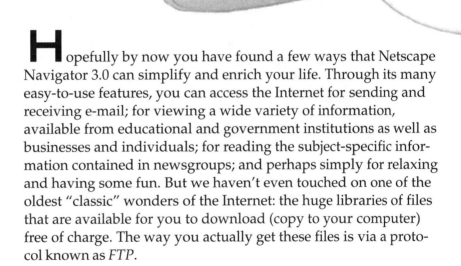

Getting Files via FTP

6

Hopefully by now you have found a few ways that Netscape Navigator 3.0 can simplify and enrich your life. Through its many easy-to-use features, you can access the Internet for sending and receiving e-mail; for viewing a wide variety of information, available from educational and government institutions as well as businesses and individuals; for reading the subject-specific information contained in newsgroups; and perhaps simply for relaxing and having some fun. But we haven't even touched on one of the oldest "classic" wonders of the Internet: the huge libraries of files that are available for you to download (copy to your computer) free of charge. The way you actually get these files is via a protocol known as *FTP*.

WHAT IS FTP?

FTP is one of the simplest and most obvious acronyms you'll come across on the Net: it simply stands for File Transfer Protocol. That sounds pretty generic, but every implementation of FTP follows the same very specific rules for sending and receiving data. The file must be broken up into pieces at one end and reassembled properly at the other; the data has to be checked for errors and stamped with the correct filename and date; and the FTP software has to enable users to navigate through the host system's directories to find the right file.

Throughout the Internet are scattered literally thousands of servers that provide files to users via FTP, and they all do their job in much the same way. Many of these sites are known as *anonymous* FTP sites, which means they allow any Internet user to log on specifically for the purpose of retrieving files. You don't need to be a registered user on the system. Typically, when logging in to anonymous sites, you specify *anonymous* as your username and your e-mail address as the password (see the sidebar, "Your Anonymous Password"). With Netscape Navigator 3.0, you don't even have to do this, since the software takes care of the login process automatically; you don't even see any prompts from the remote system.

Are there FTP sites that are not anonymous? Sure! Many corporations, for instance, maintain non-anonymous FTP sites so that employees can trade work-related files while on the road. Of course, you need an account and a real password to access files on these FTP servers. But in this chapter, we'll be dealing primarily with anonymous sites.

YOUR ANONYMOUS PASSWORD

Even when you log on to an anonymous FTP site, it's considered good form to identify yourself by using your e-mail address as your password. By default, Netscape Navigator 3.0 does not do this, but I suggest you configure the program so that it minds its Netiquette.

To configure Navigator 3.0 so that it sends your e-mail address as your password when you log on to anonymous FTP sites, select Network Preferences from the pull-down Options menu and then click the Protocols tab. Simply check the box in the lower-left section of the panel and click the OK dialog button.

➡

Of course Netscape Navigator 3.0 needs to *know* your e-mail address before it can use it. If you followed the instructions in Chapter 4, "Netscape Mail," you're all set. But if for some reason you decided not to use Netscape Mail, you can still enter your e-mail address into the program. From the Options menu, select Mail and News Preferences. Then go to the Identity tab, fill in the informational fields, and click OK. Now Navigator's FTP feature can send your e-mail address to anonymous FTP sites.

WHAT'S OUT THERE?

So what kinds of files are available at these anonymous FTP sites? You name it! There are:

- Fully functional software programs, including spreadsheets, text editors, modem programs, databases, and a dazzling variety of utilities.

- Updates and patches to most major retail software programs.

- Electronic texts ranging from Shakespeare's complete works to David Letterman's latest *Top Ten list*.

- Thousands of images, sounds, video clips, and animations.

- Technical reports, journals, electronic magazines, news summaries, and archives of user messages.

- Books and tutorials like this one that will help you get started with just about any software task.

Figure 6-1 shows some of the directories at a well-known FTP site, the University of Texas Macintosh Archive FTP site. We'll explore this site more thoroughly later in the chapter.

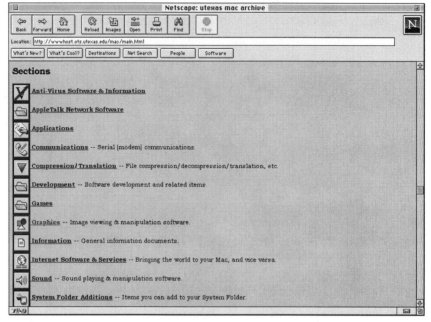

Figure 6-1: *Some of the directories of files at UTexas.*

SENDING FILES

Grabbing files from anonymous FTP sites might be the most entertaining use of Netscape Navigator 3.0's built-in FTP facility, but there are other practical applications as well. For instance, when I finish writing this chapter, I will FTP it to Netscape Press, where an editor will massage the text and then place it back on the FTP server so I can look over her changes.

To send a file via FTP, navigate to the remote FTP site and directory you want, then select Upload File from the Navigator File menu. A dialog box appears letting you choose the file to send.

You should keep in mind, though, that this feature of Netscape Navigator 3.0 can be used only to transfer files to FTP servers that support anonymous login. In order to send files to an FTP site where you have a restricted account requiring a specific username and password, you need a dedicated FTP program. Fetch 3.0.1 from Dartmouth College is a popular shareware utility for Macintosh users. It may have come with the software your access provider sent to get you on the Net, or you can download it from the UTexas FTP site.

And I can do whatever I want with all this stuff? I hear you asking. Well, yes and no. To understand why I'm waffling on this question, you need to understand that there are three broad categories of files on the Internet, and each of these categories has different rules and guidelines for usage.

PUBLIC DOMAIN

Public domain files are files that have no copyright, and there are no restrictions whatsoever on their usage. For instance, you can do whatever you want with Shakespeare's *Hamlet* or *A Winter's Tale*. Modern texts are sometimes released into the public domain as well, by authors who care more about wide distribution than about collecting any royalties or other fees. Many political polemics, for instance, are public domain.

But what about software? Sure, there's lots of public domain software on the Net. This has often been created by altruistic developers as a resource for the good of the community. The old adage "you get what you pay for" doesn't always hold true on the Net. For instance, until recently some of the very best Internet client software was public domain. Of course, there are developers who release unfinished or buggy programs into the public domain to collect feedback, as part of their development process or simply because they don't want to go through the process of refining their work. But programs like these are usually clearly marked, and in some situations they can provide a cost-effective way of dealing with very specific software tasks. And some public domain software is a true group effort: perhaps a programmer started a project years ago, and then somebody downloaded it and worked with it a bit more, then somebody else added new features, and so on. Since there are no restrictions on the redistribution or modification of public domain software, a program may evolve over the course of many years, forged as much by public scrutiny and feedback as by the work of any single designer.

FREEWARE

Freeware files are copyrighted, but there are no charges for using them. Let's say you write a program that you are very proud of, but you want to make sure anybody can use it for free. You place it on the Internet with a copyright notice and perhaps a text file explaining any restrictions on its use. For instance, you may want to make sure the software is always distributed in its original form, unmodified and bearing your name as the sole author. You may want to make it clear that nobody else may sell the software, but may only distribute it freely as you have.

Many people misunderstand freeware, confusing it with public domain files. No, they are very different. Freeware is free, but you have to play by the rules.

WHAT ABOUT VIRUSES?

In spite of all the hype it gets, the Net is no utopia—it is more like a microcosm. Just as there is a slight chance you could get mugged on your way to the corner store, there is a slight chance that you will someday download a file that "crashes your hard drive" or otherwise messes with your system, causing you that peculiarly modern form of grief known as "restoring everything from backups." (That's assuming you bothered to keep an up-to-date backup like everyone told you to!)

How common are viruses? Certainly much less than sensationalistic mass media stories would have you believe, but there are some out there. The best defense, of course, is making sure that at any given moment you could restore everything you need from backup tape or disks. If this is not the case at your house, I'd suggest you put this book down and get busy backing up files.

➡

There are other precautions you can take as well. Virus checking programs such as John Norstad's Disinfectant 3.6 are available as freeware at most Macintosh-support FTP sites, and there are a number of excellent commercial products as well, such as Norton Anti-Virus. It's a good idea to check your entire system once in a while using one of these programs. If you do discover a problem, delete all infected files from your hard drive, or follow any instructions that came with your antivirus software. You will also probably need to completely restore your hard drive from backup.

Yes, this can be a serious inconvenience. But in the interest of alleviating some of the techno-paranoia that flares up whenever the news weeklies don't have a juicy enough scandal, let's debunk a few myths:

■ Except in very rare cases, you cannot get viruses from text files or from most data files such as word processor documents. Generally speaking, something has to be *run* on your computer to infect it.

■ Most viruses do not destroy hardware, they only mess up your software so badly that it seems as though your hardware is faulty. Getting rid of all infected software and then completely restoring your system from backup will usually solve the problem.

■ Viruses do not jump from disk to disk across your office.

■ You won't catch any viruses by hanging around in particular Usenet newsgroups, though it can sometimes feel like you're coming down with something nasty!

For more information about viruses, here are a few Web sites to check out:

■ The Frequently Asked Questions (FAQ) file for the VIRUS-L/ comp.virus mailing list (http://www.cis.ohio-state.edu/hypertext/ faq/usenet/computer-virus-faq/faq.html). This FAQ contains a lot of basic information about viruses, including common symptoms and how to proceed if your system is infected.

■ Virus Information (http://csrc.ncsl.nist.gov/virus/). This page contains a comprehensive set of links to additional virus-oriented sites, as well as reviews of antivirus software.

■ University of Texas (http://wwwhost.ots.utexas.edu/mac/pub-mac-virus.html). Check out the extensive library of Macintosh-specific information.

SHAREWARE

Shareware is a great marketing innovation that came into being almost concurrently with personal computers. Shareware files or programs are distributed on a trial basis: you can download them and use them for free, but only for a short evaluation period. If you like the resource and want to keep using it, you must pay a fee (usually small) to the author or delete it from your machine. Generally it is OK to make copies for your friends to evaluate, but you, of course, can't charge.

Shareware files and programs are copyrighted. You must not copy them except as specifically allowed by the author, and you must abide by any restrictions detailed in the license or accompanying documentation. There has been plenty of litigation over misuse of shareware materials!

The advantages of shareware for the user are obvious: you get to try something out without spending a penny. But there are advantages for shareware authors as well. Distribution costs are kept to a minimum, and there are no middlemen to eat profits. The author also enjoys a direct relationship with the customer and often refines the product based on individual feedback rather than distributors' charts and graphs.

HOW TO KNOW WHAT YOU'RE GETTING

FTP sites are really just directories full of files, much like the directories on your own computer. The FTP protocol itself includes no provisions for describing the files or providing addi-

tional information, although it does let you view file details such
as size, time, and date. So how do you know what all the files in
an FTP directory really are? There are two ways:

- Many of the larger FTP sites have Web "front ends." In
  other words, you initially access them via a Web document
  that explains a little about the site and what it contains.
  When you're ready to download a file, you click on a link
  that fires up the actual FTP protocol, showing you lists of
  files and directories or going right ahead and transferring
  the file you want. Figure 6-2 shows an example of a Web
  front end to an FTP site, on the Netscape server itself.

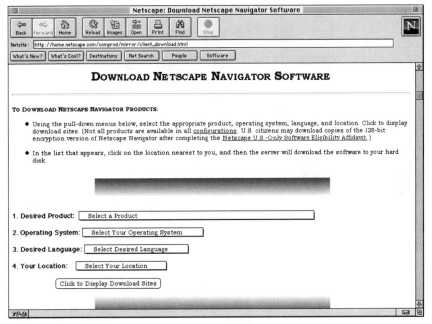

Figure 6-2: *Web front end to the Netscape FTP server.*

- Most well-established FTP sites include informational files
  that describe the rest of the available files. These informational files are often named README or INDEX (sometimes
  in lowercase), or sometimes they have names that begin with
  a dot, as in .INDEX. You may also encounter informational
  files called something like Message or ReadMe.

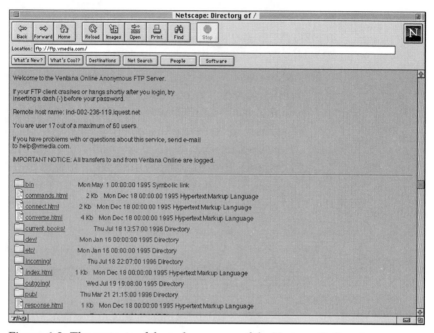

Figure 6-3: *The contents of the welcome page of the Ventana Online Anonymous FTP server.*

TIP

> *By default, Netscape Navigator 3.0 displays text files at FTP sites rather than automatically saving them to your hard drive. But what if you want to save a text file after viewing it? No problem. Just press ⌘+S or select Save As from the File menu.*

As you can see, the welcome message contains important information about the system itself, as well as the paths to many other important folders, files and messages.

COMMON FILENAME EXTENSIONS

Knowing somebody's last name won't necessarily tell you anything about the person, but the few characters that compose the extension to a filename are packed with information. For instance, if a file ends with .TXT, you can be pretty sure it's an ASCII text file, readable on virtually any system by using a simple text viewing program. But not all extensions are so obvious, so I've compiled a table of some of the most common ones you'll come across. Table 6-1 is by no means complete, but it's a good reference to keep handy as you start exploring FTP sites.

Extension	Type of File
.ASC	Probably a simple ASCII text file.
.DOC	May be a text file or a WordPerfect or Microsoft Word document.
.GZ	A file compressed using the GNU Zip program for UNIX. See note on .Z below.
.HQX	A file that has been archived using the BinHex compression program; you must use BinHex to decompress it. This compression standard is common in the Macintosh world, and chances are good that an .HQX file is intended for Mac use.
.SIT	A compressed, or "stuffed," Macintosh file. Use StuffIt Expander to decompress it. Often .SIT files are later recompressed with BinHex for transmission over the Net.
.TAR	An archive file that has been compressed using the UNIX tar facility. You don't normally need files with these extensions.
.TXT	Normally a simple ASCII text file, readable using Teach Text or Simple Text.
.Z	A file compressed using the UNIX Zip. Mac extractors are available should you need one.
.ZIP	An archive file that has been compressed using the PKZIP compression program. Normally these are from a DOS or Windows platform program, and are of limited use for Macintosh users. May be decompressed with DropStuff with Expander Enhancer (DSEE) from Aladdin Systems.

Table 6-1: *Common filename extensions on FTP sites.*

UNDERSTANDING COMPRESSION

You no doubt noticed that many of the notes in Table 6-1 refer to compression. When you look at the staggering number of files on the Internet (or the staggering number of files on your hard drive!), it is clear that it's important to shrink files so that they are as small as you can possibly make them. And of course the smaller the file, the quicker it travels from one machine on the Internet to another, reducing overall transfer time and network traffic. But what exactly is file compression?

Think about the number 20,000,000,000,000,000,000,000. Now imagine trying to read this number to another person so that he or she can write it down. You *could* say "two zero zero zero zero zero zero zero zero zero zero zero zero zero zero zero zero zero zero zero zero zero zero," but that's the stupid way to do it. If you want to maintain your friend's respect, you'll probably say "two followed by 22 zeros." You have effectively compressed the information into fewer words, and your friend can decompress it by actually writing out the 22 zeros.

There are 256 different characters that may appear in a computer file in any order, or just half that number in the case of ASCII text files. In some files, there are no repeated characters and no repeated patterns of characters, but most are full of repetitions even if the repetitions are accidental. This means that most files can be compressed. Think of a database, for instance, in which there are lots of spaces that fill out fixed-length fields. It's easy to see how you can compress a file like this by indicating the space character and the number of times it should be repeated.

Of course, I'm oversimplifying. Compression techniques have become very sophisticated and use a variety of subtle approaches, or *algorithms*, that go far beyond merely tallying repeated characters. Some try to maximize the amount of saved disk space; others try to speed up the process of compressing and decompressing files. Most try for some sort of balance between these two aspects of the process.

You have to decompress most compressed files before they can be used; compressed files are good only for transferring and storing the information. The exceptions to this are compressed graphics and sound files, which you can view or listen to directly, without running any decompression software. In this case, Netscape Navigator 3.0 (or some other viewing program) is automatically decompressing the file for you.

SMALLER + SMALLER = BIGGER

As you travel around to different FTP sites, you'll notice that graphics files such as GIFs are never "zipped up" into archives; they're always left just as they are, with their original extension. Why?

Well, GIF files are *already* compressed. The graphics standard includes an algorithm for storing these files in as few bytes as possible. Images are obvious candidates for compression, since so many pixels are repeated. Think of the background, for instance, or large patches of color. If a graphics file contained position and color information for each individual pixel that appeared onscreen, it would be gigantic!

OK, so a GIF file is already compressed. But couldn't you make it even smaller by compressing it again? Nope. Curiously, by running a GIF file through a compression program such as CompactPro or StuffIt, you actually make it *bigger*!

Kind of strange, huh? Well think about it: assuming that GIF compression is pretty tight (which it is), you're only going to eke out a few more bytes of space savings. But this added compression actually costs more space than it saves, for StuffIt has to add to the file the information about how to decompress it. In other words, it has to announce "this file has been compressed using StuffIt version *x*" as well as a bunch of other technical information. For this same reason, it may not always be worth compressing small files that are known to contain lots of nonrepeating information.

Clearly, you really need a compression program to deal with all the files you collect from the Net. In the next section, you'll kill two birds with one virtual stone: you'll learn how to use Netscape Navigator 3.0's FTP features as you download a copy of StuffIt Expander, one of the best compression/decompression programs available.

DOWNLOADING YOUR FIRST FILE

In this example, you'll access a Web page that serves as a front end for an FTP site. You will be able to download the StuffIt Expander file simply by clicking a link on the Web page, without wading through the actual directories on the FTP server itself. Later in the chapter, you'll see how Netscape Navigator 3.0 displays more "raw" FTP information.

To download StuffIt Expander using Netscape Navigator 3.0's built-in FTP:

1. Launch Netscape Navigator 3.0. The main window appears, and the Netscape home page starts loading as shown in Figure 6-4.

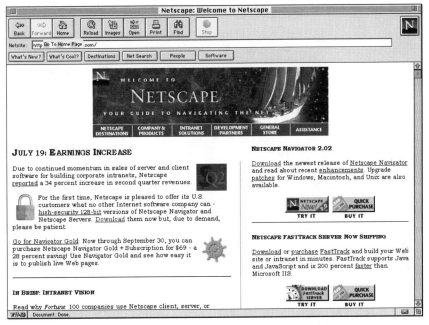

Figure 6-4: *The Netscape home page.*

2. Click your mouse inside the Location field at the top of the window to select the URL http://home.netscape.com/.

TIP

*Remember, you don't always have to type in entire URLs; in many cases you can leave off the two slashes and everything that comes before them. If you simply type in **home.netscape.com**, Navigator 3.0 is smart enough to figure out that you mean a Web site and will automatically use the HTTP protocol. Similarly, if you type in **ftp.vmedia.com**, Navigator knows you are trying to connect to an FTP site and will use FTP.*

3. Replace this URL with the one for Netscape's list of archive sites of common helper applications used on the Mac, such as StuffIt Expander, JPEGView, SoundMachine, and so forth, by typing **http://home.netscape.com/assist/ helper_apps/machelpers.html**. Once you have typed in the new URL, press Return. Netscape Navigator 3.0 retrieves the Macintosh Helpers Applications page, as shown in Figure 6-5.

Figure 6-5: *The Macintosh Helpers Applications page.*

4. You might want to take some time to look around the page. When you are ready, click the link to the University of Texas. The UTexas home page appears, as shown in Figure 6-6.

TIP

*You can save FTP sites as bookmarks just like any Web document.
Select Add Bookmark from the Bookmarks menu, or simply press
⌘+D. This is convenient if you don't have time to download a long
file immediately, but want to be able to find it easily later on.*

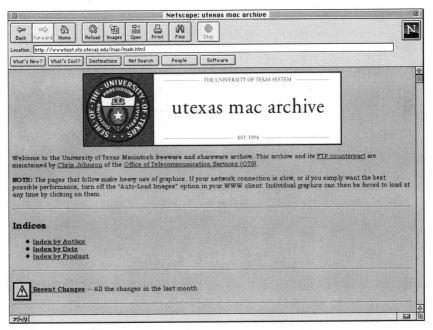

Figure 6-6: *The The University of Texas utexas mac archive page.*

5. Now let's navigate to the UTexas' FTP site by clicking on
   FTP counterpart, the link underlined and highlighted in
   the first paragraph of the now-familiar welcome message.
   The UTexas FTP site appears, as shown in Figure 6-7. Click
   on the READ-ME.Txt document for detailed information
   about what's available and how to retrieve it. Open the
   folder labeled Compression as shown in Figure 6-8 (How
   did I know? well, we're looking for a decompression
   utility— seemed logical, in a Macintosh sort of way!).

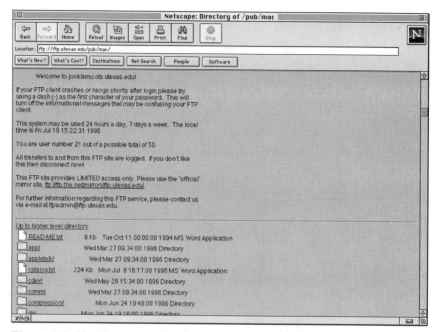

Figure 6-7: *The University of Texas directory of material available via FTP.*

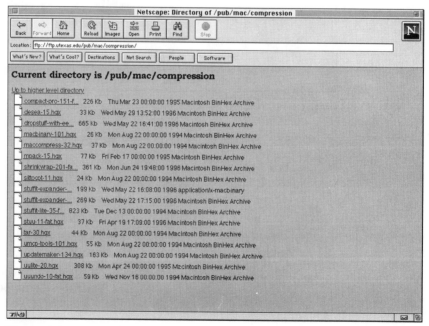

Figure 6-8: *Macintosh compression utilities available from The University of Texas via FTP.*

6. Now place your cursor (the hand) over each item, and read the material in the information bar beneath the scroll bar on the bottom of the page. Notice that the status line indicates the URL pointed to by the link. The ftp at the beginning of the URL tells Netscape Navigator 3.0 to use the FTP protocol to connect with the site, switch to the compression directory, and download the file stuffit-expander-401.hqx.

   Now, there's only one problem left—files with a .hqx extension require StuffIt Expander to decompress them. It's a chicken-and-egg dilemma. That's why we've placed a self-extracting copy of StuffIt Expander on our Netscape Press Web site. Just download that file and double-click, et viola—you can unstuff and de-BinHex like a professional. Refer to Figure 6-9. (You might also look for StuffIt Expander in the software that you were given by your access provider, and in the system software that came from Apple when you bought your computer.) Files that will self-extract have a .sea extension.

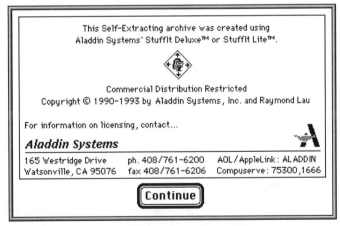

Figure 6-9: *The message displayed opening a self-extracting archive.*

7. Okay, I apologize for leading you down an elaborate trail to a seeming dead end. But there was a point to this—before you start FTP'ing all over the Net, get StuffIt Expander

installed in your Apple menu or on your desktop. Take a few minutes to do this, and let's download another file, this time with StuffIt Expander installed!

8. Go back to the compression directory at The University of Texas' Mac archive site (ftp://ftp.utexas.edu/pub/mac/compression/). This time select Drop Stuff. Here's a compression utility you can use to get your files compacted for uploading or simply to make more space on your hard drive. Click on Drop Stuff, and Netscape Navigator 3.0 will begin downloading the file. (The dialog box will show you how fast the download is taking place, how big the file being downloaded is, and how much time is remaining to complete the transmission. Go do something else while you wait for completion—this activity can take place in the background if your Mac has enough RAM!) Refer to Figure 6-10.

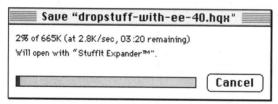

Figure 6-10: *The download progress dialog box.*

9. The next step is to determine where to put the downloaded item. Once the item is downloaded, Netscape Navigator 3.0 presents a dialog box like that shown in Figure 6-11, and gives you the opportunity to navigate through your folders to identify the place you choose. Note that expansion of the compressed file has not yet taken place; your downloaded item will be expanded as it is placed into the destination folder you select.

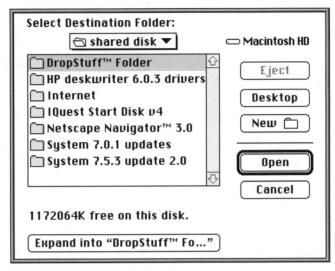

Figure 6-11: *The Destination Selection dialog box.*

10. Netscape Navigator 3.0 goes on to provide you a progress report as shown in Figure 6-12.

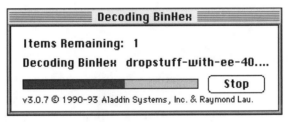

Figure 6-12: *An extraction progress report.*

UNKNOWN FILE TYPES

Sometimes when you attempt to download a file you may get an *Unknown File Type dialog box* message. This simply means that no special action or helper application (viewer) has been configured for this kind of file, and you can choose what to do with it. Netscape Navigator 3.0 can, for instance, automatically run a file like this as soon as it has been received, or it can save it to disk automatically, without popping up the dialog box. To learn how to make these configuration changes, see "Helper Applications" later in this chapter or click on the More Info button to view a tutorial document at Netscape's own Web site.

Tip: You can go to the Finder to select an application to run once a file has been downloaded, unless it starts automatically when selected. For instance, if you are downloading a Microsoft Word document, you might want to run Word right away; simply click on the document's icon, and Word will launch. Again, for more information on helper applications, see the "Helper Applications" section later in this chapter, or click the More Info button.

Congratulations! You've just downloaded your first file via FTP, and you now have an important tool for dealing with files you will download in the future.

Now let's visit an anonymous FTP site the more traditional way, without relying on a Web page as the front end.

FTP Traffic Jams

FTP sites are among the busiest resources on the Net. They may not get as many users as the most popular Web pages, but because of the way FTP works, there is a built-in traffic problem.

When you access a Web page, you quickly download the document and are off. Click a link on the page, and you bop back to the site, or to a different site. You flit from site to site, never staying longer than it takes to get the requested information. But with FTP, you remain logged in to the server while cruising and perusing directories at your own pace, and of course you remain logged in as you download files. The Web is like a fast-food joint, or like the old-fashioned automats where you walked around grabbing the dishes you wanted; FTP is like a real restaurant, with its share of customers who just never seem to stop eating!

Because of this inherent traffic problem, you might sometimes get a message telling you that too many users are already logged on when you connect with an FTP site. Sometimes, however, you will simply be unable to connect at all, and Netscape Navigator 3.0 will just seem to be spinning its wheels. The solution to either of these problems is simple: try again later. In fact, try again *much* later, at a time when there are likely to be fewer info-junkies cruising the Net (3 A.M. works pretty well).

You say you like to sleep at night? Fortunately there is another solution. For many of the larger public FTP servers, there are also *mirror sites*, FTP servers that contain the exact same files and directory structure but may experience less traffic. These mirror sites are kept in sync with the original: anything you can get at the original you can get at its mirror, and you can be sure that you're downloading the same version. Often the "sorry, we're too busy" message you get when trying to log on to an FTP server includes a list of mirror sites.

NAVIGATING FTP SITES

For this tutorial, we'll return to a site we looked at briefly earlier in this chapter, the FTP site at the University of Texas. This site houses literally thousands of programs of interest to the Internet community, from casual Net surfers to seasoned experts. This is one of many sites dedicated to Macintosh users. Another mirror site we could go to is at the University of Michigan.

1. Launch Netscape Navigator 3.0. Make sure you are connected to the Net.

2. In the Location box at the top of the window, select the currently displayed URL and replace it with **ftp://ftp. utexas.edu/pub/mac/**. Press Return. After a few moments, the top-level directory at the University of Texas site appears, as shown in Figure 6-13. Note that there is a mirror site we could also be using to get the same information and files.

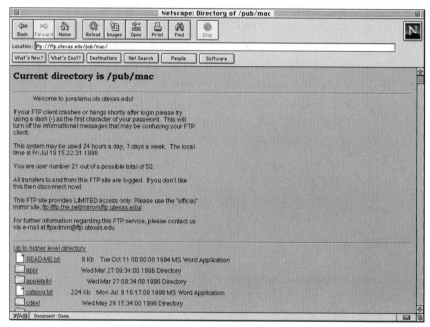

Figure 6-13: *The top-level directory at utexas.edu/pub/mac/.*

3. If there is any information at the top of the page, read it. Then scroll down. You can now see a list of several subdirectories of this top-level directory. Notice that Netscape Navigator 3.0 indicates directories with a Folder icon.

4. Maybe you're interested in graphics. Click on the graphics folder and a directory appears, as shown in Figure 6-14. Here's how to get a copy of JPEGView, which could be useful if you want to view a lot of images you've taken off the Net.

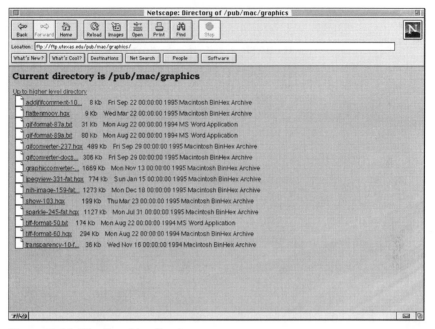

Figure 6-14: *The Graphics directory.*

TIP

If you know where you want to go on an FTP server, you can include the directory right in the URL. For instance, you could enter **ftp://ftp.utexas.edu/pub/mac/graphics/** *right in the Location box in Netscape Navigator 3.0. And if you know what file you want to retrieve (JPEGView), you can even include the filename in the URL! Look at the information bar at the bottom of the directory window—the JPEGView file is jpegview-331-fat.hqx.*

From here you can cruise around on your own for a while—Netscape Navigator 3.0 makes it so easy that you don't need me to hold your virtual hand any more. You can always back up a level using the Back button, or you can return to any level you've already seen via the Go menu. You already know that you can get to your destination by clicking your way down, level by level. But since you already know how to navigate this way, let's accelerate the process by taking a shortcut:

1. In the Location box near the top of the Netscape Navigator 3.0 window, edit the currently displayed URL so that it reads **ftp://ftp.utexas.edu/pub/mac/game/.**

   ■ A long URL like this is an excellent candidate for a bookmark. I, for one, don't want to type it again!

2. Press Return. Netscape Navigator 3.0 automatically takes you to the correct directory, as shown in Figure 6-15.

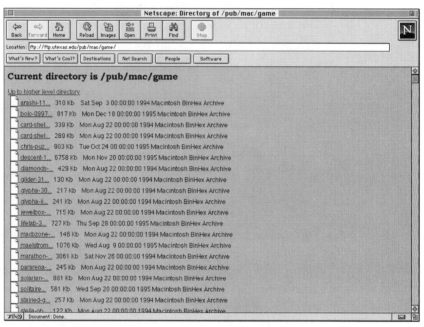

Figure 6-15: *The ftp://ftp.utexas.edu/pub/mac/game/ directory at the University of Texas.*

Try another source of Macintosh software from the UTexas host. This time, type in the URL **http://wwwhost.ots.utexas.edu/mac/ internet-misc.html** in the Location box, then press the Return key. What is displayed next is a directory of miscellaneous Internet applications for the Macintosh, with a detailed explanation of each one, along with links to their individual FTP sites as shown in Figure 6-16. Here's a good place to look for more information about that pesky communications topic we discussed in Chapter 2, "Getting Started."

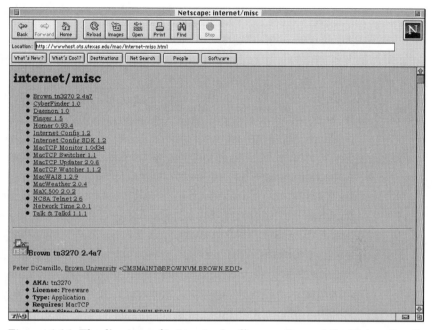

Figure 6-16: *The directory of Internet miscellaneous items at the University of Texas.*

Notice there is a 00_index.txt file at the top of a directory list. You should read this text file for capsule descriptions of all the files in this directory. Just click on it to read it, then click on the Back button in the toolbar. By default, Netscape Navigator 3.0 uses its own text utility to read text files. If you want Navigator 3.0 to use other utilities or word processors, you can set these up as "helper applications."

Now take a few moments to scroll down the list of files. Notice that these are all .hqx files, which StuffIt Expander will automatically extract for you! If the files do not have specific extensions, Navigator 3.0 uses the generic blank icon for its display. For an explanation of how to add and use these, see "Helper Applications" later in this chapter.

WHAT ARE SYMBOLIC LINKS?

As you look around FTP sites, you'll notice that in any given directory there are files, subdirectories, and something called "symbolic links." What exactly are they?

A symbolic link is really just a nickname or, more exactly, a pointer to another directory or file. Imagine you are the administrator of an FTP site, and you just put a brand new evaluation version of Netscape Navigator in the directory /pub/macintosh/system_software/www/apps/netscape. That's buried pretty far down in the directory structure, and people are going to take quite a while navigating down to that level. In addition, if they type in the entire URL, they are likely to make mistakes, taking even more time and further adding to the traffic problem. You want to make sure that users get to the new Netscape file quickly and efficiently. What to do? Create a symbolic link in the top-level directory, and call it, for instance, new_netscape. When a user clicks new_netscape, he or she is automatically transported to the directory where the file *really* lives.

The administrators of FTP sites can create symbolic links to directories or to files. If you click a link that's associated with a directory, you "teleport" to that directory; if you click a link to a file, Netscape Navigator 3.0 views the file or begins the download process. Symbolic links make it quicker, and much more pleasant, to navigate FTP sites that have complex directory structures.

SEARCHING FOR FILES

FTP is great if you know what you're looking for and where to find it. But what if all you know is that you need a particular kind of program, let's say, and you have no idea where to start looking? Or what if you can only remember part of the name of a file you want? Fortunately, the Net offers a wide variety of services for locating files in the FTP haystack. One of the old standbys, and still one of the most useful tools on the Net, is a service known as Archie.

ARCHIE

Archie is an Internet service that lets you search indexes of most of the files available at anonymous FTP sites. These indexes are maintained on special Archie servers located around the world. To use Archie effectively, you need to know part of a file's name, or at least be able to make a reasonable guess about what characters might be in its name. For instance, let's say you want to find MacTCP Watcher 2.0.6 but don't remember the exact name of its self-extracting archive file. Archie lets you specify a string of characters that appears anywhere in the name. It would be safe to guess that the string "mactcp" appears somewhere in the filename, so you can use that as your Archie search criterion and find the correct file even if its name is "latestversionmactcp."

For advanced users interested in specifying very precise search parameters, Archie even supports the full set of regular expressions that let you search for all kinds of patterns within filenames. For instance, you could look for a file that begins with a lowercase letter, followed by any number of digits, followed by the string "zsa-zsa," followed by a number greater than five, followed by an extension of either .TAR or .SH, followed by another extension of . . . Well, you get the idea. It is beyond the scope of this book to provide a tutorial on regular expressions, but I like to think of them as wild cards on steroids. If you want more information, why not use some of the Internet search tools you've learned about so far?

OK, let's give Archie a try:

1. If Netscape Navigator 3.0 is not currently running, launch it.

2. In the Location box at the top of the Netscape Navigator 3.0 window, replace the currently displayed URL with **http://www-ns.rutgers.edu/htbin/archie** and press Return. In a few moments, the Rutgers University Archie Request Form page appears, as shown in Figure 6-17.

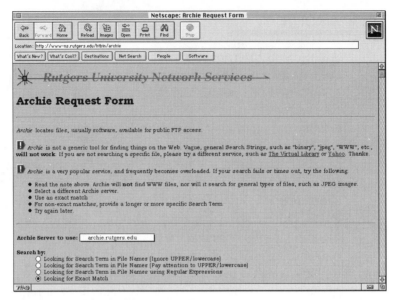

Figure 6-17: *The Archie Request Form page.*

3. Scroll down the page until you get to the search form itself. Fill it out as follows:

■ In the Search by section, click the top radio button, Looking for Search Term in File Names (Ignore UPPER/lowercase).

■ In the Search Term box, type **mactcpwatcher**.

■ Leave the other settings alone.

Your completed search form should look like Figure 6-18.

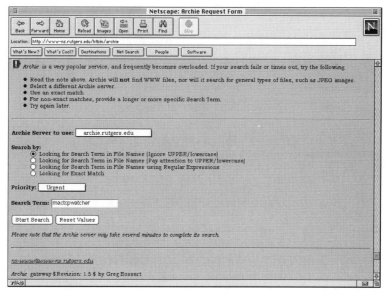

Figure 6-18: *The completed search request.*

4. Now click the Start Search button. In a few moments, the Archie Search Results page appears, as shown in Figure 6-19, providing you with links to a few different FTP sites where you can get MacTCP Watcher .

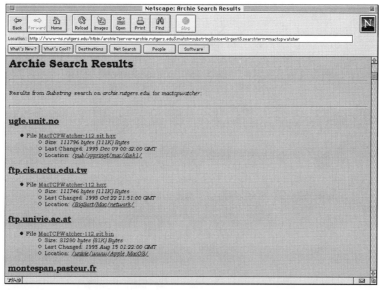

Figure 6-19: *The Archie Search Results page.*

As you can see, Archie is great if you know something—
anything—about the name of the file you are looking for. But what
if you're looking for a particular *kind* of file—a mortgage calculator, for instance—that could have any name at all? Luckily, the
Internet provides search utilities for this situation as well. One of
the best is the c | net Shareware page.

THE c|NET SHAREWARE PAGE

To get to the c | net Shareware Page:

1. If Netscape Navigator 3.0 is not currently running, launch
   it.

2. In the Location box at the top of the Netscape Navigator
   3.0 window, replace the currently displayed URL with
   http://www.shareware.com/ and press Return. In a few
   moments, the shareware.com page appears, as shown in
   Figure 6-20.

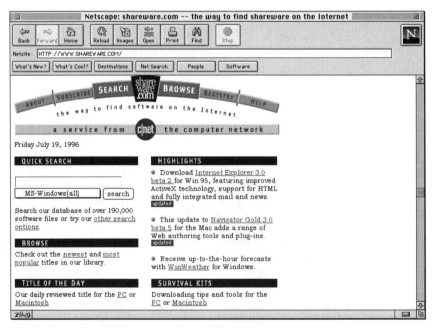

Figure 6-20: *The shareware.com page.*

3. After reading the introductory information on this page, scroll down to the search form.

4. Since we are interested in mortgage calculators for Macintosh, change the drop-down list of file categories to Macintosh. In the search word box, type **mortgage**. Your completed search form should look like Figure 6-21.

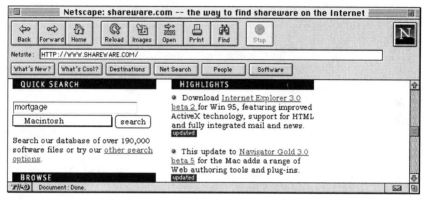

Figure 6-21: *Completed search form.*

5. Click the search button. In a few moments, the search results page appears as shown in Figure 6-22, with links to several different mortgage programs for Macintosh. You can click any one of these to retrieve the file from its FTP site.

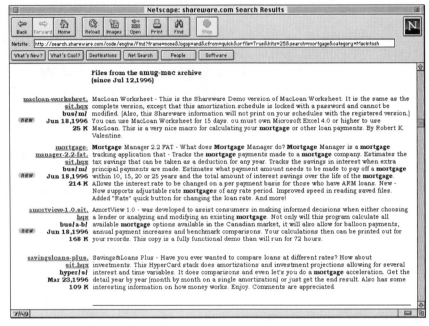

Figure 6-22: *The search results.*

The shareware.com page provides such a powerful search tool that you'll probably want to add it to your Bookmarks Directory.

USING WEB TOOLS TO FIND FILES

While there are other specialized tools for finding files on FTP sites, you may not actually need them. The World Wide Web is becoming more and more prominent as a front end for FTP servers. This means that you can find many files without specialized FTP search services; you simply use the same search engines you use for locating other types of information on the Web itself. The best of these utilities are available by clicking the Netscape Navigator 3.0 Net Search button. Whereas an Infoseek search, for instance, may not get you directly to a particular file, it will probably take you to a Web page with a link to the file you're interested in. And of course, you can find lots of files by browsing through the dozens of categories that appear when you click the Net Directory button.

As I mentioned earlier, Netscape Navigator 3.0 does more than just go out and retrieve files for you—it can actually help you start working with them right away. In the next section, you'll learn how to take advantage of this powerful feature.

WHAT ARE RFCs?

Just when you thought we were done with acronyms!

RFC stands for Request for Comment, and that's exactly what it is: a document put out on a public FTP site so that other Net users can read it and comment on the content. But an RFC contains very specialized information, technical information about the Internet itself. In fact, many of the Internet standards that have developed over the years are the result of this RFC process.

Most RFC files are slow, tedious reading, and nobody's turned them into a musical yet. But they are invaluable to anybody wanting to learn more about the Net, and a few of them are even fun. (Well, if you're a geek like me.) RFC 1208, for example, is a large glossary of networking terminology, and RFC 1325 has lots of tips for new Internet users.

How do you know what the different RFC files cover? Here are two URLs:

- ftp://isi.edu/in-notes/rfc-retrieval.txt

- ftp://isi.edu/in-notes/rfc-index.txt

The first file provides instructions on locating and downloading RFCs, and the second contains short descriptions of all the RFCs that currently exist.

HELPER APPLICATIONS

You've already seen that when you click on a text file at an FTP site, Netscape Navigator 3.0 automatically displays the contents rather than simply downloading the file to your hard drive. But that's only a small example of the automation that's possible. To understand how all of this works, let's take a look at the Helpers tab under General Preferences.

1. Select General Preferences from the Netscape Navigator 3.0 Options menu. The General Preferences dialog box pops up with the Appearance tab selected, as shown in Figure 6-23.

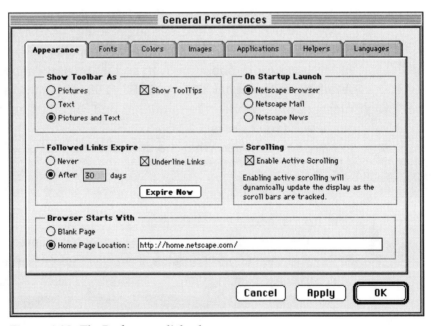

Figure 6-23: *The Preferences dialog box.*

2. Select the Helpers tab, as shown in Figure 6-24.

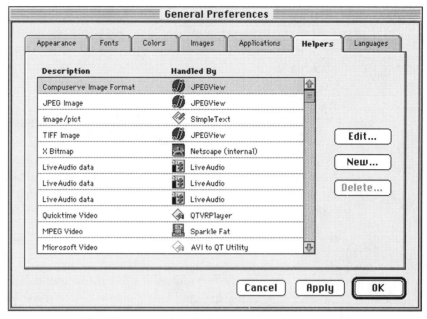

Figure 6-24: *The Helpers panel with dialog buttons for editing existing helpers, or adding new or deleting current helper applications.*

This looks like a fairly complicated dialog box at first, but once you understand the concepts, it's really pretty simple. The large scrolling list includes the names of different kinds of files you might encounter as you cruise the Net with Netscape Navigator 3.0. These file types are listed using a naming standard known as Multipurpose Internet Mail Extensions (MIME). In MIME nomenclature, for instance, files with an .EXE or .BIN extension are classified as applications, with a subtype designation of octet-stream. If you scroll down the list, you'll see many different types of files, some familiar and some unfamiliar. Usually the MIME designations make sense, as in the case of Graphics Interchange Format (GIF) files, which are classified as images with a subtype of gif.

Here's where it gets interesting. For each type of file it encounters on the Internet, Netscape Navigator 3.0 has a default action that's listed in the Handled By column of the list. For image/pict files, for example, you can see that the default action is Apple's SimpleText. X-bitmap files, on the other hand, are handled by Netscape itself. This means that X-bitmap graphics will be displayed automatically by Netscape Navigator 3.0 itself, right within the browser window. And for compressed files in BinHex or Macintosh Archive format, StuffIt Expander handles them automatically. (That's why downloaded files are expanded automatically by Netscape Navigator 3.0, even when the file does not have the .sea extension.)

Notice also that the icons have either a normal small icon appearance or are grayed out. The normal image means the application is available and Netscape Navigator 3.0 knows where to find it. The grayed-out image means Navigator 3.0 has not yet been told where to find it. Use the Edit and Browse buttons to correct this condition.

TIP

Settings in the Helpers tab also affect the way attached files are handled in Netscape Mail (see Chapter 4, "Netscape Mail").

But suppose you don't like Netscape Navigator 3.0's default action for a particular file type. Fortunately, it's very easy to change. In this example, we'll change the default action for StuffIt compressed files (.sit extension) so they are automatically saved to disk, without any "What do you want to do with this file?" dialog box popping up.

1. If you are not already in the Helpers tab, select General Preferences from the Netscape Navigator 3.0 pull-down Options menu. Select the Helpers tab.

2. Scroll down the list of file types until you find Macintosh Archive. Select this entry by clicking on it, then select Edit. The specific settings for the application/x-stuffit file type appear, as shown in Figure 6-25.

   ■ Notice that the Handled By column indicates StuffIt Expander is used for this type of file.

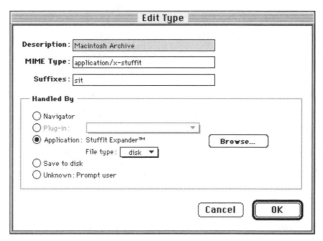

Figure 6-25: *Initial settings for application/x-stuffit (.sit extension) file type.*

3. In the Handled By section near the bottom of the dialog
   box, click the Save to Disk radio button. Then click OK.
   Now the words "Save to disk" appear in the Handled By
   column on the Helpers panel. Click OK, and return to the
   Helpers panel, which should now look like Figure 6-26.

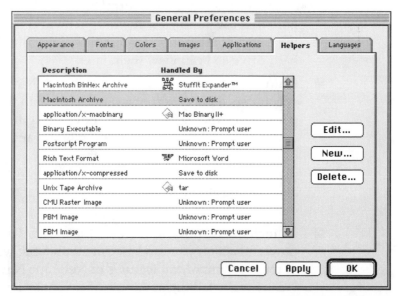

Figure 6-26: *A new action for the application/x-stuffit (.sit extension) file type.*

4. Click OK to return to the main Netscape Navigator 3.0 window. If you want to save your changes for future sessions, make sure to select Save Options from the Options menu.

That's all there is to it! Now when you click on a link to a .sit file, it will be saved to disk automatically in its compressed form.

Let's take a closer look at the other possible actions that you can associate with a file type:

- **View in Browser**. Netscape Navigator 3.0 can display several kinds of image and document files: ASCII text, Joint Photographic Experts Group (JPEG) and GIF graphics, and of course, HTML pages. Typically you'd leave these file types associated with the View in Browser action because it is the simplest and quickest way to view the information, but in some cases you may want Netscape Navigator 3.0 to launch a separate viewing or editing program as soon as the file is retrieved.

- **Save to disk**. This is obviously the most convenient option for binary files retrieved via FTP, but it can be useful in other situations as well. There are times, for instance, when I need to collect a lot of information directly from text files, but I don't want to view them right away. I temporarily set the Save to Disk option for text files, collecting them on my hard drive so I can view them later.

- **Unknown: Prompt user**. When Netscape Navigator 3.0 encounters a file type that is associated with this action, it pops up the dialog box shown above in Figure 6-7. This option is useful for file types you might want to treat differently at different times. In the case of sound files, for instance, sometimes you might want to hear them right away, while at other times you might prefer to save them to disk.

- **Launch the Application**. This is the most interesting and powerful action you can associate with a file type, and one of the most important features of Netscape Navigator 3.0. We are really talking about two different actions here:

■ If you select Navigator to handle an application that has been set to Unknown, or if you create a new MIME type and don't select a corresponding application, Navigator will download the file and present you with an alert box informing you that the selected application can't be found. You will be asked to either save the file or delete it. This also occurs if you pick an application to launch and then later decide to delete that program from your hard drive.

■ If you select the radio button and use the Browse button to select a helper application, Netscape Navigator 3.0 will run the helper application as a viewer for the associated file. The word *viewer* in this context is traditional but pretty misleading: the helper application might play the associated file rather than display it (in the case of a sound file) or even let you edit it (in the case of a Word document).

TIP

Use the Browse button to find helper applications on your hard drive.

ADDING NEW EXTENSIONS

If you want to get really fancy, Netscape Navigator 3.0 even lets you add new extensions for particular file types. For instance, you might want to add the extension .txt to the application/msword file type, so you can open files directly into Word.

To make the change:

1. If you are not already in the Helpers panel, select General Preferences from the Netscape Navigator 3.0 Options menu. Select the Helpers tab.

2. Select the dialog button marked New. The Edit Type dialog box will appear. (See Figure 6-27)

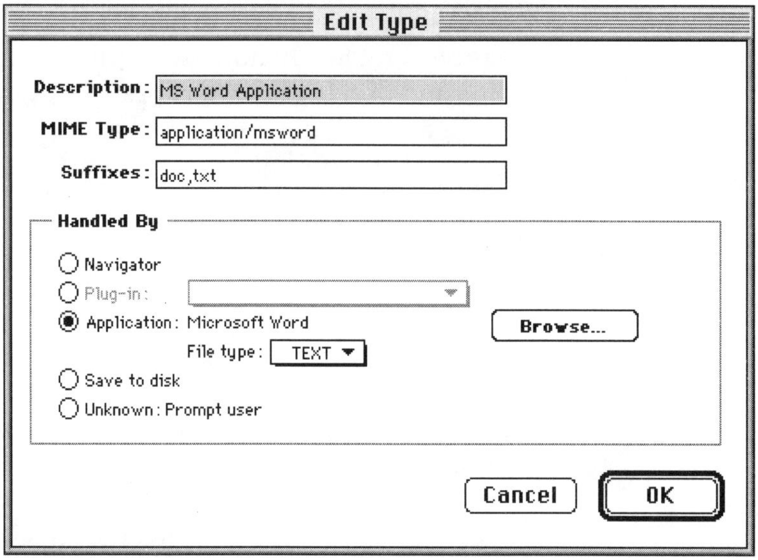

Figure 6-27: *The Edit Type dialog box associated with setting up a new helper application.*

3. In the description section, type in a description you can remember. In the MIME Type, enter **application/msword**. For Suffixes, enter **,txt**. In Handled By, use the Browse button to help you find and select the MS Word application. In File type, hold down the cursor to display all the different file types available to you. Select TEXT. The dialog box should now look like Figure 6-28.

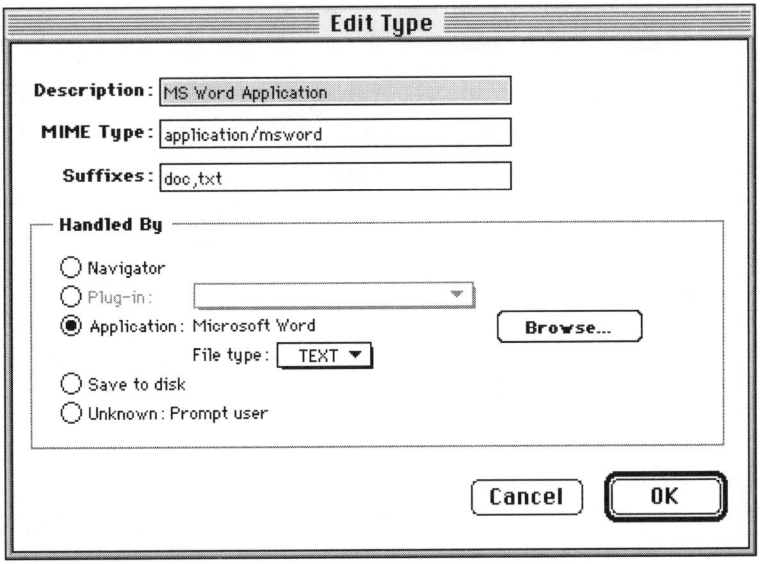

Figure 6-28: *Application/msword file type with new extension.*

4. Click OK to return to the main Netscape Navigator 3.0 window. If you want to save your changes for future sessions, make sure to select Save Options from the Options menu. Downloaded or imported documents with file extensions of .txt should now launch automatically using Microsoft Word.

TIP

When adding a new extension, make sure it's not one that is commonly associated with any other file type. For instance, many text files have the extension .DOC, but you should not add .DOC as an extension to the text/plain file type, because it is more commonly used to indicate MS-Word documents. If you do not heed my warning, you may start seeing blenderized purée de Word in your text viewer!

ADDING NEW FILE TYPES

Now if you want to get *really* fancy, you can even add new file types and subtypes to Netscape Navigator 3.0's default list. However, this is truly a propeller-head option: you should not even be thinking about it except to add a new standardized MIME type, and unless you really know what you're doing. Assuming you have the proper geek credentials, though, it's pretty easy:

1. If you are not already in the Helpers tab, select General Preferences from the Netscape Navigator 3.0 pull-down Options menu. Select the Helpers tab.

2. Select the New button. The Edit Type dialog box pops up, as shown in Figure 6-27.

3. Enter the new MIME Type and Subtype in the appropriate fields and click OK.

Netscape Navigator 3.0's Helpers facility lets you deal efficiently with just about any file on any Internet FTP site. And if you want to further automate Netscape Navigator 3.0 with new viewers, sound players, editors, or any kind of helper application, guess how you get these programs? By FTP, of course!

MOVING ON

In this chapter, you've learned the basics of navigating FTP sites and downloading files. You've also learned some strategies for finding files on the Net by name or by subject area, and you've seen how Netscape Navigator 3.0 can be customized to help you deal with your new files more efficiently. Now all you need is a bigger hard drive!

You already have most of the Web basics down, and you could easily take off at this point and start exploring on your own. But before you do that, I'd like to show you two more powerful tools that are old mainstays when it comes to exploring the Net. They are Gopher and Telnet.

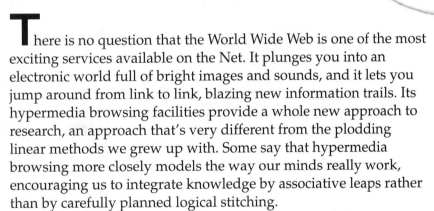

Gopher & Telnet

There is no question that the World Wide Web is one of the most exciting services available on the Net. It plunges you into an electronic world full of bright images and sounds, and it lets you jump around from link to link, blazing new information trails. Its hypermedia browsing facilities provide a whole new approach to research, an approach that's very different from the plodding linear methods we grew up with. Some say that hypermedia browsing more closely models the way our minds really work, encouraging us to integrate knowledge by associative leaps rather than by carefully planned logical stitching.

However, there are some research tasks that call for a more traditional approach to the great volume of data available on the Net; there are also some wonderful repositories of knowledge that have not yet been "Webified." Fortunately, Netscape Navigator 3.0 supports some of the older Internet services that are still very useful tools. The most important of these are *Gopher* and *Telnet*.

What Is Gopher?

What if you don't know exactly what you're looking for on the Net and want to refine your search carefully as you explore? What if you want to delve deeply into a particular area of interest, for instance, constitutional law? Typical Web sites may not help you, for often the links to other information are as arbitrary, whimsical, and wild as the imagination of the page's author.

Gopher servers, on the other hand, serve up information in tidy hierarchical menus and submenus, sticking to a subject and presenting it in top-down, outline format. Using World Wide Web documents, you leap rapidly from peak to peak. Using Gopher, you follow logically related information trails.

How Do They Come Up With These Names?

Most of the Internet services were developed not by commercial software companies, but by individuals in academia, often graduate students. This evolution is reflected in some of the jargon. If the marketing division of a software company had been involved, we'd probably be talking about Super UltraSearch Max Plus instead of Gopher. But the Golden Gopher is the mascot of the University of Minnesota, where this powerful tool was developed, and there were no people in suits calling the shots.

Once you name something "Gopher," you have to extend the metaphor. If you visit many Gopher sites, you'll discover that they are sometimes called Gopher *holes*. And avid Gopher users often talk about *burrowing* to other sites. It's all kind of quaint in this age of cyber this and surf that.

In addition to extending metaphors, computer people have a compulsive need to mix them, and so it is very common on the Net to talk about *GopherSpace*. (You can put yourself into an altered state trying to visualize that one.) GopherSpace is simply the total collection of hierarchically organized resources available to you via Gopher.

In the old days (before last year), Gopher servers were usually accessed with specialized Gopher client programs, but Netscape Navigator 3.0 makes extra software unnecessary. Netscape

Navigator 3.0 can log you on to a Gopher server and then present you with the information so that it looks very much like any Web page. Menu items are colored like other Web links, and clicking on them brings up the appropriate submenus. Let's give it a try using the *WELL Gopher* as an example.

USING GOPHER

The WELL is a large information service known for the variety of its online forums and the lively interactions of its users. It also maintains a very interesting Gopher site that's accessible to anyone on the Net. To begin exploring it:

1. Make sure you're connected to the Internet.

2. Double-click the Netscape Navigator 3.0 icon to launch the program. The main window appears, and the Netscape home page starts loading, as shown in Figure 7-1.

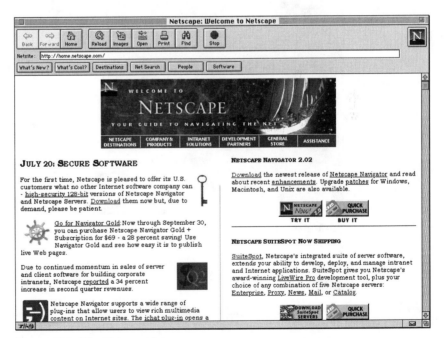

Figure 7-1: *The Netscape home page.*

3. Click your mouse inside the Netsite field at the top of the window to select the URL http://home.netscape.com/.

4. Replace this URL with the one for the WELL Gopher site by typing **gopher://gopher.well.com/**. Then press Return. Netscape Navigator 3.0 retrieves the top-level WELL Gopher menu, as shown in Figure 7-2.

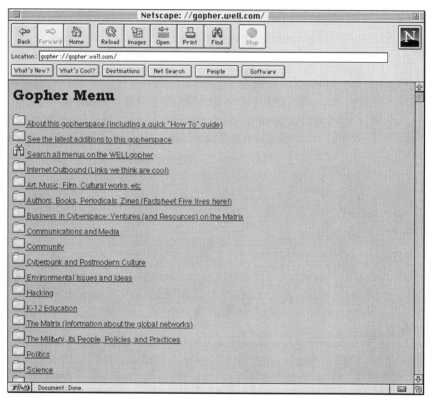

Figure 7-2: *The WELL Gopher.*

TIP

*Remember that you can type in partial URLs—Netscape Navigator 3.0 is smart enough to figure them out. Instead of typing **gopher://gopher.well.com/**, for instance, you could simply type **gopher.well.com**. Because your abbreviated URL has the word "gopher" in it, Navigator assumes this is a Gopher site.*

■ Notice that when you connect to a Gopher server, virtually all the text in the Netscape Navigator 3.0 window is composed of links. In the top level of the WELL Gopher, these are links to submenus rather than files, as indicated by the folder icons. The exception is the Search All Menus on the WELLgopher item, which brings up a searchable index of the entire Gopher server.

5. Click the top menu item, About this gopherspace (including a quick "How To" guide). A new submenu appears, as shown in Figure 7-3.

■ Notice that most of the links are to actual text files now, as indicated by the icons.

6. Click the top item, What is this place? (The basic story). This time a text file appears, as shown in Figure 7-4.

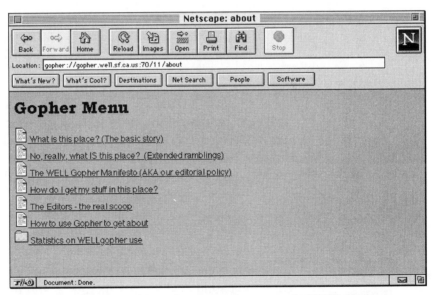

Figure 7-3: *The About this gopherspace submenu on the WELL Gopher.*

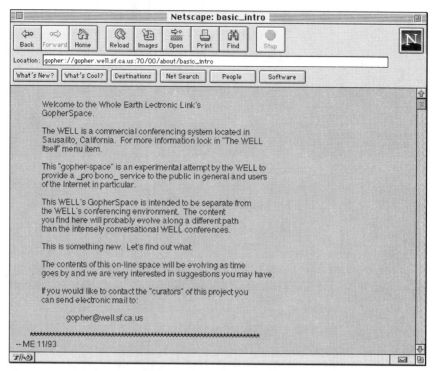

Figure 7-4: *The WELL Gopher welcome file.*

7. After reading the file, click Netscape Navigator 3.0's Back button to return to the About this gopherspace menu. You might want to read some of the other articles here, such as "How to use Gopher to get about," or the "extended ramblings" version of the "What is this place?" file. (The WELL is famous for its extended ramblings.)

8. When you're done reading, click Back again to return to the top-level WELL Gopher menu. From there you can begin to explore many different areas. Feel free to browse. The WELL Gopher is especially known for its information on media, communications, cyberpunk literature, and music.

TIP

Gopher menus can be saved, printed, copied, or made into bookmarks and shortcuts just like any other kinds of pages. In most cases, you needn't pay attention to whether you're at a Web, Gopher, or File Transfer Protocol (FTP) site. If you can see it in Netscape Navigator 3.0, you can work with it using any of the techniques you learned in Chapter 3, "A Quick Look Around."

Although the hierarchy of all Gopher sites is similar, their content varies greatly. There are Gopher sites that specialize in just about any academic field you can think of, from art to astrophysics. In addition, there are Gopher sites that are just plain fun.

But the great thing about Gopher is that it allows a site to include on its menus links to other sites as well. In other words, you are not restricted to the information available on only that particular server. Gopher is really the precursor of the Web in letting sites link to one another in a vast information net.

As you start burrowing from one site to another, you are actually creating a customized hierarchical pathway for yourself, and you can move backward and forward along it to find the information you need. Let's see how this works.

STRETCHING GOPHERSPACE

To demonstrate how you can "stretch" GopherSpace, let's use the WELL Gopher site again as a starting point (if the WELL Gopher is already displayed in your Netscape Navigator 3.0 window, skip ahead to step 3 below):

1. Make sure you are connected to the Internet. If Netscape Navigator 3.0 is not currently running, launch it.

2. In the Location box at the top of the window, select the currently displayed URL and replace it with **gopher:// gopher.well.com/**. Press Return. After a few moments, the top-level menu at the WELL Gopher site appears, as shown previously in Figure 7-2.

3. This time, click the Internet Outbound (Links we think are cool) link. The Internet Outbound Gopher menu appears, as shown in Figure 7-5.

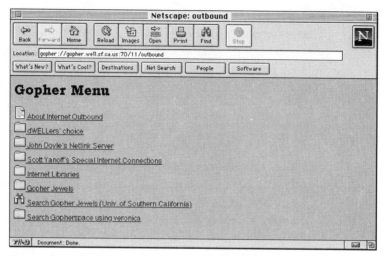

Figure 7-5: *The Internet Outbound Gopher menu on the WELL.*

4. All of the links on this menu provide useful starting points for Gopher burrowing. For this tutorial, click Scott Yanoff's Special Internet Connections. The Special Internet Connections Gopher menu appears, as shown in Figure 7-6.

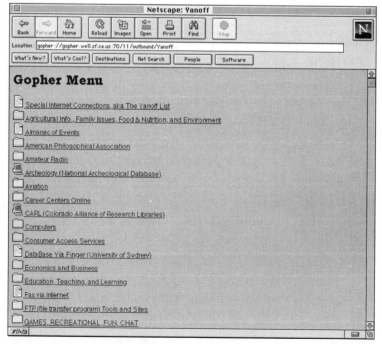

Figure 7-6: *The Special Internet Connections Gopher menu.*

■   Notice the icons depicting a computer terminal next to some of the links. This is how Netscape Navigator 3.0 indicates a Telnet connection. If you click on one of these links, Netscape Navigator 3.0 will launch a Telnet session with the host site. (More about Telnet later in this chapter.)

The Yanoff List, as it is sometimes known, offers you a wide variety of new jumping off points—or digging down points—for further Gopher burrowing. You should feel free to explore, and you might want to save this menu as a bookmark.

But before you descend into the Gopher tunnels, note that the Location box contains the URL gopher://gopher.well.sf.ca.us:70/11/outbound/Yanoff. *WELL* is still part of the site address because you've never really left the WELL; no matter how far or deep you burrow through the menus, *WELL* will still form the initial part of the URL. The URL provides a map of the path you took to get to the target information.

There are many ways to get to The Yanoff List, but you have constructed a tunnel that begins at the WELL and passes through the Internet Outbound menu. What this means is that you have a complete record of your travels, and in saving a particular URL as a bookmark, you are actually saving a map of your entire journey. With this kind of hierarchical structure, there is really no way to get lost.

This is what I mean by stretching GopherSpace. With each new link you click, you are further extending a *customized* information pathway. You can see why Gopher is a useful research tool when you're trying to refine your quest for particular information.

The WELL is only one of many tunnel entrances. In the next section, I'll list some interesting Gopher sites to begin your explorations.

GREAT GOPHER HOLES I HAVE KNOWN

Table 7-1 lists a few of the best-known Gopher sites.

URL	Description
gopher://gopher.uis.itd. umich.edu/	University of Michigan archive
gopher://ashpool.micro. umn.edu/	University of Minnesota archive
gopher://wx.atmos.uiuc.edu/	Weather maps
gopher://gopher.eff.org/	Electronic Frontier Foundation archive
gopher://gopher.well.sf. ca.us/	Whole Earth 'Lectronic Link (WELL) archive
gopher://wiretap.spies.com/	The Internet Wiretap
gopher://siggraph.org/	Conference proceedings and materials from the graphics special interest group (SIGGRAPH) of the Association for Computing Machinery
gopher://gopher.cpsr.org:70/ 11/cpsr	Computer Professionals for Social Responsibility archive
gopher://akasha.tic.com/	Sample issues of John Quarterman's Matrix News Internet newsletter, several works from Bruce Sterling
gopher://gopher.echonyc.com	Interesting information about New York City and media

Table 7-1: *Some well-known Gopher sites.*

USING GOPHER TO FIND PEOPLE

One of the most important uses of Gopher is to find people. Yes, you can use Netscape Navigator 3.0 to burrow for your long-lost Uncle Waldo—provided he's been spending some of his lost years hanging out on the Net. In fact, Gopher provides the easiest-to-use interface for a wide range of search tools.

To find Waldo, start by going to the URL gopher://gopher. micro.umn.edu/. From there, select Phone Books. Many options, including Whois searches, X.500 gateway searches, and phone books at other institutions, will appear. Searching for individuals on the Net requires that you know something about their "Net lifestyle"—where they hang out on the Net, and whether or not they are affiliated with any university or subscribe to Usenet news-groups—so at this point, you're on your own. You may not find Waldo, but at least you'll have an easy time looking.

Now that you know something about Gopher, let's take a brief look at another faithful old workhorse of the Internet, Telnet.

WHAT IS TELNET?

The World Wide Web is the showroom of the Net. It's where you'll find information in all the latest styles and colors. If you want to show a newbie what the Net is all about, you'll almost certainly start with the Web.

But a fancy new car right off the showroom floor isn't always the best way to travel. Sometimes you need an all-terrain vehicle, a rugged tool that will take you places you can't access using the newer Web protocols. Telnet dates back to the days when the information superhighway was just a two-lane blacktop, and fortunately you can still take advantage of its raw power through Netscape Navigator 3.0.

Using Telnet, you log in to other computers on the Net interactively. Once you log in, the Telnet host presents you with a command line or with text-based menus; you type menu choices or commands. Typical public Telnet sites include library card catalogs, weather information services, and a variety of specialized databases. You can also Telnet to text-based online services such as the WELL or Echo. And if you have a UNIX account on another computer on the Net, you can use Telnet to log in and run any UNIX program available on the host machine.

MUDs & MOOs

It's great to be able to access vast libraries of esoteric information via the Internet, but at some point we have to step back and take stock again of what computers are really for: playing games!

Some of the most interesting games spawned by modern information technology are MUDs and MOOs. MUDs are *Multiple-User Dimensions*, real-time, interactive role-playing games. MOOs are the object-oriented version, in which users can create their own objects, such as new rooms or features of the landscape. There are also variants of MUDs known as MUCKs, MUSHes, and MUSEs.

What all these games have in common is that several players at a time use the Internet to interact with one another as characters in a fictional world. Some of these text-based virtual worlds are full of magic and dragons, others are more like discussion forums, and some are meeting places for playing out group fantasies. Here are a couple of Web pages to get you started:

- MUDs, MOOs, and Other Virtual Hangouts (http://jefferson. village.virginia.edu/iath/treport/mud.html). Lots of info about MUDs and MOOs, and links to several sites.

- MUDs, MOOs, & MUSHes, "Hip-Waders in the CMC Swamp" (http://www.oise.on.ca/~jnolan/mud.html). Links to information and games.

Also check out the Usenet newsgroups under rec.games.mud. It's important to read the FAQs and whatever other information you can get before trying these games, as each has its own culture and rules of etiquette.

How does this remote login process work? Telnet is really a *terminal emulation* protocol. That means it makes your Mac behave like a terminal that's directly connected to the host computer. What is a terminal? A terminal is a device that can't really do anything on its own, but when it is attached to a computer it provides users with a display screen and a keyboard. In other words, a terminal provides the user interface to a host computer. Normally, terminals are attached to the host by means of cable, but terminal emulation programs allow you to connect remotely using a Mac and phone lines. With terminal emulation programs like PROCOMM PLUS and Telix, you dial directly in to a host; with Telnet, you connect via the Internet.

Figure 7-7 shows a typical Telnet session. In this example, I am logged in to the National Archeological Database, which we'll talk more about in a minute, and you can clearly see the interactive nature of this kind of connection.

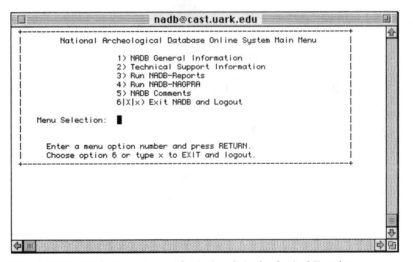

Figure 7-7: *A Telnet session with National Archeological Database.*

Telnet & Netscape Navigator 3.0

Let's see how observant you are: what's wrong with Figure 7-7?

That's right, it depicts some other software instead of Netscape Navigator 3.0. Instead of the usual toolbar and Netscape logo, you see a much simpler window. Did the author make a mistake? Did the editors miss it?

No. The fact is that Netscape Navigator 3.0 does not actually include built-in Telnet. Not only that, I don't know of any Web browser that *does* include built-in Telnet. Let me explain.

Terminal emulation programs and Web browsers are two very different kinds of software. Terminal emulation programs concentrate on interpreting ASCII character sequences on the fly, while Web browsers concentrate on displaying multimedia documents.

Since these two functions are not a good fit, the authors of most World Wide Web programs have decided to support Telnet by launching an external helper application when necessary. If you click a link that represents the URL for a Telnet connection, Netscape Navigator 3.0 launches your Telnet session by executing a separate program, passing to it the address of the site. As soon as you're finished with the Telnet session, you can return to the Netscape Navigator 3.0 window and to whatever document was last displayed in it. In fact, you don't even have to wait. If you're the kind of person who likes to do several things at once, you can go back and forth between active Telnet sessions and the main Netscape Navigator 3.0 window.

But how does Netscape Navigator 3.0 know what Telnet program to use when you navigate to a Telnet URL? It requires a little bit of setup, but fortunately the setup is very straightforward.

TN3270

Almost all public Telnet sites these days support the standard version of the protocol that uses the VT100 terminal emulation. However, there is a variant of Telnet known as *TN3270*. TN3270 sites require that you use a program that makes your Mac act like an IBM 3270 terminal instead of a DEC VT100.

Your regular Telnet program may not include TN3270 capabilities. If you plan to connect to TN3270 sites, you'll need to download a special TN3270 program from the Net. Now that you've read Chapter 6, "Getting Files via FTP," and know all about finding files on the Net, this should be no problem at all!

SETTING UP TELNET

Way back in Chapter 2, "Getting Started," we took a quick look at the Applications panel, which is where you tell Netscape Navigator 3.0 what program you want to use for Telnetting to remote sites. To get to the Applications panel:

1. In the main Netscape Navigator 3.0 window, select General Preferences from the Options menu. The General Preferences dialog box appears.

2. Select the Applications panel. The Applications panel includes fields where you can specify several supporting applications, including Telnet and TN3270, as shown in Figure 7-8.

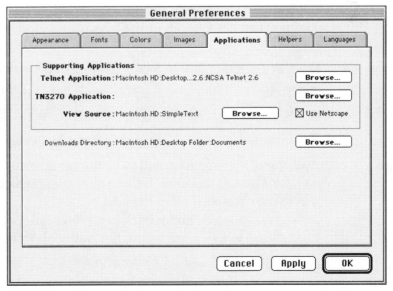

Figure 7-8: *The Applications panel.*

3. In the Telnet Application field, fill in the name of your Telnet application. Optionally, you can find the appropriate program on your hard drive using the Browse button.

4. In the same way, complete the TN3270 Application field if you plan to use TN3270.

TIP

While you're in the Applications panel, you might also want to specify an application other than Netscape Navigator 3.0 to view or edit the HTML source of any Web documents displayed in the program. You can also tell Netscape Navigator 3.0 what work directory to use for storing temporary files. We've specified the Documents folder on the Desktop.

5. Click OK.

That's all there is to it! Now you're ready to start actually using Telnet.

USING TELNET

As with any other Internet service supported by Netscape Navigator 3.0, you can get to a Telnet site by any one of several methods. You can:

■ Click a Telnet link in a Web document or at a Gopher site.

■ Type a URL in Netscape Navigator 3.0's Location box.

■ Select a Telnet link from Bookmarks.

■ Double-click a desktop shortcut to a Telnet site.

Any one of these actions will have the same result: Netscape Navigator 3.0 launches your Telnet application, which then logs you in to the site specified in the URL.

Let's give it a try by going back to a Telnet link you may have noticed earlier in a Gopher menu, the National Archeological

Database. You may not be the slightest bit interested in archeology, but I have chosen this site because it is very typical of research sites that are publicly accessible via Telnet.

For the sake of this tutorial, I'm assuming you're using NCSA Telnet 2.6. The basic instructions should be close to accurate even if you're using a different program:

1. Make sure you are connected to the Internet either directly or via your SLIP or PPP access provider. If Netscape Navigator 3.0 is not currently running, launch it.

2. In the Location box at the top of the window, select the currently displayed URL and replace it with **gopher:// gopher.well.sf.ca.us:70/11/outbound/Yanoff**. Press Return. (Hey, if you'd saved the Yanoff menu as a bookmark, you wouldn't have to type in the URL again.)

3. Click the Archeology (National Archeological Database) link. After a few seconds, the Telnet application appears with a login prompt from the remote site, as shown in Figure 7-9.

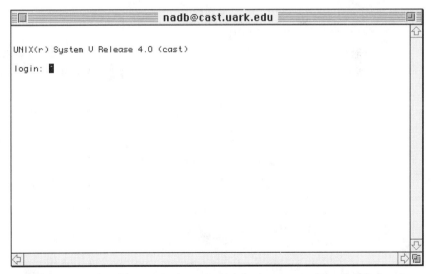

```
UNIX(r) System V Release 4.0 (cast)

login:
```

Figure 7-9: NCSA Telnet 2.6 program with login prompt from the National Archeological Database.

> **TIP**
>
> *How do you know what to enter at the login prompt? Some sites supply you with login instructions, but many don't. Depending on the exact timing of data received from the remote site, the Telnet window might cover the informational message box so that it is invisible to you. Before experimenting with different logins to see what will work, move or temporarily minimize the Telnet window to make sure you didn't miss an important message.*
>
> *If the remote system presents you with a login prompt but no information about what to enter, try typing **guest** and pressing return. In this case you'll enter **nadb** at the prompt—but we know that because we've visited this site before.*

4. Log in to this site as **nadb**, and a welcome message will greet you as shown in Figure 7-10.

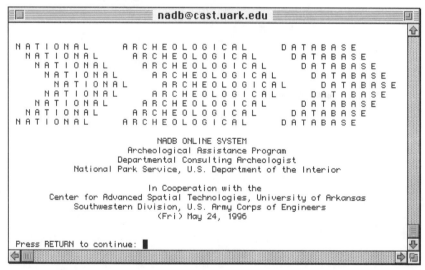

Figure 7-10: *You're logged in to the National Archeological Database via Telnet.*

5. Click OK in the message box. It disappears.

6. As directed by the remote system, press Return to continue. The NADB Connection Menu appears. Since you are connected via the Internet, select item 4, Internet to NADB, and press Return.

7. Continue following any directions that appear in the Telnet window. As is typical with research sites like this, you are asked to enter some information about yourself and to choose an ID number. Once you've gotten through this process, the NADB Main Menu appears, as shown in Figure 7-11.

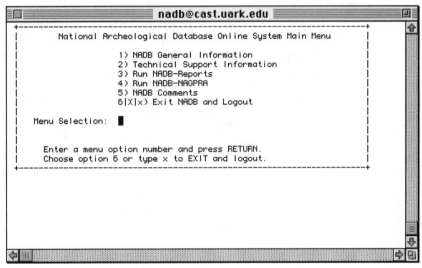

Figure 7-11: *The NADB Main Menu.*

TIP

Most Telnet programs let you copy text directly from the terminal window so that you can save it or paste it into other applications.

8. At this point, you can choose an item from the menu to get more information about the NADB or to access its search tools immediately. If you're interested in archeology, feel free to return to this site later, but for now let's select menu option 6 (or type the letter **x**), Exit NADB and Logout.

LOGGING OFF REMOTE SYSTEMS

Your Telnet program probably provides a way to disconnect from a remote site at any point, without even telling the remote host that you are leaving. In many programs, you simply choose the Disconnect option from the Connect menu.

Whenever possible, however, you should end your session cleanly by logging out from the remote Telnet site, choosing the appropriate menu options, or following instructions for quitting. Otherwise, the software at the remote Telnet site may not immediately realize you are gone and may keep the connection open for several minutes, exacerbating Net traffic jams.

Unless you're having technical problems with the connection, disconnecting without logging out is considered poor online etiquette.

9. Once you are disconnected from the remote host, you can simply quit your Telnet program.

That's all there is to it. At first it may seem awkward that Netscape Navigator 3.0 needs to launch a separate helper application for Telnet access, but there are several advantages to this system. The most significant bonus is that you can use any Telnet application you want, including ones that are much more configurable and full-featured than the program included with your basic system.

Speaking of configuration, let's take a quick look at some ways to tailor your Telnet application so that it works most efficiently for you.

CUSTOMIZING YOUR TELNET APPLICATION

Most Telnet applications offer a variety of options to make your online life easier and more productive. Since the NCSA Telnet program is typical of the simple applications that are available, we'll use it as an example. If you're using a different program, you may have to look around for some of the configuration options we're examining, but they should be there somewhere.

1. Launch Telnet by double-clicking its icon or by using the alias found in the Apple menu.

   ■ Most Telnet applications don't require you to be connected to the Net to change preferences or configuration options.

2. Select Preferences from the pull-down Edit menu, then select Global from the submenu which appears next. The Global Preferences dialog box appears, as shown in Figure 7-12.

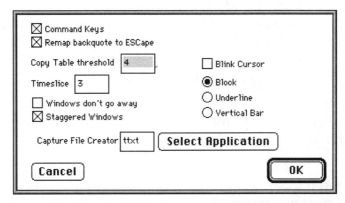

Figure 7-12: *The Global Preferences dialog box.*

The options in this dialog box are pretty typical of what's available in Telnet programs. Here are some tips for configuring these settings:

■ **Copy Table threshold**. This indicates the number of spaces NCSA Telnet 2.6 should count before placing a tab in any text you copy using the Copy Table command (⌘+T). The default is four, meaning that any text you copy from an NCSA Telnet 2.6 window that has five or more spaces in a row will have those spaces replaced with a tab. This information is handy for copying tables of information.

■ **Blink Cursor**. Check this box if you want your cursor to blink while you are in Telnet. This can help you find the cursor on remote systems that include lots of lines or underscores in their screens.

- **Block**. Check this option if you want a block cursor instead of the usual cursor. This may be much easier to see on some systems.

- **Timeslice**. This option lets you specify how much processor time to allow any other application running at the same time. It is normally best to leave this setting at the default position, although if your other programs are running sluggishly when you're in Telnet, you might try increasing this time slightly.

- **Capture File Creator**. This determines what program will open any text you capture while in NCSA Telnet 2.6. By default, it's set to ttxt, the creator designation for TeachText or SimpleText. Using the Select Application button, you can change this to Microsoft Word, WriteNow, ClarisWorks, or any other application capable of interpreting ASCII text files.

Once you have made your configuration changes, click OK to return to the main Telnet window.

MOVING ON

This has been the "back to basics" chapter—a quick look at some of the older workhorse Net services available through Netscape Navigator 3.0. Now we're going to go in the other direction and explore Netscape Navigator 3.0's multimedia capabilities. In its support of Gopher and Telnet, Netscape Navigator 3.0 provides you with a dependable off-road utility vehicle. But as you'll see in Chapter 8, its forward-looking integration of graphics and sound make it a true cyber-spaceship.

8

Graphics, Sound & Video

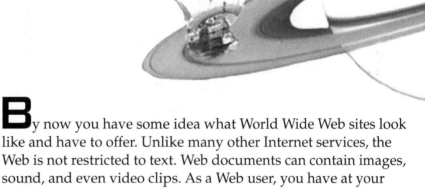

By now you have some idea what World Wide Web sites look like and have to offer. Unlike many other Internet services, the Web is not restricted to text. Web documents can contain images, sound, and even video clips. As a Web user, you have at your fingertips a vast assortment of multimedia documents that virtually come to life when you view them. Netscape Navigator 3.0 enables you to interact with these multimedia documents in a variety of ways.

 ## GRAPHICS ON THE WEB

Pictures play an important role in our lives: we hang them on our walls; we pay money to stand and look at them in museums; we take snapshots of our loved ones and favorite places. Just as pictures are a common form of communication in our society, they are an important part of the World Wide Web. In fact, much of the growth and popularity of the Web is a result of people like you and me having a new way to gather and disseminate information in a colorful and creative way.

In the following sections, you'll read about the types of graphics that are available on the Web and how you can view and download them with Netscape Navigator 3.0.

WHAT KINDS OF IMAGES ARE AVAILABLE?

Each month, thousands of new Web pages are created and placed online. Almost all of them contain some sort of graphic. Graphics can be small or large, colorful or black-and-white, tasteful or tasteless. You can probably find the exact image you're looking for on the Web if you look long enough. It may not be legally posted there, but it will be there (I discuss copyright infringement later in this chapter).

So what kinds of images can you expect to find on the Web? Almost anything. There are:

- Paintings by Renoir, Van Gogh, and little Jimmy from Ms. Wharton's first grade class.

- Publicity shots of your favorite movie and television stars, including Brad Pitt, Ricki Lake, and Bill Gates.

- Detailed weather maps like the ones you see your local weather man pointing at on the 11 o'clock news.

- More *Star Trek* and *Deep Space Nine* photos than we care to know about.

- Business logos and advertisements, from IBM and Microsoft to Absolut and Ford Motor Company.

- Cartoons and animations.

- And yes, some pictures of naked people, if you look hard enough.

GRAPHICS IN NETSCAPE NAVIGATOR 3.0— AN OVERVIEW

Fortunately for all you picture lovers, Netscape Navigator 3.0 includes features that let you view the majority of graphics on the Web. Graphics appear in a variety of sizes, shapes, and formats. In one way or another, Netscape Navigator 3.0 can either display them or provide an easy way for you to view them in another application. The best way to understand the types of graphics and how they display on Netscape Navigator 3.0 is to link to a fairly typical site.

To view a graphic in Netscape Navigator 3.0:

1. Launch Netscape Navigator 3.0. The main window appears, and the Netscape home page starts loading.

2. Click your mouse inside the Location field at the top of the window to select the URL http://home.netscape.com/.

3. Replace the URL with the one for the Ventana Online home page by typing **http://www.vmedia.com** (or simply **www.vmedia.com**). Then press Return. Netscape Navigator 3.0 retrieves the Ventana Online homepage, as shown in Figure 8-1.

Figure 8-1: *The Ventana Online home page.*

TIP

Notice that Navigator displays text first, then fills in the graphics. Sometimes you will see a description of the graphics, before it starts loading, in the top-left corner of its frame.

Have I Got the Entire Document?

Many Web pages take some time to download to your computer. How can you be sure you've received the whole thing? Netscape Navigator 3.0 provides several clues.

First, you can look at the status line at the bottom of the Netscape Navigator 3.0 window. This area indicates the transfer progress of the Web document. On the left side of the status line is a readout that displays the size, percentage downloaded, and the rate at which Netscape Navigator 3.0 is retrieving the document. You might have a difficult time reading this line because it's constantly changing, but it will give some idea of how fast your modem is transferring data. At the far right of the status line is a small graphical bar that represents the data transfer. The bar expands to the right as the new page transfers. When the document has completely transferred, this area goes blank, which tells you that no more data is being sent.

Another way to tell if a Web page is completely transferred is to look at the Stop button on the Netscape Navigator 3.0 toolbar. If it displays a red stop sign (which you can click to stop the transfer), the document is still transferring.

But probably the coolest way to see if a document is still transferring is to watch the animated Netscape logo in the top-right corner of the Netscape Navigator 3.0 window. As the document transfers, a meteor shower streams across the big Netscape *N*. When the shower ends, the document has finished downloading and all the graphics are displayed.

On a Web page like the one shown in Figure 8-1, you may see several different graphics and notice that they're used in a variety of ways. By far the most prevalent type of image you encounter in Web pages is an *inline graphic*. Inline graphics are part of the Web document itself, and not a separate file; they appear alongside the text. Inline graphics can include photos, buttons, icons, cartoons, and many other types of pictures. They are used for the following purposes:

- Logos
- Decorations
- Bullet points
- Illustrations
- Separators

Sometimes graphics are not inline, but exist only as a separate image file that you can download to your hard disk for later viewing, or one that you need to view in a separate application from Netscape Navigator 3.0. One common external viewer is JPEGView, which was used to display the graphic shown in Figure 8-2. You'll learn more about these types of images and how to view them in the section entitled "Graphics on Demand," later in this chapter.

Figure 8-2: *The Ventana home page graphic only, displayed with JPEGView. Note the statistics and comments notes, which may be turned on or off by the user.*

When you connect to a site, such as http://www.vmedia.com (Ventana's Web site), the Web document begins to transfer to your computer and appears in Netscape Navigator 3.0. As the document displays, you usually see some text first, and then the graphics begin to appear. Depending on the speed of your connection, images may seem to flow in line by line or pop right up along with the text. It all has to do with the amount of data that your modem or phone line can transmit to your computer monitor. For example, high-speed connections, such as ISDN or T1 phone lines, can transmit more data per second than modem connections.

TIP

Tired of waiting for a document's images to display? Click the Stop button on the Netscape Navigator 3.0 toolbar to stop the transfer. If you want to complete the transfer later, click Reload.

Or turn off the automatic display of graphics entirely, as described later in this chapter in the section, "Text-Only Mode."

To accommodate users with all kinds of connections, some sites now include two different versions of the same page. One page usually includes a lot of graphics that a typical modem user will not want to wait to download to his or her computer. The other usually has very few images and mostly text. When you link to a site that has these options, such as the Internet Underground Music Archive (IUMA), you must make a choice to view the page with a lot of images, or one that has been toned down a little to avoid unnecessary waiting.

Figure 8-3, shows you the site when you choose to see the graphics-intensive pages. Figure 8-4 shows what you'll see if you choose the same pages with fewer graphics. Running with a 28.8 kbps modem, the graphics-intensive page took about one minute to display. The "lite" version took only a few seconds!

Figure 8-3: *The IUMA site with lots of graphics.*

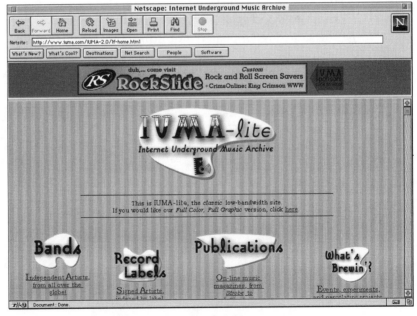

Figure 8-4: *The IUMA with very few graphics.*

TIP

Most sites include the same textual information in both their graphics version and their text-only pages—the only thing you'll miss is the images themselves.

You'll learn later how to optimize the display of graphics in Netscape Navigator 3.0, but let's first discuss a couple of special-purpose graphics often used on the World Wide Web: background images and icons.

BACKGROUND IMAGES

Background images do just what their name implies—they provide the background to the text and other graphics in a Web document. Background images typically are very small images that are repeated again and again over the entire background. (This technique sometimes is referred to as *texture mapping* in graphics design programs.) The images can be solid colors, textures, patterns, or whatever the Web author comes up with. For example, the Graphion home page pictured in Figure 8-5 shows a gray granite background. Some other backgrounds you may encounter include marble, wood grain, and metallic, but occasionally you'll even see the same logo repeated a hundred times across your screen.

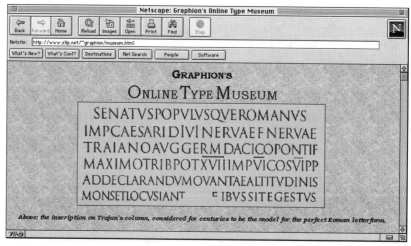

Figure 8-5: *Graphion's home page, showing gray granite background.*

When Web page authors create a page, they can enter HTML code (the language of Web pages) to include an image as the background. Not all Web sites use backgrounds, but these days it's becoming the norm. Backgrounds offer the Web author a way to set a standard color, texture, or image for the entire Web site. This eliminates the need to rely on the Web browser to provide a color (using the Options | General Preferences | Colors panel) for the Web page.

ICONS

Icons are another type of graphic you'll encounter on almost all Web pages. Icons are small images or buttons, sometimes miniatures of larger images you can find at that site. Icons are used to highlight certain points on the page, lead you to another Web page or site, or let you view or download a larger image. Let's look at each of these uses.

In Figure 8-6, you see a set of icons to the left of some text on the Web page. These icons serve the same purpose that bullets do in a book or business document: to distinguish key points. Icons can also be used to highlight special text on a page.

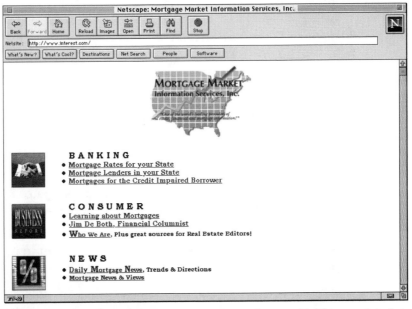

Figure 8-6: *Icons emphasize important text on the page (© Mortgage Market Information Services, Inc.).*

The second type of icon is actually a hotspot that links to another page or another site, sometimes to graphics of products or announcements. This type of icon works the same as linked text on a page—when you click it, you connect to that other site or page. Icons of this type often have a small blue border around them to indicate they are links. Figure 8-7 shows examples of icons that you click to advance to another related site.

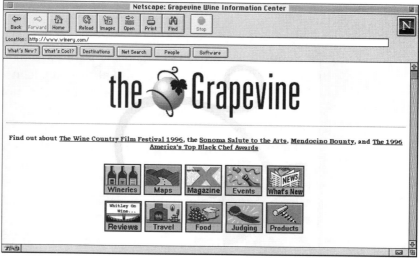

Figure 8-7: *Icons that provide links.*

WHAT IS THE NETSCAPE NOW ICON?

After your first 10 or 15 minutes on the Web, you're bound to run into a Web page that includes the Netscape Now icon (see Figure 8-8). Netscape provides this icon for Web page authors to include on pages designed especially for Netscape Navigator 3.0. This icon, or button, links the user to Netscape's home page so that users who don't have Netscape Navigator 3.0 installed can order or download a copy of it. For more information on obtaining permission to use this icon, see http://home.netscape.com/comprod/mirror/netscape_now_ program.html.

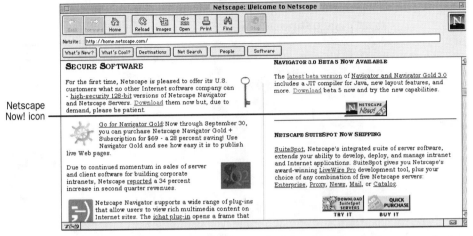

Netscape
Now! icon

Figure 8-8: *Web page authors can use the Netscape Now icon on pages designed for Netscape Navigator 3.0.*

Icons are also used as small "try-before-you-download" versions of larger graphics. When you click this kind of icon, often called a *thumbnail*, the larger image begins to transfer. The advantage of this approach is obvious: the smaller thumbnails transfer to your machine much more quickly than full images you may not even be interested in.

For example, the Web page in Figure 8-9 shows small icons of Renoir paintings (http://sunsite.unc.edu/wm/paint/auth/renoir/). You can scroll down the page and click the painting you'd like to see in full size. Now a larger painting displays in Netscape Navigator 3.0, as shown in Figure 8-10.

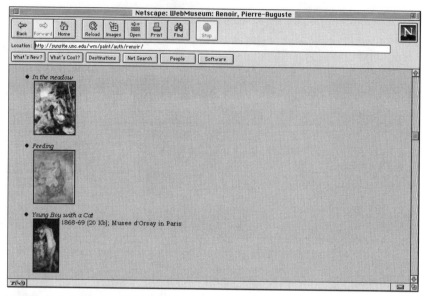

Figure 8-9: *Thumbnail of several of Renoir's paintings.*

TIP

Netscape Navigator 3.0 can be set to automatically open the JPEGView application, if it' not already open, and use JPEGView to permit you to see an enlarged version of the thumbnail. You could save the graphic image on your desktop or in a folder you have designated for it, or you can discard the image if you no longer want to view it. See the section "Setting up Helper Applications" later in this chapter.

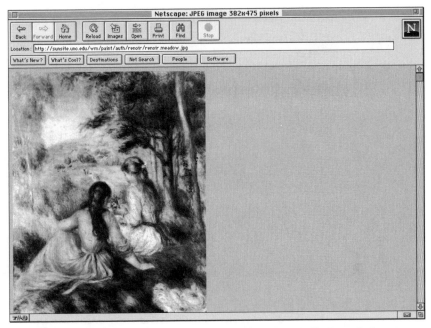

Figure 8-10: *Full view of Renoir's painting of Mademoiselle Romain Lacaux.*

TIP

Conscientious Web page authors include file sizes and estimated transfer times next to icons or thumbnails. (JPEGView uses the shortcut command ⌘ +0 to show statistics which you might find useful.) Use these estimates to determine if the wait is going to be worth it. When I am on these sites, I find the smallest file and download it first. If I don't like the quality, I probably will not download another one.

GRAPHICS FORMATS SUPPORTED BY NETSCAPE NAVIGATOR 3.0

The graphics in Web documents typically come in standard file formats that most Web browsers, such as Netscape Navigator 3.0, can understand and display on your computer. The standard file formats include Graphics Interchange Format (GIF), Joint Photographic Experts Group (JPEG), and XBM. GIF and JPEG are the most common graphics you'll encounter in Web pages. XBM is a UNIX graphics format and is more likely to be found at university or research areas that generally work with high-speed computing applications.

ANY OTHER FORMATS OUT THERE?

Many other types of graphics formats are available on the Web, including Macintosh PICT, BMP, PCX, TIFF, and encapsulated PostScript (EPS), but the most common image formats are GIF and JPEG.

Both GIF and JPEG files are compressed to save transmission time and to limit their storage size. It is beyond the scope of this book to get into the technical differences between JPEGs and GIFs, but the two formats excel in different areas. JPEG compression is often used for ultra-realistic photographic images, while GIF is used for colorful graphics. GIFs can start to display on your screen while they are still downloading, while with JPEG images you must wait for the entire image before it appears (although a new standard called "progressive JPEG" is emerging, which displays images while they are loading). GIF images may also be *transparent*. Transparent GIF images are graphic files that have been customized to eliminate the background color of the image. Thus they appear to "float" on top of the Web page instead of being stuck inside a rectangular prison.

TIP

Since many graphics on the Web come for the DOS world, they will often carry the DOS-standard three-letter file extension. While you can ignore this for most purposes on the Mac, it's a handy way to distinguish GIFs from JPEGs at a glance. JPEG files generally have an extension of .JPG (on the Mac, sometimes extended to .JPEG); GIF files always have an extension of .GIF. JPEGView may be set to save in PICT format by default. Open the Preferences menu from the pull-down File menu.

When authors create Web pages, they make sure the images they place as inline graphics can be displayed by the most popular Web browsers. Because Netscape Navigator is such a popular browser, Web authors almost always try to develop pages that are compatible with it. This means that they use GIFs and JPEGs. You should not have any problem viewing most Web pages.

GRAPHICS ON DEMAND

Some Web sites offer images you can download to your computer for subsequent viewing. These differ from inline graphics because they are not part of the text of the Web page display, but are only linked to in the document. You can still view many of these files in Netscape Navigator 3.0, using it simply as a file viewer instead of a Web browser. Or, if you want to edit the file or save it in a different format, you can view it in a stand-alone graphics application such as GIFConverter or JPEGView.

At the Saturn Web site shown in Figure 8-11, for example, you can download a picture of one of the auto new models and then view it in Netscape Navigator 3.0.

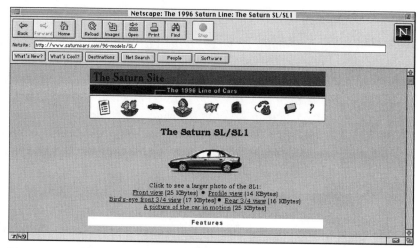

Figure 8-11: *The Saturn Web site.*

To download a picture:

1. Make sure you are connected to the Internet. If Netscape Navigator 3.0 is not currently running, launch it.

2. In the Location box at the top of the window, select the currently displayed URL and replace it with the address for the Saturn Web site, which is **http://www.saturncars.com/96-models/SL/**, and press Return.

TIP

Remember, you can abbreviate URLs. You can leave off the http:// if you want.

3. After the Web document transfers to your computer and displays, click on a link to a full-size picture. These are listed underneath the picture of the car on the home page. The links describe the view of the image, such as Front View or Rear View. Next to a hot link is the approximate size of the image in kilobytes. The larger the image, the more time it takes to display.

4. Click on the A picture of the car in motion link. Notice that Netscape Navigator 3.0 opens a new page where the image will be displayed, provided helper applications have been set to use Netscape Navigator 3.0 for the image format being transferred. Figure 8-12 shows the completed version of this picture, using Netscape Navigator to open the image.

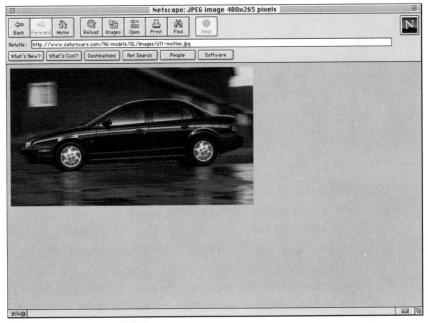

Figure 8-12: *The Saturn SL/SL1 in motion.*

Now that the image is onscreen, what can you do with it? Not much, at this point. Netscape Navigator 3.0 is not designed to be a graphics editor, but only a viewer for certain types of graphics., What you can do is save the image to your hard disk for later viewing. If you enjoy a particular image and you've waited several minutes for it to transfer to your machine, you owe it to yourself to save it to disk.

1. To save an image to disk, Select Save As from Netscape Navigatgor 3.0's File menu. The Save As dialog box appears.

2. Choose a location for the file and then click the Save button. The Saving Location dialog box appears, showing the progress of the file transfer.

TIP

To save a graphic quickly, hold down the mouse button on the image and select Save This Image As from the context menu that pops up here.

■ Because the file already has been downloaded to your computer (but not saved to disk), it takes only a few seconds to save it to disk.

3. Click on the Back button to return to the previous Web page.

Who Owns the Image?

The easy answer to this question is "probably not you." Almost every image on the World Wide Web and the Internet is owned by someone or by a legal corporation. Don't think that just because you can download an image to your computer's hard disk you own the rights to the file. In most cases, you do not. In fact, some images have been placed on the Web illegally, without permission from their owners. By downloading these images, you may also be breaking the law.

Fortunately most sites comply with international copyright laws and make available only those images they own or have legally licensed from another party. These images are provided for you to view but not reuse or sell in any form.

Some sites legally allow you to download graphics for use in commercial or noncommercial ways. Clip art images, for example, fall into this category. Many sites offer downloadable images that ➡

you can incorporate in business documents, Web documents, and other sources. But remember, you are still responsible for making sure that the images you download are indeed owned or licensed by the person providing them.

Other sites require that you first pay a fee to acquire the rights to view and download images. Sites such as MTV, Sony, and Playboy offer repositories like this. Again, copyright laws restrict you from reselling these images as your own. You can only look at them, you can't plaster them all over Usenet newsgroups.

Netscape Navigator 3.0 makes graphic configuration quite simple—there is only one setting in the General Preferences | Images panel. It specifies whether or not images will be displayed before they have been completely transferred. To change this setting, select from the following choices:

- **While Loading.** Instructs Netscape Navigator 3.0 to display partial images while they are being transferred. This is the default setting.

- **After Loading.** Tells Netscape Navigator 3.0 to wait until the entire image has transferred before displaying it. On very fast networks, this *may* be slightly faster than the other method, but I'm a child of the visual age and get anxious if I don't see something happening on my screen right away.

After you make changes to the Images panel, click OK to save them and return to the main Netscape Navigator 3.0 window. Or click Cancel if you want Netscape Navigator 3.0 to disregard any changes you have made.

TEXT-ONLY MODE

They say a picture is worth a thousand words, but we writers have never bought that. In spite of all the dire warnings of bow-tied professors, we have not degenerated into an illiterate society that worships only images. In fact, as technology gets better and better at surrounding us with imagery, more and more *words* get published!

You really see how important words are when you have a modem connection to the Net. If you have a slow modem and have been following the various links in this chapter, you're probably growing tired of waiting for some of the documents to transfer. In fact, if you have a modem that operates at less than 28.8 kbps, you may already be working on next year's letter to Santa. But besides speeding up your Internet connection, there is another approach: you can bypass graphics altogether.

Netscape Navigator 3.0 gives you the option of turning off the automatic display of graphics by deselecting the Auto Load Images option on the Options menu (see Figure 8-13). When this option is turned off, a small icon appears as a placeholder wherever an image is supposed to display. Figure 8-14 shows a Web document in text-only mode, with several placeholders for graphics.

Figure 8-13: *Unchecking Auto Load Images turns off the automatic display of graphics.*

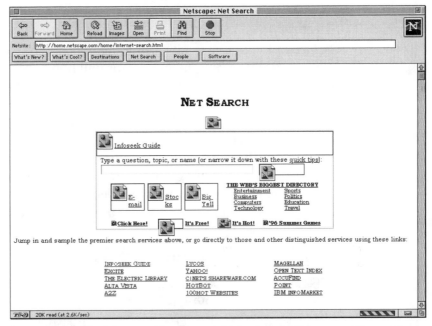

Figure 8-14: *The Netscape Navigator 3.0 Net Search Web page with graphics turned off.*

If you then come across a particular document whose graphics you want to view, you can easily display them by clicking the Images button. This reloads the document with graphics displayed.

If you want to display graphics other than those supported directly by Netscape Navigator 3.0, there is one more configuration step: setting up helper applications.

SETTING UP HELPER APPLICATIONS

You read earlier in this chapter about how you can download images to view in another application, such as JPEGView or GIFConverter. When configured to work with Netscape Navigator 3.0, these applications are called *helper applications*. To make them work with Netscape Navigator 3.0, you must set them up using the Helpers tab of the General Preferences dialog box. In Navigator 3.0, new plug-ins can be loaded by simply dragging them to the Plug-ins folder within your Netscape folder, before startup. At start-up, the Navigator will record the data types for that plug-in in its preferences file. You can view these on the Helpers panel of the General Preferences tabs using the pull-down Options menu.

If you disable a plug-in, Navigator will remember its data types, and automatically mark the plug-in as disabled. If you later return that plug-in to the folder, you will need to re-enable the plug-in using the General Preferences settings.

First, obtain a helper application and install it on your system. Applications that let you view or edit graphics are available from various sources, including third-party books, software stores, FTP and Gopher sites, and World Wide Web sites. Some of the applications that you might want to obtain are listed in the Table 8-1.

Viewer Name	Supports File Types
JPEGView	GIF, JPEG/JPG, TIFF, PICT, BMP, MacPaint, Startup Screen
GIFConverter	GIF, EPS, JPEG/JPG, JFIF, TIFF, RIFF, MacPaint, Thunderscan
Acrobat	PostScript*
*Adobe Acrobat is a commercial product in two parts: Acrobat Reader and Acrobat Distiller. The Distiller is capable of converting Portable Document Format files into a format readable by Acrobat Reader. For more information, check http://www.adobe.com/.	

Table 8-1: *Some graphics viewers that can be used as helper applications.*

TIP

Virtually any program that can run on your system can be used as a helper application in Netscape Navigator 3.0. In Chapter 9, "Power Navigator 3.0," you'll also learn about plug-ins, *which are another type of application that can extend Navigator's graphics capabilities.*

Netscape Navigator 3.0 natively displays GIF and JPEG files, so unless you're interested in editing or format conversion you won't gain much with a helper application that supports only these formats. You need one that offers the capabilities to read those formats and others, such as TIFF and PICT. These file types are fairly common, and some Web sites may include these types of graphics in their documents or file archives.

Once you acquire and install a helper application on your system, use the following steps to configure it to work with Netscape Navigator 3.0 to display any TIFF files you encounter:

1. Select General Preferences from the pull-down Options menu. The General Preferences tabbed panels appear.

2. Select the Helpers panel, shown in Figure 8-15. If you feel overwhelmed by this screen, see the upcoming sidebar "What Are All Those Funny Settings?"

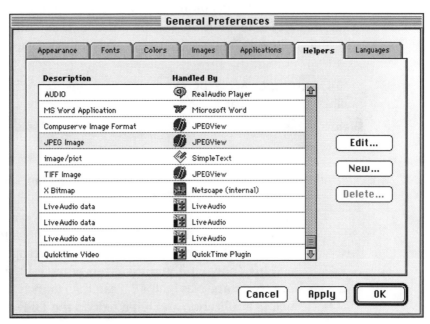

Figure 8-15: *The Helpers panel.*

WHAT ARE ALL THOSE FUNNY SETTINGS?

The Helpers panel looks fairly complicated at first, but once you understand the concepts, using it is really pretty simple. The large scrolling list includes the names of different kinds of files you might encounter as you cruise the Net with Netscape Navigator 3.0. These file types are listed using a naming standard known as *MIME*. In MIME nomenclature, for instance, files with an .SND are classified as audio, with a subtype designation of "basic." If you scroll down the list you'll see many different types of files, some familiar and some unfamiliar. Usually the MIME designations make sense, as in the case of GIF files, which are classified as images with a subtype of gif.

Here's where it gets interesting. For each type of file it encounters on the Internet, Netscape Navigator 3.0 has a default action that's listed in the Handled By column of the list. For more details, select the Edit button. For image/gif files, for example, you can see that the default action is Jnetscape (internal). This means that GIF graphics will be displayed automatically by Netscape Navigator 3.0, right within the browser window. And for RGB files, the default is Prompt User. When you click on a link to an .RGB file, you will be prompted for a solution.

3. In the long scrolling list at the top of the tab, scroll down until you see the TIFF Image entry. Double-click it. This will take you to the Edit dialog box in which you can set up how you want to handle these files. The extensions for TIFF images that Netscape Navigator 3.0 will recognize are tif and tiff, shown in the suffixes box of the Edit Type dialog box. Netscape Navigator 3.0 can then launch the associated helper application and tell it to load the TIFF image.

4. Select the Handled by Application radio button, which is below the File Extension box. This tells Netscape Navigator 3.0 to launch your helper application, in this case JPEGView, when it encounters a TIFF image.

5. Now you need to tell Netscape Navigator 3.0 where on your computer to find the helper application. Use Browse to navigate through your folders to locate the helper application. Once you've found the application, select it and click the Open button.

`TIP`

Use the Browse button to find helper applications on your system. Or if you lose things a lot, like I do, use the Find command from the pull-down File menu in the Finder.

6. Click OK to save your changes and return to the main Netscape Navigator 3.0 window.

Now when you encounter a site that includes TIFF images, Netscape Navigator 3.0 automatically starts the helper application and lets you view and manipulate the image.

The subject of graphics on the Internet is a very large one, and we've covered only the basics in this chapter. Chapter 9, "Power Navigator 3.0," will go into more advanced uses of graphics through VRML and Netscape Navigator 3.0 *plug-ins* as well as Java and JavaScript, but for now let's see—or rather, hear—what's up with sound in Netscape Navigator 3.0.

SERVER PUSH & SIMPLE ANIMATION

Most Web pages require that you interact with them in some way. They usually include links to other pages, graphics to click, animation to view, or sound objects to download and listen to. All of these items are initiated in some way by the user, the person using the client application (Netscape Navigator 3.0, in this case).

Another type of HTML instruction enables Web authors to design pages that deliver an updated version of the page without interaction from the user. This technology is called *server push*. Using server push, the server transmits Web page instructions and

➡

information to your browser window. As you navigate to various Web sites that support server-push technology, the connection between you and the server on the other end remains open. The server can continue to "push" updated information and data to your computer continuously. By pushing several different images into the same location on a Web page, for instance, a server can give the impression of a single animated image. The connection between you and the server closes when you leave the site.

An example of a Web site that supports server push is the Word site at http://www.word.com. It uses server push in a variety of ways, often to display advertisements during the time you are moving from one page to another. The advertisement appears, gives you a few moments to read it, and then disappears so that you can continue on to the item that you originally selected.

Throughout Word, there are clever icons that rely on server push for animation. But there are all kinds of uses for server push. A sports site, for instance, can use server push to keep a scoreboard updated with the latest scores and team highlights.

SOUND ON THE WEB

All Macs play sound, and new models include stereo capabilities. This has helped to fuel the growth of sound capabilities on the Web. Thousands of Web sites now include sound files that offer a new way to experience online content. Radio stations, public television stations, and network news shows are providing sites that feature sound recordings. Some sites even include *live* performances of rock bands or the play-by-play of weekly football games. As the Web matures, you'll be able to sit back and listen as you work on that marketing proposal or college term paper.

AT WHAT COST SOUND?

If a picture is worth a thousand words, what's the value of the spoken word? It may or may not be worthwhile to spend the time it takes to download a file with sound in it and listen to it.

Sound files have been available on the Internet and the World Wide Web for years, but for the most part have been impractical to use. They are generally huge files, which offer only a short segment of actual content. A 30-second sound recording may occupy over 5MB of disk space. That's a lot of transmission time and disk space to waste for a little excitement.

Sound on the net has also been hampered until recently by the unavailability of PCs equipped with sound devices. Since we've had sound on our Macs for a long while, that's not a problem for us, but most Netsurfers are still PC-based and it's the masses that drive the market.

New applications are becoming available that allow you to listen to sound files as they are transmitted to your computer. That means you don't have to wait forever, racking up online charges to see if you even like the thing. One of the packages that offers this incremental sound playing is RealAudio, which is discussed later in this chapter. What these packages offer users is a sense of real-time interaction across the Internet. If you don't like what you hear, you can immediately stop the transmission of the sound file before you invest a lot of your time.

SUPPORTED SOUND FILES IN NETSCAPE NAVIGATOR 3.0

Netscape Navigator 3.0 includes built-in support for the following sound file formats: AU, SND, AIF, AIFF, AIFC, MIDI, and WAV. It's not important to know what all these acronyms mean, but you *should* know that the three most popular sound types on the Web are AU, SND, and WAV. MIDI files are really music files rather than sound files— digital "scores" that can be played correctly on any electronic musical instrument that supports the General MIDI standard.

WHAT IS LIVEAUDIO?

Until Netscape Navigator 3.0, Web browsers required special helper applications such as SoundApp in order to play audio files. LiveAudio is what Netscape calls Navigator 3.0's ability to play audio files *without* any external helper application. Similarly, the built-in video features I cover later in this chapter are known as LiveVideo.

LISTENING TO SOUND IN NETSCAPE NAVIGATOR 3.0

When you connect to a Web site that contains sound files, you generally will see a speaker icon indicating that it is a sound file. If the sound file is of a type that Netscape Navigator 3.0 supports, you can click the icon. Netscape Navigator 3.0 automatically plays the file. If a sound file is embedded directly into an HTML page, you won't even have to click a link. Let's look at an example.

1. Make sure you are connected to the Internet either directly or via your SLIP or PPP access provider. If Netscape Navigator 3.0 is not currently running, launch it by double-clicking its icon.

2. In the Location box at the top of the window, select the currently displayed URL and replace it with **http://www.spottedantelope.com/wander.htm**. Press Return. After a few moments, the Wandering Italy page appears, as shown in Figure 8-16.

Figure 8-16: *The Wandering Italy page.*

Notice the sound control panel in the top-left frame. That's what Netscape Navigator 3.0 displays whenever it encounters a sound file. The controls are pretty much like those on any electronic device: click the left button to start playing, click the right button to stop. You can adjust the volume of the selection by dragging the slider below the buttons to the right or left. Assuming your sound card is working properly, hit the play button and you'll hear a man with a beautiful Italian accent telling you "Good morning."

When the sound file ends, it stops automatically and you can do one of two things: play it over and over again or get a life. If you want, you can save the sound file to your hard drive by selecting Save Frame As from the File menu.

USING REALAUDIO WITH NETSCAPE NAVIGATOR 3.0

As I'm sure you just discovered, sound files can take a while to download to your machine. But fortunately there are some new *streaming* standards that speed up the process. What do I mean by streaming? Suppose the sound file starts playing over your computer's speakers before it's completely downloaded. That's streaming. Instead of clicking a link and twiddling your thumbs, you can click a link and start shaking your booty. Not quite instant gratification, but close.

By far the most prominent streaming sound format on the Web is RealAudio. Using the RealAudio plug-in, which is available from the RealAudio Web site at http://www.realaudio.com, you can hear news, sporting events, music, and much more. The RealAudio format almost makes you feel as though you're listening to the radio, right on the Net. In fact, some traditional radio stations have started to supplement their broadcasts with RealAudio files on the Web.

The complete RealAudio system consists of two pieces. The first piece is one you'll probably never have to use unless you become a Web site administrator. The *RealAudio Server* is the software that enables Web sites to offer RealAudio files.

The other piece of the RealAudio puzzle is the client software that enables users like you to listen to RealAudio recordings. In this case it's a plug-in that works seamlessly with Netscape Navigator 3.0, just as if it were a built-in feature.

WHAT'S A PLUG-IN?

You've already learned about helper applications—programs that Netscape Navigator 3.0 can launch in order to display a particular graphics format or play a sound. Plug-ins are like helper applications in that they extend Navigator's abilities, but they do it seamlessly. When you install a plug-in, it almost becomes a part of

➡

Navigator. You can't tell that it isn't just another feature. For instance, a plug-in supporting an unusual graphics format might display images right within Navigator 3.0's browser window, just like a GIF or JPEG file. And once you install the RealAudio plug-in, it will behave very much like Navigator's built-in sound support.

OBTAINING REALAUDIO

The RealAudio plug-in, which is what you want to install on your system, is currently free of charge. To get a copy of RealAudio, connect to RealAudio's Web site (http://www.realaudio.com/) and download the software to your computer. You will be asked to fill out a short form before downloading it.

Make sure to read the list of system requirements to run the program. The requirements include a Macintosh with a 25 MHz 68030 or higher processor, or the Macintosh Power PC. You also need 8MB of RAM, but Virtual Memory is acceptable according to Progressive Networks, the software provider. You also need at least 2MB of free disk space. In order to install the RealAudio Player, you will need Apple System 7.5, 7.1, or 7.0. With System 7.0 you will also need QuickTime version 1.6.1 or later. If you do not already have 16-bit sound capability, install Sound manager 3.0 or 3.1. Sound Manager 3.*x* will automatically convert the 16-bit audio output from the RealAudio Player to the 8-bit sound produced by some Macintosh computers. A free upgrade to Sound manager 3.1 is available from Apple at ftp://ftp.info.apple.con?Apple.Support. Area/Developer_Services/System_Software_Extensions//Sound_Manager_3.0.sit.hqx. Sound Manager 3.1 is available from Apple at http://www.support/apple.com/pub/apple_sw_updates/US/Macintosh/system_sw/Other%20System%20Software/Sound_Manager_3.1.hqx.

INSTALLING & CONFIGURING REALAUDIO

OK, you've completed the forms, chosen the correct version of RealAudio, and downloaded it to your computer. StuffIt Expander downloaded and decompressed the application, and placed it in the Applications folder in your system. It's sitting on your computer and ready to install. Navigate to the folder in which you decompressed the RealAudio programs, and double-click on the RA Player Installer icon. The RealAudio Installer tests your machine to verify that it can play RealAudio, installs the application software, scans your disk for installed WWW browsers and inserts the RealAudio Player as a viewer for the audio/x-pn-realaudio MIME type of file.

If you wish, the Installer will insert the RealAudio home page in Netscape Navigator 3.0's bookmarks folder. Installer does not care if you begin this process with Netscape Navigator 3.0 in operation. Through a series of information windows, RealAudio Installer will advise you that it must close your active browsers in order to complete its installation, and if you choose you can let Installer work in a very seamless Macintosh-style fashion. To check up on Installer, follow these steps:

1. Navigate to the Helpers Application panel. Select General Preferences from the pull-down Options menu, and go to the Helpers panel.

2. Double-click on the Description titled "Audio, Handled By RealAudio Player." This will open your Edit Type dialog box, which should look like Figure 8-17.

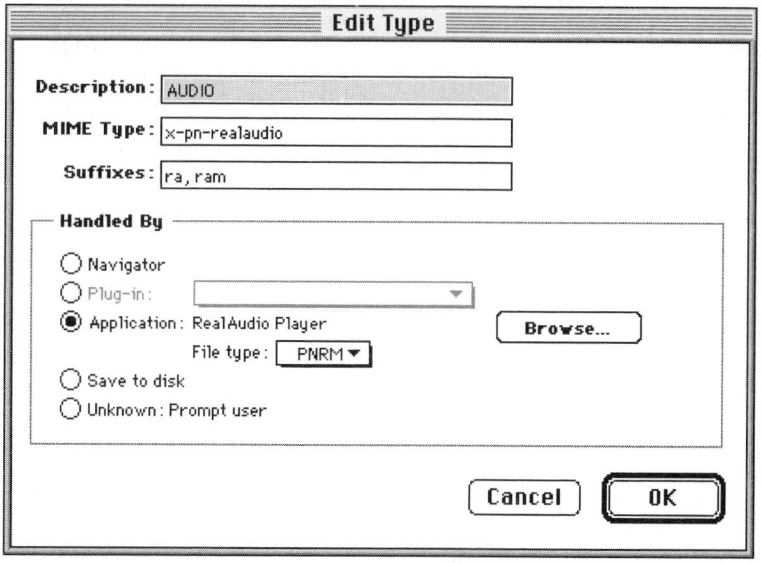

Figure 8-17: *The RealAudio Player application in the Edit Type dialog box in the Helpers panel.*

CAN I CREATE MY OWN REALAUDIO FILES?

Yes, you can, but you'll need some extra software. Specifically, you must download a copy of the RealAudio Encoder from the Progressive Networks Web site. Using Encoder, you start with a WAV or AU audio file and convert it to the RealAudio file format, with the extension .RA. Within the RealAudio file you can insert a name of the file, author, and copyright information. This information is displayed on the user's machine when he or she is playing it back. Of course, the file you've created doesn't do you much good unless you have a way to distribute it to the public. You must copy it to a site that has the RealAudio server software. For more information on RealAudio servers, see the RealAudio Web site at http://www.realaudio.com/.

TRYING OUT REALAUDIO

When you connect to sites that contain RealAudio links, you can listen to a link by clicking it. It's that easy. The RealAudio player first contacts the host computer that contains the audio file. After a few moments during which it downloads the initial section of the file, it starts to play it over your system speakers. You can adjust the volume of the playback by using the slider control on the right side of the player.

TIP

RealAudio links are often indicated with an icon of a radio or boom box, sometimes with the letters "RA" on it. Take a look at National Public Radio (http://www.npr.org) for a typical use of links with icons like this and for an example of RealAudio used effectively in conjunction with articles and stories.

So that you can try out RealAudio, Table 8-2 lists some sites that include RealAudio files. In the future, look for events such as football games, rock concerts, speeches, and the like to be simulcast as RealAudio events that you can listen to live.

Site Name	Address
National Public Radio	http://www.npr.org/
ABC Radio Network	http://www.abcradionet.com/
Delta Dream Vacations	http://pwr.com/LEISURE/ DELTA.html
Advanced Digital Services	http://206.65.169.39/
Grace Hour	http://www.smart.net/~ggwo/
Nightstand	http://www.nightstand.com/
Tabernacle Baptist Church	http://www.tabernacle.org/~tbc/
Toyota Motor	http://www.toyota.co.jp/
North Carolina News Network	http://www.capitolnet.com/ncnn/

Site Name	Address
QuikQuitz Stop Smoking	http://www.mindspring.com/ ~wbarnes/health/quikquitz.html
Adtek Web Services	http://www.adtek.com/
Tech Talk Radio Network	http://ttn.nai.net/
BBC Radio 3: Facing the Radio	http://www.bbc.co.uk/ftr/
Black Cat Radio	http://www.pulver.com:80/thecat/
MusicNet	http://www.man.net/~musicnet/
OneWorld	http://www.oneworld.org/realaudio/ index.html
I-Net LIVE!	http://www.pennet.net/inetlive/

Table 8-2: *Some sites that have RealAudio files.*

Once you have installed RealAudio Player, you can adjust the volume and the start-and-stop activity by using the control panel shown in Figure 8-19.

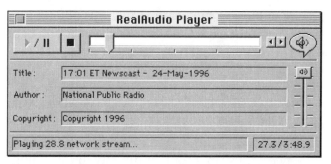

Figure 8-18: *The RealAudio Player control panel from which you can start and stop play, adjust volume, and monitor progress of the audio message.*

THE REALAUDIO PRESIDENT

Politicians of every stripe are clamoring over the new telecommunications technologies, though they frequently misunderstand them. It is no surprise that several of President Clinton's speeches are available on the Web via RealAudio. Just point Navigator 3.0 to http://www.whitehouse.gov/WH/EOP/OP/html/OP_Speeches.html and start looking around—or listening around. If you have a good sound card and listen carefully enough, you might even hear Bill inhale.

VIDEO IN NETSCAPE NAVIGATOR 3.0

We geeks spend so much time on the Web that sometimes we forget what Real Life is. Real Life is an operating environment that includes mountains, oceans, trees, crying babies, barking dogs, Big Macs, and the Menendez brothers. It's not the greatest user interface, but it sure beats anything Bill Gates could come up with. And one of the most interesting features of Real Life is that things move! We do not experience life as a succession of still images such as those you usually encounter on the Net, but as a constant ebb and flow of matter through space.

Now you can come a little closer to Real Life on the Web. Apple Computer has arranged for Apple's QuickTime plug-in for Netscape Navigator 3.0 to be included, so that when you run Navigator 3.0 the plug-in will be ready for use. This will let you experience QuickTime content directly in the Navigator 3.0 browser window. You no longer need a helper application like MoviePlayer to view QuickTime content. You can also view QuickTime VR Panoramas and Objects inline, after downloading the QuickTime VR component from Apple.

VIDEO WITH SOUND

The QuickTime plug-in works with existing QuickTime movies, and with movies prepared to take advantage of the plug-in's "fast start" feature. The "fast start" feature will present the first frame of the movie almost immediately and can begin playing even before the movie has been completely downloaded.

Netscape Navigator 3.0 uses the QuickTime plug-in automatically to play any QuickTime movie while browsing the Internet. The plug-in can play many kinds of QuickTime movies (.mov files) including movies with text, MIDI, and other kinds of data. If you have installed the QuickTime VR component, it will also let you interact with QuickTime VR Panorama and objects.

Here's a nice example of an AVI clip that includes sound, put out by the government of Newfoundland and Labrador..

1. Make sure you are connected to the Internet either directly or via your SLIP or PPP access provider. If Netscape Navigator 3.0 is not currently running, launch it by double-clicking its icon.

2. In the Location box at the top of the window, select the currently displayed URL and replace it with **http:// www.gov.nf.ca/itt/business/people.avi**. Press Return. After a few moments, the first image of an AVI file appears in the center of your browser window.

TIP

Large AVI files and AVI files that include sound may take a while to download. And I mean quite *a while. Keep that crossword puzzle and knitting project nearby.*

3. Click the image. Immediately it begins playing, complete with music and voice-over.

The current version of Navigator only plays AVI and QuickTime files automatically, but the Netscape developers were smart enough to make the program extensible. If you want Navigator 3.0 to play other animation formats right in the Browser window, all you have to do is find a plug-in for that particular media type. We've talked about plug-ins earlier in the sections on RealAudio, and we'll come back to them in the next chapter, "Power Navigator 3.0."

TIP

To play QuickTime movies on your system, you need to have the latest version of Apple QuickTime installed. The software is available at http://quicktime.apple.com/qt/sw/sw.html.

MOVING ON

In this chapter, you've learned the basics of viewing graphics and listening to sound in Netscape Navigator 3.0. You've also learned how to play video clips, or movies, right in the Browser window. By now you should have a sense of how vast the possibilities are when it comes to incorporating new media into Web pages. Advertising executives are jumping up and down with excitement, scheming all kinds of ways to inundate you with the latest multimedia innovations.

In the next chapter I cover some of the most powerful features of Netscape Navigator 3.0: VRML, plug-ins, Java, and JavaScript. This is where the ride gets wild, so hang on tight.

9

Power Navigator 3.0

As you learned in the last chapter, Netscape Navigator 3.0 is one of the most robust tools available for displaying a wide range of multimedia content. But the story doesn't end there. As new technologies develop, Netscape is quick to incorporate them. And Navigator 3.0 even includes methods by which developers can tack new modules onto the program, seamlessly integrating powerful new multimedia features. This open architecture ensures that Navigator 3.0 will keep looking young as the world at large comes up with ever more exciting ways to package information.

In this chapter we'll look at four ways in which Navigator 3.0 is keeping up with all the changes in multimedia presentation:

- VRML support, letting you navigate the three dimensional virtual worlds that are starting to crop up all over the Net. VRML is the best legal way to get dizzy without leaving your desk chair.

- Plug-ins, which allow developers to extend Navigator 3.0's power in all kinds of imaginative ways. Thanks to a couple of plug-ins my computer is now playing MIDI music files off the Net while it displays 3D models of agricultural chemicals. Did somebody say something about *work*?

- Support for the hundreds of Java applets available on the Web, as well as the thousands waiting to be written. Java is a full-featured, general-purpose programming language, and Navigator 3.0 is designed to execute any programs written in Java. This means that the ways to extend Navigator 3.0 are virtually limitless.

- JavaScript, a much simpler language that can be thrown right into HTML files to extend Navigator's capabilities. JavaScript can make sure you've entered a valid zip code in a Web form, make text scroll across your screen, or even replace the status information at the bottom of the browser window with a joke. I think of JavaScript as the tool of choice for "stupid Navigator tricks."

Feeling adventurous? Let's start right in with VRML.

VRML

First, how do you say it? Some people say V-R-M-L, carefully articulating each letter, but they're not the cool people. The cool people say *VER-MUHL*, with the stress on the first syllable just like in *thermal*.

And what exactly does it stand for? *V*irtual *R*eality *M*odeling *L*anguage. It's really a pretty simple concept. Just as HTML is a markup language that tells a Web browser to display various elements such as headings, italic text, and links, VRML is an extension that tells a Web browser to display various components of three-dimensional virtual worlds. These include objects that rotate or otherwise move through space in a "realistic" way, as well as graphical backgrounds that make you feel as if *you're* moving as you manipulate your mouse. To get technical, VRML is a standard for encoding computer-generated graphics into a file format for transmission across the Net or an intranet; it is also the standard a Web browser uses to interpret and display these graphics so that you can interact with them. Many people see VRML as an eventual replacement for HTML itself, offering a more intuitive and life-like way of navigating the Web.

Moving Worlds? Live3D?

Here's some more terminology you might encounter, but first a little history.

Originally, Silicon Graphics (SGI) came up with Open Inventor, a file format that became the basis for VRML; they also developed QvLib, which was the software component responsible for "understanding" and interpreting the file. Gavin Bell of SGI then wrote the proposal for the VRML 1.0 standard. The standard was adopted, and developers began implementing it.

Of course as soon as version 1 of any standard is accepted by the technology community, somebody starts working on version 2. There have been several rival proposals, but the one that really caught on is called *Moving Worlds*. Developed and supported by a broad consortium of software and hardware vendors, it provides many new features including full motion, live content and animation, enhanced audio, and the ability to connect with databases. Most importantly, it has strong support for multi-user interactivity. You won't need to get dizzy alone any more. At this point it looks like Moving Worlds will become VRML 2.0.

Just as the HTML standard doesn't specify exactly what a heading or footnotes should look like in every Web browser, VRML doesn't specify exactly how to display graphical objects such as wire-frame models. Virtual worlds may look and feel a bit different from one VRML browser to another. *Live3D* is simply Netscape's own particular implementation of VRML, and it's widely considered one of the best available.

Trap

Before we move ahead to have some fun with Live3D, please make sure you are working with the newer Power Macintosh PowerPC system and not a 68000 configuration computer. The Live3D version of Netscape Navigator 3.0 has been developed to run on any PowerPC Macintosh with 24MB of RAM and 6MB (10MB during installation) of hard disk space. If you are working with a 68000 Mac, you should be using the standard version of Netscape Navigator 3.0, and looking forward to the release of Live3D on the 68K and UNIX configurations later.

If you're running a Power Macintosh, you need to take some memory management steps before proceeding with our next exercise. Make sure Navigator 3.0 is shut down, and select Finder in the Apple application menu bar. In your Netscape Navigator 3.0 folder, from the desktop select the Navigator 3.0 application icon, then choose Get Info from the File menu. In the dialog box, adjust the figure in the Preferred Size box to at least 16MB. Navigator 3.0 with Live3D will run with 16MB of physical RAM plus at least 8MB of Virtual Memory. Make sure you have set Virtual Memory to On by opening the Memory Control Panel and adjusting the Virtual Memory selection buttons. When Virtual Memory is on, with System 7.5.3 Update 2, your Macintosh will automatically double working memory by the amount of physical RAM present on your system.

Be as generous as you can with physical RAM settings for Navigator 3.0. When Navigator 3.0 runs out of memory (which can happen frequently if you are working with very large files) it simply crashes. Remember to restart your computer after you have reset your memory allocation for Navigator 3.0. After restart, choose About This Macintosh from the Apple menu to make sure you have allowed sufficient memory for both the application and your System Software.

OK, let's go ahead and try some VRML navigation.

VRML NAVIGATION

1. Make sure you are connected to the Net. (I'm assuming you don't have any virtual worlds on your office intranet yet, but if I'm wrong simply make sure they're accessible to you.)

2. In the Navigator folder or program group, work your way through the Live3D folder to the Apple folder, and double-click on the abounce.wrl icon. Netscape Navigator 3.0 appears, but instead of the usual home page there's a different three-dimensional one, as shown in Figure 9-1.

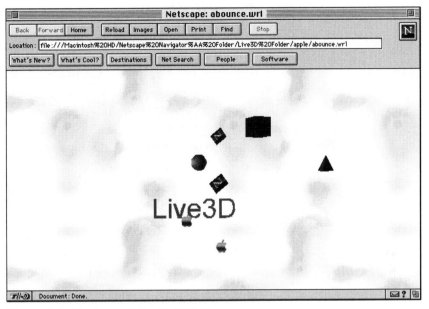

Figure 9-1: *Navigator 3.0 with VRML page.*

TIP

There's nothing magical about the Live3D icon. It simply loads Netscape Navigator 3.0 with a sample VRML file. You could have retrieved the file yourself by typing the location in the Browser window's Location box; the Live3D icon is simply a convenient shortcut.

Let's take a few minutes to get oriented.

There are five buttons along the bottom of the window, labeled Walk, Fly, Point, Help, and Reset. Each of these buttons represents a different operational mode for your controls. In other words, if you click Fly, your mouse and keyboard might act differently in the window than they do when you click Walk.

Since you've got to walk before you can fly, let's start there:

1. Make sure the Walk button is depressed.

2. Move your mouse around the window. Notice whenever your pointer rests on the large N it becomes a hand, and the word *Netscape* appears.

- This is a simple link to the Netscape home page. Links in VRML do not appear as underlined text, but as a temporary element in the graphic.

3. While the word is displayed, double-click your mouse button. You are transported to the regular old Netscape site, as shown in countless illustrations in this book. When you are done at the Netscape site, click the Back button on the toolbar to return to the VRML page.

4. Now click your mouse button and while holding it down drag your mouse slowly around the window. Notice that you seem to move in relation to the N.

- As you drag to the right or left, you seem to move right or left in relation to the object.

- As you drag up, you seem to move toward the object.

- As you drag down, you seem to move away from the object.

TIP

You can also use your arrow keys to move left, right, forward, and back. We'll put it all together in a table at the end of this section.

5. Ready for some fun? Try dragging with both your mouse button and command key depressed. Immediately you see the power of VRML: you are now moving around the object as if it's three-dimensional.

6. One more move: hold down the Alt key while dragging with the left mouse button. The object "slides" in the window in a two-dimensional manner. In other words, the up-and-down component of your mouse movement does not change your apparent distance from the object.

TIP

In Walk mode, the A and Z keys slide you up and down.

7. OK I was lying. There's still one more move I want to show you. Click the Reset button. (*Wait!* The one on your screen, not the one on your computer!) The VRML window returns to its original state.

How do you remember all these navigational techniques? That's easy: just click the Help button. A convenient legend appears in the window, staying visible until you click the Help button again.

Most navigation can be done with the mouse and keyboard, without using the buttons on the navigation toolbar. Click on a VRML world to enable keystrokes for that world. Hold down the mouse button, and keep the mouse in one place, to invoke the Live3D pop-up menu. Select Walk mode, which is the default position, and you will be able to navigate using the following combinations:

Action	Reaction
Mouse drag	Walk forward/backward, or turn left/right.
Up/Down arrows	Walk forward and backward
Left/right arrows	Turn left or right
Control+mouse click	Point: Animate viewpoint toward the object.
Control+drag	Pan left/right or up/down.
Command+drag	Spin (orbit about the entire scene). To automate the spin, release the mouse button before the command key.
Mouse click	Stop spinning
A/Z	Tilt the object up or down.
Shift (with mouse click or keystroke)	Move faster
Double click	Pending

If navigation is slow, use Optimize Window Size from the Options section of the Live3D menu. A smaller window can speed up that action on your screen by about 20%.

Lost in Cyberspace

Thank God for the Reset button. I was born in the early fifties and never saw a video game until I was an adult. My idea of fast-paced action was when the Lone Ranger and Tonto discovered a hideout, one that looked suspiciously like the hideout they found in the previous episode. Now drop me into a VRML page, and in a matter of seconds I'm hopelessly lost, wandering the far reaches of space looking for something—*anything*—recognizable.

My kids, on the other hand, seem to find virtual worlds utterly familiar, warm, and homey. So if you were born before the Kennedy assassination, here's my number one hint for exploring VRML effectively: bring a kid along!

The VRML Context Menu

One of the most powerful features of VRML is that it lets *you* control the way the graphic information appears on your screen. You can do this by clicking your mouse button anywhere within the browser window. A Context menu pops up.

From the Context menu there are a number of ways to reconfigure your navigation environment. I'm not going to cover all of these, mainly because they're a lot harder to describe than they are to explore. You can have some fun checking them out on your own, but here are a few things to try:

- Want to make your travels more realistic in Fly mode? Select Bank when Flying from the Navigation submenu. Your imaginary craft will tilt in the direction of your turns.

- Want to see what a 3D object looks like in wireframe instead of solid? Click Wireframe from the Detail menu.

- Want to turn off the buttons at the bottom of the window for a better view of your virtual world? Uncheck the Navigation Bar item on the Options submenu.

If you want to preserve the changes you have made, simply click Save All Settings As Default in the Options submenu.

WHAT'S THE POINT?

So far VRML applications have concentrated on pretty, imaginative pictures. You can see some great examples of individual images, sometimes known as *models*, at http://www.tcp.ca/gsb/VRML/vrml-modelshop.html. (Don't miss the rotating zebra head!) But what about more serious applications?

Well, just about everything you can do with ordinary HTML you can do with VRML as well. Or at least you'll be able to when all the VRML 2.0 features are adopted. VRML pages can include links to other documents, enhance sites with sound and video, and even collect user information for online transactions. You can think of the added dimension as providing yet more ways to organize information.

In addition, VRML provides a visual analog for the "real" world. Imagine an online real estate company providing three dimensional models of houses. You could check out the frontyard, then the backyard, then go inside and wander through the rooms. You could click on various appliances to find out what brand they are, or how old they are. And think of the educational possibilities: kids in school wandering through three-dimensional depictions of the human body, clicking to get more information on their favorite organs.

No, you're not going to see that in 1996, but it's quite likely in 1997. VRML is just emerging from its "proof of concept" stage, and real-world applications haven't caught up with the technology yet. In addition, VRML pages are still pretty slow to load over modem connections. But for a taste of things to come, check out Netscape's own Media Showcase site at home.netscape.com/comprod/products/navigator/version_3.0/showcase/index.html.

PLUG-INS

Right out of the box (or the CD sleeve), Netscape Navigator 3.0 lets you experience most of what is available on the Net. But as the Web becomes more popular and the technology improves, more sophisticated multimedia content is becoming available all the time. You just saw, for instance, how VRML is adding new dimensions to Web content—literally. Movies, desktop-published documents, and video conferencing are slowly making their way onto the Web as well. Not only are these new types of data putting strains on the infrastructure of the Internet, they are also is forcing Web browsers to evolve from text and graphics displayers to real-time, interactive multimedia viewers.

Not to worry. Your investment in Netscape Navigator 3.0 is a good one. The Netscape developers have come up with an open-extendible architecture that lets the program evolve as technology itself evolves. Through plug-in applications developed by independent software vendors, Navigator 3.0 enables you to experience most of what is currently available online.

Plug-ins extend Netscape Navigator 3.0's capabilities so that it can display or play a wide variety of documents and file types, such as Adobe Acrobat PDF (Portable Document Format) files, Macromedia Director movies, and MIDI music files. It uses what's known as its *Live Objects* technology to enable developers to create rich multimedia content for the Internet or office intranets.

Up until Netscape Navigator 2.0, Web users were required to configure separate helper applications that worked independently of their Web browsers to view and control most multimedia documents. Now when you download and configure plug-ins to work with Netscape Navigator 2.0 or later, the plug-ins become part of the browser itself. Movies, sound events, presentation graphics, and more display directly in the Netscape Navigator 3.0 window. In fact, plug-ins are so well integrated with the program that you'll quickly forget you're using them.

How Plug-ins Display in Netscape Navigator 3.0

When you use a plug-in with Netscape Navigator 3.0, it may not always be apparent that the plug-in is a separate application. With helper applications, you always know when a graphics program or a media player starts because you see it display in a separate window. Plug-ins, however, can interact with Netscape Navigator 3.0 in one of three modes of operation:

- **Full-screen plug-ins.** Full-screen plug-ins are just that—plug-ins that take up the entire Netscape Navigator 3.0 browser window. These are less common than embedded plug-ins.

- **Embedded plug-ins.** Embedded plug-ins are referenced in HTML documents so that when a user clicks on the reference, the plug-in activates and displays the object. Although this is similar to the way in which other objects, such as embedded graphics, are handled, embedded plug-ins can respond to user events, including mouse motions. Figure 9-2 shows a typical embedded plug-in, an interactive Shockwave tic-tac-toe game.

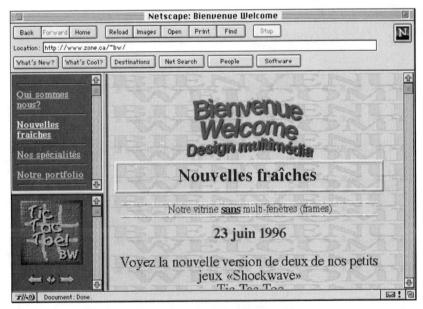

Figure 9-2: *A plug-in tic-tac-toe game in the left-hand frame.*

As a Web author, you specify embedded plug-ins by using the <EMBED> HTML tag, as shown in the following syntax:

```
<EMBED SRC="trailer.mpg", WIDTH=150,
HEIGHT=250 CONTROLS=TRUE>
```

In this example, when the user clicks on the plug-in reference on the Web page, an MPEG player activates automatically and plays a film clip named "trailer.mpg."

- ■ **Hidden plug-ins.** Hidden plug-ins are ones that users cannot see or otherwise control, such as plug-ins that play music files in the background.

There are dozens of excellent plug-ins available for Netscape Navigator 3.0, and many of them are available in shareware or beta versions right on the Net. The Online Companion for this book, available at http://www.netscapepress.com, includes a thorough list of currently available plug-ins for all versions of Netscape Navigator 3.0.

Just to show you how easy it is to work with plug-ins, here's some more detailed information on one of the most exciting, the Macromedia Shockwave plug-in.

SHOCKWAVE & NETSCAPE NAVIGATOR 3.0

The Shockwave plug-in lets you view Macromedia Director movies and multimedia files in Netscape Navigator 3.0. Developers can include Director movies in HTML documents by using the <EMBED> tag. Documents can even include more than one movie per HTML page.

When you access a site that includes a Director file, you can scroll through the Web page even while the movie is playing. You can interact with the movie by clicking on it, and you can enter text from the keyboard into text fields within the movie. And the movie itself can access information from the Internet and open URLs.

To download a copy of Shockwave, enter **http://www.macromedia.com/Tools/Shockwave/shock.html** in the Netscape Navigator 3.0 Location field and press Return. Next, click the link Get the Shockwave Plug-In for Your Browser. On the next page, click the link for your appropriate operating system, such as Macintosh PowerPC. You now can download the file by clicking one of the links provided.

After you download the Shockwave plug-in file, Navigator 3.0 automatically launches StuffIt Expander to decompress the file and extract the archive. It creates a folder called nppz0001.sea.hqx, where it places the Shockwave plug-in and a Readme document.

The folder may also contain other files for viewing shockwaved files using Navigator 3.0.

If you cannot decompress the file nppz0001.sea.hqx, or if you see a warning from Navigator 3.0 saying "No Viewer Configured for File Type," choose "Save To Disk" to save the Shockwave folder onto your hard drive. Then you can go to the Netscape Utilities Page to download a decompression utility.

Assuming you are using a Power Macintosh, double-click on the Shockwave installer icon for the PPC version of the applications. StuffIt Expander 4.0.2 will automatically decompress the files and place them in appropriate folders within your Netscape Navigator 3.0 folder.

You should close any applications that you have open prior to starting the Setup program, including Netscape Navigator 3.0. You may also want to verify that you have allocated enough physical RAM to Navigator 3.0; be as generous as you can be!

Once Shockwave is installed, you can start Netscape Navigator 3.0 and test out its new capabilities. One site that uses a multimedia image to enhance its appeal is the Welcome To Netscape page for Shockwave. The URL for this page is: http://home.netscape.com/comprod/products/navigator/version_2.0/plugins/director_examples/director_example1.html. (Think they could have made that URL any longer?) Here's what it looks like:

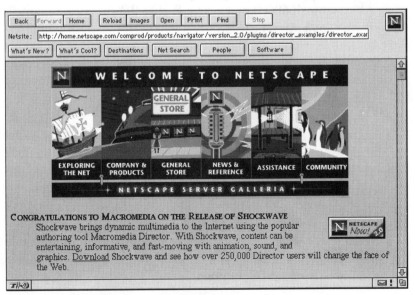

Figure 9-3: *The Welcome to Shockwave page.*

The interesting part of this page is that the normally static image at the top of Netscape's page is now animated. It includes a moving marquee, has hyperlinked buttons, and even highlights a button as you pass your mouse pointer over it.

You can see other uses of Shockwave at the Macromedia Shockwave Vanguard Gallery at http://www.macromedia.com/ Tools/Shockwave/Vanguard/index.html. Listed here are companies that are integrating Shockwave-compatible images into their Web sites, including *Advertising Age*, c | net, and the American Cancer Society.

Java

When you get older and your grandchildren ask you about the good old days of the World Wide Web, you'll tell them about Java. You'll tell them that Java was the technology that got us one step closer to bringing real-time interaction between people on the Internet. Java not only enhances Web pages with impressive graphics, it enables software developers to create secure two-way Web applications in a straight-forward fashion. These applications are called *Java applets*. With release of Netscape Navigator 3.0, Java support has been added to the Macintosh Power PC and Macintosh 68000 platforms. Figure 9-4 shows an example of what a Java applet can do.

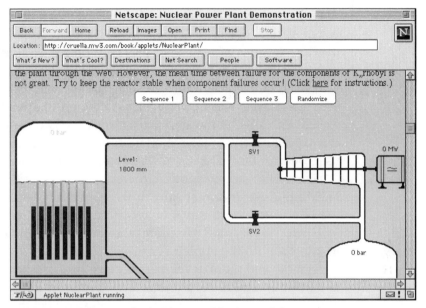

Figure 9-4: *A Java applet in Netscape Navigator 3.0.*

SO WHAT ARE APPLETS?

Java applets are the hottest new eye-candy on the Web. But what exactly are they? They are simply small applications written in the Java programming language. Yes, Java is an entire programming language developed by Sun Microsystems, Inc. (For the propeller-heads reading this, it's similar to C++ but without pointers.) Java lets developers create platform-independent multimedia applications for distribution on the Web. With Netscape Navigator 3.0, you can visit sites that include Java applets (or even full-blown applications) and actually run them.

Since Java applets are cross-platform, you run the same code on a Macintosh as you do on a Windows 3.1 or Windows NT machine. When you get to a Web page that includes Java applets, you don't have to choose which version to link to. And since Netscape was in the technological vanguard in supporting Java, you don't need a special helper application to interpret the Java code—Navigator 3.0 does it all.

With traditional Internet and World Wide Web content, the focus is mainly only one-way—from the server to the user. It's similar to the cable television that comes into your house. You can receive data from this cable, but you cannot transmit data back through it. We've seen that forms allow for some two-way interactivity, but Java really opens up the possibilities. When Java applets are integrated with a Web browser, such as Netscape Navigator 3.0, you can experience live information updating, interaction with other users, and instant interaction with Internet servers.

Java applets are embedded in Web pages (using the <APPLET> HTML tag) and automatically downloaded by Netscape Navigator 3.0 to your computer. A Java run-time application included in Netscape Navigator 3.0 executes the Java applet and enables you to interact with the applet.

As more and more developers acquire Java programming skills, and more and more people start using browsers like Netscape Navigator 3.0 that support Java, Web sites will begin to include them. In fact, they may become as plentiful as graphics and other files you encounter on the Web now. For this reason, you need to know how to interact with Java applets when you encounter them.

INTERACTING WITH JAVA APPLETS

When you arrive at a site that includes a Java applet, you really don't have to do anything special. Netscape Navigator 3.0 does all the work. Information that Navigator needs for running the Java applet is embedded in the HTML documents using the <APPLET> tag. Netscape Navigator 3.0 automatically downloads and interprets the applet. A complete download may take several minutes. Once the applet arrives on your machine, you interact with it per the individual applet's instructions.

Figure 9-5 shows a Java crossword puzzle that lets you actually enter words.

Figure 9-5: *A Java crossword puzzle that enables real-time interaction.*

If you scroll up the window you'll see that this Java applet, like many others, includes a list of instructions, as shown in Figure 9-6.

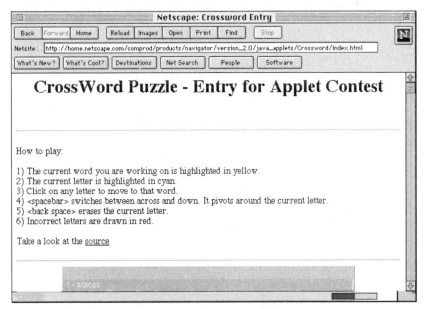

Figure 9-6: *Instructions for the Crossword Puzzle applet.*

As you can see, you fill out the crossword puzzle right while it's displayed in Netscape Navigator 3.0. You can type in letters, delete letters, and move from one box to another using your mouse and keyboard. The main difference between this type of application and a crossword puzzle that may have appeared earlier on the Internet is that the Java applet lets you interact with it directly in Netscape Navigator 3.0. Previously you would have had to download a file that runs separately from Netscape Navigator 3.0.

If you're interested in taking a look at some more Java applets, you can do so by visiting one of the sites listed in Table 9-2. These sites include one or several applets that automatically display in the Netscape Navigator 3.0 window. Remember that most Java applets are interactive, so get in there with your mouse.

Applet	Where You Find It
Blinking Text	http://www.javasoft.com/applets/applets/ Blink/example1.html
Curve	http://fas.sfu.ca:80/1/cs/people/ GradStudents/heinrica/personal/curve.html
Crossword	http://home.netscape.com/comprod/ products/navigator/version_2.0/java_applets/ Crossword/index.html
Financial Portfolio Demo	http://www.javasoft.com/applets/applets/ StockDemo/standalone.html
Imagemap	http://www.javasoft.com/applets/applets/ ImageMap/example1.html
Modern Clock	http://www.wsrn.com/southern/java/ DateClock.html
Pythagoras	http://home.netscape.com/comprod/ products/navigator/version_2.0/java_applets/ Pythagoras/index.html

Simple 3D Viewer	http://www.javasoft.com/applets/applets/WireFrame/example1.html
StarField	http://home.netscape.com/comprod/products/navigator/version_2.0/java_applets/StarField/index.html
Traditional Clock	http://www.javasoft.com/applets/applets/Clock/index.html

Table 9-2: *Some Java applets and where to find them.*

Another great resource that has sprung up over the past few months is the Gamelan Java Directory at http://www.gamelan.com/. This Web site is full of links and resources to Java sites and development news. If you're serious about Java, either as a developer or end user, you need to check out this site every so often to see what's new on the Java front.

ARE JAVA APPLETS SAFE?

Yes, for the most part. Applets are written in a Java language subset that includes several security precautions. For instance, applets can't perform most file system access or file I/O routines. These precautions, however, do not absolutely guarantee that a developer intent on breaking into your system can't do so.

Another form of security is in the Netscape Navigator 3.0 browser itself. Select Network Preferences from the Options menu and then click the Languages tab, shown in Figure 9-7. Notice the Enable Java checkbox. Netscape Navigator 3.0 offers this option so that you can disable Java support for those times you want to download a Java applet to your machine but then cut off the network transactions *back* to the server (you also can disconnect from the Internet and run the applet locally). When you leave the option checked, this means you want full access to Java applets so you can initiate a two-way communication between your client and the server machine. By default, this setting is checked to enable full Java access.

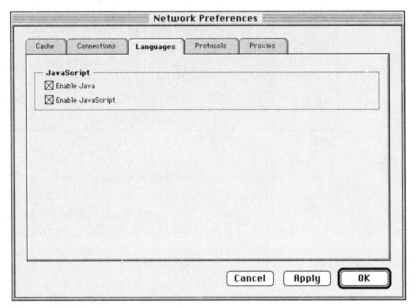

Figure 9-7: *The Languages panel.*

You can disable JavaScript here as well. Refer to the section on JavaScript later in this chapter.

CREATING YOUR OWN APPLETS

For those interested in developing Java applets, you can obtain Sun's official documentation and the Java API (application programming interface) from http://java.sun.com/. Remember, this is a serious programming language. If you don't have any previous experience with C++ or a similar object-oriented language, now's the time to go out and buy a book about programming in Java.

When you arrive at the Sun site, notice the small Java applet at the bottom of the Web page. It's an animated cup of steaming coffee (you know, hot java). The first place you'll probably want to visit at that site is the documentation area. This area includes a full introduction to Java and starts you on your way to understanding how to create your own applets.

Java is what's known in the computer industry as a "cool new feature." It's not just something that's needed to perform a particular task—it also looks toward the future and has a strong element of fun to it. What you can do with Java is limited only by your imagination.

TIP

For detailed technical information on a particular Java applet, click the Show Java Console item in Netscape Navigator 3.0's Options menu.

JavaScript

As you travel around the Web, you may notice some user interface niceties that don't seem part of regular old HTML. For instance, there might be some text in your Navigator 3.0 status bar that ties in with the Web page you're viewing. Or words may scroll across the browser window. Or when you type a bogus area code into a form, a message pops up telling you your entry isn't valid.

TIP

Some of the following material may be of interest to you only if you are planning to create your own Web pages (see Chapter 11, "Your Personal Workspace & Web Page"). Once you have a basic understanding of what JavaScript is, feel free to skip over the technical stuff!

If you wonder how the author of the Web page is pulling off these tricks, a good guess would be JavaScript. You can think of JavaScript as "Java Lite": a language that's less powerful than Java but easier to use. While Java programs are independent binary files compiled using special Java programming tools, entire JavaScript programs may be entered directly into an HTML page with a simple text editor. Navigator 3.0 simply interprets the new commands on the fly. Table 9-3 points out some of the differences between Java and JavaScript.

JavaScript	Java
Code is human-readable and embedded right in HTML file.	Java applets are separate from HTML pages.
Interpreted by Navigator 3.0—not compiled.	Compiled on server.
Uses objects, but does not support classes or inheritance.	Completely object-oriented. Applets are made up of object classes that support inheritance.
No need to declare data type of variables.	Strong typing: data types need to be declared.
References to objects checked dynamically at run-time.	Static binding at compile time.

Table 9-3: *Differences between Java and JavaScript.*

Whoa! In case you're not a programmer, let me put that in plain English: Java is for the big stuff, JavaScript is for smaller effects. Java requires special development tools and a solid understanding of object-oriented programming concepts, whereas you can probably add some simple JavaScript to your own Web pages after a few hours of playing around.

LIVECONNECT

LiveConnect is a new Navigator 3.0 technology that lets plug-ins, JavaScripts, and Java applets interact with each other. For example, thanks to LiveConnect, clicking a button in a Web page could start up separate video and audio plug-in files that are perfectly synced. Or it might start a brief movie, which could then trigger a sound file. In other words, LiveConnect allows for real-time integration of various separate media files and interactive Java scripts or applets.

JavaScript Nuts & Bolts

There are two ways that JavaScript can be embedded in HTML scripts. First, a Web author can use the <SCRIPT> tag. Here's a simple example:

```
<HTML>
<HEAD>
<SCRIPT LANGUAGE="JavaScript">document.write("Everybody →
loves")
</SCRIPT>
</HEAD>
<BODY>
Netscape Navigator 3.0!
</BODY>
</HTML>
```

Yep, you guessed it: what appears on your screen is the phrase "Everybody loves Netscape Navigator 3.0!" OK, you would never really *do* it that way, but at least this gives you an idea of how it works. As you can see, the <SCRIPT> tag is inside the HEAD area of the document. Now just imagine that instead of using the predefined *document.write* function, we had used something more interesting. How about a function that scrolls the words across your browser window in rainbow colors?

Or here's a more practical example using a square function you define yourself:

```
<HTML>
<HEAD>
<SCRIPT LANGUAGE="JavaScript">
function square(i) {
    document.write("What number is to be squared: ",return i * i
   }
  document.write("The result of this calculation is:
",square(2),".")
</SCRIPT>
</HEAD>
<BODY>
<BR>
```

```
The script is all finished calculating the square.
</BODY>
</HTML>
```

The result?

```
What number is to be squared: 2
The result of this calculation is 4.
The script is all finished calculating the square.
```

If you study the code a little, you can see that it defines the square function as one that first prints the phrase "What number is to be squared?", then accepts a number from the user, then multiplies that number by itself and returns the result. Once defined like this, the function may be used anywhere later in the document.

The <SCRIPT> tag is pretty convenient, but there is also an even more powerful way of working with the language: *event handlers*. This sounds pretty techie, but it's actually quite simple. Netscape Navigator 3.0 obviously recognizes when a user performs some action such as clicking on a word or phrase. With JavaScript, you can associate chunks of code with actions (or events). In other words, when a user clicks on a word, JavaScript knows to do something. Take a look at this example:

```
<INPUT TYPE="button" VALUE="Add It Up Now"
onClick="AddItUp(this.form)">
```

This snippet of code executes a function called AddItUp whenever you click on the button labeled "Add It Up." It could be used to add all the numbers you'd previously entered in a form.

JavaScript can use *properties* such as "visible" and "color" to return your specified response. You might, for example, design a Web page that includes listings and descriptions of your products. Let's say you sell countertops, and each model of countertop comes in various styles, textures, and colors. Customers to your site may want to design a virtual kitchen by mixing and matching colors and textures with different countertops and other fixtures. With JavaScript, you can include a selector that enables users to adjust the colors and textures of specific countertops. You could create the entire site as a Java applet, but why not use Java only where necessary (such as for creating the virtual kitchen and countertop and the selector). Then use JavaScript to change the colors and textures of the countertop in the applet.

WHAT'S NEW IN JAVASCRIPT FOR NAVIGATOR 3.0?

If you've already done some JavaScript programming with earlier versions of Netscape Navigator, you might be interested in what's changed for version 3.0. Besides general improvements in performance, here's two very exciting new features:

- JavaScript can now change JPEG and GIF images "on the fly." Imagine staring at a picture of Warren Christopher that suddenly turns into Madonna. Graphics can change automatically at a particular interval or when the viewer clicks a button or icon.

- JavaScript can now detect whether or not a plug-in is available and adjust the Web page accordingly. For instance, suppose a page includes a fancy 3D-animated image, which requires a plug-in you don't have. JavaScript could figure this out and substitute a plain old GIF or JPEG.

TIP

For a more comprehensive and up-to-date user reference on JavaScript, see the Netscape Navigator 3.0 reference at http://home.netscape.com/comprod/products/navigator/version_3.0/script/script_info/index.html. You can find the JavaScript Authoring Guide at that location.

MOVING ON

In this chapter we've looked at some of the advanced capabilities of Netscape Navigator 3.0; forward-looking extensions such as VRML that put you at the cutting edge of Web browsing. We've also seen how plug-ins and Java can extend the power of Navigator 3.0 in ways that are hard even to imagine.

There's another new trend on the Net as well: an increased interest in security. As more and more companies set up shop on the Web, more and more of us will start purchasing all kinds of products electronically. I don't know about you, but when I type in my credit card information I want to be sure it gets to the right place without any side trips onto someone else's hard drive. Netscape navigator 3.0 provides some of the most flexible security features available, and in the next chapter we'll take a close look at them.

10

Commerce & Security

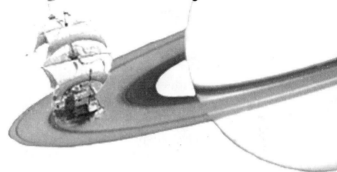

The Internet has displayed a colorful history. The military started it, the academic world helped to develop and refine it, and thousands of individuals began using it for everything from research to interactive games. But as with every other innovation, at some point somebody says, "Well that's just great, but how do I make a buck with it?"

Freed from past restrictions on commercial activity, the modern Internet provides countless ways to make—and to spend—a buck. Businesses large and small maintain Web pages that promote their products and services. And these are not just businesses that deal with software or computers. Virtually every type of major enterprise is represented with a Web page.

Many companies go beyond merely promoting themselves on the Net—they actually sell products. Yes, the Internet is the Home Shopping Network of the future. You no longer have to wander over to your couch to go shopping for that Hummel figurine or autographed baseball; you can do it right at your keyboard. And the variety of products available is staggering. You can buy everything from mouse pads to MIGs.

Let's take a quick look at how online commercial transactions work.

THE MECHANICS OF ONLINE TRANSACTIONS

Way back in Chapter 3, "A Quick Look Around," you saw an example of a Web page that included various forms elements, or *forms widgets*, as they are sometimes known. These are screen objects that accept input from you—push buttons, radio buttons, check boxes, drop-down lists, and edit fields that you fill in with information. You have seen objects like these in the preferences dialog boxes for virtually every Macintosh program, but the forms widgets are different. Forms widgets are not really part of Netscape Navigator 3.0 or of any other software; they are components of the Web document you're viewing. If you select By Document Source from the Netscape Navigator 3.0 View menu, you'll see that these fancy interactive objects are really just simple HTML tags. Figure 10-1 shows a typical forms document, the Rutgers University Archie Request Form you saw earlier in the book, and Figure 10-2 shows its source.

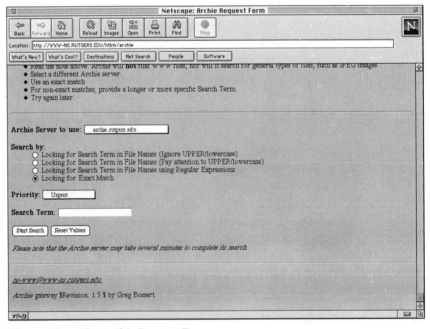

Figure 10-1: *The Archie Request Form.*

```
                              archie-2136
<!doctype html public "-//IETF//DTD HTML //EN//2.0">
<HTML>
<HEAD>
<TITLE>Archie Request Form</TITLE>
</HEAD>
<BODY>
<IMG SRC="/doc-images/logos/ns_net_bar.gif" ALT="Rutgers University Network Services">

<H1>Archie Request Form</H1>
<HR>

<P><EM>Archie</EM> locates files, usually software, available for
public FTP access.</P>

<P><IMG SRC="/doc-images/icons/bang_arrow_icon.gif" ALT="NOTE:">
<EM>Archie</EM> is not a generic tool for finding things on the Web.
Vague, general Search Strings, such as "binary", "jpeg", "WWW", etc.,
<STRONG>will not work</STRONG>.  If you are not searching a specific
file, please try a different service, such as
<A HREF="http://www.w3.org/hypertext/DataSources/bySubject/Overview.html">
The Virtual Library</A> or <A HREF="http://www.yahoo.com/">Yahoo</A>.
Thanks.</P>

<P><IMG SRC="/doc-images/icons/bang_arrow_icon.gif" ALT="NOTE:">
<EM>Archie</EM> is a very popular service, and frequently becomes
overloaded.  If your search fails or times out, try the following:</P>

<UL>
<LI> Read the note above.  Archie will <STRONG>not</STRONG> find WWW files, nor
will it search for general types of files, such as JPEG images.
<LI> Select a different Archie server.
<LI> Use an exact match
<LI> For non-exact matches, provide a longer or more specific Search Term.
<LI> Try again later.
</UL>
```

Figure 10-2: *The HTML source for the Forms page in Figure 10-1.*

Almost every page that includes forms widgets also includes a button marked Submit or Send. When you click this button, all the information you've entered is sent out on the Net to a particular site specified in the Web document. Once it reaches this site, a special piece of server software known as a *Common Gateway Interface* (CGI) collects your data and processes it. Perhaps the gateway simply dumps your information into a database file, or perhaps it immediately starts checking your credit history. It may even send some new information back to you, such as an acknowledgment that it has received your order.

I know what you're thinking. The whole idea of sending addresses and phone numbers and especially credit card information across the Net to some distant company sounds risky. When you press the Submit button, your personal data goes bopping from computer to computer across the vast reaches of cyberspace. How can you be sure it gets to the right place, or that technically savvy criminals don't nab it en route?

And that brings us to the huge and controversial topic of security.

In this chapter I'll first cover the basic concepts of security in Netscape Navigator 3.0. After that, starting with the section called "Security Preferences," I'll show you how to customize the program for your particular needs.

SECURITY ON THE NET

When I was a kid, the mix of technology and commerce was already cause for panic. "Some companies encourage you to order products by telephone," complained the news media. "When you place your order, they'll try to get you to tell them your credit card number instead of mailing a check. Don't do it!" they warned. "Don't give *anyone* your credit card number over the phone!"

Twenty-something years later these fears seem quaint. The American public has become used to home shopping and 800 numbers and has clearly decided that convenience is worth a little risk. Did the nightmare scenarios come true? Did unscrupulous employees at companies all over the country steal thousands of credit card numbers and spend all your money at the track? Of course not. Most employees want to keep their jobs.

Security is about people, not technologies. No matter what methods you use to transfer information, somebody can steal it if he or she wants it badly enough. Germany under Hitler was home to some of the world's greatest cryptographers and information scientists, and yet the Allied powers were able to crack the secret codes. Right now hundreds or perhaps even thousands of workers—telephone sales agents, customer service representatives, data entry personnel, managers, bank tellers, system administrators—have access to your financial records or your credit card information. The operator could even listen in on your phone calls. And yet how often do you get ripped off?

The people who handle Internet transactions are really no different from the workers who already know or have access to your credit card numbers. Let's dispel a few myths:

■ The Internet is *not* a den of hacker-thieves looking for a quick buck. There are easier ways to steal.

- Sending data across the Net does *not* give everyone on the Net access to that data.

- Most businesses set up shop on the Net because it offers a new, cost-effective point of sale, *not* because it enables them to collect more personal information about their customers.

- The Internet is *not* a leaky old boat full of giant security holes that can never be plugged.

That said, the security of information on the Net is still an important issue. Even though the biggest security hole is people rather than software or hardware, and even though abuses have been exaggerated by weekly magazines and so-called news shows, there's nothing wrong with making the Internet as secure a medium as possible for financial transactions. Netscape, recognizing from its inception as a company that commercial transactions were the Next Big Thing on the Net, has taken a lead in bolstering the security of transmitted data.

NETSCAPE & SECURITY—SSL

To understand what Netscape has done to address security issues, you have to understand the issues it is addressing. In other words, in what ways is it even possible to improve Internet security?

Information traveling between your computer and another machine, such as a Web server, is routed from Internet node to Internet node until it finally reaches its destination. It may pass through a handful or even dozens of computer systems. At any one of these sites, it is possible for a technically proficient but unscrupulous individual to access the stream of data for ulterior motives. Somebody could eavesdrop on you, collecting personal or financial information; somebody could copy your intellectual property, such as a great new idea for a patent; or somebody could even change your data before it reaches its destination, causing all kinds of mayhem. The Internet itself provides no built-in mechanism for preventing activities like these.

Netscape's response to this lack of security was to develop the *Secure Sockets Layer (SSL) protocol*. The SSL protocol enhances Internet security in four ways:

■ It provides a mechanism for server authentication. This means that you can be sure you're really connected to the Web site you intended to connect with.

■ It provides for user authentication as well. A secure Web site can make sure it's really dealing with you, not some cheap imitation.

■ It provides privacy by using a powerful encryption technique on transmitted data.

■ It provides data integrity, ensuring that the information you send arrives exactly as you sent it.

If you think about it for a moment, you'll realize that for SSL to work, both ends of the link—the client and the server—must run software that supports these features. If your Web browser encrypts your credit card information, for instance, the server you're talking to must be able to decrypt it. Currently SSL is supported by Netscape Navigator 3.0 and all of Netscape's Web servers, which are rapidly becoming a standard for businesses on the Net.

How does SSL work? The Internet can be seen as a layered set of protocols. In Chapter 1, "The Net & the Web," you learned that everything rests on TCP/IP, the protocol suite that actually divides your data into packets and ships them out to the right destination. Above this there are application protocols such as Telnet, FTP, and HTTP. These are the support protocols for the various services available on the Net. SSL actually provides a new protocol layer, situating itself between TCP/IP and the application protocols. That way it is not dependent on any of these other protocols in order to do its job. Figure 10-3 is a diagram of how a message you type is processed by the various protocol layers, then travels across the Net to a Web server that "unprocesses" the information.

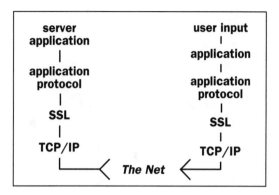

Figure 10-3: *A secure message sent to a Web server.*

SSL uses a powerful mechanism for protecting data known as
public key encryption. Each Netscape Commerce server has its own
unique pair of digital keys, which are really just long strings of
random bytes. One of these keys is private and kept secret at the
server site; the other is made public. When you send a message to
a secure server, it is encrypted and automatically includes the
public key for that site. The private key at the server end must be
the one that "fits" this public key; otherwise, your data will not be
decrypted and you will not be able to communicate. Since these
pairs of keys are guaranteed to be unique, you can be certain that
your information has reached the right destination before it is
decrypted.

CAN'T SOME HACKER CRACK SSL?

Sure, hackers can break anything. It's just a matter of how much work it takes.

SSL uses authentication and encryption technology that was developed by RSA Data Security. The export version of Netscape Navigator 3.0, which is required by the United States Government to use a weaker version of encryption than the U.S.-only version, relies on what is known as RSA's "40-bit key RC4 algorithm." Even in this weaker implementation, the security is pretty impressive. Let's say your neighbor knows you are about to transmit your credit card number. He goes outside with a ladder and a bunch of equipment and manages to capture the encrypted data from your phone line. If you're a forgiving sort of person, you should go out and warn him that it takes an average of 64 MIPS-years to break the code. This means that if he gets a 64-MIPS computer to work round the clock on deciphering your information, he'll probably have the answer in about a year. By that time, your credit card will be maxed out anyway.

SITE CERTIFICATES

Besides public key encryption, SSL offers another level of security called *site certification*. Here's how it works:

In order to operate in secure mode and use the features of SSL, anyone who sets up a Netscape server in secure mode must have requested and been sent a special Digital Certificate, a unique pattern of bytes that "unlocks" these features. RSA Certificate Services, a division of RSA Data Security, Inc., handles the certification process. Before issuing a certificate (which of course is sent encrypted), RSA makes sure that the requesting organization is "for real." Digital certificates, in conjunction with public key encryption, help to protect you from fraud, pranks, and theft of intellectual property.

PERSONAL CERTIFICATES

Starting with version 3.0, Netscape Navigator also supports *Personal Certificates*. These are the mirror images of Site Certificates: they assure a secure Web site that you are really you. Personal Certificates may eventually make it unnecessary for you to type in a name and password each time you access a secure site—the Web server will get more complete authentication information automatically from your personal certificate. Within the next year or so, you'll even be able to obtain Personal Certificates that are specific to particular payment methods. You may have a Visa Personal Certificate, for instance, as well as a Mastercard one.

PASSWORDS

OK, let's say you have several Personal Certificates. That means that you might be able to log into a secure site without typing in a special password—the software handles authentication for you. But suppose somebody else can access your machine. Since the authentication process is automatic, hasn't this whole system made online transactions less rather than more secure?

Not really. If you think that somebody else might access your machine, Netscape lets you create a personal password that you must type in every time you launch the program. You can change this password as often as you like, and there is no way for another user to discover it. In fact, it is so secure that it may even cause *you* some headaches: if you forget what it is there is no way to find out, and you have to get all new Personal Certificates!

SSL IN ACTION

As I said, for Netscape's SSL security protocol to do its job, both the server and the client must support it. You already know that Netscape Navigator 3.0 supports it, so how do you know when you're connected to a secure server? Let's take a look:

1. Make sure you are connected to the Internet, either directly or through a SLIP or PPP connection with your access provider. If you are using a SLIP or PPP connection and are not currently connected, double-click the Dial-Up Networking icon for your access provider.

2. Launch Netscape Navigator 3.0. The main window appears, and the Netscape home page starts loading as shown in Figure 10-4.

Figure 10-4: *The Netscape home page.*

3. Click your mouse inside the Netsite box at the top of the window to select the URL http://home.netscape.com/.

4. Replace this URL with **https://www.att.com/**, the URL for AT&T's secure home page. (No, that's not a typo. To access documents on secure servers, you type **https** instead of **http** in the protocol section of the URL.) A Security Information alert appears, as shown in Figure 10-5.

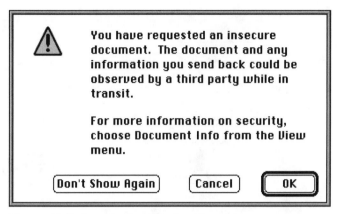

Figure 10-5: *Security Information alert.*

■ Whenever you are presented with a notification dialog box like this, you have the option of selecting the Don't Show Again button. If you select it, a corresponding check box is unchecked in the General tab of Netscape Navigator 3.0's Security Preferences. You can also change these options directly in the General tab. To learn how to do this, see the section called "Security Preferences."

TIP

*Netscape's news servers also provide SSL security. The URL for a secure Usenet news site would begin with **snews:** instead of **news:**.*

5. After reading the Security Information alert, click OK. The AT&T home page appears, as shown in Figure 10-6.

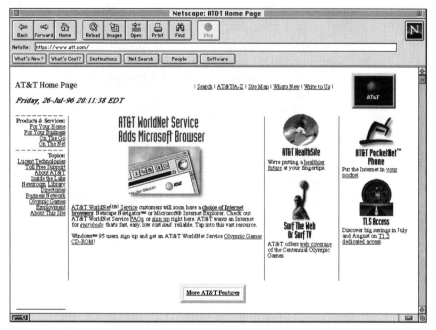

Figure 10-6: *The AT&T home page.*

There are some new details to notice in the Netscape Navigator 3.0 window:

- The security icon in the bottom left corner no longer depicts a broken key on a gray background, but an unbroken one on a blue background.

- There is a blue color bar across the top of the content area.

TIP

Check out the number of teeth on the key icon while displaying a secure document. If the key has two teeth, you are using high-grade encryption, the kind that cannot be exported from the United States to other countries. If it has one tooth, you are using the lower-grade encryption sanctioned by U.S. law for export.

These visual cues are great for letting you know that SSL security is in effect, but what if you want more detailed information about a particular secure document? Netscape Navigator 3.0 also provides a specific Document Information page for every site you visit. Let's take a look at the information that's available for the AT&T home page.

THE DOCUMENT INFORMATION PAGE

To view the Document Information page for the AT&T site:

1. With the AT&T home page still displayed in the Netscape Navigator 3.0 window (as shown in Figure 10-6), select Document Info from the View menu. The Document Info page appears, as shown in Figure 10-7.

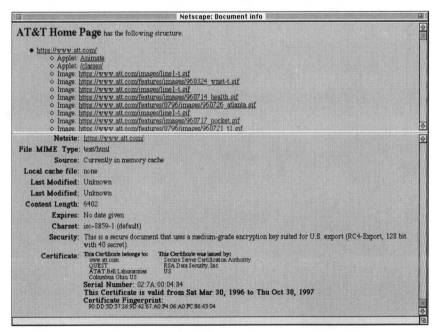

Figure 10-7: *Document information for the AT&T home page.*

- ■ The top panel of the Document Info page identifies the actual documents currently displayed in the Netscape Navigator 3.0 window, including the URLs for the HTML file itself and for any inline graphics.

- ■ The bottom panel is comprised of a miscellany of information about the document, including security information.

2. Scroll through the bottom panel to view information about the AT&T home page. Not all of this information is directly related to security issues, but even the more general items can help you determine the authenticity of a document. Here's a list of the fields and their meanings:

- **Netsite**. This is simply the URL of the document. Obviously, this should be the same as the URL you entered or the link you clicked.

- **File MIME Type**. Since this is an HTML file, the MIME type is text/html.

- **Source**. This tells you how Netscape Navigator 3.0 is currently accessing the HTML source for the document. In this case, it has been cached to disk, and Netscape Navigator 3.0 is reading the cached version.

- **Local cache file**. This is the name of the file on your local hard drive that contains the source for the cached document. By default, Web pages you retrieve via SSL are not cached to your hard drive.

- **Content Length**. This is simply the size of the file, if available.

- **Expires**. This indicates when the cache file expires, based on your Preferences settings.

- **Charset**. This indicates the character set used by the document. In most cases the Charset will be iso-8859-1, which is the technical name for ISO-Latin (the character set used for Western European languages).

- **Security**. This field indicates the type of security used for this document. In this case, it's the medium-grade RSA algorithm.

Next there are several items specifically about the Digital Certificate issued to the server site:

- **This Certificate belongs to**. RSA requires that each applicant for a certificate submit a registered organization name and a variety of other identifying information. Obviously if you think you're at an AT&T

site, but the owner of the Digital ID is not AT&T, you may have found a security problem.

- **This Certificate was issued by**. For now, this field should indicate that the certificate was issued by RSA. Other organizations might be involved in the certification process in the future, but if this field reads something like "Hacker d00d," you probably shouldn't submit your credit card number.

- **This Certificate is valid from**. As an added protection, Digital Certificates are issued for set lengths of time. This field indicates when the current certificate expires.

- **Certificate Fingerprint:** This is a special digital signature that helps assure the authority of the certificate.

You shouldn't need to access this information very often, but if you suspect a security problem, the Document Info page offers you ample opportunity to play digital detective.

MIXED SECURITY DOCUMENTS

The SSL protocol allows for Web documents that contain a combination of secure and insecure information. When you access such a document using **https** in the URL, the insecure information is hidden and replaced by a special mixed security icon. If you want to access the insecure information, you should try connecting to the same address, but using **http** instead of **https** in your URL.

In addition, when you submit forms information in a secure or mixed document by pressing a Submit button or activating some other widget, Netscape Navigator 3.0 can pop up a message letting you know about the security of the submission process itself. This message is similar to the Security Information alert shown earlier in Figure 10-5, and you'll learn how to configure this option in the next section, "Security Preferences." With this added step, you can always know whether or not the information you want to send will be protected by SSL.

SECURITY PREFERENCES

Netscape Navigator 3.0 includes several options for customizing its security features. These can be accessed by clicking Security Preferences from the Options menu. Let's begin by looking at the general security preferences.

GENERAL SECURITY PREFERENCES

To access the general security preferences, simply select Security Preferences from the Options menu. The General panel appears, as shown in Figure 10-8.

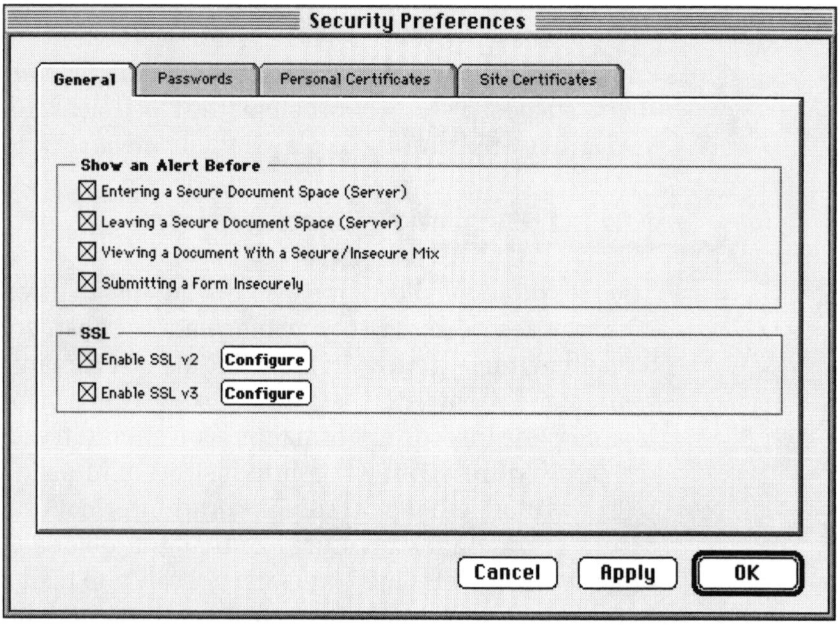

Figure 10-8: *The General panel.*

Earlier in the chapter, you saw that Netscape Navigator 3.0 pops up special security alert messages to inform you of changes in the security status of your connection. It's a good idea to leave these alerts enabled, but the top section of the General tab lets you turn off any that you don't want to see. Here are the results of unchecking each of these boxes:

- **Entering a Secure Document Space (Server)**. Unchecking this box means that you will not receive notification when you are about to access a document on a secure server. If you spend a lot of time on secure servers and know what you are doing, you might want to uncheck this box.

- **Leaving a Secure Document Space (Server)**. Unchecking this box means that you will not be notified when you are about to *leave* a secure server and access a document that is not secure.

- **Viewing a Document With a Secure/Insecure Mix**. Unchecking this box means that you will not receive an alert when you are about to access a document that contains both secure and insecure information.

- **Submitting a Form Insecurely**. Unchecking this box means that you will not receive notification when you are about to submit information insecurely over the Net. If you do a lot of online shopping and are concerned about credit card fraud, I would not recommend unchecking this item.

The bottom section of the General tab lets you check which versions of SSL you want to use. Unless you know what you're doing and have very specific reasons for disallowing any of the protocols, you should *leave these settings alone!*

TIP

SSL 3.0, which is new with this version of Netscape Navigator, has several advantages over earlier implementations. Besides being more efficient, it includes an extra encryption mechanism, better Digital Certificate management, and better support for hardware devices.

TWO MORE ALERTS

There are two more situations in which security alerts can pop up.

■ Suppose you're on a Web page that uses e-mail rather than HTTP or HTTPS to submit a form. In this case, when you click a Submit button, the information you entered is sent to an e-mail address rather than the Web server. By default, Netscape Navigator 3.0 warns you of this.

■ Netscape Navigator 3.0 includes a feature that allows a Web server to temporarily store a small piece of information (called a "cookie") on your system. For instance, suppose you're shopping at a virtual shopping mall and piling goodies into your virtual shopping cart. The Web server you're connected to can tell Navigator to store the names of items you've already decided to purchase. You can configure Navigator so that it warns you before a server tries to send you any of this "cookie" information.

Where do you change these settings? Select Network Preferences from Navigator 3.0's Options menu and click the Protocols tab, as shown in Figure 10-9.

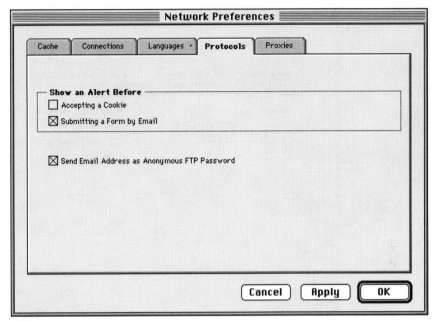

Figure 10-9: *The Protocols panel.*

PASSWORDS

As I mentioned before, Netscape Navigator 3.0 lets you create a personal access password. You may have already done this when you installed the program, but in case you didn't, or in case you want to change your password, follow these directions:

1. From the Options menu, select Security Preferences.

2. Click the Passwords tab, as shown in Figure 10-10.

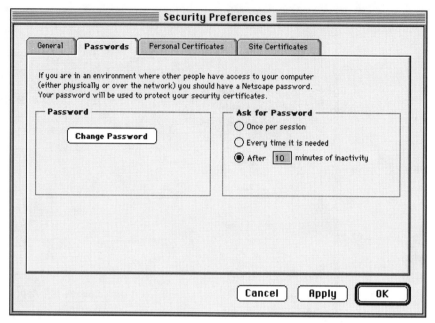

Figure 10-10: *The Passwords panel.*

> **TIP**
>
> *If you've already configured a password for Navigator 3.0, you'll see a Change Password button instead of a Set Password button.*

3. Select one of the Ask for Password options.

   ■ Select Once per session if you want Netscape Navigator 3.0 to ask you for your password only once, when you first launch the program.

   ■ Select Every time it is needed if you want Navigator to ask for your password before each time it transmits your Personal Certificate information.

   ■ Select After 10 minutes of inactivity if you want Navigator to ask you for your password after 10 minutes of idle time. You can also change the number of minutes if you want.

4. Click the Set Password button. The Change Your Netscape Password dialog box appears, as shown in Figure 10-11.

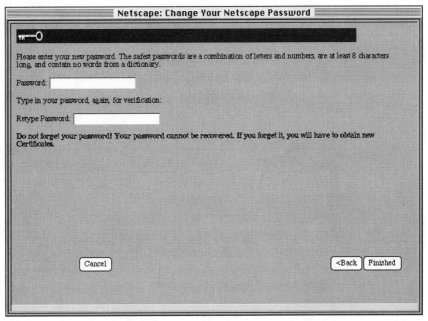

Figure 10-11: *The Change Your Netscape Password dialog box.*

5. Enter your new password in both boxes.

6. *MEMORIZE YOUR PASSWORD!* This is so important I'll repeat it. *MEMORIZE YOUR PASSWORD!* Oh, and one more thing: *MEMORIZE YOUR PASSWORD!*

7. Click Finished. You are returned to the Passwords panel shown in Figure 10-10.

Now that your Personal Certificates are protected, it's time to get one!

PERSONAL CERTIFICATES

As I mentioned before, Personal Certificates are special electronic keys that identify you to a secure Web server. There's a good chance that they will become a common means of authenticating users for financial transactions over the Web. They may also be used within an organizational intranet to protect sensitive documents, since Web servers can be configured to accept or reject particular digital certificates.

To obtain and configure a new Personal Certificate:

1. Make sure you are connected to the Internet.

2. From the Options menu, select Security Preferences.

3. Click the Personal Certificates tab, as shown in Figure 10-12.

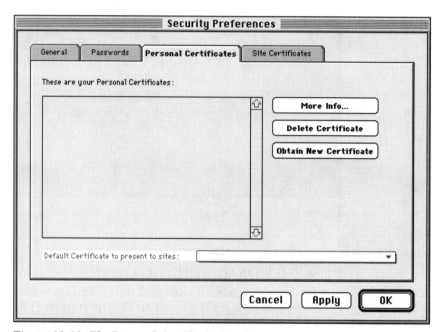

Figure 10-12: *The Personal Certificates panel.*

4. Click the Obtain New Certificate button. Follow all the instructions that appear for obtaining your certificate, and make sure to fill out the forms with correct information.

TIP

You can also obtain a Personal Certificate directly from VeriSign, Inc., who is the current Certifying Authority for Personal Certificates. It's URL is http://www.verisign.com.

5. Once you have a Personal Certificate, take another look at the Personal Certificates panel. It should now contain your new Personal Certificate.

6. To view the digital information contained in your new certificate, select it and click the More Info button. You may invoke the automatic connection to VeriSign, Inc.'s home page, shown below in Figure 10-13.

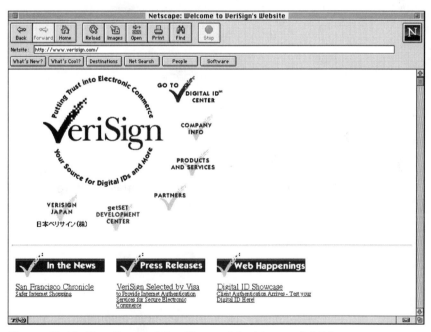

Figure 10-13: *New Personal Certificate with nickname "phil."*

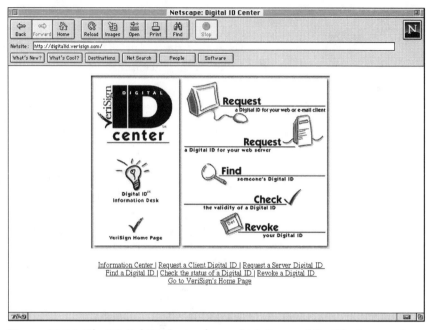

Figure 10-14: *The Digital ID Center from which Personal Certificates may be obtained.*

7. To set a particular Personal Certificate as the default certificate that is presented when you access a secure Web site, select it from the drop-down list at the bottom of the tab. You may have several certificates for different purposes, such as particular kinds of online credit card transactions.

WHAT ABOUT CACHED INFORMATION?

As you know, one of the ways that Netscape Navigator 3.0 operates quickly and efficiently is by caching information you've retrieved from the Net. By storing Web pages either in memory or on your hard drive, you avoid having to re-download this material each time you connect to a particular site.

However, you probably don't want sensitive financial or personal information hanging out on your drive. For this reason, Netscape Navigator 3.0 does *not* cache to disk any documents that you have retrieved using the SSL protocol. For instance, a fresh copy of the secure AT&T page we saw earlier will be retrieved every time you restart Navigator and link to the site. Nobody can poke around your hard drive and discover your secrets—at least your SSL secrets!

But what if your machine is relatively secure and you're not worried about hard drive hackers? Why should you twiddle your thumbs while Navigator downloads fresh copies of SSL documents that haven't changed? Well, Navigator 3.0 lets you be more lax if you want. To configure the program so that it *does* cache SSL information to your hard drive, select Network Preferences from the Options menu and then click the Cache tab. At the bottom of the Cache tab, check the Allow Persistent Caching of Pages Retrieved Through SSL check box. Now you're in the fast lane and living a little more dangerously.

Warning: Do not check this check box if you're thinking about running for President some day.

SITE CERTIFICATES

Now select the remaining tab in the Security Preferences dialog box, the one labeled Site Certificates. Figure 10-15 shows what you should see.

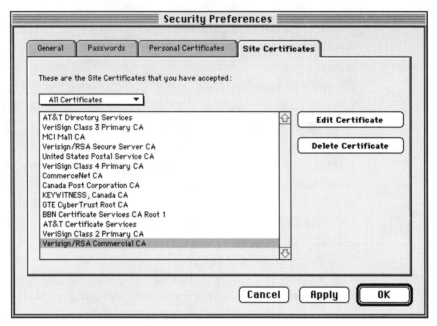

Figure 10-15: The Site Certificates panel.

To operate in secure mode, a Web server site must obtain a special certificate, and you are sent a copy of the certificate information when you connect using SSL. The Site Certificates tab lets you view this information to verify that any data you send goes only to the certificate owner. In addition, this tab lets you specify whether or not to allow connections to the owners of specific Site Certificates or to sites that have been certified by particular certifying authorities.

Let's take a closer look:

1. In the Site Certificates tab, make sure that All Certificates is selected in the drop-down list near the top.

2. From the list of certificates, select VeriSign RSA CA and click the Edit Certificate button. The certificate information for the Secure Server Certification Authority appears, as shown in Figure 10-16.

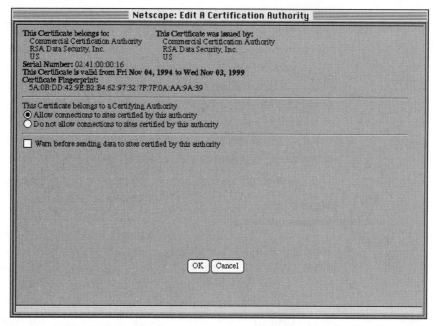

Figure 10-16: *Certificate information for the RSA Secure Server Certification Authority.*

■ This is the identifying information for a certifying authority rather than for a single site.

3. If you wish to allow connections to sites certified by the RSA Secure Server Certification Authority, leave the Allow connections to sites certified by this authority radio button checked. If you don't want to connect to sites certified by RSA, select the Do not allow connections to sites certified by this authority radio button.

   ■ If you check the Do not allow connections to sites certified by this authority radio button, you will be eliminating your ability to connect securely to any site certified by RSA, including the Netscape site itself!

4. If you want a warning to pop up before you send data to sites certified by RSA, check the Warn before sending data to sites certified by this authority check box.

5. When you're finished, click the OK button.

You can also delete a certificate from the Site Certificates panel by selecting it and clicking the Delete Certificate button.

So far we've looked at some of the recent security enhancements developed by Netscape. They go a long way toward protecting sensitive information both for people browsing the Web and for people developing sites. But if you work in an office that's on a LAN or WAN, or if you are thinking of implementing one, you're probably interested in a slightly older technique for protecting data and network resources—proxies.

PROXIES

Proxy gateways are a security feature deployed by many businesses. System administrators set up proxy gateways so that users on a LAN are not actually connected directly to the Internet. Instead, any Internet data they send or receive is handled by the proxy computer, which passes the information on. The proxy may be completely transparent, allowing all data in and out of the organization and simply monitoring activity, or it may be part of a *firewall* that restricts both inbound and outbound access in various ways. The proxy settings in Netscape Navigator 3.0 allow the program to pass on a network request (in the form of a URL) to an outside agent through a firewall, which performs the request for Netscape Navigator 3.0. The proxy agent then returns any Internet information to Netscape Navigator 3.0.

WHAT IS A FIREWALL?

You've probably read horror stories about hackers who get online only to sabotage or destroy data. As the new information technologies mature, acts like these probably won't have the same thrill they used to, but cyber-criminals will never disappear completely.That's why businesses, universities, government agencies, and other sites that have sensitive data on their networks are forced to think of ways to keep these types of users away. Firewalls are software and hardware solutions that provide a layer or several layers of protection between the Internet and a network. These layers are designed to keep the bad guys out, but they also restrict users within a network from getting out on the Internet directly. For this reason, proxies were created to enable users to work through firewalls and access the outside world.

By the way, the term *firewall* comes from the days when brick walls were built between apartment buildings to keep fires from spreading from one building to the next. The metal between the engine and the passenger compartment of a car is also called a firewall.

Users of a Netscape Navigator 3.0 software client using a proxy gateway still think they are on the Internet even though they technically are not. Proxy gateways are implemented based on the type of service in use, such as FTP, Gopher, WAIS, news, and HTTP (the World Wide Web). Each URL access method can send its requests to a different proxy.

CONFIGURING PROXY SETTINGS

Your first task is to ask your system administrator if a proxy is even necessary or available. If you are running Netscape Navigator 3.0 on an internal network from behind a firewall, you then need to know the names and associated port numbers for the server running proxy software for each network service. You'll need this data so that you can fill out the Proxies panel in the Network Preferences page in Netscape Navigator 3.0, as shown in Figure 10-17.

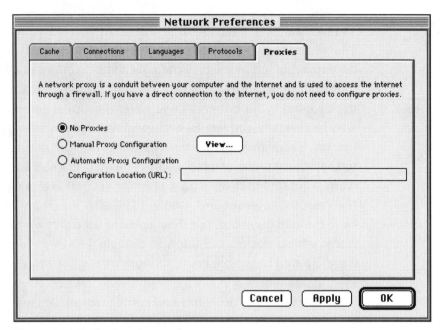

Figure 10-17: *The Proxies panel.*

The Proxies panel includes the following items:

■ **No Proxies**. Configures Netscape Navigator 3.0 to run without a proxy. This is the default setting.

■ **Manual Proxy Configuration**. This option allows the most flexible configuration of proxy gateways for each type of URL. If you want to configure the proxy settings yourself, use this option, as described under "Configuring a Proxy Manually."

■ **Automatic Proxy Configuration**. Instructs Netscape Navigator 3.0 to configure your proxies automatically based on a configuration file designed expressly for your proxy server. Click the radio button and then provide the file's URL in the Configuration Location (URL) field.

If you're interested in automatically configuring proxies for several (or many) users on an office network, you should take a look at the Netscape Administration Kit. This product not only lets you configure proxies on an enterprise-wide basis, it also lets you configure every copy of Navigator 3.0 with standard mail server and news server addresses. It even lets you redefine the Directory buttons and add your own animated corporate logo to the program. For more information on the Netscape Administration Kit, see Appendix C of this book or navigate to the URL http://home.netscape.com/comprod/products/navigator/version_3.0/enterprise/index.html.

CONFIGURING A PROXY MANUALLY

To set a proxy using the Manual Proxy Configuration choice, follow these steps:

1. Launch Netscape Navigator 3.0. The main window appears, and if you are using a starting page located on your hard drive it will display in the Netscape Navigator 3.0 window. Otherwise, you will see a blank window. This is because you are not yet connected to the World Wide Web (remember, that's what you're trying to establish by configuring the proxy settings). Click the Stop button to stop Navigator from looking for the home page it isn't going to find.

   ■ If a message box pops up telling you that Netscape Navigator 3.0 cannot find a domain, go ahead and click OK. This message box is telling you something you already know!

2. Select Network Preferences from the Options menu, then select the Proxies panel, shown in Figure 10-17.

3. Click on the Manual Proxy Configuration radio button.

4. Click the View button to display the Network: Proxies: Manual dialog box, as shown in Figure 10-18.

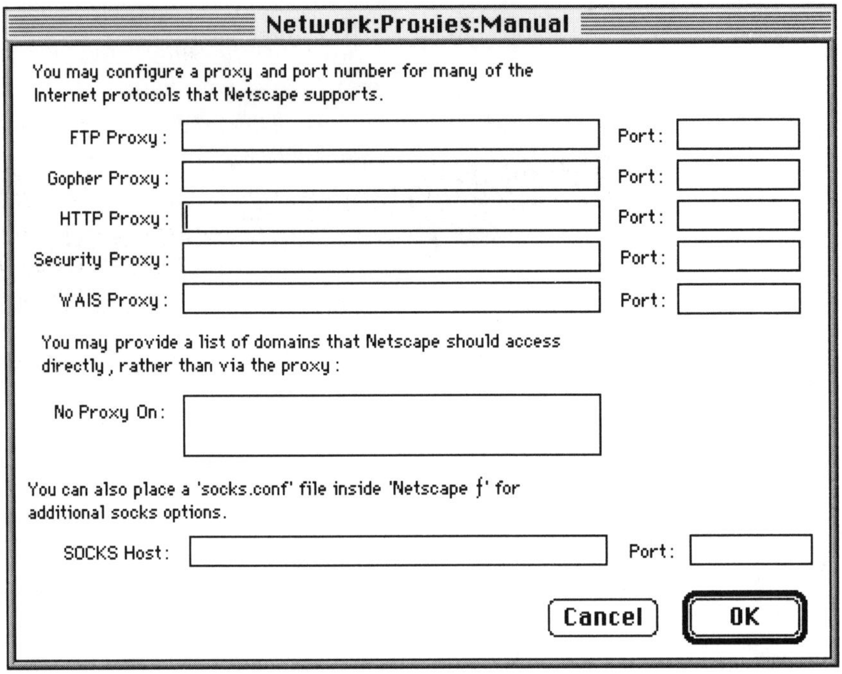

```
┌──────────── Network:Proxies:Manual ────────────┐
│                                                 │
│  You may configure a proxy and port number for  │
│  many of the Internet protocols that Netscape   │
│  supports.                                       │
│                                                 │
│     FTP Proxy: [                ]  Port: [     ] │
│  Gopher Proxy: [                ]  Port: [     ] │
│    HTTP Proxy: [|               ]  Port: [     ] │
│ Security Proxy:[                ]  Port: [     ] │
│    WAIS Proxy: [                ]  Port: [     ] │
│                                                 │
│  You may provide a list of domains that Netscape │
│  should access directly, rather than via the     │
│  proxy:                                          │
│                                                 │
│   No Proxy On: [                ]                │
│               [                ]                │
│                                                 │
│  You can also place a 'socks.conf' file inside   │
│  'Netscape ƒ' for additional socks options.      │
│                                                 │
│   SOCKS Host: [                ]  Port: [     ] │
│                                                 │
│                      ( Cancel )  [[  OK  ]]     │
└─────────────────────────────────────────────────┘
```

Figure 10-18: *The Network: Proxies: Manual dialog box.*

■ The long list of Proxies should be blank unless already configured by your network administrator. The Port settings will all have zeros in them, with the exception of the SOCKS host port, which should read 1080. If you see some other data already listed, stop and ask someone if these are the proper settings. If so, you're done.

5. Fill in each of the proxy fields with the following information:

TIP

You can put the Internet addresses for multiple hosts in each field. If your network administrator provides you with multiple proxy addresses for each protocol, they should be separated by commas. Do not use wildcards for multiple addresses!

- **FTP Proxy**. Enter the Internet address of the system running the proxy software and the port number for FTP protocol access. When set correctly, you'll be able to access anonymous FTP sites.

- **Gopher Proxy**. Enter the Internet address of the system running the proxy software and the port number for Gopher protocol access. When set correctly, you'll be able to access Gopher menus.

- **HTTP Proxy**. Enter the Internet address of the system running the proxy software and the port number for HTTP protocol access. When set correctly, you'll be able to access Web pages and sites.

- **Security Proxy**. Enter the information for your Secure Sockets Layer (SSL) protocol resource.

- **WAIS Proxy**. Enter the Internet address of the system running the proxy software and the port number for WAIS protocol access. When set correctly, you'll be able to access WAIS databases.

- **SOCKS Host**. If your network uses a SOCKS Host gateway as part of a firewall, enter its Internet address here.

6. Your network may be configured to allow you to access certain sites directly, without going through a proxy. If so, enter the addresses for these sites in the No Proxy on box. The format of these entries is the Internet address followed by the port number for the allowed protocol. For instance, the standard port number for Gopher is 70, so to allow direct access to the Gopher server at pjames.com you would type **pjames.com:70**.

TIP

Unless you have a photographic memory, take this book or page with you when you talk to your site administrator. Have him or her fill out the correct addresses and ports for each setting. Then enter the information yourself in your copy of Netscape Navigator 3.0. Why? Because you need to make sure all these settings are perfect before trying to use Netscape Navigator 3.0. Otherwise you'll experience problems and won't be able to access anything on the Net.

7. Click OK, then click OK again in the Proxies panel to return to the main Netscape Navigator 3.0 window.

Now that you've got this all set up, you should be able to connect to the Internet via your company's LAN. Give it a try by clicking the Home button. If it doesn't work, you'll need to talk once more to your network administrator. Every network is configured a little differently, so we can't give you any easy answers here.

SECURITY AND JAVA APPLETS

In Chapter 9, "Power Navigator 3.0," you read about Java applets. Since these are programs that you download and run on your system, you may be concerned about security. In most cases Java applets are not a security risk. They are written in a Java language subset that includes several security precautions. For instance, applets can't perform most file system access or file I/O routines. These precautions, however, do not absolutely guarantee that a developer intent on breaking into your system can't do so.

If you're worried, Netscape Navigator 3.0 provides another safeguard. Select Network Preferences from the Options menu and then click the Languages tab, shown in Figure 10-19. Notice the Java Enable check box. By unchecking the box, Netscape Navigator 3.0

offers the option to disable Java support for those times you want to download a Java applet to your machine but then cut off the network transactions *back* to the server (you also can disconnect from the Internet and run the applet locally). When you leave the option checked, this means you want full access to Java applets so you can initiate a two-way communication between your client and the server machine. By default, this box is checked to enable full Java access.

This tab also lets you disable JavaScript, adding one more measure of security to your system.

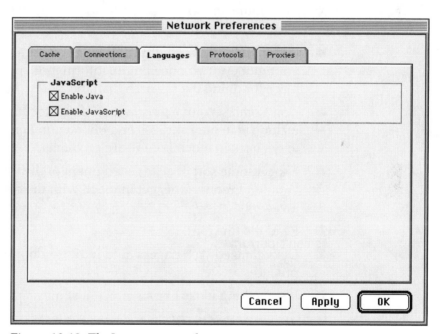

Figure 10-19: *The Languages panel.*

THE MOST POWERFUL SECURITY— COMMON SENSE

There is no question that Netscape Navigator 3.0, when used in conjunction with the Netscape Web servers that are springing up all over the Net, provides very powerful protection from theft, fraud, and abuse of sensitive electronic information. I applaud Netscape for working so diligently toward making online commerce a safe and sensible option. It wouldn't surprise me if electronic transactions become the norm a few years from now. Enhanced security such as SSL is paving the way for this new way of doing business.

But you already possess a powerful security tool, more powerful than even the 128-bit key RC4 version of RSA's stream encryption algorithm—your common sense. I hate to get Forrest Gumpish on you, but here are a few things your mama should have always said:

- If you don't know anything about a company, don't send it your money. If you need more information, what better place for doing the research than the Net?

- Don't send sensitive information if the document doesn't include an e-mail address or a phone number you can use to get back in touch if there are problems.

- Expect some sort of acknowledgment of the transaction. If you don't receive one, get in touch with the company right away.

- Read the fine font.

- Disorganized Web pages could indicate sloppy business practices as well.

- If something looks like a scam, it just may *be* a scam.

Add these truisms to SSL, and you've got *real* security.

Moving On

By now you know how to cruise the Net (or your own intranet) pretty well using Netscape Navigator 3.0. You know how to jump from document to document on the Web, how to send and receive e-mail, how to read and post Usenet news, how to get files, and how to tap the power of hypermedia. In this last chapter, you learned a little about commerce on the Web, and how Netscape Navigator 3.0 provides security for online transactions.

But what about developing your *own* Web pages? Even if you don't want to become the Spielberg of the Net, you might want to put together a simple page just for yourself, with links to some of your favorite sites. In the next chapter, I'll show you how to do it.

11

Your Personal Workspace & Web Page

One of the great things about working at home is that I can keep my desk as messy as I want. I like to surround myself with piles of paper: printouts of interesting articles I've found on the Net, invoices, research documents, my own writing, reference books, today's newspaper, phone lists, unopened mail, you name it. Nobody else can find anything on my desk, but I have no problem at all. I've grown used to it, and I like it the way it is. So there!

You can use Netscape Navigator 3.0 to set up what's known as a *PowerStart* page, and you can make it as neat or as messy as you want. Because the software provides excellent organizational tools, it's a little bit harder to make it messy, but believe me, you can do it! Each morning Navigator 3.0 will drop your favorite electronic newspaper on your desk, automatically updating the headlines; it will provide links to all the search engines and other resources you need for the work you're currently doing; and it'll even remind you to pick up the kids from school today. But no, I'm afraid it can't clutter your desk with empty coffee cups. Wait for version 4.0.

Netscape's PowerStart feature relies on JavaScript to dynamically update the information on your virtual desktop. Once you set it up, all you need to do is click a button to make sure you have the latest news or stock quotes sitting in front of you in Navigator 3.0's browser window. And because your PowerStart page is not a static document out on the Net somewhere, nobody else can access it. All the setup information about what kinds of news and other elements should be included in your personal workspace are stored locally, in a file called cookies.txt.

TRAP

*Do **not** try to edit your cookies file (cookies.txt) directly—you are almost sure to get yourself in trouble!*

In addition to creating a PowerStart page, you may want to create a different kind of Web page for yourself, one that is even more customized or specifically targeted. It might contain nothing but links to sources for legal information, for instance, or your favorite artwork. In this chapter you'll not only learn how to create a general PowerStart page, you'll also learn the very basics of "hand-rolling" your own Web page that you can even share with the rest of the cyberworld.

First, let's set up a PowerStart page.

TIP

Netscape's PowerStart feature requires a connection to the Internet, since it uses JavaScript to communicate with the Netscape server and update information. If you are using Navigator 3.0 on an intranet and do not have direct access to the Net, you will not be able to use this feature. You should skip ahead to the section "Rolling Your Own Web Page."

CREATING YOUR POWERSTART PAGE

OK, get ready for a fun ride.

Note: Netscape's PowerStart feature was brand new when this book went to the printer—we literally had to stop the presses to include this information! By the time you read this, some of the features may have changed or been enhanced, but the general instructions that follow should work fine.

1. Make sure you are connected to the Net. If you are not already running Netscape Navigator 3.0, launch it by clicking its icon.

2. After the Netscape home page appears, click the PowerStart link or button. Netscape changes the home page regularly, but this link probably appears near the bottom. After a few seconds the Netscape PowerStart setup page appears, as shown in Figure 11-1.

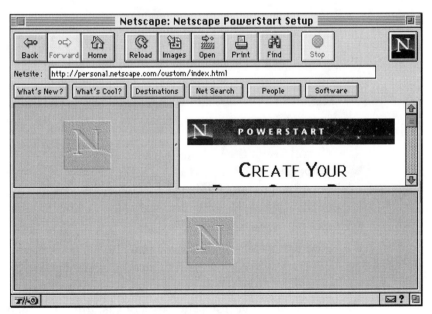

Figure 11-1: *The Netscape PowerStart setup page.*

3. Scroll down the frame that contains text and read the description of the PowerStart feature. When you're done reading, click the Continue button. Now some instructions appear in the left-hand frame, as shown in Figure 11-2, and the right-hand frame contains a preview of the workspace you are building.

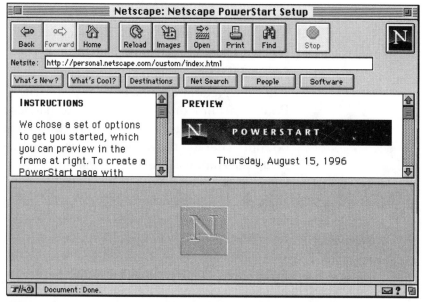

Figure 11-2: *Two new frames activated in the PowerStart setup page.*

Scroll down the left-hand frame. As you can see, it contains a number of links that are actually options for customizing your PowerStart page. Here's the rundown on how the three frames in the browser window will operate as you start to create your personal workspace:

- In the left-hand frame, you choose particular options you want to configure. We'll call this the *Options frame*.

- Once you click one of these links, the bottom frame will display various choices. For instance, if you click on a link labeled Background Color, various background color choices appear in the bottom frame. We'll call this bottom frame the *Selection frame*.

■ The right-hand frame, where we started this whole process, shows you a preview of your personal workspace. As you choose new elements in the Options and Selection frames, this *Preview frame* is automatically updated to reflect your latest changes.

The left-hand Options frame always contains the same information. That means if you don't like a change you've made, you can always go back and click that option again.

OK, we're about to start messing up your virtual desk. Let's start with content.

> **TIP**
>
> *You can create a simple default PowerStart page by clicking the Quick Start button in the Options frame. You might want to give it a try to see what it looks like. You can always go back and personalize your PowerStart page later, following the instructions that follow.*

CHOOSING YOUR CONTENT

Start by scrolling down to the Choose Your Content section in the left-hand frame and read the text. You'll discover that by clicking the Collection link, you can choose from a variety of PowerStart page templates suited to particular interests. For instance, if you're an armchair jock, you can choose a template that includes lots of sports links, or if you're a geek like me, you can choose to litter your desktop with lots of technology information. You can experiment with different collections on your own, but for now simply leave the default General selection button selected, as shown in Figure 11-3.

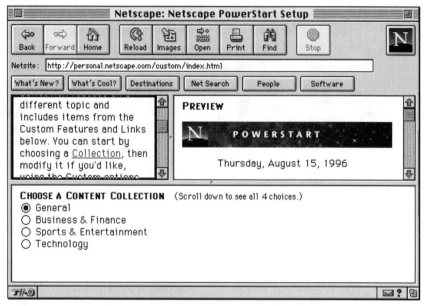

Figure 11-3: *The General collection selected.*

This collection provides your PowerStart page with a broad range of features, but you may want to customize your content more specifically. Let's start with Netscape Headline News.

NETSCAPE HEADLINE NEWS

Netscape is one of the most productive companies I've ever encountered. Their programmers and product designers are the rabbits of the software world. They're always coming up with new stuff, including important upgrades and add-ons, and they generally announce their products via their Web site. If you choose the latest news from Netscape link as shown in Figure 11-4, the latest Netscape headlines will be dropped right onto your PowerStart page automatically!

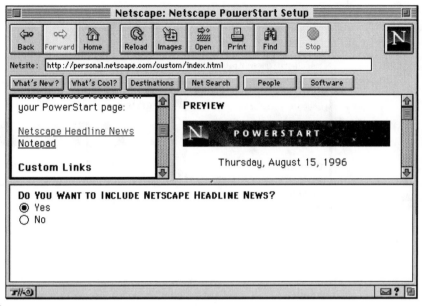

Figure 11-4: *The Netscape Headline News option.*

NOTEPAD

The Notepad is a simple but powerful feature. It is a blank area in your workspace within which you can jot notes to yourself. These notes are preserved even when you leave Netscape Navigator 3.0, so the Notepad is great for daily reminders such as "Get a life."

Figure 11-5 shows where you choose to add the Notepad to your PowerStart page.

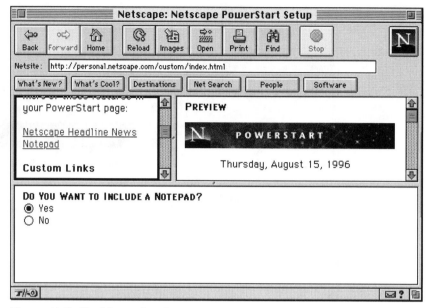

Figure 11-5: *The Notepad option.*

STOCK TICKER

If you own shares in any publicly traded company, you can get the latest information on how rich or poor you are—right within your PowerStart page! To add this cool feature, simply click Stock Ticker in the Options frame. Then in the Selection frame specify the symbols for companies you're interested in.

CUSTOM LINKS

Most importantly, you can enhance your personal workspace with links to a variety of information resources. The Options frame offers many choices, from Sports to Technology. In each case, the method of selecting links is the same, so I'll just highlight a few:

- ■ If you click Daily News in the Options frame as shown in Figure 11-6, you can select from a variety of electronic sources for daily news.

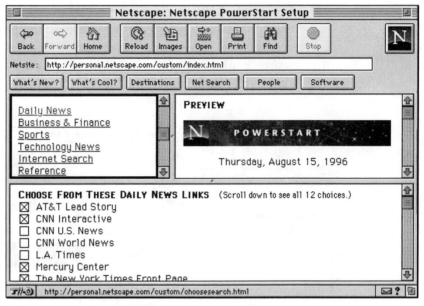

Figure 11-6: *The Daily News option.*

■ Clicking Reference, as shown in Figure 11-7, lets you select some common reference books to pile onto your virtual desktop.

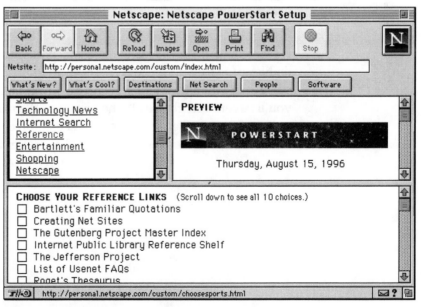

Figure 11-7: *The Reference option.*

■ Powerful search engines are becoming one of the most common ways to access information on the Internet, and it can be a real convenience to include links to your favorite search engines right in your PowerStart page. Figure 11-8 shows you how.

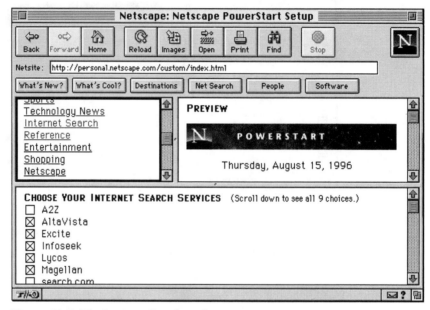

Figure 11-8: *The Internet Search option.*

■ If you're like most Navigator 3.0 users, you spend a lot of time on Netscape's own Web server. There are probably some pages that you return to again and again, and others that you'll never even glance at. The Netscape Web Site pages option shown in Figure 11-9 lets you customize your personal workspace with the Netscape pages that matter to *you*.

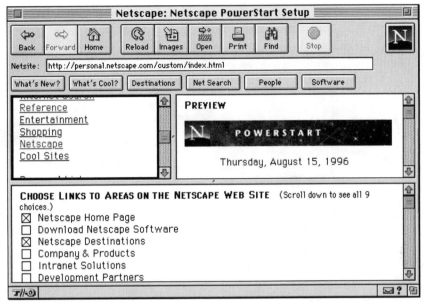

Figure 11-9: *The Netscape Web Site option.*

■ We all know what the Web is really for—finding cool sites. If you enhance your desktop with some of the links shown in Figure 11-10, you're well on your way to lots of high-quality time wasting.

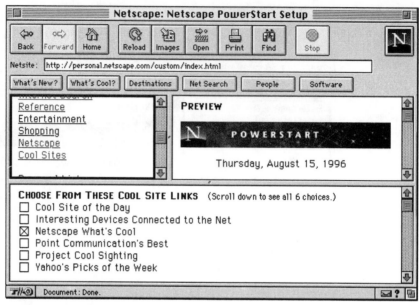

Figure 11-10: *The Cool Sites option.*

■ Finally, you can add your own personal links to sites you've discovered. Let's give this a try:

1. Click the Personal Links option in the Options frame. A Personal Links form appears in the Selection frame, as shown in Figure 11-11.

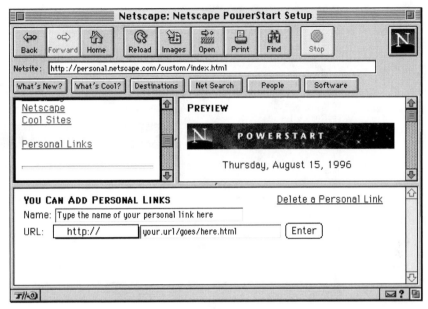

Figure 11-11: *The Personal Links form.*

2. Type in the name that you want to appear in your PowerStart page, and then type in the correct URL for the site. For example, if you want to include a link to Netscape Press, your Personal Links form should look something like Figure 11-12.

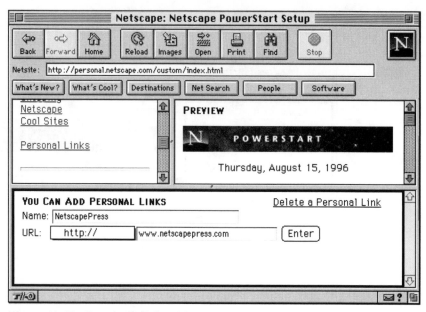

Figure 11-12: *Creating a link to Netscape Press.*

3. Click Enter. The information is added to your personal workspace and you are returned to the Personal Links form. You can add as many personal links as you want, simply clicking Enter after you type the information for each one.

TIP

To delete the links from your page, simply click Delete Personal Links.

OK, now that you've added some clutter to your desk, let's make it pretty.

CONFIGURING YOUR PAGE'S APPEARANCE

Back in the left-hand Options frame, scroll down to the Style Sheets link and click it. As you can see in Figure 11-13, you are given a choice of style sheets to choose from.

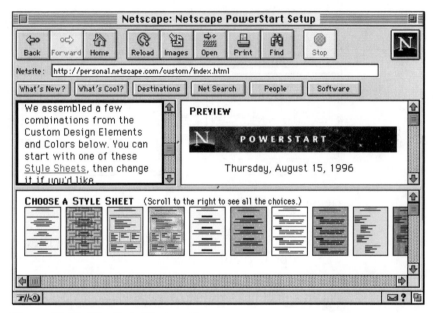

Figure 11-13: *The Style Sheets option.*

Style sheets include elements such as background colors, page layout, etc. Simply click the style you like. The Preview window is updated based on your choice. But you can still customize all the individual visual elements of your PowerStart page.

CUSTOM DESIGN ELEMENTS

To change the custom design elements on your PowerStart page:

1. Scroll down the Options frame until you reach the Custom Design Elements section.

2. Now scroll down the Options frame a little further to the Layout link and click it. Figure 11-14 shows the Layout options available in the Selection window.

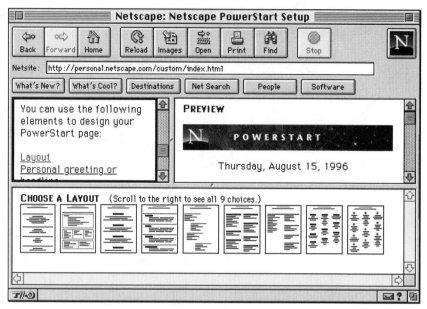

Figure 11-14: *The Layout option.*

3. Click one of the available options. The Preview window is updated automatically.

Want to change the headline for your page? Go ahead and click the Headline link. The Headline choices appear in the Selection frame, as shown in Figure 11-15.

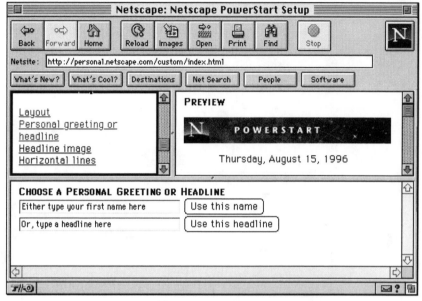

Figure 11-15: *Headline choices.*

Type in either your own name or a new headline for your personal workspace, then click the appropriate button. As you can see in Figure 11-16, the Preview frame is automatically updated.

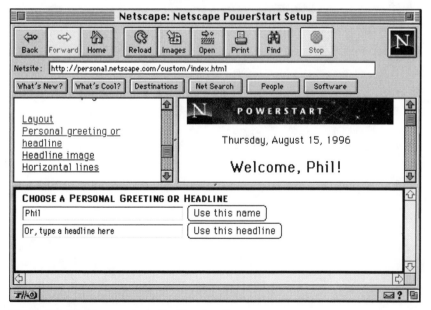

Figure 11-16: *New name in the Preview frame.*

You can also add a graphic to your new headline:

1. Back in the Options frame, click Headline image. The Selection frame now displays several images, some of them animated and many of them depicting the Netscape mascot, Mozilla, as shown in Figure 11-17.

Figure 11-17: *Headline image choices.*

WHO'S MOZILLA?

You may have noticed that Netscape uses the image of a friendly-looking dragon all over the place. And you may have wondered why.

Netscape Navigator was the brain-child of several developers who had previously worked on a Web browser called NCSA Mosaic. Mosaic was the standard for graphical Web access for several years. As the developers started to expand the capabilities of Mosaic, they code-named the beta versions Mozilla, which is short for "Mosaic meets Godzilla." In other words, they thought of Netscape as a supercharged or mutant version of Mosaic. Though they decided not to release the commercial product under this name, Mozilla stuck around as a mascot. Netscape artists have developed dozens of pictures of Mozilla: you see him (or is it a her?) everywhere.

Try this for fun: type **about:mozilla** in the Netsite/Location box and press Enter. You should get an interesting quote from the "Book of Mozilla."

2. Select a graphic. Again, the Preview frame is updated. (In the following illustrations you'll notice that I chose Mozilla riding a little bicycle. I am easily amused.)

There are a few more choices in the Configuring Design Elements section. Let's go through them all now:

1. Click the Horizontal lines link in the Options window. Now several choices for a horizontal line appear in the Selection window, as shown in Figure 11-18. Some of available lines may even be animated.

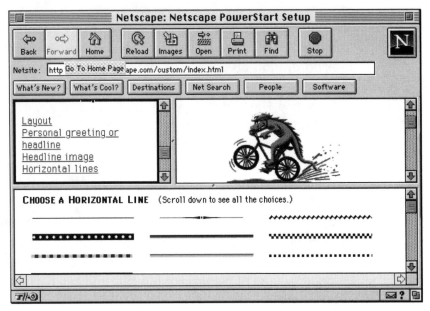

Figure 11-18: *The Horizontal lines option.*

■ The horizontal line you choose is the line that will separate the various areas of your PowerStart page.

2. Click one of the horizontal lines. Again, your Preview frame is updated.

3. After scrolling down to the Custom Colors section in the Options frame, click Background color or pattern. A number of background colors and patterns appear in the Selection frame, as shown in Figure 11-19.

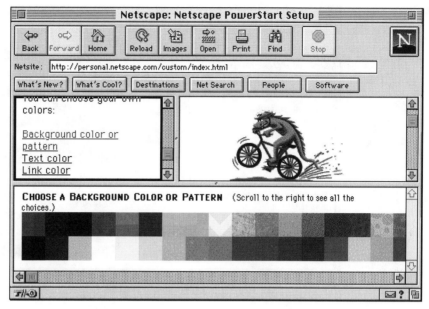

Figure 11-19: *Available background colors and patterns.*

4. Select one of the color combinations. As usual, the Preview frame immediately reflects your choice.

What if the background color you choose makes links, visited links, or even regular text hard to see on your page. No problem! Navigator 3.0 lets you choose custom colors for all these display elements. Simply click the appropriate links in the Options frame and then choose from the Selection frame. As always, the Preview frame will reflect your choices.

PUTTING IT ALL TOGETHER

We're almost ready to actually create your PowerStart page. But first, make sure you like all the choices you've made. You can go back to any option in the Options frame, click it again, and make whatever changes you want. Nothing has been set in electronic stone, so feel free to play around. When you finally think you've got it the way you want it, scroll down to the very bottom of the Options frame. You'll see two buttons, as shown in Figure 11-20.

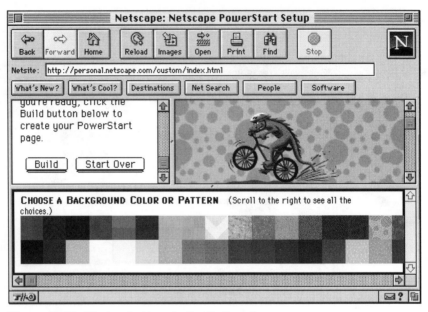

Figure 11-20: *The two buttons in the Options frame.*

The buttons are pretty self-explanatory. To go ahead and create your personal workspace, click the Build button. To "zero out" all the options and start over again, click Start Over.

Let's assume you click the Build button. Your machine huffs and puffs, maybe grumbles a bit, and finally lands you in your newly built PowerStart page, as shown in Figure 11-21. (*Note:* If you choose a different layout, your personal workspace might look quite different from mine.)

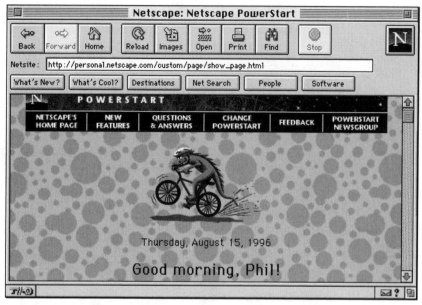

Figure 11-21: *A new PowerStart page.*

Now scroll down and take a look around. As you can see in Figure 11-22, your Netscape Headline News and Notepad are there.

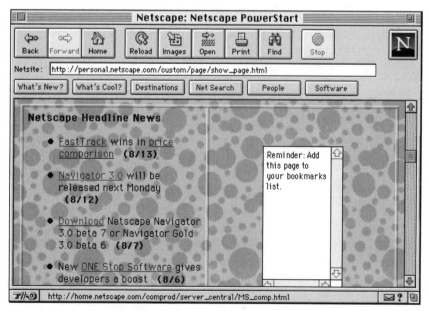

Figure 11-22: *Netscape Headline News and Notepad.*

And if you scroll down further, you get to the Netscape Web Site links and the Cool Site Links as shown in Figure 11-23.

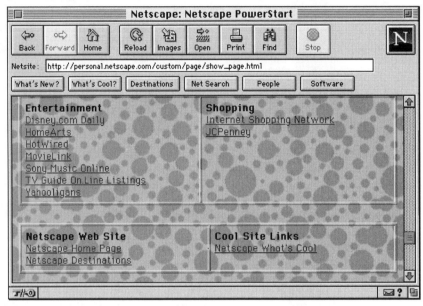

Figure 11-23: *Netscape and Cool Site links.*

Scroll further still and you'll hit your Search and Directory links, Daily News links, and any Personal Bookmarks links you added.

But what if you want to change your PowerStart page? That's easy. Scroll back up and look at the PowerStart imagemap at the very top of the page. You'll see that one of the options is Change PowerStart, as shown in Figure 11-24.

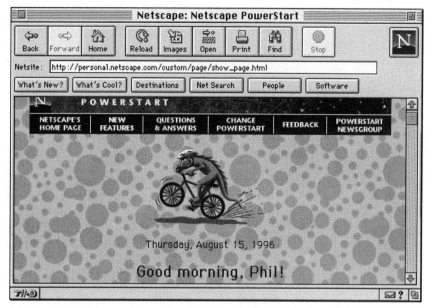

Figure 11-24: *The top of your PowerStart page, with Change PowerStart link.*

Well, you've got a personal workspace all right. But how do you access it in the future? Easy. Here comes one of the shortest sections I've ever written:

ACCESSING YOUR POWERSTART PAGE

To access your PowerStart page:

1. Make sure you are connected to the Net.

2. If Netscape Navigator 3.0 is not currently running, launch it by double-clicking its icon.

3. If the Netscape home page does not appear automatically, navigate to **http://home.netscape.com.** Scroll down to the PowerStart button or link, as shown in Figure 11-25.

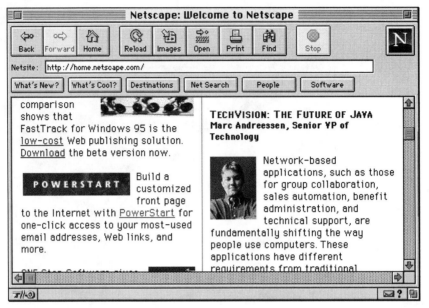

Figure 11-25: *The PowerStart link.*

4. Click the PowerStart link. The Netscape Web server and Navigator 3.0 work together to update your personal workspace with the latest information and display it in your browser window.

TIP

Make sure to create a bookmark or desktop shortcut for your PowerStart page. You might even want to specify it as your default home page, the page that appears when you first load Netscape Navigator 3.0. To do this, go to the Appearance tab under General Options, make sure the "Home Page Location" option button is selected, and type **http://home.netscape.com/custom/page/show_page.html**.

ROLLING YOUR OWN WEB PAGE

Netscape's PowerStart feature is a great convenience, but you can also create a new Web page for yourself several other ways. Your Web page can contain all the links you want in it, though unless you're a pretty skilled Web author, it will not provide some of the niceties of PowerStart such as a Notepad or Netscape Headlines that update automatically.

Given that it's more work to roll your own Web page, why would you want to do this instead of relying on Netscape's PowerStart feature? There are several possibilities:

- You might want to include complete descriptions of your favorite links rather than just one-line labels.

- You might want more flexibility in the look-and-feel of your Web page. For instance, you may prefer pictures of Madonna to pictures of Mozilla. Or you might want to add more advanced interface elements such as client-side image maps.

- If you're not on the Internet itself but on an office intranet, the PowerStart feature will not work.

And there is one more compelling reason to roll your own page, perhaps the most important one of all: you might want to share your page with others by making it available on the Net or on your intranet. You cannot share your PowerStart page, only independent Web pages.

CLIENT-SIDE IMAGE MAPS

As you learned in Chapter 3, "A Quick Look Around," many Web sites feature graphical maps you can click on to access different services or documents, such as the one at the top of Netscape's own home page. This graphic is actually an image map that you can click on to move to different parts of the Netscape Web site.

Most image maps as they are now written are server-side maps. This means that the map stays on the server; when you click an area of the map, the request travels back to the server to be processed. As you might guess, it takes time just for the server to figure out where you want to go; then it has to process the transaction.

With client-side maps, however, the image map is embedded in the Web page and processed directly by Netscape Navigator 3.0. This means you can include image maps in a Web page that sits right on your own home machine. There is no need for a Web server. If you already know something about HTML, read on.

The new tags used to create client-side image maps are <MAP> and <AREA>. The basic syntax is as follows:

```
<MAP NAME="name"> <AREA [SHAPE="shape"] COORDS="x,y,..."
[HREF="reference"] [NOHREF] </MAP>
```

You can design image maps that are specified in only one file, such as your Web page, and then reused by other Web documents on your site. To update this type of map you only edit one file, whereas the older server-side maps require a separate map for each page. Another place you may start seeing this HTML extension is on non-HTTP media such as CD-ROMs. Developers could use the <MAP> and <AREA> tags to help users locate data on their CDs.

Information on image maps as well as other HTML features is available at Netscape's own "Creating Net Sites" page. The URL is http://home.netscape.com/assist/net_sites/index.html.

HTML Basics

Now that you've learned how to create pages using PowerStart, let's take a look at what's going on behind the scenes.

All Web pages are written in a language called HTML (HyperText Markup Language), a subset of SGML (Standard Generalized Markup Language). HTML is nothing but ASCII text with embedded codes representing instructions for the proper display of that text, or for initiating actions such as linking to another site. The most basic HTML commands tell the Web browser program what font size and style to use, how to break up paragraphs, when to use bulleted lists, and so forth.

Netscape's PowerStart feature actually generates HTML code based on your requirements. But as you get more serious about Web authoring, you'll probably want to create some pages without using this facility.

I've found that the best way to start learning HTML is to study the content and structure of the pages you visit. You can look at the source code for the page you're on simply by selecting Document Source from Netscape Navigator 3.0's View menu. You can even save the source under a different filename on your own system by choosing Save As from the File menu. You can then use it as a template for your new HTML file, which can be edited in Notepad or any other text editor. If you get really serious, you should pick up the latest version of Netscape Navigator Gold, which includes a specialized full-featured editor for Web pages.

TIP

If you get Navigator Gold, check out Netscape's Gold Rush Tool Kit (available at Netscape's Web site). The Gold Rush Tool Kit provides wizards and templates that automate the process of creating HTML pages, making it as easy as creating a PowerStart page. Unfortunately, the Tool Kit will only work with Navigator Gold, not with the standard version of Navigator 3.0.

HTML files on most Web servers have the extension .HTML. Since DOS and versions of Windows prior to Windows 95 do not support extensions of more than three characters, however, Windows HTML files end with the extension .HTM. If you do not use the .HTM extension, Netscape Navigator 3.0 will not recognize your files as valid HTML pages.

Netscape Navigator 3.0 lets you preview or test any HTML documents you create. To view a local HTML file, choose Open File from the File menu.

There are several excellent HTML reference areas online, as shown in Table 12-1. These pages will teach you the basics of HTML authoring.

Site	URL
HyperText Markup Language: Working and Background Materials	http://www.w3.org/hypertext/WWW/MarkUp/MarkUp.html
Peter Flynn's "How to Write HTML"	http://kcgl1.eng.ohio-state.edu:80/www/doc/htmldoc.html
Introduction to HTML Documentation	http://www.hprc.utoronto.ca/HTMLdocs/NewHTML/intro.html

Table 12-1: *Popular HTML references.*

There are also lots of other resources available right from the Netscape site. But if you want to start with more general information regarding the World Wide Web (straight from the horse's mouth), the best resource is the W3 Consortium Web server (http://www.w3.org/). The European Laboratory for Particle Physics (CERN), the folks who developed the Web, created this site and recently handed the task of maintaining it over to the W3 Consortium. This is a great clearinghouse for software information.

To show you how simple HTML coding can be, here's a template for the beginning of a customized Web page. Type the following text into any text editor such as Notepad:

```
<HTML>
<TITLE>My Favorites</TITLE>
<H1>My Favorite Sites</H1>
<UL>
<LI><A HREF="http://www.netscapepress.com">Netscape Press</A>
<LI><A HREF="http://www.vmedia.com">Ventana Online</A>
<LI><A HREF="http://home.netscape.com/">Netscape</A>
</UL>
</HTML>
```

Save this file with an .HTM extension. For instance, you can call it FAVE.HTM. Then, next time you're in Netscape Navigator 3.0, select Open File from the File menu, select your new file in the File Open dialog box that appears, and click Open. Voilà, you're a Web author!

WHAT ARE TARGETED WINDOWS?

In Netscape Navigator 3.0, browser windows can now have names associated with them. You can have a link in one window refer to another window by using its name. When you click on the link, the document appears in the named window. If the named window is not open, Netscape Navigator 3.0 opens it and names if for you.

For HTML authors reading this, here's a sample of the syntax:

```
<A HREF "something.html" TARGET "TEST"> Click to open the
TEST window</A>
```

PUBLISHING YOUR WEB PAGE ON THE NET

Once you've created the world's best Web page, you may become eager to share it with the world. Fortunately, many Internet access providers are happy to rent out space on their servers. Some might not charge any extra for this, as long as you keep your storage needs down to a meg or two. Give your ISP a call to see what the deal is.

And of course if you get *really* serious, you can even set up your own Web server. The quickest and easiest way to do this is using Netscape's FastTrack product. And of course, you'll need the *Official Netscape FastTrack Book*, which I worked on and may be in print by the time you read this. Hey, what's wrong with a little shameless self-promotion?

MOVING ON

Browsing the Web is half the fun. The other half is starting to create your own content. You don't have to be a graphic designer or a programmer to create your own personal workspace or Web pages. All it takes is a little imagination, some good ideas, and of course some cool links.

And speaking of cool links, wait till you see Chapter 12, "Our Favorite Sites." (Can you believe I resisted the temptation to call it "My Favorite Pings"?) Of course you can find plenty of great Web sites using tools available from Netscape's own site: the What's New and What's Cool lists, the Destinations page, and the search engines on the Net Search page. But it always helps to have a few pointers from someone you know, or at least from somebody who wrote a book you're reading. Now let's get cruising—or surfing—or whatever it is this year!

12

Our Favorite Net Resources

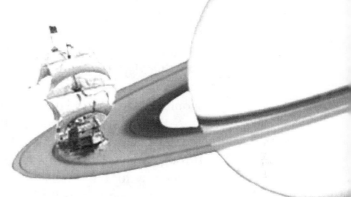

Now that you can use Netscape Navigator 3.0 effectively, it's time to get out there and discover some really cool sites! You already know the best ways to get started:

- Netscape's own What's Cool? page.
- Netscape's What's New? page.
- Some of the directories such as Yahoo! that are accessible from Netscape Navigator 3.0's Net Directory button.
- Netscape's Destinations page.

These are great resources. But I thought I'd let you in on some of my own favorite pages and hangouts. This is a very personal list. It is by no means exhaustive, as that would be impossible, nor have I attempted to cover a broad range of topic areas. These are sites that I've found useful, instructive, inspiring, amusing, or just a bit peculiar. I've divided the entries into categories and listed them in alphabetical order, from Art to Web Info. But hypermedia tends to defy categorization. If you don't find a site you're looking for under one category, try a related one. And if you have purchased the version of this book that comes with a CD-ROM in the back cover, you can browse an electronic version of this chapter, clicking on links to go directly to sites that interest you.

Except for e-mail and newsgroup resources, I've included an address in the standard URL format so that you can use it directly in Netscape Navigator 3.0. For many of the Gopher sites listed, I've also included path information. This path simply guides you to the appropriate area by following the Gopher's menu system.

A word of warning: The Internet is constantly under construction. A site that was there yesterday may have outgrown its current server and moved, or the person maintaining the site may have decided it was too much trouble and closed it down. All of the addresses included were accurate at time of publication, but it wouldn't surprise me if some sites had moved or closed down since then. Yes, the Internet really *is* that changeable! In many cases, if a site has moved, you'll be able to get to the new location through a link that's kept at the old location. And you can always try looking for the site using Navigator's Net Search page. But if a site's gone, sometimes it's just plain gone. The best advice is simply to move on. There are plenty more out there!

TIP

Don't forget to create bookmarks or desktop shortcuts for your favorite sites.

The beauty of the Net is that you can't get too lost, so feel free to follow paths that lead away from our suggestions. With Netscape Navigator 3.0 and a willingness to explore, you'll soon be discovering all sorts of wonders that I've never even heard of!

ART: VISUAL

@art

Type: WWW

Address: http://gertrude.art.uiuc.edu/@art/gallery.html

Summary: An interesting "gallery" of new visual art that explores some of the possibilities inherent in the Web. This site is a must-see for electronic artists as well as anyone interested in visual information and Web design.

Arts Online

Type: FTP

Address: ftp://nic.funet.fi/pub/doc/library/artbase.txt.Z

Summary: A list of arts-related resources on the Net.

Australian National University Art History Server

Type: WWW

Address: http://rubens.anu.edu.au/imageserve/

Summary: Michael Greenhalgh, professor of art history at Australian National University, compiled this collection of over 2,800 print images from the 15th to 19th centuries and another 6,000 images of classical and European architecture and architectural sculpture. Some highlights: a tutorial on the Palace of Diocletian at Split, a survey of the architecture of Islam, and a tour of classical sites in Turkey.

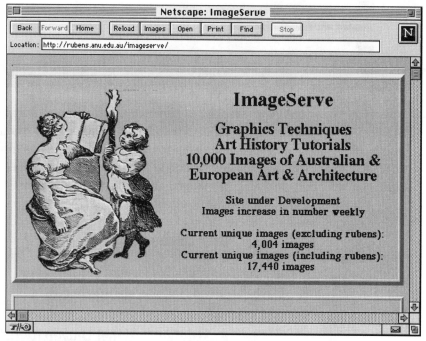

The Australian National University Art History Server.

Carlos' Coloring Book

Type: WWW

Address: http://robot0.ge.uiuc.edu/~carlosp/color/

Summary: A fun site, especially for younger kids, though they will need lots of help from an adult. By pointing and clicking you can choose virtual crayons and color in any one of several pictures. This is great for artistically challenged people like me, because there is no way to color outside the lines. After your masterpiece is finished, you can download it.

Fractals

Type: FTP

Address: ftp://csus.edu/pub/alt.fractals.pictures/

Summary: Tons of fractal images in GIF format. They're arranged in directories by date; as of this writing, the latest is 1991, but there's a lot of cool stuff.

Fractals Fractals Fractals . . .

Type: WWW

Address: http://www.fishnet.net/~ayb/

Summary: Yes, another fractals page. I never get tired of them, and so this is a favorite site. Here you can find over 500 beautiful computer-generated graphics as well as links to other fractal sites. Enjoy.

Art Baker Fractal Images.

Gallery of Interactive On Line Geometry

Type: WWW

Address: http://www.geom.umn.edu/apps/gallery.html

Summary: Use Kali to learn about the 17 crystallographic symmetry groups of the plane. This work is similar to that seen in some of M. C. Escher's woodcuts. Play a pinball-style game to explore the effects of negatively curved space. Much more involving symmetry groups and angle geometries. This page is maintained by The Geometry Center at the University of Minnesota.

Institute of Egyptian Art and Archaeology

Type: WWW

Address: http://www.memst.edu/egypt/main.html

Summary: Take a color tour of Egypt or view the exhibit of Egyptian artifacts at the University of Memphis. The Institute of Egyptian Art and Archaeology is part of the Department of Art at the University of Memphis.

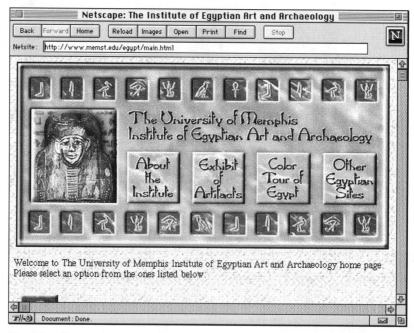

Egyptian Art.

Kaleidospace

Type: WWW

Address: http://kspace.com

Summary: A commercial site, but well worth a look. Independent artists gather here to display and sell their work.

Kaleidospace.

Kodak's Sample Digital Images Page

Type: WWW

Address: http://www.kodak.com/digitalImaging/ samples/samples.shtml

Summary: Beautiful photographs, slickly presented. There's also valuable information on how the images were prepared.

Origami

Type: FTP
Address: ftp://nstn.ns.ca/listserv/origami-l/
Summary: Learn new folding techniques, get display ideas, tips, and bibliographies. Subscribe to mailing lists by sending e-mail to origami-l-request@ntsn.ns.ca.

The Planet Earth Home Page

Type: WWW
Address: http://white.nosc.mil/info_modern.html
Summary: Another good index to what's out there on the Web, with an excellent Getting Started page for novices.

Strange Interactions

Type: WWW
Address: http://amanda.physics.wisc.edu/show.html
Summary: An online art exhibit by John Jacobsen. From his artist's statement, "My work is an attempt to give a concrete aspect to the subconscious." Definitely worth checking out!

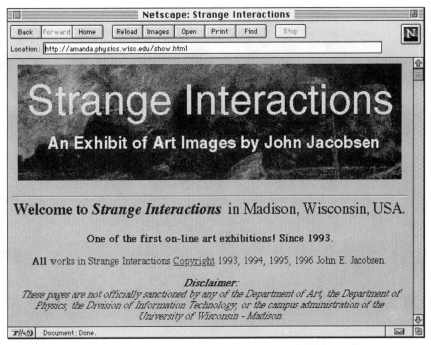

Strange Interactions.

The Thing

Type: WWW

Address: http://www.thing.net/thingnyc

Summary: Serious talk about serious contemporary art. I like to have a glass of red wine in my hand when I visit this site.

WebMuseum

Type: WWW

Address: http://mistral.enst.fr/

Summary: Great art classics right on your computer screen! It takes a while to download some of the paintings, but it's still quicker and cheaper than flying to Paris.

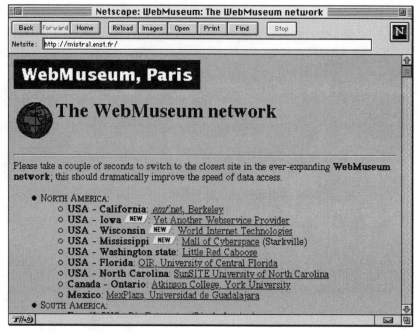

WebMuseum.

Some Related Newsgroups

alt.artcom   rec.arts.misc

alt.postmodern   sci.fractals

rec.arts.fine

Arts: Multidisciplinary

The Fluxus Page

Type: WWW

Address: http://www.panix.com/~fluxus/

Summary: A grab-bag of art, music, and writing by the Fluxus pioneers of the early sixties (George Maciunas, Wolf Vostell, LaMonte Young, Yoko Ono, Philip Corner, etc.) and by later neo-Fluxus artists. A must-visit site for anybody interested in the history of contemporary art or interested in forms of expression that are innovative and fun at the same time.

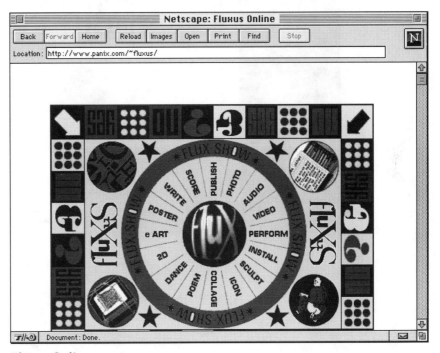

Fluxus Online.

IAMfree

Type: WWW

Address: http://www.rahul.net/iamfree/

Summary: This "Internet Arts Museum for free" offers interesting art, music, and literature in a virtual museum setting. All of the work included was specifically intended for this form of free Internet distribution.

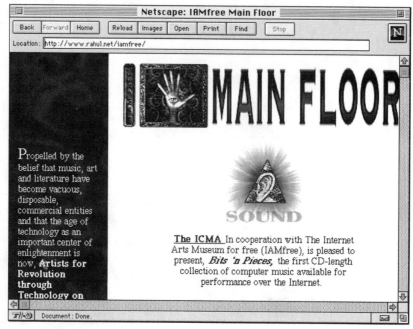

Internet Arts Museum.

Life With Father

Type: WWW

Address: http://www.art.uiuc.edu/ludgate/the/place/stories/life_with_father/myfather.html

Summary: This is a poetic, autobiographical story-with-pictures by the artist Joseph Squiers. It shows some of the possibilities for highly personal and highly professional artwork on the Web.

Megadeth, Arizona

Type: WWW

Address: http://caprec.com/Megadeth/megadeth.html

Summary: A well-designed and media-rich site maintained by the band Megadeth. Some of the highlights include a "HorrorScopes" service and a set of links to peculiar freeware programs. This is a good site for those who like their entertainment slightly spooky.

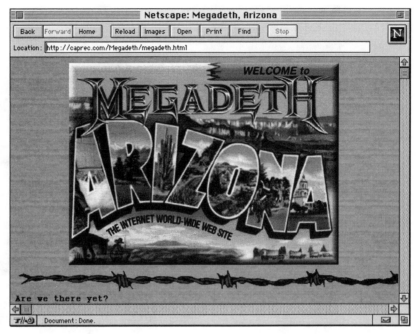

Megadeth, Arizona.

Postmodern Culture

Type: WWW

Address: http://jefferson.village.Virginia.EDU/pmc/

Summary: Postmodern Culture is an interesting, heady e-zine exploring recent developments in culture and the arts. It includes some poetry and fiction as well as essays.

The Singapore Graffiti Page

Type: WWW

Address: http://davinci.technet.sg/BOG/

Summary: This is an odd one. Remember Michael Fay, the American boy who was caned for scrawling graffiti in Singapore? This Web site, apparently sponsored in part by the Singapore government, lets you spray-paint *virtual* walls to your heart's content. (I didn't play around for too long, though, because I don't like even virtual spankings.)

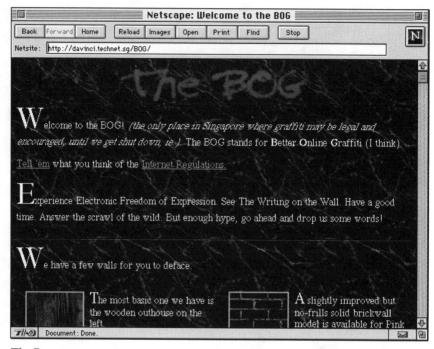

The Bog.

BOOKS, LITERATURE & ZINES

Alternative-X

Type: WWW

Address: http://www.altx.com/althome2.html

Summary: This is *the* place to visit if you want to catch up on recent trends in literary fiction, especially the so-called "avant-pop" phenomenon. This site includes stories and polemics by such great, innovative writers as Derek Pell, Euridice, and Harold Jaffe. Rather than playing with the visual possibilities of HTML, Alt-X serves up prose by the bucket-load, so if you're a literary type, there's an excellent bang/buck ratio.

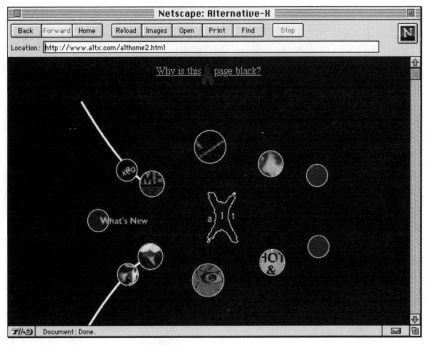

Alternative-X.

The Asylum
Type: WWW
Address: http://asylum.cid.com/
Summary: This adventurous site exploits the interactive possibilities of the Web. It includes collaborative stories and poems that you can add to as well as a "lite brite" that lets you exercise your imagination by creating pictures out of little circles of color.

Basement Full of Books
Type: FTP or WWW
Address: ftp://ftp.greyware.com/pub/Literature/BFoB/ basement_full_of_books.txt

http://www.greyware.com/bfob/

Summary: Get autographed books (with personal inscrip-
tions) directly from their authors. Lots of science
fiction authors like Ursula K. Le Guin, Harlan
Ellison, David Brin, and Joe Haldeman. The list is
updated every month. You get a short synopsis of
each book, along with ordering information.

You can also get this list by sending an e-mail
message to mail-server@rtfm.mit.edu. Put "send
usenet/news.answers/books/basement-full-of-
books" (without the quotes) in the body of the
message.

Bookstore List

Type: WWW
Address: http://www.cis.ohio-state.edu/hypertext/faq/
usenet/books/stores/top.html
Summary: This site presents, in hypertext form, lists of the
best bookstores around the world. (They are
taken from Usenet FAQs.)

Bordeaux and Prague

Type: WWW
Address: http://www.freedonia.com/~carl/bp/
Summary: Carl Steadman, the creator of the Bordeaux and
Prague page, is a story writer and artist whose
unusual work was influenced by postmodern
French thought and Situationism. He uses the
richness of HTML to present complex works
effectively and with humor. This material is not
everybody's cup of espresso, but I love it!

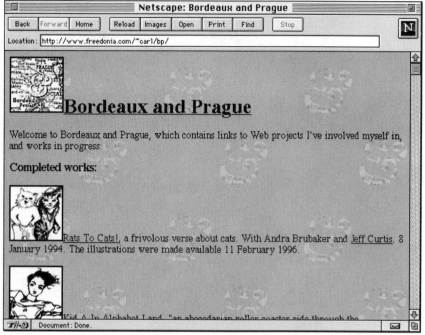

Bordeaux and Prague.

Crisp

Type: WWW

Address: http://www.crispzine.com

Summary: A nicely designed general interest zine featuring articles, fiction, and poetry. Crisp is geared toward the under-thirty Web-head crowd.

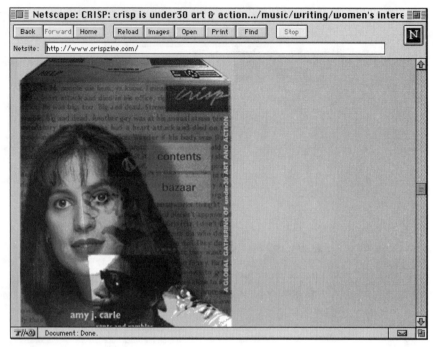

Crisp.

Delirium

Type: WWW

Address: http://pathfinder.com/twep/Features/
Delirium/DelTitle.html

Summary: *Delirium*—a novel that utilizes the interactivity of
the Web—is an interesting example of hyper-
media in a literary context. Worth checking out if
you're interested in how technology creates new
possibilities for the arts.

Feed

Type: WWW

Address: http://www.feedmag.com

Summary: Cultural, political, and artistic commentary with
a technological bent. Good solidly designed site.

Foxy

Type: WWW

Address: http://www.tumyeto.com/tydo/foxy

Summary: Got a teenage daughter? Send her here. Oh wait a minute, you *are* a teenage daughter? Check it out!

The Hypertext Fiction Page

Type: WWW

Address: http://www.ugcs.caltech.edu/~benedett/hyper.html

Summary: A good introduction to the theory and practice of hypertext fiction, including a few interesting examples. This page is maintained by students at Caltech.

Hypertext Fiction.

John Labovitz's E-ZINE LIST

Type: WWW
Address: http://www.meer.net/~johnl/e-zine-list/index.html
Summary: A directory of over 175 zines available on the Net.
Contact: John Labovitz
johnl@meer.net

Libido Magazine

Type: WWW
Address: http://www.indra.com/libido/cover3.html
Summary: In its print version, *Libido* is one of the best and "classiest" magazines that focuses on erotic art, photography, and writing. The electronic version is just as good. This is erotica for people who are not afraid to think.

The Nancy Drew Page

Type: WWW
Address: http://sunsite.unc.edu/cheryb/nancy.drew/ktitle.html
Summary: I love this site! Nancy Drew from a historical perspective. From a psychological perspective. From a sociological perspective. From an artistic perspective. This is pay dirt for pop culture fans and deconstructionists. By the time you're done here, you'll know Nancy better than you know yourself.

Nancy Drew, Eternal Prom Queen.

Online Fairy Tales

Type: FTP

Address: ftp://info.umd.edu/inforM/EdRes/ ReadingRoom/Fiction/FairyTales

Summary: I always enjoyed telling my kids stories when I put them to bed, but quite often I couldn't remember exactly how a particular fairy tale went and ended up improvising my own bizarre plots. If only I'd had Internet access I could have FTPed to this site and quickly brushed up on any of the almost 100 tales provided!

STIM

Type: WWW

Address: http://www.stim.com/

Summary: This is one of the most interesting new zines on the Web. It features good solid writing, lots of ear and eye candy, and some excellent regular columns including Daniel Radosh's perceptive analyses of the Web itself.

Urban Desires

Type: WWW

Address: http://desires.com/

Summary: An *excellent* and intelligent zine full of provocative articles, interviews, reviews, and artwork. The masthead says it all: "An Interactive Magazine of Metropolitan Passions."

Word Magazine

Type: WWW

Address: http://www.word.com/

Summary: No, this has nothing to do with Microsoft Word. It's a big, intelligent New York–based zine that emphasizes high-quality writing and colorful graphics. It's sort of an East Coast *HotWired*, but with more of an emphasis on the arts and pop culture and less of an emphasis on things cyber. Great animation. Definitely worth a look!

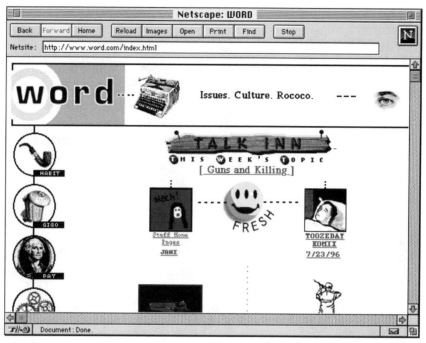

Word *magazine.*

Some Related Newsgroups

alt.books.reviews	bit.listserv.literary
alt.books.technical	misc.writing
alt.etext	rec.arts.poems
alt.mythology	rec.arts.prose
alt.usage.english	rec.mag
alt.zines	

 **BUSINESS**

Doing Business With Hong Kong

Type: WWW
Address: http://www.hk.super.net/~rlowe/consult/
Summary: Basic trade information, a trade contacts service, and a list of companies by trade.

Downtown Anywhere

Type: WWW

Address: http://www.awa.com/

Summary: Businesses can establish a Net presence in this virtual community. But it's not all business. Lots of Net and general reference info. Check out the library and newsstand, museums, the financial district, the sports arena and, of course, Main Street.

Marshall Space Flight Center Procurement Home Page

Type: WWW

Address: http://procure.msfc.nasa.gov

Summary: Advanced procurement information and small business assistance documents. Learn about federal streamlining initiatives. Pointers to other federal procurement sites such as the Johnson Space Center and Kennedy Space Center home pages.

Contact: Jim Bradford
GP01/Procurement Office
NASA/Marshall Space Flight Center
Huntsville, AL 35812
205/544-0306
jim.bradford@msfc.nasa.gov

STO's Internet Patent Search System

Type: WWW

Address: http://sunsite.unc.edu/patents/intropat.html

Summary: Do a title search through all U.S. patents issued since 1970.

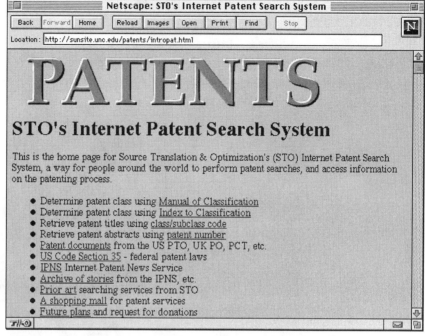

Patent Search System.

Some Related Newsgroups

alt.business.misc
alt.business.multi-level
misc.entrepreneurs

COMPUTING

Free OnLine Dictionary of Computing

Type: WWW
Address: http://wombat.doc.ic.ac.uk/
Summary: Searchable dictionary that includes terms related to general computing, programming languages, networks, domain theory, acronyms, computing history, and just about anything else that has to do with computers.

Global Monitor

Type: WWW
Address: http://nccr.monitor.ca:80/monitor/
Summary: A cool electronic mag loaded with computer-related info.

Global Monitor *magazine.*

PC's and Macintoshes

Type: Gopher
Address: gopher://wiretap.spies.com
Path: Wiretap Online Library / Technical Information / PC's and Macintoshes
Summary: Lots of articles and tips for both PC and Mac users.

Toll-Free Numbers

Type: FTP

Address: ftp://oak.oakland.edu/pub/misc/telephone/ tollfree.num

Summary: Toll-free numbers for a bunch of computer companies.

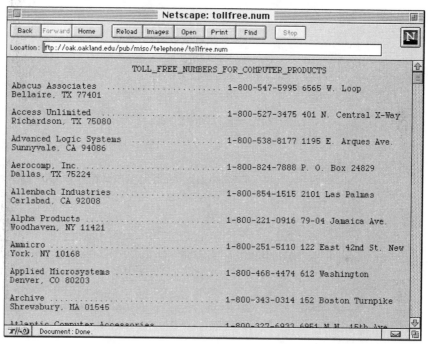

Toll-free number index.

UNB Graphic Services Desktop Publishing Resource Base

Type: WWW

Address: http://degaulle.hil.unb.ca/UNB_G_Services/ GSHomePage.html

Summary: Plenty of plugs for UNB's services, but enough pointers to clip-art collections, font banks, and other DTP resources to make it a valuable site.

Virus Information

Type: FTP
Address: ftp://oak.oakland.edu/pub/misc/virus
Summary: Technical information about most known viruses. Includes DOS and Mac data.

Some Related Newsgroups

alt.cad.autocad	comp.misc
alt.cyberpunk.tech	comp.theory
alt.privacy	comp.virus
clari.nb.general	comp.sys.misc

CULTURE & DIVERSITY

American Memory From the Library of Congress

Type: WWW
Address: http://rs6.loc.gov/amhome.html
Summary: A nicely done glimpse of America's past, including collections of photographs, text, and even sound recordings. Lots of material on American culture and history, most of it from special collections of the Library of Congress.

Native American Net Server

Type: Gopher
Address: gopher://alpha1.csd.uwm.edu
Path: UWM Information, Native American Net Server
Summary: Articles and cases on Indian law, book reviews, job openings, education, Native American newsletters, even Native American fonts.
Contact: Michael Wilson
University of Wisconsin at Milwaukee
mwilson@alpha2.csd.uwm.edu

Resources for Diversity

Type: WWW

Address: http://www.nova.edu/Inter-Links/
diversity.html

Summary: This page has links to the African Studies Web,
Chicano-LatinoNet, Disability Information,
Diversity at the University of Michigan, the Inter-
Tribal Network for Native Americans, the Latin
American Network Information Center, Minority
Online Service (MOLIS), Omni-Cultural Aca-
demic Resource, Gay/Lesbian Resources, and
Women's Studies at the University of Maryland.

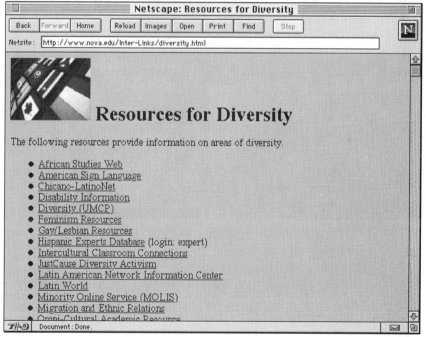

Resources for Diversity.

Women's Resource Project

Type: WWW

Address: http://sunsite.unc.edu/cheryb/women/wshome.html

Summary: *Women's studies:* Pointers to women's studies programs at several colleges and universities. *Women and literature:* Bios of female authors from Harriet Beecher Stowe to Marge Piercy, from Jane Austen to Maya Angelou. A guide to women's resources on the Net.

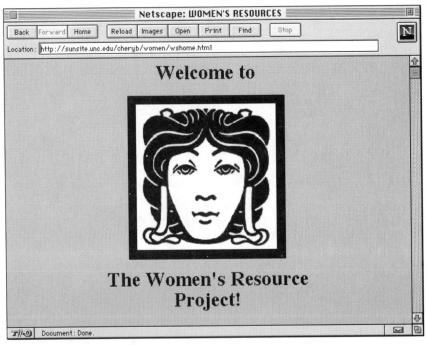

Women's Resource Project.

Some Related Newsgroups

alt.discrimination
soc.culture.african.american
soc.women

EDUCATION

Higher Education Resources and Opportunities

Type: Telnet

Address: telnet://fedix.fie.com

Login: new

Summary: The Minority OnLine Information Service is an online database service with all sorts of information about scholarships, grants, fellowships, conferences, research opportunities, and other opportunities for minorities and women.

Hillside Elementary School

Type: WWW

Address: http://hillside.coled.umn.edu/

Summary: Every student in Mrs. Collins' sixth grade class has created his or her own home page. Lots more planned for this site, a joint project of Hillside Elementary School in Cottage Grove, Minnesota, and the University of Minnesota College of Education.

Reading Disabilities

Type: FTP

Address: ftp://ftp.spies.com/Library/Article/Misc/disable.rd

Summary: Extremely clear and well-written paper, "Neuropsychological Bases of Educational Disabilities," by Robert Zenhausern, Ph.D., professor of psychology at St. John's University. It's a scholarly paper, but its style makes it accessible to the lay public.

Schoolnet Resource Manual

Type: FTP

Address: ftp://schoolnet.carleton.ca/pub/English/ Manuals/

Summary: This is a huge file with about a kazillion pointers to science, technology, and education resources on the Net.

The manual's directory is full of Net information. Check out the Big Dummy's Guide to the Internet, Electric Mystic Guide to Internet, FTP Introduction, E-Mail Intro, Gopher_FAQ, Internet Basics, and Guidelines-Netiquette.

U.S. Department of Education

Type: WWW

Address: http://inet.ed.gov/

Summary: Get press releases and information about funding opportunities, speeches prepared for the U.S. Secretary of Education, Teachers' and Researchers' Guides to the U.S. Department of Education, and links to other educational resources.

ENTERTAINMENT

eye magazine

Type: WWW

Address: http://www.eye.net

Summary: This is Toronto's premier arts-listings weekly. Not only does it inform you of what's going on in Toronto, it also presents interesting features on musicians and other artists. This is a well-thought-out Web page.

Interlog EYE.NET.

The East Village

Type: WWW

Address: http://www.theeastvillage.com/

Summary: *The East Village* is the premier example of an entirely new category of Internet entertainment: the Web soap opera. Of course instead of suburban neurotics the regulars in this drama are a bit closer to home, or to home page: they are Noo Yawkers dealing with the vicissitudes of passionate bohemianism. The producers have really done a good job with this. Let's hear it for the Internet, offering us better and better ways to keep from getting any work done.

ENVIRONMENT

Ask-a-Geologist

Type: e-mail

Address: ask-a-geologist@octopus.wr.usgs.gov

Summary: Ever wonder what kind of rock is the most common in your area? How the mountains were formed? When the next earthquake is likely to hit your town? I'm not sure how the U.S. Geological Survey has time for this, but if you send your question to the address above you'll receive an answer within a couple of days. And since this service is free, you won't lose your chert. (Sorry about that.)

Cascades Volcano Observatory Home Page

Type: WWW

Address: http://vulcan.wr.usgs.gov/home.html

Summary: Arm yourself with information about volcanoes and other natural hazards. Get hazard assessments and warnings during volcano crises. Find out about the International Volcano Disaster Assistance Program. Links to Alaska and Hawaii volcano observatories.

The EnviroLink Network

Type: Gopher

Address: gopher://envirolink.org

Summary: As you'd guess, this site is full of information about ecology, environmental groups, endangered species, and environmental law.

Institute for Global Communications (IGC)

Type: Gopher

Address: gopher://gopher.igc.apc.org

Summary: From the welcome message: "IGC runs four computer networks known as PeaceNet(TM), EcoNet(TM), ConflictNet, and LaborNet. IGC is the U.S. member of the Association for Progressive Communications, a 16-country association of computer networks working for peace, human rights, environmental protection, social justice, and sustainability."

TIOTS! (This is one terrific site!)

Contact: Institute for Global Communications
18 De Boom St.
San Francisco, CA 94107
415/442-0220
igc-info@igc.apc.org

Linkages Home Page

Type: WWW

Address: http://portal.mbnet.mb.ca/linkage/

Summary: Provided by the International Institute for Sustainable Development, publishers of the Earth Negotiations Bulletin. Links to information about international environment and development meetings such as the World Summit for Social Development, the International Conference on Population & Development, and the Earth Negotiations Bulletin.

Linkages.

Ozone Depletion

Type: FTP

Address: ftp://rtfm.mit.edu/pub/usenet/news.answers/ozone-depletion/

Summary: FAQ files about the depletion of the ozone layer are posted monthly. There's a special section for the Antarctic ozone hole.

Students for the Exploration and Development of Space

Type: Gopher

Address: gopher://seds.lpl.arizona.edu

Summary: This site includes the latest information about celestial events as well as a wealth of material related to space exploration.

The Virtual Desert

Type: WWW

Address: http://www.well.com/user/vegas/desert/Top/index.html

Summary: If you love the American desert as much as I do, you'll love this Web page.

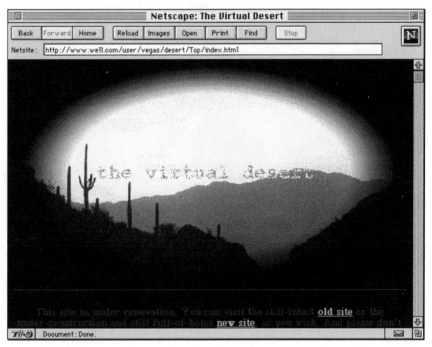

The Virtual Desert.

Some Related Newsgroups

bit.listerv.biosph-1

sci.environment

FINANCE

Credit Info

Type: FTP

Address: ftp://rtfm.mit.edu/pub/usenet/news.answers/
consumer-credit-faq/

Summary: Is Mastercard better than Visa? What is a secured
card? Do I want a fixed-rate or floating-rate card?
Why is a discount better than a rebate? The
answers to these and many other burning consumer questions can be found in the consumer
credit FAQ, which was compiled from questions
asked on the misc.consumers newsgroup.

Economics

Type: Gopher

Address: gopher://nysernet.org

Path: Special Collections:Business and Economic
Development

Summary: If the world of business is your world, have a
blast exploring these resources. Among them: a
FAQ on advertising on the Internet, the Basic
Guide to Exporting, Commerce Business Daily,
and a U.S. Patent database.

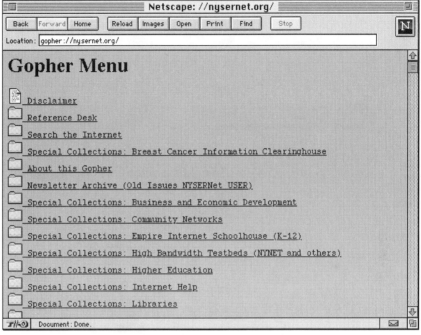

NYSE Gopher.

Foreign Exchange Rates

Type: Gopher

Address: gopher://una.hh.lib.umich.edu

Path: ebb /monetary statistics/ FRB foreign exchange rates

Summary: These figures from the Federal Reserve Bank of New York are updated weekly.

Koblas Currency Converter

Type: WWW

Address: http://bin.gnn.com/cgi-bin/gnn/currency

Summary: This page is updated weekly. By default, the page shows the currency rates of over 50 countries relative to U.S. currency (e.g., one U.S. dollar is worth 1.3605 dollars in Australia). To get currency rates relative to another country, just click the country you want.

Some Related Newsgroups

clari.biz.currencies.us_dollar
clari.biz.finance
clari.biz.economy.world

FOOD & DRINK

The Chocolate Lovers' Page

Type: WWW
Address: http://bc.emanon.net/chocolate/
Summary: Lots of links to information about everybody's favorite designer drug.

Food Recipes Database

Type: Gopher
Address: gopher://gopher.aecom.yu.edu
Path: Internet Resources / Miscellaneous / Search the Food Recipes Database
Summary: Huge searchable recipe list.

HOT HOT HOT

Type: WWW
Address: http://www.hot.presence.com/g/p/H3/
Summary: No, it's not another one of those virtual sex sites you keep reading about. This one's a highly organized list of hot sauces from around the world. If you like your food spicy, check this out!

Hot Hot Hot.

Over the Coffee

Type: WWW

Address: http://www.cappuccino.com/

Summary: If you're a coffee lover, it's all here. Coffee trivia and factoids, a travelers' guide to coffee houses, a list of coffee-related Usenet groups, a coffee recipe collection, lists of coffee (and tea) books, a glossary of coffee terminology, and resources for coffee professionals.

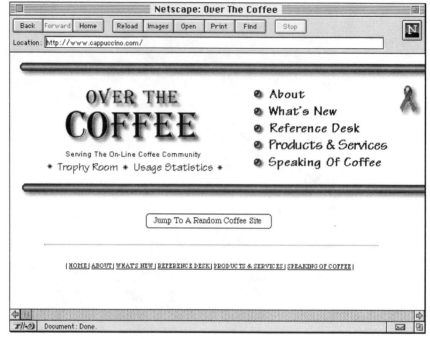

Over the Coffee.

Patriots' Trail Girl Scout Council

Type: WWW

Address: http://www.ptgirlscouts.org/ptgirlscouts.html

Summary: I've listed this Boston-area scouting page with other food-related Web sites because it lets you order your cookies online! Of course, the Scouts advise that you should support your local troop first, but if nobody comes knocking on your door and you've got a Thin Mints jones that just won't go away . . .

The Real Beer Site

Type: WWW
Address: http://realbeer.com/
Summary: If you want to hear about Coors and Anheuser-Busch products, watch football; if you want to find out about micro-breweries and carefully hand-crafted beers, check out this Web page. The emphasis here is on old-fashioned *quality*, and there is a wealth of information about beers from all areas of the country.

Real Beer.

Recipes

Type: FTP
Address: ftp://gatekeeper.dec.com/pub/recipes
Summary: A collection of over 500 recipes.

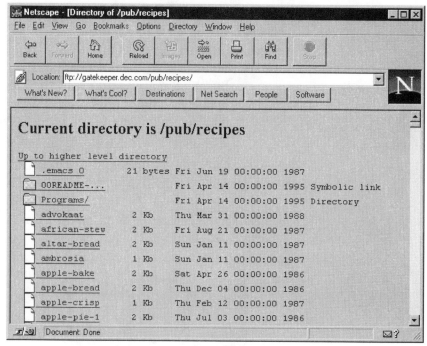

Recipes.

The Recipes Folder

Type: WWW

Address: http://english-www.hss.cmu.edu/recipes.html

Summary: If you're a vegetarian, you'll feel right at home here. If you're a flesh eater, you'll have to put up with the following subject headings: "Vegetarian Stuff," "Dead Animals," and "Things Possibly Involving Dead Animals and Possibly Not." Whatever your culinary predilections, this is a terrific list of recipe sources.

The Single Malt Page

Type: WWW

Address: http://www.dcs.ed.ac.uk/home/jhb/whisky/

Summary: I hate to admit it, but I've spent a lot of time at this site. Here you can learn everything there is to know about fine, single malt Scotch whiskey, or *whisky*, as they say over there. This is a serious, professionally designed Web page that includes a clickable map of the different whiskey-producing regions and even an Excel spreadsheet! As a concession to the nonpurists of the drinking world, there is even some recently added information on blended whiskeys.

Whisky!

Vegetarianism

Type: FTP

Address: ftp://flubber.cs.umd.edu/other/tms/veg

Summary: All kinds of info for vegetarians and would-be vegetarians—FAQs, recipes, and so on. Another vegetarian resource to check out is the rec.food.veg newsgroup.

Veggies Unite!

Type: WWW

Address: http://www.honors.indiana.edu/~veggie/recipes.cgi/

Summary: A searchable index of over 900 vegetarian recipes. Links to other nutrition and health sites.

Some Related Newsgroups

alt.college.food	rec.food.historic
alt.folklore.herbs	rec.food.recipes
alt.food.fat-free	rec.food.restaurants
alt.gourmand	rec.food.sourdough
alt.support.diet	rec.food.veg
rec.crafts.winemaking	sci.med.nutrition
rec.food.cooking	

FUN & GAMES

The Beavis and Butthead Home Page

Type: WWW

Address: http://calvin.hsc.colorado.edu/

Summary: Heh—heh heh heh—heh heh—.

Chiba Woo

Type: WWW

Address: http://sensemedia.net/sprawl/

Summary: What do you get when you cross a MOO with a Web document? A WOO, of course. As you may know, a MOO is an interactive online game with object-oriented extensions. This site is an interesting experiment in extending MOOing to the Web. It also contains some excellent links to other sites.

Chiba Woo.

Ferret Central

Type: WWW

Address: http://www.optics.rochester.edu:8080/users/pgreene/central.html

Summary: I keep threatening to get one of these wonderful animals, and after browsing this site, which includes a thorough FAQ, beautiful photos, and links to other ferret-related sites, you might want one too. Remember: *They are not rodents!*

Fly With Us!

Type: WWW

Address: http://www.interedu.com/mig29/

Summary: Have you ever wanted to climb into the cockpit of a MiG-29, roar down the runway and then fly at supersonic speeds to the edge of space? We're not talking virtual reality here, this is the real thing! For a price—make that a *hefty* price—Fly With Us!, Inc., offers you a first-class vacation in Russia that includes a flight with a "co-pilot" who hopefully knows more about the aircraft than you do. The Web site provides you with a description of the various vacation packages and even an in-flight video clip. I dare you to do this!

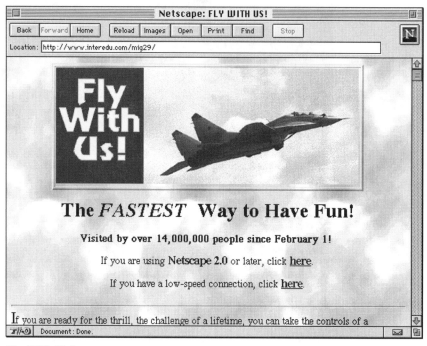

Fly With Us!

Games Domain

Type: WWW
Address: http://www.gamesdomain.com/
Summary: If you have any interest in games, check out this page. It has links to Usenet groups and games FAQs, a Walkthroughs link that can get you unstuck from several popular games, and over 100 links to games-related Web pages and FTP sites.

Hollywood Online

Type: WWW

Address: http://www.hollywood.com/

Summary: This is the place to find out about the latest Hollywood movies. Not only does it include listings and discussion boards, it exploits the multimedia power of the Web by offering up sound clips and video trailers.

Hollywood Online.

Killer List of Video Games

Type: Gopher

Address: gopher://wiretap.spies.com

Path: Wiretap Online Library/Mass Media/Games and Video Games/The Killer List of Video Games

Summary: Get the inside scoop on your favorite games through files like Definitive Arcade Video Cheats,

SEGA Genesis Secrets, Killer List of Video Games, Home Video Games History, and (yes, this is for real) The Rules of Tiddlywinks.

Roller Coasters

Type: FTP

Address: ftp://gboro.rowan.edu/pub/Coasters

Summary: FAQs, reviews of parks and coasters, animations, JPG, and GIF images.

Sony

Type: WWW

Address: http://www.sony.com

Summary: As you would expect, this is a large, well-done, slick site that includes lots of information on movies, CDs, concerts, electronic equipment, and so on. It's a nice mall to visit.

Sony (no baloney).

TV Net

Type: WWW

Address: http://tvnet.com/TVnet.html

Summary: Want to find out what's on tonight? TV Net can tell you! This page also includes a wealth of TV-related information and links to other sites. Put your computer near the couch and you'll never have to get up again.

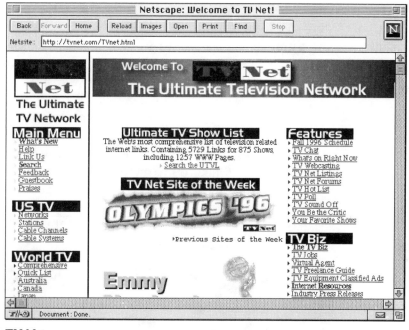

TV Net.

TV2NITE

Type: e-mail

Address: listserv@necom.com (type **subscribe tv2nite-l** in message)

Summary: You're at work, but you can't keep your mind off what you're going to do when you get home. *Baywatch . . . Melrose Place . . .* a new miniseries about OJ . . . Wait a minute, was that tonight or tomorrow? Better check. But why should you have to get up from your desk just to find out what's on TV tonight? There's really no reason to work so hard at work—now you can have tonight's TV lineup e-mailed to you every day. Tip: If you work at home, you can avoid trudging over to your desk by keeping a laptop PC right by the couch!

Virtual Vegas

Type: WWW

Address: http://www.virtualvegas.com/vvhome.html

Summary: Lost Wages is one of those love-it-or-hate-it cities. Since this site does a nice job of capturing all the gaudiness and tackiness, I suspect it may be one of those love-it-or-hate-it Web pages. There are layers of annoying registration forms to get through, and the process is made even slower by traffic (Virtual Vegas has received some mass-media attention). Once you're there, though, you'll see a well-crafted piece of glitzy Americana.

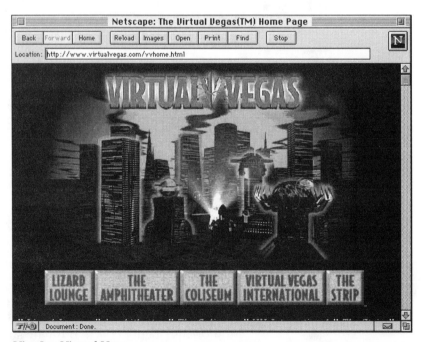

Viva Las Virtual Vegas.

WebMind Crosswords

Type: FTP

Address: ftp://rtfm.mit.edu/pub/usenet/news.answers/crossword-faq/

Summary: Crossword aficionado heaven. Guides, dictionaries, solution tips, software info, and so on. Also try ftp://pub/usenet/news.answers/puzzles/faq for a collection of mindbenders.

Zarf's List of Interactive Games on the Web

Type: WWW

Address: http://www.leftfoot.com/realgames.html

Summary: Just what it sounds like. A good hotlist.

HEALTH, MEDICINE & RECOVERY

Americans With Disabilities Act

Type: Gopher

Address: gopher://scilibx.ucsc.edu

Path: The Library / Electronic Books and Other Texts

Summary: Get the full text of the 1990 Americans with Disabilities Act.

Cornucopia of Disability Information (CODI)

Type: Gopher

Address: gopher://val-dor.cc.buffalo.edu

Summary: A great resource for those with disabilities and health professionals. Lots of digests, info on legal issues and assistance, college guides, independent living centers, and employment resources.

Dr. Greenson's Gastrointestinal and Liver Pathology Home Page

Type: WWW

Address: http://www.pds.med.umich.edu/users/greenson/

Summary: Just what you've been waiting for! It even includes pictures of a GI Case of the Month and an Infectious Case of the Month. I'm thinking of making a musical of this page.

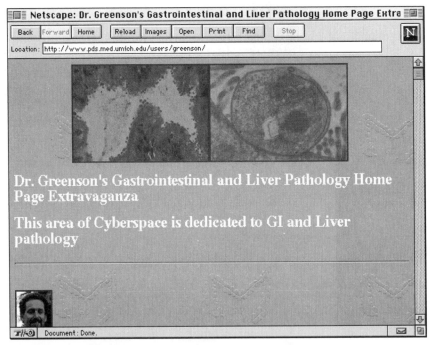

GI and Liver Pathology.

The Heart Page

Type: WWW

Address: http://sln2.fi.edu/biosci/preview/heartpreview.html

Summary: All kinds of physiological information about the human heart, with great illustrations. No, you won't learn how to keep people from breaking it.

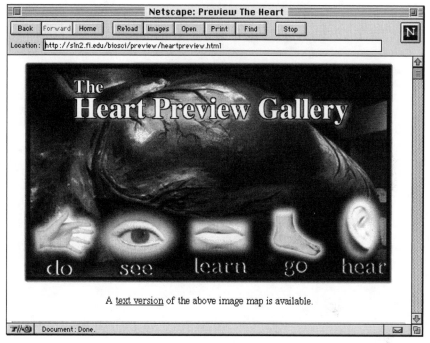

Preview the Heart.

Institute for Molecular Virology

Type: WWW

Address: http://www.bocklabs.wisc.edu/

Summary: Info about the AIDS virus, 3D images and animations of virus structures, 2D electron micrographs of viruses, online virology course material, phone book of virologists on the Net, and virology-related journal articles.

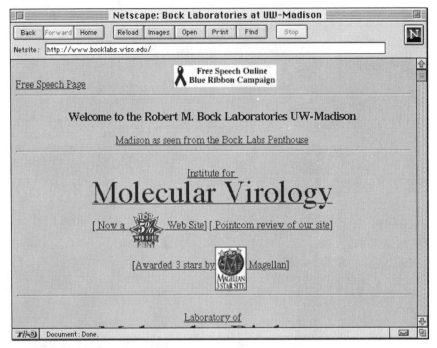

Bock Laboratories.

Midwifery and Birth Information Page

Type: WWW

Address: http://www.efn.org/~djz/birth/birthindex.html

Summary: This is my wife's favorite Web site. It includes articles on midwifery as well as prenatal and postnatal care. This is not a flashy site, but it's full of valuable information that can't be obtained elsewhere.

Midwifery, Pregnancy, and Birth-Related Information

National Toxicology Program (NTP) Home Page

Type: WWW

Address: http://ntp-server.niehs.nih.gov/

Summary: Established by the Secretary of Health and Human Services "to coordinate toxicology research and testing activities within the Department, to provide information about potentially toxic chemicals to regulatory and research agencies and the public, and to strengthen the science base in toxicology. In its 16 years, the NTP has become the world's leader in designing, conducting, and interpreting animal assays for toxicity." The annual plan describes current work being done in carcinogenesis, toxicology, genetic toxicology, and chemical disposition.

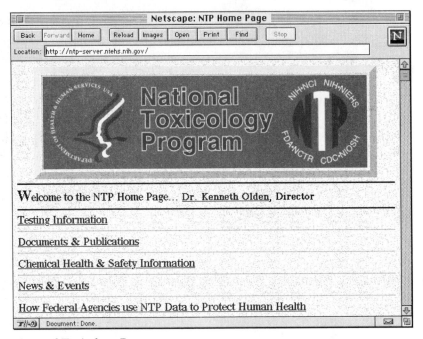

National Toxicology Program.

New York State Breast Cancer Information Clearinghouse

Type: Gopher

Address: gopher://nysernet.org/

Path: Special Collections: Breast Cancer Information Clearinghouse

Summary: A great resource for breast cancer patients, family members, and health professionals. Lots of info on treatment and rehabilitation, a list of names and phone numbers of support groups throughout the United States, and pointers to other cancer resources.

Psycoloquy

Type: WWW

Address: http://www.w3.org/hypertext/DataSources/bySubject/Psychology/Psycoloquy.html

Summary: An electronic journal sponsored by the American Psychological Association. Contains reports on new ideas and findings in all areas of psychology. Contributors solicit peer feedback, and contributions are refereed by members of Psycoloquy's Editorial Board.

Usenet: sci.psychology.digest

Or, to get articles automatically, send e-mail to listserv@pucc.bitnet or listserv@pucc.princeton.edu. Leave the Subject line blank and put the following in the body of the message: **sub psyc *Firstname Lastname*** (where *Firstname* and *Lastname* are your own names, *not* your Internet address).

Sexual Assault Recovery Service

Type: Gopher
Address: gopher://wilcox.umt.edu
Summary: Documents and discussions on dealing with sexual assault experiences and prevention.

You can also Telnet to selway.umt.edu and use the login *health*.

12-Step

Type: e-mail
Address: muller@camp.rutgers.edu
Summary: The purpose of this group is to share experiences about 12-step programs.

The Wellness List

Type: mailing list
Address: majordomo@wellnessmart.com
Summary: This list includes discussions of health, nutrition, wellness, and life expectancy. Lots of healthy recipes, nutrition and fitness-related product announcements, book reviews, and nutrition-related position papers.

To subscribe, send the following one-line message in e-mail: **subscribe wellnesslist** *your name* (where *your name* is your full name, *not* your e-mail address).

Some Related Newsgroups

alt.folklore.herbs	clari.tw.health.aids
alt.health.ayurveda	misc.fitness.misc
alt.med.cfs	misc.health.diabetes
alt.support.diet	talk.politics.medicine
bit.listserv.c+health	sci.med.aids
clari.tw.health.misc	sci.med.pharmacy

HISTORY

The History Resources Page

Type: WWW

Address: http://history.cc.ukans.edu/history/ WWW_history_main.html

Summary: The University of Kansas maintains this excellent collection of links to history resources around the Net. If you can't find out about it starting from here, it might not have happened.

MEDEIV-L

Type: mailing list

Address: listserv@ukanvm.cc.ukans.edu (send message with **SUBSCRIBE** in body)

Summary: This mailing list is for discussing all aspects of the middle ages.

Contact: Jeff Gardner jgardner@ukanvm.ukans.edu

Time's Man of the Year

Type: WWW

Address: http://pathfinder.com/time/special/moy/ moy.html

Summary: Each year since 1927, *Time* magazine has chosen somebody to appear on the cover as Man of the Year. Can you guess who was chosen in 1984? That's right, Peter Ueberroth. How about 1955? You guessed it, General Motors president Harlow Hubert Curtice. Once you get past the overwhelming male bias, this is actually a pretty interesting stroll down memory lane. While the articles about the individuals are informative, this site really says more about our values, about what types of achievement we have considered important over the course of recent history.

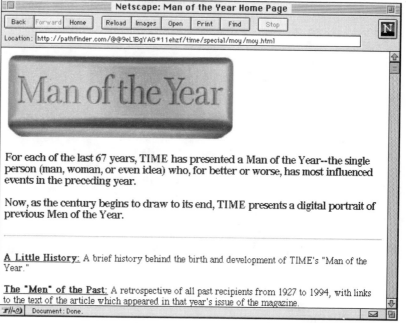

Man of the Year Home Page.

Some Related Newsgroups

alt.history.what-if	alt.war.civil.usa
alt.revisionism	bit.listserv.history
alt.war	soc.history

HUMOR

BRETTnews

Type: WWW

Address: http://pathfinder.com/vibe/vibeart/brettnews/index.html

Summary: *Brettnews* is a well-done, idiosyncratic personal humor zine. It always makes me laugh, and sometimes it even makes me think.

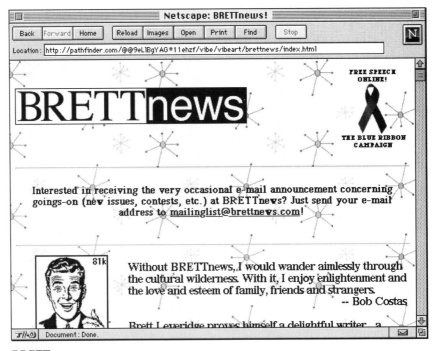

BRETTnews.

Cartoons

Type: Usenet

Address: alt.toon-pics

Summary: Download pictures of your favorite cartoon characters.

The Comic Strip Page

Type: WWW
Address: http://www.unitedmedia.com/comics/
Summary: The home for United Artists cartoons.

The Comic Strip. (Copyright UFS, Inc. 1995. Reprinted with permission of United Features Syndicate. All rights Reserved.)

Netwit

Type: mailing list
Address: help@netwit.cmhnet.org
Summary: If stupid Internet humor is your thing, send a message with your Internet address in the body of the message.

The Unofficial Tank Girl WWW Site

Type: WWW
Address: http://www.cs.ucl.ac.uk/staff/b.rosenberg/tg/index.html

Summary: Tank Girl is a creation of Jamie Hewlett and Alan Martin. On this page, you'll find a gallery of Tank Girl pictures, a Tank Girl FAQ, and everything else you need to be Tank Girl–literate.

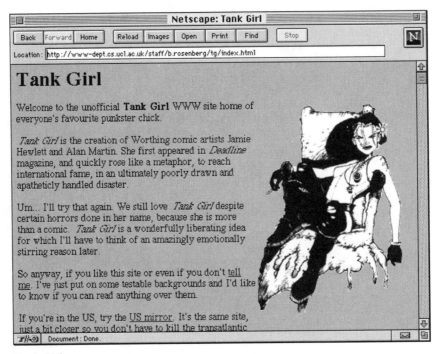

Tank Girl.

Some Related Newsgroups

alt.comedy.british
alt.comics.buffalo-roam
alt.comics.superman
alt.fan.firesign-theatre
alt.fan.wodehouse
alt.fan.tank-girl
alt.folklore.college
alt.humor.best-of-usenet
clari.feature.foxtrot
rec.arts.comics.marketplace

rec.arts.comics.strips
rec.humor.d
rec.humor.funny

INDEXES, HOTLISTS & SEARCH TOOLS

Archie Request Form

Type: WWW

Address: http://hoohoo.ncsa.uiuc.edu/archie.html

Summary: Archie is a utility for locating files at anonymous FTP sites. You used to need your own Archie client to connect with an Archie host, or alternatively you could Telnet to a site that provided a text-based UNIX client. Now it's much simpler. This site lets you specify your request in a simple Web form and then does the rest of the work for you.

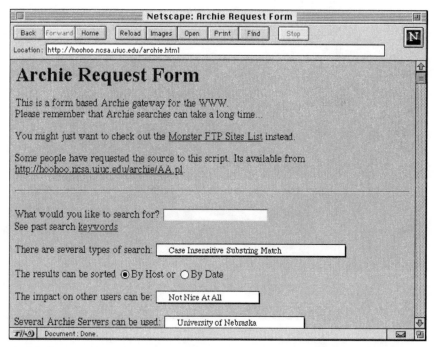

Archie Request Form.

ARGUS ClearingHouse for Subject-Oriented Resource Guides

Type: WWW
Address: http://www.clearinghouse.net/
Summary: A well-organized collection of hotlinks, grouped by subject area.

Best of the Net

Type: WWW
Address: http://gnn.com/wic/botn/index.html
Summary: Part of the excellent GNN site, this document includes hotlinks to a variety of interesting Web pages.

Best of the Net.

Best of the Web

Type: WWW
Address: http://wings.buffalo.edu/contest/

Summary: This is the Academy Awards for Web pages, voted on by thousands of Internet users. There are a variety of categories, and you can jump right over to the winners via the provided hotlinks.

CityLink

Type: WWW
Address: http://www.usacitylink.com/
Summary: More and more city governments and civic organizations are establishing a presence on the Web. CityLink points you to many of these. It also includes a wide range of information that may be important to travelers. For instance, the New York link includes a brief guide to treating gunshot wounds.

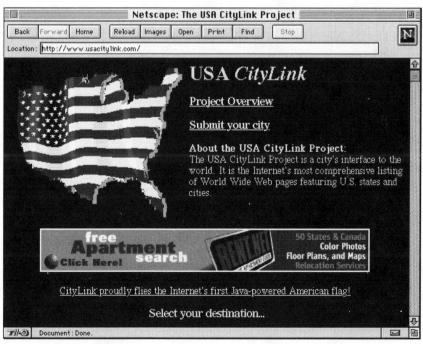

The USA CityLink Project.

Cool Site of the Day

Type: WWW

Address: http://cool.infi.net/

Summary: On the Web, as in "real life," there's always someone who's willing to tell you where to go. This home page includes a new link each day to a particularly interesting and original site. There are also links to previously chosen cool sites.

Cool Site of the Day.

Cool Sites to Visit

Type: WWW

Address: http://kells.vmedia.com:80/alternate/vvc/ onlcomp/mosaicqtw/hyperguide/ CoolSite4.html

Summary: Ventana's own collection of cool stuff. The home page has a list and descriptions of current cool happenings. Go to General Net Resources (from the TOC page) for a terrific collection of information about the Net.

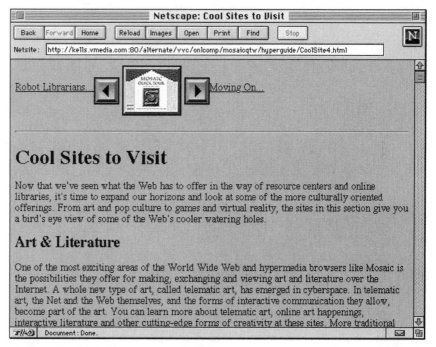

Ventana Cool Sites.

CUI W3 Catalog

Type: WWW

Address: http://cuiwww.unige.ch/w3catalog

Summary: This site, administered by the University of Geneva, provides a searchable front-end for several excellent Internet catalogs.

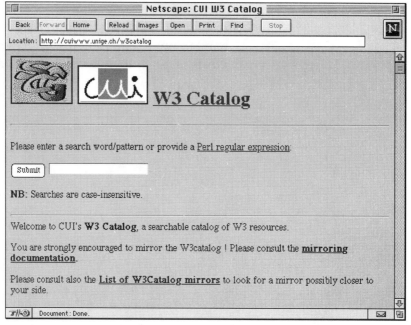

University of Geneva Catalog.

ECHO!

Type: WWW

Address: http://www.echonyc.com/

Summary: This is a collection of interesting home pages by members of the Echo online service. The documents vary from technology hotlists to experimental art.

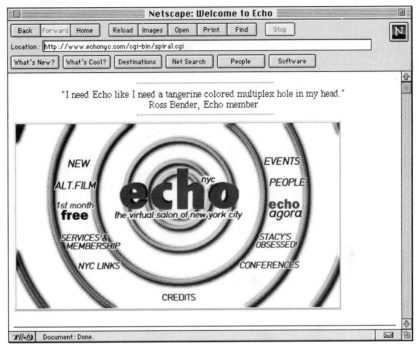

ECHO!

The EINet Galaxy

Type: WWW

Address: http://www.einet.com

Summary: EINet Galaxy is an easy-to-use and thorough hotlist. A good starting point for Web novices.

E-ZINE LIST

Type: WWW

Address: http://www.meer.net/~johnl/e-zine-list/

Summary: John Labovitz maintains the most thorough and up-to-date list of electronic zines currently available.

451f

Type: WWW

Address: http://hakatai.mcli.dist.maricopa.edu/451f/index.html

Summary: Another great collection of Web links.

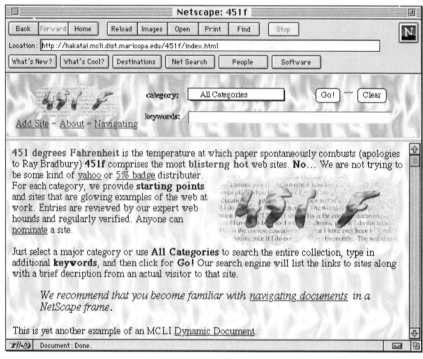

451f.

GNN Select

Type: WWW

Address: http://gnn.com/wic/wics/index.html

Summary: Another giant hotlist organized into dozens of categories. It's worth checking out the ever-changing What's New section once in a while.

GNN Select.

Harvest

Type: WWW

Address: http://harvest.cs.colorado.edu/

Summary: This is one of the best Web "search engines," including indexes of home pages, public domain software, newsgroups, and so on. It is easy to use and thorough, one of the best places to go when you want to "harvest" specific information.

Index Librorum Liberorum

Type: WWW

Address: http://www.fourmilab.ch/

Summary: John Walker has amassed a large, interesting collection of public domain electronic texts, technical papers, and programs. Not only does he make these materials available to you, he has organized them so that it's easy to find what you're looking for.

Infomine

Type: WWW
Address: http://lib-www.ucr.edu/govpub/
Summary: Links to a variety of federal government Web sites.

Infoseek

Type: WWW
Address: http://www.infoseek.com/
Summary: This claims to be the largest set of searchable indexes to WWW pages and to USENET newsgroups. After a quick look around I have no reason to doubt it. Infoseek also maintains indexes to over 80 computer periodicals. A great place to start your research.

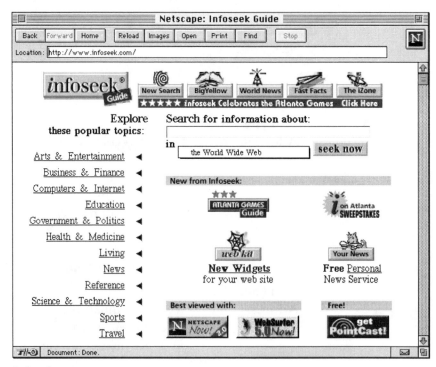

Infoseek.

Inter-Active Yellow Pages

Type: WWW
Address: http://netcenter.com/yellows/index.html
Summary: Commercial products and services on the Net. Everything from consumer electronics to travel to "The World's First Totally Useless 900#s."

Internet Resources Meta-Index

Type: WWW
Address: http://www.ncsa.uiuc.edu/SDG/Software/ Mosaic/MetaIndex.html
Summary: This page has links to most of the resource directories and indexes on the Net.

The Internet Services List

Type: WWW
Address: http://www.spectracom.com/islist/
Summary: This is Scott Yanoff's absolutely huge list of World Wide Web hotlinks. It is well-organized and updated regularly. Another great place to start browsing!

InterNIC Directory

Type: WWW
Address: http://ds.internic.net/
Summary: InterNIC provides several very large searchable databases of Internet resources. Definitely worth checking out.

Justin's Links From the Underground

Type: WWW
Address: http://raptor.swarthmore.edu/jahall/
Summary: This is an almost legendary hotlist of interesting and unusual Internet sites.

List of American Universities

Type: WWW

Address: http://www.clas.ufl.edu/CLAS/
american-universities.html

Summary: Many major colleges and universities now have Web pages, and this site provides links to over 150 of them.

TILE.NET/*LISTSERV*

Type: WWW

Address: http://www.tile.net/tile/listserv/index.html

Summary: There are hundreds of special-interest e-mail lists, but how do you find them? This site provides an organized overview of what's available.

Lycos

Type: WWW

Address: http://www.lycos.com/

Summary: Lycos lets you search for specific Web documents based on keywords you enter. It maintains a database of over 800,000 URLs. There are some other interesting resources here as well, including a list of the frequency of over six million words used on the Web. Lycos is one of those facilities that's almost too good, presenting you with more information than you really need, but it's a great resource if you use it carefully to narrow down your search.

Lycos search engine.

Marius Watz' WWW Pages

Type: WWW
Address: http://www.hok.no/marius/
Summary: Links focus on philosophy, the avant-garde, cyberculture, and the computer underground. Check out his NEXUS project.

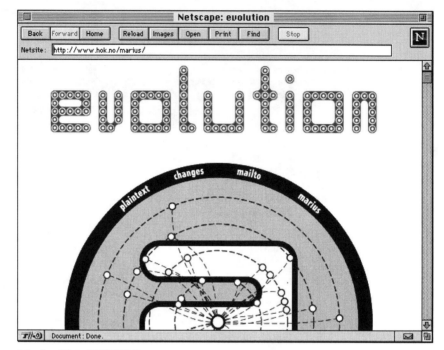

Marius Watz' WWW Pages.

Mirsky's Worst of the Web

Type: WWW

Address: http://mirsky.com/wow/

Summary: Not all of us have the time to cruise around the Web each day looking for the worst sites we can find. Fortunately, Mirsky does. Actually, some of his award winners I found more interesting than atrocious. I wonder what that says about me?

Mirsky's Worst of the Web.

The Mother-of-all BBS

Type: WWW

Address: http://wwwmbb.cs.colorado.edu/~mcbryan/
bb/summary.html

Summary: Links to just about everything on the Web. You
can perform a WAIS search on the Bulletin Board.

NetManage WWW Starting Points

Type: WWW

Address: http://www.netmanage.com/netmanage/
nm11.html

Summary: Yet another set of links organized by subject.

Nexor Public Services

Type: WWW

Address: http://web.nexor.co.uk/public/welcome.html

Summary: Yet another good search tool, letting you find information on the Web by keyword.

Open Market's Commercial Sites Index

Type: WWW

Address: http://www.directory.net

Summary: Businesses of all sizes are flocking to the Web to promote and even sell products and services. This site contains literally thousands of links to commercial sites; it also includes links to government and not-for-profit Web pages.

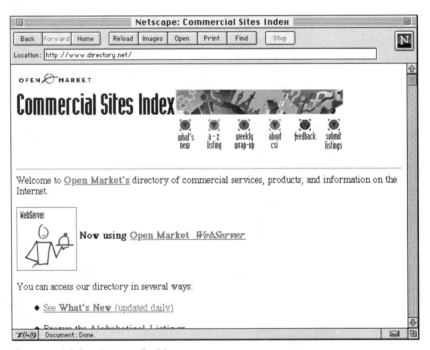

Commercial Services on the Net.

The Rumor Mill

Type: WWW

Address: http://asylum.cid.com/

Summary: A small, highly selective collection of fun and bizarre hotlinks.

The SenseMedia Surfer

Type: WWW

Address: http://www.picosof.com:8080/html/scott.html

Summary: This is one of my favorite hotlists. It includes links to hundreds of different sites in many different categories. A great place to begin a day of Web surfing.

The Source

Type: WWW

Address: http://hakatai.mcli.dist.maricopa.edu/smc/ml/source.html

Summary: A great selection of philosophy, religion, and psychology resources.

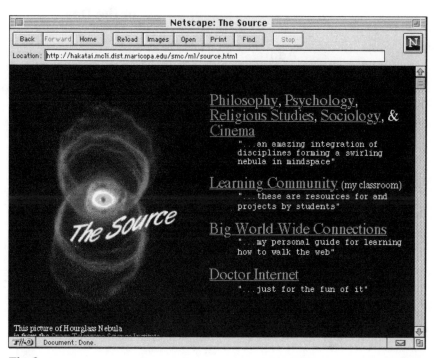

The Source.

Special Internet Connections

Type: FTP

Address: ftp://ftp.csd.uwm.edu/pub/inet.services.txt

Summary: A *huge* list of Internet resources, updated regularly. Better than a lot of other resource lists because it gives descriptions of each site. Print it out and start browsing—there's enough to keep you busy at least until the next edition of this book comes out.

Also available by mailing list by sending a subscription request to yanoff@csd4.csd.uwm.edu. The list is also posted regularly to several Usenet newsgroups including biz.comp.services and alt.internet.services.

Spider's Pick of the Day

Type: WWW

Address: http://gagme.wwa.com/~boba/pick.html

Summary: This is another "Cool Site of the Day"-type page, giving you yet another starting point each morning for wasting your precious work time on self-betterment and frivolity.

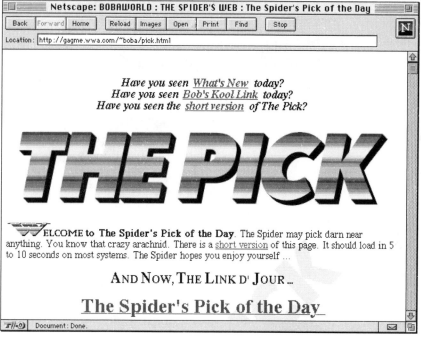

Spider's Pick of the Day.

The Internet Town Hall

Type: WWW

Address: http://town.hall.org/

Summary: This is a real grab-bag of electronic information and interesting links, a good starting point for a leisurely stroll around the Web.

The UCMP Subway

Type: WWW

Address: http://ucmp1.berkeley.edu/subway.html

Summary: A large hotlist of interesting sites, presented in a slightly unusual way: "The subway will take you to many virtual destinations throughout the Internet. Below you will see a map. Please touch a place on the map and you will receive a seat on the next train." Yes, yet another travel metaphor for browsing the Web!

UNC-CH Heliocentric Information Map

Type: WWW

Address: http://sunsite.unc.edu/heliocentric.html

Summary: I'll bet you didn't know that the University of North Carolina, with its SunSITE, is the center of the information universe—or at least the information solar system. Check out this interesting example of Web design, which provides lots of valuable information as well.

URouLette

Type: WWW

Address: http://www.uroulette.com:8000/

Summary: Overwhelmed by the sheer number of sites on the Web? Can't decide where to go next? You need the Web Roulette Server. Click on a roulette wheel and God knows where you'll end up. Given the nature of the Web, chances are it will be somewhere strange and fascinating, perhaps the home page of a nine-year-old particle physicist who likes cha cha music.

Usenet Launchpad

Type: Telnet

Address: telnet://launchpad.unc.edu

Summary: Not everybody has access to a good Usenet news server. Perhaps your service provider doesn't provide one as part of your account. Perhaps it is difficult to access due to traffic. Or perhaps it only includes a limited set of hand-picked "tasteful" newsgroups so that you can't post to some of your favorites such as alt.sex.bestiality.barney. Launchpad provides you a temporary shell account that you can use to launch one of the text-based UNIX newsreaders such as rn. You can also send e-mail and connect to Gopher or WAIS servers.

Vibe's World Map

Type: WWW

Address: http://pathfinder.com/vibe/vibeworld/
worldmap.html

Summary: While this seems to be mainly an ad for Timex, it is actually a pretty useful page. Click on any area of a world map and you will be presented with a comprehensive list of Web sites in that area. Since it's Timex, you also get the local time.

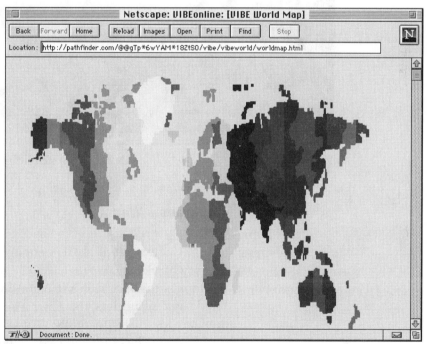

Vibe's World Map.

Virtual Town

Type: WWW

Address: http://wwwcsif.cs.ucdavis.edu/virt-town/
welcome.html

Summary: Plenty of good Web links presented in the form of a virtual town. You click on the area that you want to visit.

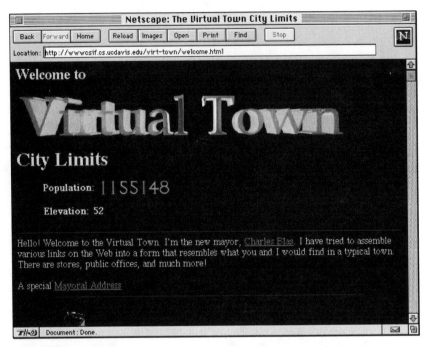

Virtual Town.

net.Genesis Wandex

Type: WWW

Address: http://www.mit.edu:8001/people/mkgray/mkgray.html

Summary: Wandex is the World Wide Web Wanderer Index. This magic wand lets you enter a keyword and then locates the appropriate Web documents for you. Wandex has indexed over 27,000 Web documents from more than 12,000 sites.

Washington & Lee University's Netlink Server

Type: WWW

Address: http://honor.uc.wlu.edu:1020/

Summary: Links to high-level Internet sources, database of links to public login Telnet sites, WWW servers, WAIS servers—tons of stuff!

WebAnnounce

Type: WWW

Address: http://wwwac.org/WebAnnounce/

Summary: Once you've created your own Web page, you probably want to announce it to the online world. Many large public hotlists let you add your site, but it's inconvenient to keep track of all these promotional venues. That's where WebAnnounce comes in: now you can do all your self-publicizing from one page. This is a great time-saving utility!

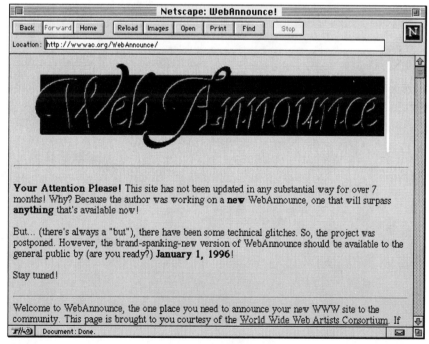

WebAnnounce!

The Webcrawler

Type: WWW

Address: http://www.webcrawler.com/

Summary: This excellent search engine indexes the contents of Web documents, so you can find pages that contain a particular word or phrase.

The Web's Edge

Type: WWW

Address: http://kzsu.stanford.edu/uwi.html

Summary: "UnderWorld Industries' Cultural Playground." Lots of alternative stuff. Check out "Stream of Conscience," an art/poetry Web-zine.

What's Hot and Cool on the Web

Type: WWW

Address: http://kzsu.stanford.edu/uwi/reviews.html

Summary: Lots of cool (and hot) alternative-type stuff.

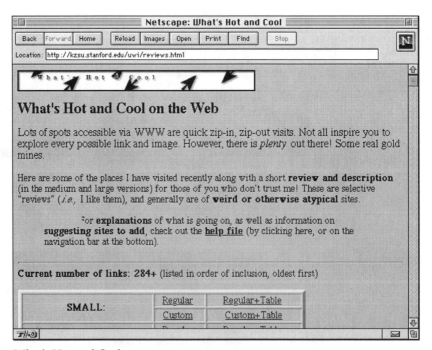

What's Hot and Cool.

NCSA What's New

Type: WWW

Address: http://www.ncsa.uiuc.edu/SDG/Software/ Mosaic/Docs/whats-new.html

Summary: Get the latest Web info here. Descriptions of and links to new home pages.

NCSA What's New.

World Birthday Web

Type: WWW

Address: http://www.boutell.com/birthday.cgi/

Summary: Andy Warhol said that in the future everybody will be famous for 15 minutes. Well if you're a Web traveler, you can be famous for at least an entire day. Enter your name and birthday here and you will appear in the birthday list on that day. If you enter a URL for your home page, a hotlink to that site will be included as well.

The World Wide Web Consortium

Type: WWW

Address: http://www.w3.org/pub/WWW/

Summary: This is one of the best starting points for exploring the Web, although the sheer volume of information can be overwhelming.

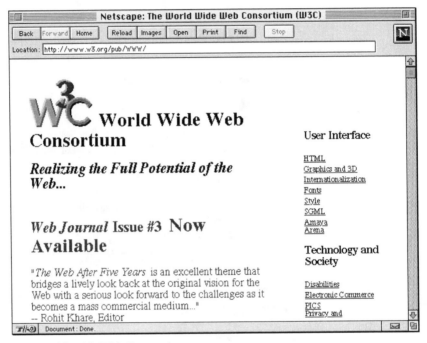

The World Wide Web Consortium.

World-Wide Web Worm

Type: WWW

Address: http://wwww.cs.colorado.edu/wwww

Summary: The "WWWW" is becoming one of the most popular tools for searching the Web. It is extremely flexible, allowing regular expression searches on URL, subject, and content. In spite of its flexibility, it's not difficult to use, and the site even includes a straightforward tutorial.

The World Wide Yellow Pages

Type: WWW

Address: http://www.yellow.com/

Summary: This is exactly what it sounds like—a directory of businesses that have home pages on the Web. What makes this different from the kind of yellow pages we're used to is that it is constantly updated, and you can even add entries yourself. A very useful tool.

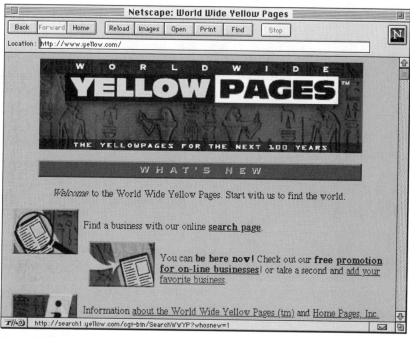

World Wide Yellow Pages.

Yahoo!

Type: WWW

Address: http://www.yahoo.com (or Net Directory button)

Summary: Yahoo! may be the best-known of the large public hotlists sprinkled around the Web. It includes a good search facility, and since it allows users to enter new sites it is always up-to-date. This is an excellent place to start exploring.

INTERNET STUFF

A Beginner's Guide to HTML

Type: WWW

Address: http://www.ncsa.uiuc.edu/demoweb/html-primer.html

Summary: Learn to create HTML documents that can be placed on the Web.

Community Computer Networks: Building Electronic Greenbelts

Type: FTP

Address: ftp://ftp.apple.com/alug/communet/

Summary: Steve Cisler's excellent overview of community networks examining what kinds of information and services can be found on these systems, what groups are running community networks and cost aspects. The essay discusses current models for community networks and the impact these networks have on their local (physical) environment.

Contact: Steve Cisler
Apple Library
4 Infinite Loop
MS 304-2A
Cupertino, CA 95014
408/974-3258
sac@apple.com

Good Internet Books

Type: Gopher

Address: gopher://nysernet.org

Path: Special Collections: Internet Help / Good Books About the Internet

Summary: A great list of books about the Net. There's a short summary, the ISBN number, and the price.

Internet Society

Type: WWW

Address: http://info.isoc.org/home.html

Summary: The Internet Society was created in 1991 to be the international organization that promotes global cooperation and coordination for the Internet and its technologies. Individuals and organizations can join. There's a great general info Internet FAQ.

Contact: Internet Society
org-membership@isoc.org
800/468-9507 (U.S. only)
703/648-9888

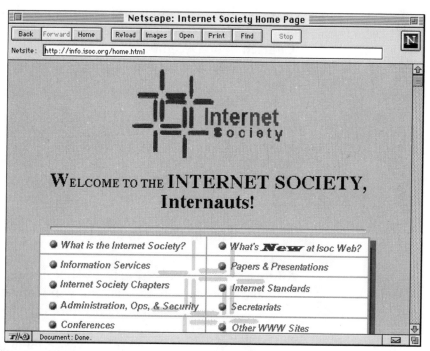

Internet Society.

Internet Web Text

Type: WWW

Address: http://www.december.com/web/text/index.html

Summary: Created in spring of 1994 (but updated since) by John December for a course in Computer-Mediated Communication at Rensselaer Poly-technic Institute. His goal: to create an interface students could use to familiarize themselves with the Internet—how to use it, how to find information, how to connect with people. He makes use of icons to create memory aids to remembering sources. This page also has links to lots of online Internet guides and resources, such as *Zen and the Art of the Internet*.

Contact: John December
decemj@rpi.edu

IRC Thesis

Type: FTP

Address: ftp://ftp.spies.com/Library/Cyber/electrop.txt

Summary: This honors thesis by E. M. Reid, "Electropolis: Communication and Community on IRC," explores the culture of Internet Relay Chat.

List of New Mailing Lists

Type: mailing list

Address: request-NEW-LIST@VM1.NoDak.EDU

Summary: Subscribe to this list and you'll always be on top of the latest mailing list info. Whenever a new mailing list is formed or an old one is updated, you'll receive a message describing the additions or changes.

To subscribe, send the following one-line message in e-mail: **subscribe New-list** *your name* (where *your name* is your full name—*not* your e-mail address).

NCSA Mosaic

Type: WWW

Address: http://www.ncsa.uiuc.edu/SDG/Software/ Mosaic/NCSAMosaicHome.html

Summary: Download the latest release of NCSA Mosaic, get installation and configuration instructions, info about bugs and bug fixes, FAQs, and an online users' manual. Also get graphics viewers, HTML editors, Pkunzip, and winsocks.

Netnews Filtering Service

Type: e-mail

Address: netnews@db.stanford.edu

Summary: Sign up with this Stanford service to help you zero in on the Internet stuff you want. You send a profile to the service, and they send you relevant news articles.

Send an e-mail message with the command HELP in the body of the message to get more information.

Why Are Internet Resources Free?

Type: Gopher

Address: gopher://wiretap.spies.com

Path: Wiretap Online Library / Cyberspace / Why are Internet Resources Free?

Summary: Ever wondered why you can get to most of the stuff on the Net without having to pay? This article explains it all for you.

Some Related Newsgroups

alt.answers	alt.security.pgp
alt.culture.internet	bit.listserv.new-list
alt.culture.usenet	misc.answers
alt.newbie	misc.legal.computing
alt.online-service	news.software.readers

Jobs

Federal Jobs

Type: Gopher

Address: gopher://gopher.Dartmouth.EDU:70/11/ Careers

Path: Job Openings in the Federal Government

Summary: Lists of federal job opportunities and information that'll help you apply for a federal job.

Online Career Center

Type: Gopher

Address: gopher://msen.com

Path: The Msen Career Center/The Online Career Center

Summary: You can post your resume and search job lists at no charge, get career counseling, and connect with recruiting agencies.

Contact: occ@mail.msen.com

Some Related Newsgroups

bionet.jobs
bionet.women-in-bio
biz.jobs.offered
info.wisenet
misc.jobs.contract

misc.jobs.misc
misc.jobs.offered
misc.jobs.offered.entry
misc.jobs.resumes

Journals & Zines

Boardwatch Magazine

Type: WWW

Address: http://www.boardwatch.com/

Summary: A taste of what's in the print version of this wide-ranging monthly about BBSing and the Internet.

Boardwatch *Magazine.*

Career Magazine

Type: WWW

Address: http://www.careermag.com/careermag/

Summary: Tired of cruising the Net and want to get a job instead? Need money to support your online addiction? About to get fired for playing games on the Web instead of selling widgets? You need to check out this site quickly.

Career *Magazine.*

Computer Mediated Communication Magazine

Type: WWW

Address: http://www.december.com/cmc/mag/current/toc.html

Summary: An interesting electronic magazine filled with information and opinion about the technology and culture of the Internet.

dimFLASH

Type: WWW

Address: http://www.well.com/user/futrelle/dflash.html

Summary: An interesting zine with excellent graphics and hotlinks to other peculiar sites.

Editor & Publisher Interactive

Type: WWW
Address: http://www.mediainfo.com/edpub/
Summary: This is an extensive and constantly changing list of newspapers that offer online services. The list only covers large mass-media papers, not zines or electronic newsletters.

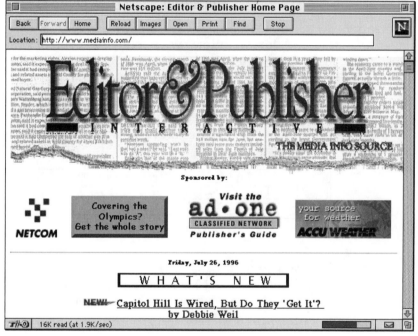

Editor & Publisher Home Page.

The Fiore Report

Type: mailing list
Address: sept4yu@ix.netcom.com
(send e-mail saying you want to subscribe)
Summary: Sex therapist Tony Fiore writes this monthly electronic newsletter that offers advice on improving or enhancing your sex life.

Fringeware

Type: WWW

Address: http://www.fringeware.com/

Summary: Fringeware is an interesting bunch of people in Austin who offer cutting-edge cyberinfo, cyberart, and cyberproducts. This is the place to go when *Wired* looks tired.

HotWired

Type: WWW

Address: http://www.hotwired.com/

Summary: This is one of the biggest tourist attractions on the Internet, a sort of new-media Disney World for plugged in twenty-somethings. You'll find a little of everything here, though most of the material focuses on various aspects of cyberspace itself.

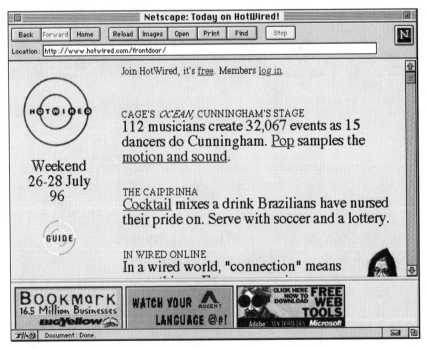

HotWired.

iWorld

Type: WWW

Address: http://www.iworld.com/

Summary: This is the Web home of Mecklermedia, the folks who publish *Internet World*. Here you can find a special hypermedia version of the magazine.

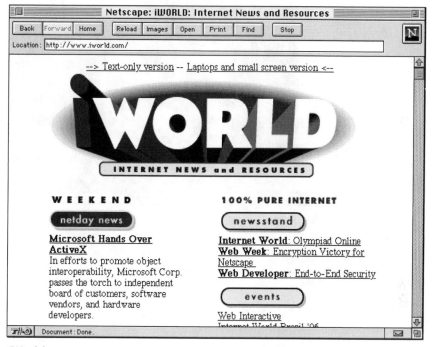

iWorld.

Link Digital Campus

Type: WWW

Address: http://www.linkmag.com/

Summary: In addition to the interesting *Link* zine, this site contains a thorough index to student publications from universities around the country. A valuable resource!

Link *Digital Campus.*

Mediamatic

Type: WWW

Address: http://www.mediamatic.nl/home.html

Summary: This is an interesting Dutch magazine about interactive media and its cultural implications. Well-written and well-produced.

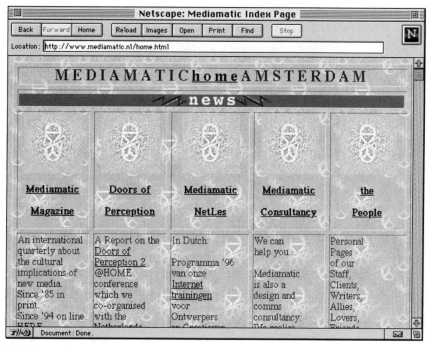

Mediamatic.

Mercury Center

Type: WWW

Address: http://www.sjmercury.com

Summary: Many newspapers now offer electronic versions. This is one of the best, developed by *San Jose Mercury News*.

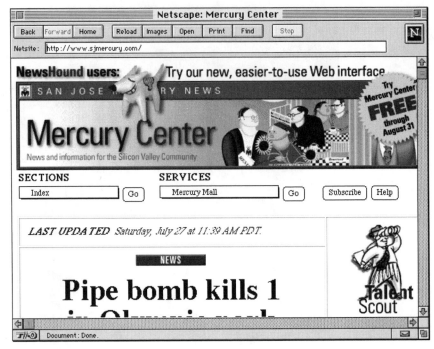

Mercury Center.

The Netly News

Type: WWW

Address: http://www.pathfinder.com/Netly

Summary: Internet expert Josh Quittner runs this one. "There are 35 million stories in cyberspace. We give you a new one every day." That's the basic idea, a new and usually excellent feature article every day, mainly about Web and Internet issues.

Netsurfer Digest

Type: WWW

Address: http://www.netsurf.com/nsd/index.html

Summary: This is an interesting electronic zine about the Net and interactive communications. Zines like this are popping up daily, but this one has more substance than most.

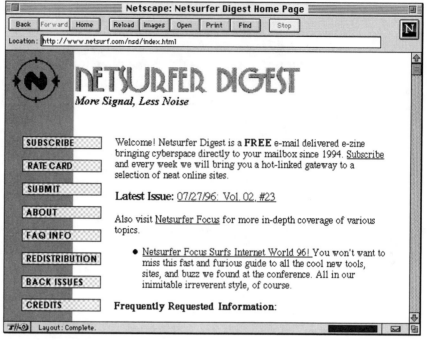

Netsurfer Digest.

Ziff-Davis Publishing

Type: WWW

Address: http://www.ziff.com

Summary: Ziff-Davis is the General Motors of computer magazine publishing. This site lets you access *PC Magazine* and eight others.

 KIDS

The Cisco Educational Archives

Type: WWW

Address: http://sunsite.unc.edu/cisco/cisco-home.html

Summary: Lots of hotlinks to Web pages of interest to school-age kids as well as teachers.

Explora-Net

Type: WWW

Address: http://www.exploratorium.edu/

Summary: This is the home page for the Exploratorium, a fascinating hands-on science museum in San Francisco. It includes areas of interest to both children and adults.

Global Show-n-Tell

Type: WWW

Address: http://www.telenaut.com/gst/

Summary: It is difficult to find good sites for younger children on the Web, but this is one of the best. It's an interactive exhibition of children's art; everything on display was created by kids and e-mailed in. I'd like to see more ideas like this!

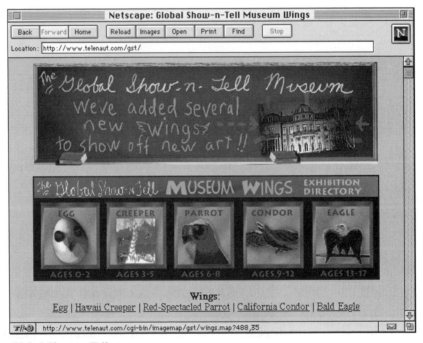

Global Show-n-Tell.

Interesting Places for Kids

Type: WWW
Address: http://www.crc.ricoh.com/people/steve/ kids.html
Summary: This Web page includes links to literally hundreds of entertaining and educational sites for children. Don't stick them in front of the TV, drop them off here!

IPL Youth

Type: WWW
Address: http://ipl.sils.umich.edu/youth/
Summary: This is the kids' section of the University of Michigan's Internet Public Library, and it's a wonderful site. Kids can submit their own stories to a contest, check out a book, explore math and science, chat about books they like, even submit questions to authors.

Yahooligans

Type: WWW
Address: http://www.yahooligans.com/
Summary: This may be the only kids' site you ever need. It's the junior version of Yahoo!, with hundreds of neatly categorized links to other pages. A great starting place for exploration on a rainy afternoon.

LANGUAGES

Esperanto-English Dictionary

Type: Gopher
Address: gopher://wiretap.spies.com
Path: Wiretap Online Library / Articles / Language / Esperanto English Dictionary

Summary: Next time your boss tells you what to do, why not answer in Esperanto!

Foreign Language Resources

Type: WWW

Address: http://www.itp.berkeley.edu/~thorne/HumanResources.html

Summary: This is a large collection of links to sites that can help you learn a foreign language.

Human-Languages Page

Type: WWW

Address: http://www.willamette.edu/~tjones/Language-Page.html

Summary: This page currently contains more than 100 links to over 40 different languages. Tutorials, dictionaries, software, and literature.

Japanese/English Dictionary–Gateway

Type: WWW

Address: http://www.wg.omron.co.jp/cgi-bin/j-e

Summary: This page is also available in Japanese. The dictionary entries can be viewed with text-based browsers or with Japanese text sent as images.

Travelers' Japanese with Voice

Type: WWW

Address: http://www.ntt.jp/japan/japanese/

Summary: Learn some simple Japanese before that next business trip.

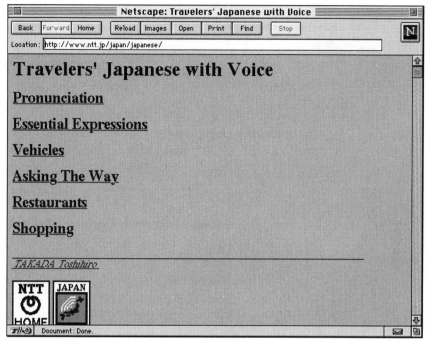

Travelers' Japanese with Voice.

Web Italian Lessons by Lucio Chiappetti

Type: WWW

Address: http://www.willamette.edu/~tjones/
languages/Italian/Italian-lesson.html

Summary: Lessons are available as PostScript files, as well as
in HTML format.

Some Related Newsgroups

alt.chinese.text
alt.japanese.text
k12.lang.francais
k12.lang.russian
sci.lang
soc.culture.esperanto
soc.culture.french

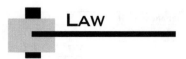

LAW

Advertising Law Internet Site

Type: WWW

Address: http://www.webcom.com/~lewrose/home.html

Summary: Legal aspects of marketing. Stuff about info-mercials, home shopping, and 900 number regulations. You can also get FTC guides and consumer advisories.

Criminal Justice Country Profiles

Type: Gopher

Address: gopher://uacsc2.albany.edu

Path: United Nations Justice Network / U.N. Criminal Justice Country Profiles

Summary: Find out how the criminal justice system works in different countries.

Legal Information Institute

Type: WWW

Address: http://www.law.cornell.edu/

Summary: Get information about recent Supreme Court decisions, search an e-mail address directory of faculty and staff at U.S. law schools. Lots of links to other law-related stuff.

West's Legal Directory (WLD)

Type: Gopher

Address: gopher://wld.westlaw.com

Path: West's Legal Directory via WAIS

Summary: Search for attorneys or law firms by specialty in any area in the United States or Canada. Profiles include information on such things as years of practice and offices held. You can also search for former students of law schools. E-mail questions to wldhelp@research.westlaw.com. Phone 800/777-7089.

Some Related Newsgroups

bit.listserv.lawsch-l
clari.news.usa.law
misc.int-property
mis.legal
misc.legal.computing

MISCELLANY: UNCLASSIFIABLE WONDERS

The Advanced Nerdity Test
Type: WWW
Address: http://gonzo.tamu.edu/nerd-backwards.html
Summary: If you're reading this book instead of *Proceedings of the ACM* you're probably not a total nerd. On the other hand, if you're reading this book at all, you're probably a little bit of one. Find out just how nerdy you really are.

Animals
Type: FTP
Address: ftp://rtfm.mit.edu/pub/usenet/news.answers
Summary: You'll find all sorts of animal stuff here. A few of the subdirectories to check out:
cats-faq
pets-birds-faq
fleas-ticks
dogs-faq

The Digital Confession Booth
Type: WWW
Address: http://anther.learning.cs.cmu.edu/priest.html
Summary: It's so much easier this way. And, you can scroll through everybody else's sins, too!

Find-the-Spam

Type: WWW

Address: http://sp1.berkeley.edu/findthespam.html

Summary: Some people have too much time on their hands, and I'm glad they do. This is by far the goofiest, stupidest Web page I've come across. I love it.

Find-the-Spam.

The Froggy Page

Type: WWW

Address: http://www.cs.yale.edu/HTML/YALE/CS/ HyPlans/loosemore-sandra/froggy.html

Summary: This is one of my favorite sites. It includes many beautiful photographs of frogs as well as a variety of frog-related information. From the Froggy Page you might also want to jump to Sandra Loosemore's home page, which contains some other interesting links.

The Grouchy Café

Type: WWW
Address: http://www.echonyc.com/~cafephrk/cafe.html
Summary: This is a warm friendly hangout with a real sense of *place*. Cafephreak, the proprietor, serves up recipes, anecdotes, information on coffee, a list of angst-ridden teenage books, fun artwork, and the memorable advice "Never fall in love with a lesbian who read Sartre instead of Judy Blume. She will rip out your heart."

The Groucy Café.

Hacker Barbie

Type: WWW
Address: http://www.catalog.com/mrm/barbe/barbe.html
Summary: An amusing and interesting home page focusing on a transformed and far more interesting version of Mattel's Barbie doll. Not for everybody, but I really enjoyed this site.

InterJackie

Type: WWW
Address: http://www.echonyc.com/~interjackie
Summary: A sort of cyber-club from the people who publish the always interesting *Verbal Abuse* magazine. Great graphics.

Mr. Edible Starchy Tuber Head

Type: WWW
Address: http://winnie.acsu.buffalo.edu/potatoe/
Summary: Yes, this is what it sounds like. You add various features to a potato-shaped outline, coming up with "hilarious" distorted faces. This is where you come to relive a vital part of your 1960s childhood.

The MIT Gallery of Hacks

Type: WWW
Address: http://fishwrap.mit.edu/Hacks/Gallery.html
Summary: At MIT the word "hack" means a clever prank such as putting a phony police car on top of the Great Dome (Building 10) on the last day of classes. Many descriptions of hacks are accompanied by photographs. This site is an inspiration to college students everywhere.

Net Chick Clubhouse

Type: WWW
Address: http://www.cyborganic.com/People/carla
Summary: "Psst!–Over here! We're in the Net Chick Clubhouse—spreading gossip, telling secrets, relishing pop culture, luxuriating, and playing hard." What more could you want if you're a Net Chick?

Paul Haas' Appliances

Type: WWW
Address: http://hamjudo.com/

Summary: Paul Haas is a UNIX consultant. He also maintains a Web page that includes constantly updated information on his refrigerator (temperature, contents) and hot tub (temperature, contents). This is the age of information. Can you really afford to miss any?

The Really Big Button That Doesn't Do Anything

Type: WWW

Address: http://www.wam.umd.edu/~twoflowr/ button.htm

Summary: This is another one of those useless sites, a giant push button that does not respond to your clicks. It includes, however, numerous philosophical musings on the nature of the button, and it allows you to add your own. A great site to visit if you've already figured out every other way to waste time.

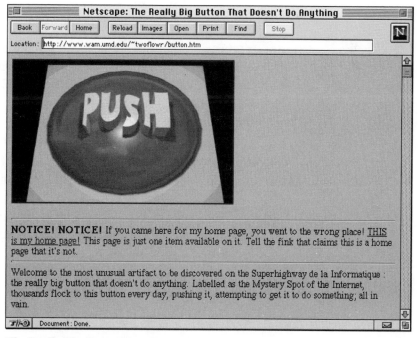

The Really Big Button.

SCHWA™

Type: WWW

Address: http://fringeware.com/SchwaRoot/Schwa.html

Summary: I've always felt that the Internet wouldn't really be the same without Schwa. This crazy alien conspiracy think-tank typifies the wide range of viewpoints available to Netsurfers. Crackpots are one of America's greatest products, and I'm glad they have a voice on the Web.

SpingoWorld

Type: WWW

Address: http://www.echonyc.com/~spingo/ SpingoWorld

Summary: A fun and very unclassifiable site that includes chatting via Time-Warner's Palace. Lots of sounds, too.

SteveC's Pages

Type: WWW

Address: http://ftp.std.com/homepages/stevec/ index1.html

Summary: Inspired silliness, including the Sofasphere II Project ("How will mankind absorb 500 channels?") and a collection of Stephen Hawking's favorite pick-up lines.

The Surrealist Compliment Generator

Type: WWW

Address: http://pharmdec.wustl.edu/cgi-bin/ jardin_scripts/SCG

Summary: This Web page presents you with a unique randomly generated compliment each time you reload it. For instance, the first time I visited it told me, "Sound barricades into rolls of peanut butter when you speak." It was the nicest thing anybody had said to me all day, so I decided to try again. This time I got, "Ever so slightly, you remind me of a staircase falling exotically into a sea of spilled macaroni." There is also a slightly more serious side to this site, as it includes lots of fascinating information on the Surrealist Movement in the arts.

The TiReD-WiReD Server

Type: WWW

Address: http://www.cs.odu.edu/~bianco/bin/tired-wired.cgi

Summary: Every month devoted members of the *cyberhipoisie* thumb as quickly as they can to *Wired* magazine's TiReD-WiReD list to find out what's cool to be talking about this month and what's oh-so-five-minutes-ago. This site offers an amusing take off on this cyberculture chestnut, an almost Dadaist list generated by some secret mathematical formula. Good clean fun.

The Wall O' Shame

Type: WWW

Address: http://www.milk.com/wall-o-shame/

Summary: A fun but humbling look at humankind, the Wall O' Shame presents examples of stupidity and inanity culled from newspapers, magazines, even the Net. This is not fiction; it's way too strange.

MACINTOSH MANIA

mirror.apple.com

Type: WWW

Address: http://mirror.apple.com

Summary: This is the Web front end for the Apple mirror site. From here, you can access mirrors of some of the Internet's largest software archives, including Stanford's Info-Mac archive and the mac files at the University of Michigan. The Apple site is also one of the most reliable and easiest to access.

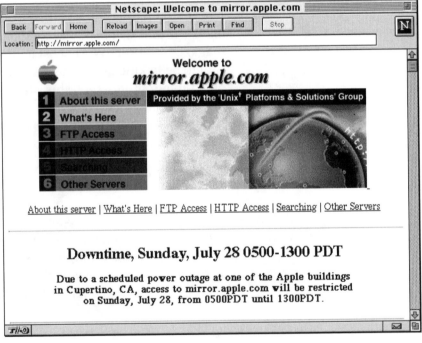

The Apple mirror front end.

The Apple Computer Home Page

Type: WWW

Address: http://www.apple.com

Summary: This is Apple's official corporate presence on the Web. From here you can retrieve official information on Apple, its products and its plans. There are links of special initiatives for publishers, students, and other key Apple marketers, cool new Apple technologies, developer information, software updates (via FTP), third-party Web sites, and much more. This site also includes a list of resources demonstrating why the Macintosh beats Wintel boxes in productivity, ease of use, and cost.

Apple Computer Inc.'s home page.

info.apple.com

Type: FTP

Address: ftp://ftp.info.apple.com

Summary: This is the place to go to download the latest software releases, publications, and other information from Apple. Here's where I found Update 2 for System 7.5.3, for example. Cyberdog, Newton, Apple plug-ins, and FAQ headquarters may all be reached through this valuable FTP site.

Boston Computer Society

Type: WWW

Address: http://www.bcs.org/bcs

Summary: The Boston Computer Society (BCS) is one of the oldest and best-known computer groups in the country. Their Web site provides information on computers in general, answers to technical questions, information on recycling your old computers, lists of computer classes and instructional sessions, as well as links to local BCS groups and chapters. A great place to go for ideas about upgrades, add-ons, or a new system!

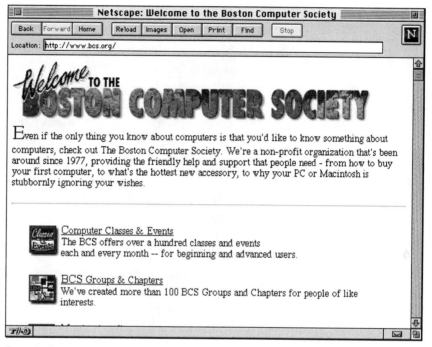

Boston Computer Society's home page.

BMUG Online

      Type: WWW

  Address: http://www.bmug.org

 Summary: The Berkeley Macintosh Users Group (BMUG) is the world's largest Mac users group, and their Web site can help answer just about any question you have on Macintosh things. In addition, they have a large archive of publicly distributable software, and links to lots of cool Mac sites.

Macintosh Helper Applications

Type: WWW

Address: http://home.netscape.com/assist/helper_apps/mac_helpers.html

Summary: A quality page provided by Netscape which gets Macintosh users directly to applications and plug-ins which will help them use Navigator 3.0 most efficiently. A must-visit site if you are going to make the most of Navigator's features!

Macintosh Tips & First Aid

Type: WWW

Address: http://hypatia.dartmouth.edu/~tcurtin/mac/mac.html

Summary: A nicely-arranged, comprehensive collection of tips and emergency advice, from those arcane key combinations to a listing of Mac error codes. Maintained by Tim Curtin.

The Best of the Macintosh Universe

Type: WWW

Address: http://www.netaxs.com/people/bluesky/Mac.html

Summary: While the page itself is unremarkable, Jeff Bubis' site contains an amazing number of Mac-related links. An excellent starting point for some random Mac-related surfing.

TidBITS

Type: WWW

Address: http://www.dartmouth.edu/pages/TidBITS/TidBITS.html

Summary: This is the home page for the weekly TidBITS electronic newsletter, a publication which compiles information on "interesting products and events in the computer industry." The site has a definite Mac slant and bias!

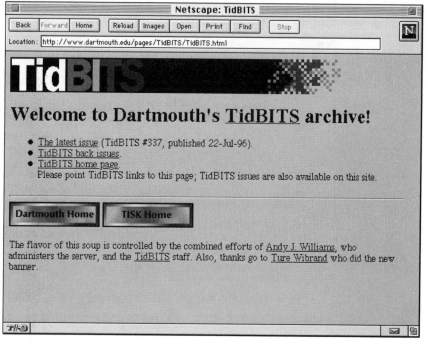

Dartmouth's electronic newsletter for Macintosh.

EvangeList and MacAddict

Type: WWW

Address: http://www.evangelist.macaddict.com/

Summary: Guy is one of the original Macintosh evangelists, a Mac Fellow, a widely-read columnist and book author, software investor, and just about anything else you can imagine. If the Mac had a face, it could be Guy Kawasaki's! The purpose of this site is to evangelize the world about the good news of Macintosh and Newton and Apple, and help the world become a better place! Contains links to important Apple Macintosh sites and information.

The EvangeList home page.

The University of Texas

Type: WWW

Address: http://wwwhost.ots.utexas.edu/mac/main.html

Summary: A very well organized and informative site for all things Macintosh. This is one of my favorite mirror sites for Mac software from Apple, as well as a comprehensive repository for shareware and freeware. If you design and create Web sites using a Macintosh, please show the world by placing a "Made with Macintosh" badge on your site's home page, using high-quality graphics from this very supportive site!

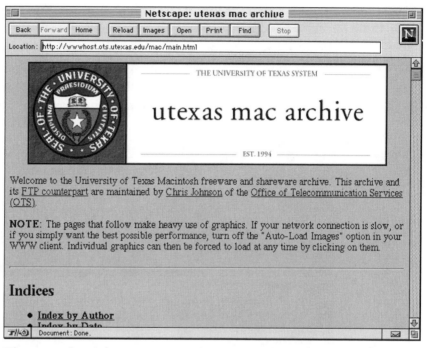

The utexas home page.

MULTIMEDIA

Index to Multimedia Information Sources

Type: WWW

Address: http://viswiz.gmd.de/MultimediaInfo

Summary: Links to film and video resources, media archives, MPC specs, cable regulations, desktop publishing, art, music, zines, publishers, MIDI, MPEG, satellite TV, Nielsen ratings, the Billboard chart, hypertext and hypermedia, multimedia software, newsgroups, and about a zillion other multimedia-related resources. Multimedia FAQ heaven and lots of conference announcements.

Silicon Graphics' Serious Fun Page

Type: WWW

Address: http://www.sgi.com/Fun/fun.html

Summary: As you would expect from this pioneering high-tech company, this site is loaded with fascinating computer-generated images and video clips.

Serious Fun with SGI.

MUSIC

Addicted to Noise

Type: WWW

Address: http://www.addict.com

Summary: The title says it all.

Classical Music

Type: Usenet

Address: rec.music.classical.performing

Summary: Lots of interesting and serious discussions (low garbage ratio).

The Death of Rock 'n' Roll

Type: WWW

Address: http://alfred1.u.washington.edu:8080/~jlks/pike/DeathRR.html

Summary: *The Death of Rock 'n' Roll: Untimely Demises, Morbid Preoccupations and Premature Forecasts of Doom in Pop Music*, by Jeff Pike, was published by Faber & Faber in 1993. This site contains lots of samples from the book. They're meant to entice you to buy the book, but you'll find plenty of info about your favorite dead rock stars even if you don't plan to make a purchase.

Contact: Faber & Faber
800/666-2211

Digital Tradition Folk Song Database

Type: WWW

Address: http://pubweb.parc.xerox.com/digitrad

Summary: A searchable database containing words and music to thousands of folk songs collected by Dick Greenhaus and friends.

Hyperreal—the Techno/Ambient/Rave Archive

Type: WWW

Address: http://hyperreal.com/

Summary: The Rave Archive will take you to the alt.rave FAQ, The List of Rave Lists, and pointers to tons of Rave home pages.

Contact: Brian Behlendorf, founder of the SFRaves mailing list
brian@hyperreal.com

Hyperreal.

Internet Underground Music Archive (IUMA)

Type: WWW

Address: http://www.iuma.com/IUMA/

Summary: IUMA is a huge catalog of artists, albums, and songs, including reviews and many MPEG samples. This site keeps getting bigger and better. It was founded by Rob Lord and Jeff Patterson to showcase unsigned musicians. Listen to clips from over 140 independent rock bands.

Intrrr Nrrrd

Type: WWW

Address: http://nervecore.com/e-zine

Summary: A classic. "Saving souls with punk rawwk since August 1994." What else can you say?

Knitting Factory

Type: WWW

Address: http://knittingfactory.com

Summary: The Knitting Factory is both a performance space and record label in New York City. For many years they have been devoted to some of the most interesting music around, including the work of adventurous composers and performers who bridge whatever gap there used to be between innovative jazz and avant-garde "classical" music.

List of Coordinators

Type: WWW

Address: http://www.update.uu.se/pub/cathouse/lyrics/Coordinator.html

Summary: Reviews and tech info about coordinators (a piece of equipment which can be used to control and/or program the performance of either an internal or an external sound source). Some coordinators: drum machines, sequencers, bass machines, MIDI arpeggiators. A major site for electronic music aficionados. Specifications, performance notes, and personal reflections concerning the categorized equipment. Regularly updated.

Random Band Names

Type: WWW

Address: http://www.terranet.ab.ca/~aaron/band_names.html

Summary: Everyone who has started a band, except maybe Courtney Love, has struggled with the difficulty of coming up with a good name. Should you be "Stuck Pig" or would "Timex Junk-Monkies" make more sense? This site solves the problem by offering you a unique randomly generated band name. If you're not musical, you could probably use it as your handle on AOL or some other information service.

SonicNet

Type: WWW
Address: http://www.sonicnet.com
Summary: One of the most popular music sites on the Web, SonicNet, features great visuals, news and reviews, and RealAudio sound clips. Alternative rock is the style here.

The Ultimate Band List

Type: WWW
Address: http://american.recordings.com/wwwofmusic/ubl/ubl.shtml
Summary: Want to find the Nick Cave Web site? This claims to be the largest listing of Internet resources for specific bands, and I have no reason to doubt it. What makes this a great site is that it can be updated by users and that it includes not just Web links but links to all kinds of resources: lyric files, newsgroups, mailing lists, digitized songs, and so on.

VANGELIS—The Man and the Music

Type: WWW
Address: http://bau2.uibk.ac.at/perki/Vangelis.html
Summary: Pictures, sounds, and digitized film sequences. Biographical information, as well as info about his solo and collaborative works, including motion picture scores.

Violin and Bow Makers

Type: WWW
Address: http://www.eskimo.com/~dvz/violin-makers.html
Summary: Get a regularly updated list of e-mail addresses for bowed stringed instrument makers throughout the United States. There's a short bio for each person. This site also includes info about The American Federation of Violin and Bow Makers.

The Voodoo Lounge: Rolling Stones Web Site

Type: WWW

Address: http://www.stones.com/

Summary: Be the first on your block with a "black polar fleece ear warmer with embroidered tongue." Yes, folks, this is where you'll find the official Stones merchandise catalog. Also tour schedules, music clips, picture collections, and interviews.

Rolling Stones Web Site.

WNUR-FM Jazz Information Server (The Jazz Web)

Type: WWW

Address: http://www.acns.nwu.edu/jazz/

Summary: Discographies, jazz media info (radio stations, etc.). History of jazz, live performance schedules, biographical info on artists, FAQ, lots of info on other jazz resources.

Woodstock '94 Internet Multimedia Center

Type: WWW

Address: http://www.well.com/woodstock/

Summary: Woodstock '94 is immortalized in this site. Everything in here was created during Woodstock by on-site participants and the Internet community. Over 300 pages of pictures, sounds, and text. Peace, dude.

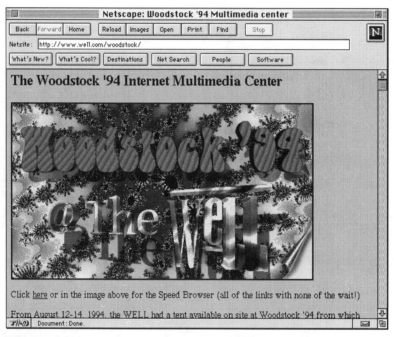

Woodstock '94.

Some Related Newsgroups

alt.emusic	rec.music.bluenote
alt.guitar.tab	rec.music.celtic
alt.music.a-cappella	rec.music.christian
alt.music.filk	rec.music.classical
alt.music.jewish	rec.music.country.western
alt.rock-n-roll.hard	rec.music.funky
alt.rock-n-roll.metal	rec.music.indian.misc
rec.music.afro-latin	rec.music.marketplace.cd

NEWS

Commercial News Services on the World Wide Web

Type: WWW

Address: http://www.jou.ufl.edu/commres/webjou.htm

Summary: Links to all the newspapers on the Net, campus as well as commercial, and to other newspaper and journalism-related resources.

The New South Polar Times

Type: WWW

Address: http://139.132.40.31/NSPT/ NSPThomePage.html

Summary: Do you ever wake up wondering what's going on at the South Pole right now? Before this Web site opened its virtual doors it wasn't very easy to get the latest news from the bottom of the world, but it's fascinating stuff. You won't read about OJ, Newt, or Whitewater; instead, it's scientific research and life in one of the most beautiful and difficult environments. In more ways than one, this is a truly cool site.

OCCULT

Dark Side of the Net

Type: mailing list

Address: carriec@eskimo.com

Summary: Subscribe to this list if you want to find out about all sorts of occult-related resources, including stuff about vampires.

To subscribe, send the following one-line message in e-mail: **subscribe dark side of the net** *your name* (where *your name* is your full name— *not* your e-mail address).

Freud's Studies of the Occult

Type: FTP
Address: ftp://ftp.spies.com/Library/Fringe/Occult/freud.occ
Summary: Freud actually dug into paranormal studies, and this paper gives all the spooky details.

Occult

Type: FTP
Address: ftp://ftp.funet.fi/pub/doc/occult/
Summary: Lots of pictures and documents—everything from astrology to wicca to magic.

Real Astrology

Type: WWW
Address: http://www.realastrology.com
Summary: Horoscopes for the rest of us. It doesn't matter if you believe in the stuff or not, Rob Brezsny is a writer with a wonderful upbeat style. I've known hardcore astrology-haters who love this page.

ONLINE SERVICES

Echo

Type: WWW
Address: http://www.echonyc.com/
Summary: Echo, an online service in New York structured somewhat like the WELL, has often been compared to a salon where artists and media professionals gather for stimulating conversation. This is not far from the truth. Echo has its own unique style and culture, "very New York" according to some users and certainly very different from most Internet forums. The Web site gives you a small taste of this uniqueness.

The WELL

Type: WWW

Address: http://www.well.com/

Summary: The WELL is a large West Coast online service that for many years has provided users with some of the most stimulating conferences in cyberspace. The Web page is like a snapshot, giving you a good picture of the unique WELL culture. This site is full of fascinating information and links, definitely worth a visit.

The WELL.

PHILOSOPHY

The American Philosophical Association
Type: Gopher
Address: gopher://apa.oxy.edu
Summary: Lots of philosophy stuff. Check out the International Philosophical Preprint Exchange, a collegial gathering of philosophers circulating pre-publication drafts of their work and commenting on the work of others.

POLITICS, GOVERNMENT & SOCIAL ISSUES

ACLU
Type: WWW
Address: http://www.aclu.org/
Summary: Even if I completely disagreed with the beliefs and aims of the American Civil Liberties Union, I would still highly recommend this page. It is well organized, colorful, and thought provoking. In addition, it contains many valuable links to other political and human rights resources. The ACLU page is one indication that the Web has come of age, that it is able to deal with serious material as effectively as it presents the latest eye candy to Net surfer d00dz.

Amnesty International
Type: WWW
Address: http://www.amnesty.org
Summary: News, contact information, and software pertaining to the organization for prisoners of conscience everywhere.

Contact: Hilary Naylor
AIUSA PeaceNet Coordinator
hnaylor@igc.apc.org
Amnesty International USA
500 Sansome St. #615
San Francisco, CA 94111
415/291-9233

Anarchist Electronic Contact List
Type: WWW
Address: http://www.cwi.nl/cwi/people/Jack.Jansen/
spunk/Spunk_Resources.html
Summary: Spunk Press maintains this collection of anarchist
and alternative resources. Newsgroups such as
alt.society.anarchy, alt.society.revolution, and
misc.activism.progressive. A Marx and Engels
Gopher hole. Alternative literature and mailing
lists.

Bibliography of Senate Hearings
Type: FTP
Address: ftp://ftp.ncsu.edu/pub/ncsu/senate/
Summary: Monthly bibliographies of Senate hearings.

The California State Senate
Type: WWW
Address: http://www.sen.ca.gov
Summary: As you would expect from the most computer
literate state in the nation, California has done a
great job making important government information available to the public. Here you can search
for pending bills in a particular area of interest,
view the actual content including proposed
changes, get updates on the bill's status, and so
on. If you leave an e-mail address you will be
notified automatically when the bill's status
changes. It would be nice if every state provided
this service!

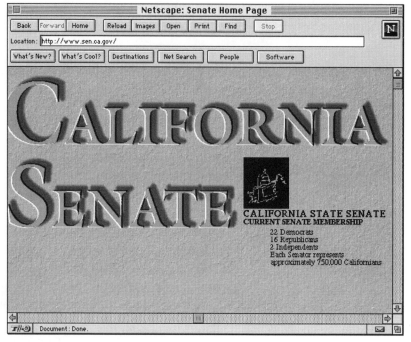

The California State Senate Web Site.

Censorship

Type: FTP

Address: ftp://ftp.spies.com/Library/Article/Rights/censored.bk

Summary: A list of books that have been banned, burned, or otherwise challenged in the last 15 years.

Center for Civic Networking

Type: FTP

Address: ftp://ftp.std.com

Path: Choose /associations/civicnet

The CIA

Type: WWW

Address: http://www.odci.gov

Summary: Yes, they're here too. The World Fact Book, included at this site, is an excellent reference for general information on specific countries.

Declassified DOE Documents

Type: WWW

Address: http://www.doe.gov

Summary: The Federal government recently declassified hundreds of Department of Energy documents, including those dealing with nuclear experiments and the possible exposure of American citizens. Not only has the DOE made these documents available to professional researchers, they've put them up on the Web with an online index. Now you can find out the *real* reason you have three arms.

DIANA: An International Human Rights Database

Type: WWW

Address: http://www.law.uc.edu:80/Diana/

Summary: This site is dedicated to "completing the pioneering work in human rights information of Diana Vincent-Davis." It's a searchable database of human rights and law-related resources. As of this writing, there were over 10,000 pages available, with the volume increasing daily.

The FBI

Type: WWW

Address: http://www.fbi.gov/

Summary: Now that J. Edgar Hoover's gone they might not be everywhere anymore, but they do have their own presence on the Web. This is a surprisingly interesting home page. Of course there's a long warning not to copy their opening logo.

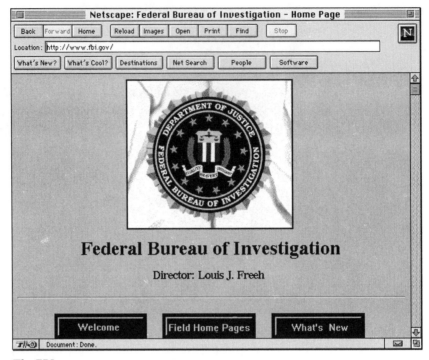

The FBI.

Fedworld

Type: WWW

Address: http://www.fedworld.gov/

Summary: Fedworld serves as a clearinghouse for information on federal agencies. It also contains links to dozens of government sponsored information servers. An important resource.

Government Documents

Type: Gopher

Address: gopher://wiretap.spies.com

Path: Government Docs (US: World)

Summary: Get full text files of government acts such as the Americans with Disabilities Act, the Brady bill and the Fair Credit Reporting Act. This area also has world constitutions, as well as NATO and White House press releases.

The MoJo Wire: Mother Jones Interactive

Type: WWW

Address: http://www.mojones.com/mojo_interactive/
mojo_interactive.html

Summary: The Mother Jones Interactive page is organized
into ten "campaign" areas such as Making Our
Democracy Work, Waging Peace, Curbing Vio-
lence in America, Fostering Diversity and Community, Improving Our Nation's Education, and
Keeping the Media Honest. You'll find articles
from *Mother Jones Magazine*, resource guide
listings, and "chat" rooms.

National Child Rights Alliance

Type: WWW

Address: http://www.ai.mit.edu/people/ellens/NCRA/
ncra.html

Summary: A collection of documents about the NCRA and
issues pertaining to child abuse.

Contact: Jim Senter
JIMSENTER@delphi.com

Silent Witness

Type: WWW

Address: http://gn2.getnet.com:80/silent/

Summary: Wanted Posters go interactive! This site is not
tremendously relevant unless you live in Phoe-
nix, but it demonstrates an interesting new use of
the Web. Police reports are presented with photographs, sketches, and lots of information. Viewers
are encouraged to call in anonymous tips if they
have any information about the particular crime
or missing person. I suspect this idea will spread
to other cities.

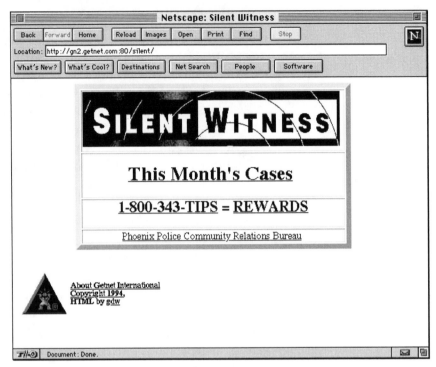

Silent Witness.

SLATE

Type: WWW

Address: http://www.slate.com/

Summary: This is Microsoft's initial foray into the world of mainstream politically-oriented journalism. A hair left of center, this paper-magazine-in-Web-clothing reads a lot like *Harper's* or *The Atlantic Monthly*. Yeah, the kind of stuff your dad called "a good read." If you like hearing what pundits have to say about the state of the world, curl up in front of your monitor and enjoy.

United Nations

Type: Gopher
Address: gopher://nywork1.undp.org:70
Summary: Info about UN conferences, session highlights and press releases, UN System directories, UN Development Programme documents, links to other UN and related Gophers.

United States Department of Justice Home Page

Type: WWW
Address: http://www.usdoj.gov
Summary: Links to several Justice Department organizations concerning litigation, investigatory, and law enforcement offices. Also pages for various DOJ issues and links to other Federal government and criminal justice information sources.

U.S. Bureau of the Census

Type: WWW
Address: http://www.census.gov/
Summary: Census Bureau news releases, population information and projections, tips on genealogy, financial data for state and local governments and schools, and summarized demographic data.

The Census Bureau.

The U.S. Constitution

Type: WWW

Address: http://www.law.cornell.edu/constitution/constitution.overview.html

Summary: Yep, just what it sounds like. See it while it lasts.

U.S. Department of Health and Human Services

Type: WWW

Address: http://www.os.dhhs.gov/

Summary: A starting point for accessing DHHS organizations. Cancer and AIDS related information, NIH grants and contracts, molecular biology databases, poverty guidelines, and links to other federal government resources.

U.S. Government Today

Type: Gopher

Address: gopher://wiretap.spies.com

Path: Government Docs (US & World) / US Government Today

Summary: Current membership lists for the House and Senate, phone and fax numbers for members of Congress.

Voice of America (VOA)

Type: Gopher

Address: gopher://gopher.voa.gov

Summary: Check out the International News and English Broadcasts radio newswire reports. You'll get daily reports, features, and documentaries on worldwide news events.

Contact: Chris Kern
202/619-2020
ck@voa.gov

Welcome to the White House

Type: WWW

Address: http://www.whitehouse.gov

Summary: As of the writing of this book, this is still where Bill and Hillary live. Tour the White House, check out Al Gore's favorite political cartoons, download a picture of Socks, read the electronic citizens' handbook, get detailed info about Cabinet-level and independent agencies, daily press releases, briefings on economic and environmental policy, information on government funded child care and disaster assistance, and lots more.

Some Related Newsgroups

alt.activism	alt.society.conservatism
alt.censorship	alt.society.revolution
alt.politics.greens	bit.listserv.politics
alt.politics.libertarian	bit.org.peace-corps
alt.politics.media	talk.politics.soviet
alt.save.the.earth	talk.politics.theory

PRIVACY

PRIVACY Forum

Type: WWW
Address: http://www.vortex.com/privacy.htm
Summary: Discussions of privacy in the information age. This directory includes all issues of the Privacy Forum Digest, as well as lots of related reports and materials.

  The home page gives complete instruction for subscribing to the PRIVACY Forum.

Type: FTP
Address: ftp://ftp.vortex.com/privacy
Type: Gopher
Address: gopher://cv.vortex.com
Path: *** PRIVACY Forum ***

Privacy Information

Type: WWW
Address: http://www.eff.org/
Summary: The latest information on personal privacy online from the Electronic Frontier Foundation.

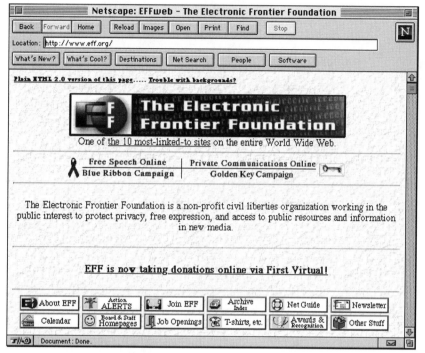

The Electronic Frontier Foundation.

REFERENCE

IoQtus

Type: WWW

Address: http://pubweb.ucdavis.edu/Documents/ Quotations/homepage.html

Summary: Jason Newquist at the University of California at Davis has put together a comprehensive quotations resource. It includes his own quotations list and pointers to a whole bunch of other quotations sources.

Contact: Jason Newquist jmnewquist@ucdavis.edu

Online reference works

Type: WWW

Address: http://www.cs.cmu.edu:8001/Web/references.html

Summary: A great collection of links to dictionaries, geographical information, legal and governmental references, phone books, and other reference resources.

RELIGION & SPIRITUALITY

The Bhagavad Gita

Type: WWW

Address: http://www.cc.gatech.edu/gvu/people/Phd/Rakesh.Mullick/gita/gita.html

Summary: The Hindu scripture in the original Sanskrit. Each chapter is a separate PostScript document. An English translation and a summary are also available from this page.

Buddhist Studies

Type: WWW

Address: http://coombs.anu.edu.au/WWWVL-Buddhism.html

Summary: Buddhist organizations, several Buddhist studies databases, links to Gopher and Web resources. A good place to start. From here, you should be able to find out whatever you want about Buddhism. This page also contains links to other religion resources.

Catholic Resources on the Net

Type: WWW

Address: http://www.cs.cmu.edu/Web/People/spok/catholic.html

Summary: Some of the sections: Liturgy and Worship, Scripture, Writings from the early Church, Vatican II documents (1962-1965), selected papal encyclicals and pronouncements, history and culture, and related resources.

Full text of several books such as *Confessions of St. Augustine, The Imitation of Christ,* and *The Practice of the Presence of God.*

Electric Mystics

Type: Gopher
Address: gopher://wiretap.spies.com
Path: OO/Library/Article/Religion
Summary: Complete bibliography of online religious studies resources. Electronic documents, conferences, serials, software, and archives.

Hindu Names

Type: FTP
Address: ftp://ftp.spies.com/Library/Article/Language/hindu.nam

Israel Project

Type: FTP
Address: ftp://israel.nysernet.org/israel
Summary: Information about all aspects of Judaism and the state of Israel.

Never forget. Change to the /israel/holocaust directory for a wealth of information, including data, on the neo-Nazi movement.

Spirituality & Consciousness

Type: WWW
Address: http://zeta.cs.adfa.oz.au/Spirituality.html
Summary: Pointers to info about channeling, meditation, yoga, Veda, Theosophy, astrology, Bhakti-Yoga, Free Daism, paranormal phenomena, and lots more having to do with metaphysical and alternative views.

Netscape: WWW-VL: Spirituality & Consciousness

Location: http://zeta.cs.adfa.oz.au/Spirituality.html

Spirituality & Consciousness.

SCIENCE

Alfred Wegener Institute for Polar and Marine Research

Type: WWW

Address: http://www.awi-bremerhaven.de/

Summary: The Alfred Wegener Institute has laboratories in Bremerhaven and Potsdam, bases in the Arctic and Antarctic, and research ships and aircraft. Lots of GIFs, maps, and charts of the polar region. Includes a detailed hydrographic atlas of the Southern Ocean. There's a database of polar and marine related docs on the Web, pointers to other WWW servers related to polar, marine, and global change research.

AMSAT: The Radio Amateur Satellite Corporation

Type: WWW

Address: http://www.qualcomm.com/amsat/AmsatHome.html

Summary: If you're one of those people who makes and launches satellites in your backyard, this is *the* site for you.

Avion Online

Type: WWW

Address: http://avion.db.erau.edu/avion/avionhome.html

Summary: The first online aviation/aerospace newspaper. The Space Technology section covers activity at Kennedy Space Center, including shuttle launches and landings. The Aeronautica section routinely covers activity in the aviation and aeronautics industry, including aviation trade news and special flying events.

Biological Sciences Resources

Type: FTP

Address: ftp://ksuvxa.kent.edu/library/acadlist.file5

Summary: This is a list of a whole bunch of mailing lists that have to do with the biological sciences.

Center for Coastal Studies

Type: WWW

Address: http://www-ccs.ucsd.edu/

Summary: The Center for Coastal Studies is a research unit of UC San Diego's Scripps Institution of Oceanography. You'll find all sorts of studies on subjects like global warming, long-term climate change, earthquake prediction, coastal protection, and sediment management.

Type: Gopher

Address: gopher://gopher-ccs.ucsd.edu

Comet Shoemaker-Levy 9

Type: WWW

Address: http://newproducts.jpl.nasa.gov/sl9/sl9.html

Summary: When Comet Shoemaker-Levy 9 collided with Jupiter in July 1994, it was the first time the collision of two major solar system bodies was observed and recorded. This page contains lots of background information and animations, and takes you to photo files from NASA and world-wide observatories. There's a whole section full of links to other Comet Shoemaker-Levy home pages (currently there are seven).

Lunar Institute of Technology

Type: WWW

Address: http://sunsite.unc.edu/lunar/index.html

Summary: The Lunar Institute of Technology was estab-lished in 2032, and its School of Starship Design is renowned throughout the Solar System. If you are one of the lucky few to attend this prestigious institution, you will participate in the design of a manned interstellar vehicle. Pick a specialty— Mission/Operations, Structure/Shielding, Payload/Sciences—and become part of the design team.

My description may be somewhat tongue-in-cheek, but you'll find some serious science here.

The Mercury Project

Type: WWW

Address: http://cwis.usc.edu/dept/raiders/

Summary: Ever since the first text-based adventure computer games, we have been the masters of virtual worlds, engaging in all kinds of exciting activities from the comfort of our desk chairs. But no matter how deeply we immersed ourselves in these alternate realities, a part of us always knew they weren't really real. What if you could type something on your keyboard and have an immediate effect on a robot made of wires and metal, not just electronic information? Well, the Mercury Project lets you do just that. In real-time you control the movements of a robot arm that's busy excavating an actual physical site as part of some academic research. Not exactly Star Wars, but it's a fascinating project that demonstrates the power of the Internet and makes you feel like a you're driving a big electronic bulldozer.

The Myers-Briggs Test—Kiersey Temperament Sorter

Type: WWW

Address: http://sunsite.unc.edu/jembin/mb.pl

Summary: Take this short psychological test to determine what makes you tick or tock. For instance, I found out that I'm the same kind of guy as Socrates, Gerald Ford, and Henry Mancini.

The NASA Newsroom

Type: WWW

Address: http://www.gsfc.nasa.gov/hqpao/ newsroom.html

Summary: All sorts of NASA press releases, press kits, status reports, fact sheets, and official statements.

NASA Online Information

Type: WWW

Address: http://mosaic.larc.nasa.gov/nasaonline/ nasaonline.html

Summary: NASA's home page, huge and full of interesting information. It includes links to specialized FTP sites, Gopher sites, and much much more.

Numerical Aerodynamic Simulation: The NASA Supercomputer

Type: WWW

Address: http://www.nas.nasa.gov/

Summary: This is the ultimate computer geek page, full of information on the NAS large-scale supercomputing system used by NASA and other agencies. It is a rich and fascinating site.

Primate Info Net

Type: Gopher

Address: gopher://night.primate.wisc.edu:70/11/

Summary: This entire gopher is devoted to primate biology. You'll find stuff about animal welfare legislation and behavioral patterns. Lots of newsletters and discussions.

Smithsonian Institution's Natural History Gopher

Type: Gopher

Address: gopher://nmnhgoph.si.edu

Summary: This Gopher contains newsletters, projects, and lots of pointers to other natural history resources. If you're interested in botany, vertebrate zoology, biodiversity, biological conservation, global volcanism, or anything else involving natural history, check out this cool site.

Space Movie Archive

Type: WWW

Address: http://www.univ-rennes1.fr/ASTRO/ anim-e.html

Summary: We're not talking science fiction here. We're talking solar eclipses, meteorology, and space exploration. (With some science fiction thrown into the mix for good measure.) Tons of animations and instructions for getting animation viewers if you don't already have one.

Type: FTP
Address: ftp://ftp.univ-rennes1.fr/pub/Images/ASTRO/ anim

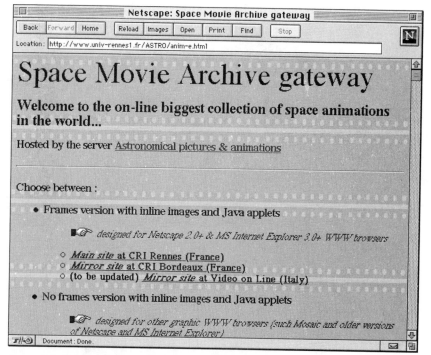

Space Movie Archive.

Stephen Hawking's Black Hole Theory

Type: Gopher
Address: gopher://wx.atmos.uiuc.edu
Path: Documents / fun / hawking.black.holes
Summary: The full text of Hawking's 1988 presentation, "Baby Universes, Children of Black Holes."

United States Geological Survey

Type: WWW
Address: http://info.er.usgs.gov/

Summary: Geologic map of the United States and information about public issues, education, and environmental research.

Midcourse Space Experiment

Type: WWW
Address: http://msx.nrl.navy.mil
Summary: A GUI system developed at the Backgrounds Data Center in Washington D.C. to "bring visualization to its databases of multiple remote sensing platforms." Users can query, visualize, and analyze geophysical and celestial data and metadata.

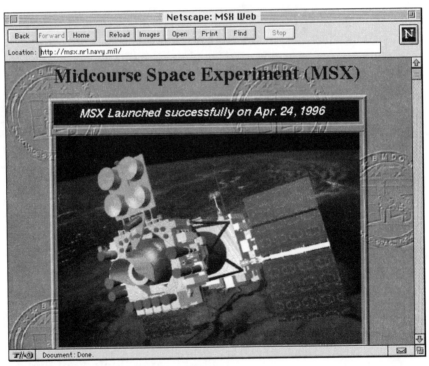

The VISTA Midcourse Space Experiment.

Some Related Newsgroups

alt.sci.planetary	bionet.women-in-bio
bionet.genome.arabidopsis	sci.astro
bionet.genome.chromosome	sci.astro.hubble
bionet.molbio.ageing	sci.bio.ecolog
bionet.plants	sci.astro.planetarium
bionet.photosynthesis	sci.bio.technology
bionet.population-bio	sci.engr.chem

SCIENCE FICTION

Isaac Asimov FAQ

Type: WWW

Address: http://www.lightside.com/SpecialInterest/asimov/asimov-faq.html

Summary: This FAQ is full of fascinating stuff about the master and his works.

J. R. R. Tolkien Information Page

Type: WWW

Address: http://www.csclub.uwaterloo.ca/u/relipper/tolkien/rootpage.html

Summary: This page, put together by Eric Lippert, is an amazingly complete Tolkien resource. In addition to FAQs, book lists, Newsgroups, language resources, info about the Tolkien Society, a Middle-Earth map, Noldor and Great Houses family trees. There are several query tools.

Contact: Eric Lippert

relippert@descartes.uwaterloo.ca

The Klingon Language Institute

Type: WWW

Address: http://galaxy.neca.com/~soruk/tlhIngan/

Summary: In learning most foreign languages, there is no substitute for visiting the actual country. If you want to learn Klingon, however, there is no substitute for the Web pages maintained by the Klingon Language Institute. Even if you're not a *Star Trek* fan you'll get a kick out of this site, a labor of love for some very dedicated Klingon enthusiasts.

The MIT Science Fiction Library Pinkdex

Type: WWW

Address: http://www.mit.edu:8001/pinkdex

Summary: This is a thorough catalog of science fiction books that lets you search by keyword.

Science Fiction Resource Guide

Type: FTP

Address: ftp://gandalf.rutgers.edu/pub/sfl/sf-resource. guide.html

Summary: From the SF-Lovers Archives at Rutgers University. The ultimate SF link. It's all here—authors, awards, bookstores, fandom, fiction, movies, zines, conventions, and more.

Speculative Fiction Clearing House

Type: WWW

Address: http://thule.mt.cs.cmu.edu:8001/sf-clearing-house/

Summary: Science fiction, fantasy and horror archives, authors, awards, conventions, zines, and newsletters. Also resources for SF writers.

Unofficial Xanth Page

Type: WWW

Address: http://www.best.com/~wooldri/awooldri/Xanth.html

Summary:

For fans of Piers Anthony's Xanth world novels. Some highlights: a cheat list for Companions of Xanth, a Qbasic program that allows you to generate Xanth-like talents, the Piers Anthony FAQ, a Xanth family tree, the Xanth calendar, and a color image of Piers and his dog. Newsgroup: alt.fan.piers-anthony

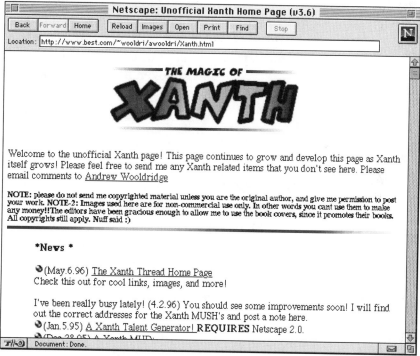

The Magic of Xanth.

SHOPPING

Aircraft Shopper Online

Type: WWW

Address: http://aso.solid.com/

Summary: Looking for a P51 Mustang fighter? Or is an old DC-3 more your style? Or do you want to sell your rusting 172 and upgrade to something a bit newer? Whether you want to buy or sell a plane, this is the best place on the Web to get started.

The Classified Advertising Page

Type: WWW

Address: http://www.imall.com/ads/ads.html

Summary: Whether you're looking for a computer, a job, or a date (or even if you're looking for all three), this is the site to visit. The listings, many of them links to Usenet newsgroup announcements, are well organized and current.

The Future Fantasy Bookstore

Type: WWW

Address: http://futfan.com/

Summary: Digital maintains this excellent online book catalog full of SF and fantasy titles. This is probably the best Web source for this kind of material.

Hall of Malls

Type: WWW

Address: http://nsns.com/MouseTracks/HallofMalls.html

Summary: I *hate* malls! Malls fall somewhere between rats and taxes on my list of the 10 Worst Things in the World. But I have to admit that electronic malls on the Web aren't *quite* so annoying—at least you're not bombarded with endlessly repeating Muzak versions of "Little Drummer Boy."

If there's something you can't get online, it's probably pretty hard to get any other way. Malls are springing up all over the Web. And because there are so many malls, the Web has generated a new kind of virtual hell: the meta-mall, somewhere you can go to choose which mall you want to visit. Here it is, a glimpse of the Jetsonesque future. Shop till your hard drive drops.

Offworld Metaplex

Type: WWW

Address: http://offworld.wwa.com/

Summary: Oh no, a cyber *theme* mall! Let the mysterious Mr. Sin lead you through a "unique shopping experience." There's actually some pretty neat stuff here if you're in a consumerist mood.

The Virtual MeetMarket(sm)

Type: WWW

Address: http://vmm.ravenna.com/

Summary: "Wild and crazy netsurfer dude seeks female UNIX tigress for some fun with a SUN." That sort of thing.

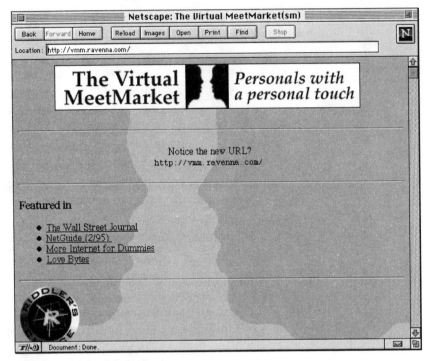

The Virtual MeetMarket(sm).

SHOWBIZ

Elvis Lives!

Type: WWW

Address: http://128.194.15.32/~ahb2188/elvishom.html

Summary: Created by superfan Andrea Berman to "honor his cultural and musical legacy." Take a tour of Graceland, inspect Elvis's shopping list, and check out the results of an online seance conducted in January 1994.

Gossip

Type: Usenet

Address: alt.showbiz.gossip

Summary: Don't get bogged down with the facts—this is pure unadulterated gossip.

Sports

Aquanaut

Type: WWW

Address: http://www.aquanaut.com:8080/

Summary: Everything scuba—a database of diveable ship-wrecks, reviews of dive gear and equipment, reviews of popular dive destinations, and underwater pictures.
Newsgroup: rec.scuba

The Art of FENCING

Type: WWW

Address: http://www.ii.uib.no/~arild/fencing.html

Summary: Articles, fencing clubs and associations, events lists, the Internet Fencing Encyclopedia (a collection of links to pages about fencing).

Footbag WorldWide

Type: WWW

Address: http://www.cup.hp.com:80/~footbag/

Summary: Footbag is a new sport, similar to the game of Hacky Sack. Get tournament results, equipment information, images, and video clips of footbag action.

To join the mailing list and chat with other players at all levels, send e-mail to ba-footbag-request@cup.hp.com (include your first and last name somewhere in the message).

George Ferguson's Ultimate Page

Type: WWW

Address: http://www.cs.rochester.edu/u/ferguson/ultimate/

Summary: Ultimate Frisbee is a non-contact team sport. Get the official rules and tournament handbook here.

Hawaii's NHL Home Page

Type: WWW

Address: http://maxwell.uhh.hawaii.edu/hockey/
hockey.html

Summary: Welcome to the world of hockey. From here, you can get to all of the NHL team home pages, the NHL Statserver, game schedules, and Stanley Cup info. Currently, there are plans to provide daily statistical updates on teams and players.

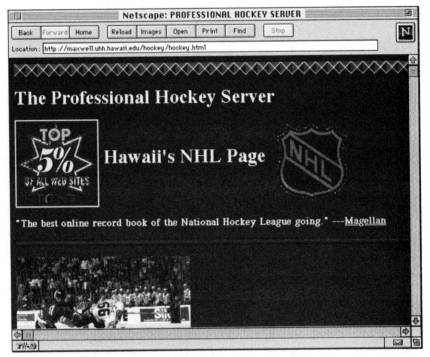

Professional Hockey Server (Author: Richard Crowe, The University of Hawaii at Hilo).

Korfball

Type: WWW

Address: http://www.earth.ox.ac.uk:80/~geoff/

Summary: Korfball is a mixed team sport that's kind of like basketball, but without backboards or dribbling. Get the latest information about this rapidly growing sport.

Mountain Biking

Type: WWW
Address: http://xenon.stanford.edu/~rsf/mtn-bike.html
Summary: Info about biking trails in various parts of the United States, as well as a link to a mountain bike page in the UK.

NBA.com

Type: WWW
Address: http://www.nba.com
Summary: My 11-year-old son lives here. This site solves the problem of what to do with your life when the game is over.

Orienteering and Rogaining Home Page

Type: WWW
Address: http://www2.aos.Princeton.EDU:80/rdslater/orienteering/
Summary: Get out your old scout compass and hit the road. Announcements about these two popular sports, federation and club information, and links to related pages.

The Running Page

Type: WWW
Address: http://sunsite.unc.edu/drears/running/running.html
Summary: Info about upcoming races, race results, places to run, running related products, and running publications.

Check out the Exercise Trails Network. Members of the American Running and Fitness Association have been contributing maps of their favorite running and exercise trails. You can get a free map by contributing one of your own, even if you're not a member. Otherwise, maps cost $1.

Sports World BBS

Type: WWW
Address: http://debussy.media.mit.edu/dbecker/docs/
swbbs.html
Summary: Stats for NHL, NFL, NBA, and Major League
Baseball pools.

Volleyball World Wide Service

Type: WWW
Address: http://www.volleyball.org/
Summary: This page was created by Tom Jack, a software
design engineer who coaches volleyball in his
spare time, as a way of centralizing information
about the sport. You'll find FAQs, info about the
volleyball newsgroup, equipment, TV coverage,
and coverage of Olympic and professional teams.
Because Tom lives in Cupertino, California,
there's lots of info about classes, clubs, tourna-
ments and such in the San Jose/San Francisco
area. Links to volleyball sites throughout the
United States.
Contact: Tom Jack
taj@cup.hp.com
408/447-4239

STAR TREK

Star Trek Files

Type: FTP
Address: ftp://ftp.spies.com/Library/Media/Trek
Summary: Tons of Trek-related files, including a Klingon
vocabulary and a *Deep Space Nine* bibliography.

British Starfleet Confederacy

Type: WWW

Address: http://deeptht.armory.com/~bsc/

Summary: If you join the British Starfleet Confederacy, you'll get a certificate of commission, officers' manual, identity card, stardate calendar, and six bimonthly newsletters and chapter bulletins. Even if you don't want to join the fleet, this page contains comprehensive links to all things Trek.

Contact: starfleet@subspace.demon.co.uk

Klingon Language Institute

Type: WWW

Address: http://www.kli.org/

Summary: The Klingon Language Institute was founded in 1992 "to promote, foster, and develop the Klingon language, and to bring together Klingon language enthusiasts from around the world." You'll find sound files, information about their postal course and how to subscribe to the mailing list, and a fascinating background on the development of the language. (It's one of the few artificial alien languages actually developed by a trained linguist.)

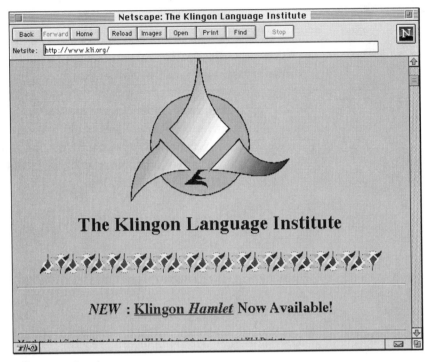

Klingon spoken here.

STRANGE USENET NEWSGROUPS

alt.angst
alt.barney.dinosaur.die.die.die
alt.buddha.short.fat.guy
alt.flame.roommate
alt.food.sugar-cereals
alt.geek
alt.happy.birthday.to.me
alt.pantyhose
alt.religion.santaism
alt.spam
alt.tasteless
alt.wesley.crusher.die.die.die

talk.bizarre

TECHNOLOGY

Telecom Information Resources on the Internet
Type: WWW
Address: http://www.ipps.lsa.umich.edu/ telecom-info.html
Summary: A plenitude of pointers to telecommunications Net resources. It's all here—voice, data, video, wired, wireless, cable TV, satellite. You can find info about aspects of telecom issues, from technical to public policy, from economic to social impacts.
Contact: Jeff MacKie-Mason jmm@umich.edu

THEATRE & FILM

Drama
Type: Gopher
Address: gopher://english-server.hss.cmu.edu
Path: Drama
Summary: Play scripts, drama-related materials, reviews, Shakespeare info. Follow path to Shakespeare-Glossary for glossary of Shakespearean terms.

Home Page of Theatre
Type: WWW
Address: http://www.cs.fsu.edu/projects/group4/ theatre.html
Summary: Follow the links on this page to find myriad theatre resources. Some highlights: Ray Bradbury's Theatre Episode Guide, ruins of the Roman Theatre, The Fire Sign Theatre, and Computers in Theatre.

Internet Movie Database

Type: WWW

Address: http://www.msstate.edu/Movies/

Summary: This is the Web's most complete searchable database of films. If you're a movie buff, don't miss this site!

Screenwriters' and Playwrights' Home Page

Type: WWW

Address: http://www.teleport.com/~cdeemer/ scrwriter.html

Summary: As of this writing, this page is still under construction, but there are already lots of resources for screenwriters and playwrights. There's a guide to screenplay structure, scripts, discussion groups, and tips from the pros.

Weird Movie List

Type: FTP

Address: ftp://ftp.spies.com/Library/Media/Film/ weird.movi

Summary: Alphabetical list of weird movies, with descriptions. You can also get this list via Gopher. The address is wiretap.spies.com, then choose Wiretap Online Library / Mass Media / Film and Movies / Weird Movie List.

TRAVEL

City.Net

Type: WWW

Address: http://www.city.net

Summary: Good information on the largest and best-known cities around the world.

Clothing Optional

Type: FTP

Address: ftp://rtfm.mit.edu/pub/usenet/rec.answers/
nude-faq/beaches

Summary: Get naked! Lists of clothing-optional beaches, hot
springs, parks, and resorts worldwide.

Downwind

Type: Telnet

Address: telnet://downwind.sprl.umich.edu 3000

Summary: Traveling? Why not check out the current
weather and the forecast for your destination city.

The Global Network Navigator/Koblas Currency Converter

Type: WWW

Address: http://bin.gnn.com/cgi-bin/gnn/currency

Summary: This page is updated weekly. By default, the page
shows the currency rates of over 50 countries
relative to U.S. currency (e.g., one U.S. dollar is
worth 1.3605 dollars in Australia). To get currency rates relative to another country, just click
the country you want.

GNN TC Internet Resources — Planning & Research

Type: WWW

Address: http://nearnet.gnn.com/gnn/meta/travel/res/
planning.html

Summary: Even if the longest trip you ever take is from your
computer to your printer, check out this page. It'll
take you to all sorts of travel-related resources.
You'll find U.S. Army Area Handbooks on Egypt,
Indonesia, Israel, Japan, the Philippines,
Singapore, Somalia, South Korea, and Yugosla-
via. And get an inside peek at the documents the
State Department gives its people before they
travel to a country. Get the latest U.S. State

Department travel warnings and consular information sheets. A few more highlights: The Internet Guide to Hostelling; Travel Health—Staying Healthy in Asia, Africa, and Latin America; the CIA World Factbook; Travel Tips for Less Developed Countries; and the Worldwide Telephone Codes list, which is a searchable list of area codes for the entire world.

The Hawaiian Islands

Type: WWW

Address: http://www2.hawaii.edu/visitors/visit.hawaii.html

Summary: This one's maintained by the Hawaii Visitors Center. There's a link to each of the islands.

The Jerusalem Mosaic

Type: WWW

Address: http://www1.cc.huji.ac.il/jeru/

Summary: Listen to the song of Jerusalem, view Jerusalem from the sky, read about events in the history of Jerusalem.

Local Times Around the World

Type: Gopher

Address: gopher://austin.unimelb.edu.au

Path: General Information and Resources/Local Times Around the World

Summary: Connect to computers in cities around the world to get local time reports.

PCTravel

Type: Telnet

Address: telnet://pctravel.com

Summary: PCTravel makes it easy for you to view and select schedules and fares for all major airlines. All you need to know is where and when you are going. You can even buy your tickets online.

The Perry-Castañeda Map Collection

Type: WWW

Address: http://www.lib.utexas.edu/Libs/PCL/
Map_collection/Map_collection.html

Summary: This is a great collection of electronic maps from
the Perry Castañeda Library at UT. It even includes National Park maps and a map of the
South Pole. Needless to say, there are maps of
Texas, too.

The Rec.Travel Library

Type: WWW

Address: http://rec-travel.digimark.net/

Summary: The rec.travel Usenet newsgroups have always
been a great source of travel information, but far
from convenient when it comes to tracking down
the facts you need. This Web site serves up a
tremendous amount of up-to-date information on
destinations, transportation, and even travel
agents. It also includes links to other travel-
related pages.

Subway Maps

Type: Gopher

Address: gopher://vishnu.jussieu.fr

Path: Indicateur des metros (don't worry, there's a file
in English too)

Summary: Download color maps of the Paris and Lyon
subways.

UT-LANIC

Type: Gopher

Address: gopher://lanic.utexas.edu

Summary: This is the University of Texas Latin American
Network Information Center. Here you can
access a wealth of information about Latin
America, including catalogs, databases, FTP
archives, other gopher sites, and so on.

Virtual Paris

Type: WWW

Address: http://www.paris.org/

Summary: Well, it's not quite the real thing, but it's a lot cheaper.

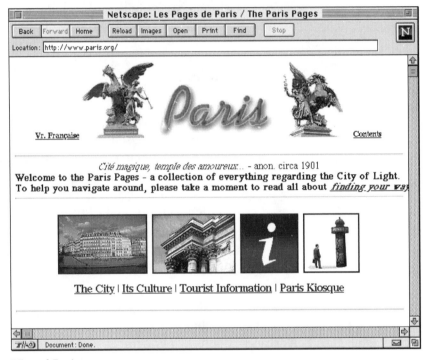

Virtual Paris.

Virtually Hawaii

Type: WWW

Address: http://www.satlab.hawaii.edu/space/hawaii/

Summary: This is a NASA site that includes lots of remote sensing satellite and aircraft images of Hawaii. It also provides real-time satellite data and links to several related pages. While it's not exactly the same as sunning on a beach in Maui, this is a great educational site.

Virtually Hawaii.

Welcome to Eurogopher

Type: WWW

Address: http://www.sunet.se/eurogopher/eg.html

Summary: This is a great starting point for information about Europe.

A Related Newsgroup

rec.travel.marketplace

UTILITIES & SPECIALIZED INFORMATION

The AT&T 800-Number Directory

Type: WWW

Address: http://www.tollfree.att.net

Summary: This is a wonderful convenience that I use all the time. Simply type in the name of a company and you will be presented with the 800 number much more quickly than you could look it up in a phone book.

Electric Postcard

Type: WWW

Address: http://persona.www.media.mit.edu/Postcards/

Summary: This is a great idea, really exploiting the interactive possibilities of the Web. You choose from a large collection of "postcards," beautiful and interesting graphics files, and address one to a friend. Your friend can then log into this site and based on a tracking number pick up the postcard you "sent."

FedEx

Type: WWW

Address: http://www.fedex.com/

Summary: This site is about as sexy and inspiring as the U.S. Senate, but it lets you find out where your package is.

The Global Network Navigator/Koblas Currency Converter

Type: WWW

Address: http://bin.gnn.com/cgi-bin/gnn/currency

Summary: Find out what your dollar's worth in many major nations. An excellent tool for business travelers.

The IRS

Type: WWW

Address: http://www.irs.ustreas.gov/prod/

Summary And you thought you could get away from them on the Web! Actually this is a very useful site that provides forms, instructions, and answers to common questions. ("Do I really have to give you my money?" "Yes.")

The Jargon File

Type: WWW

Address: http://www.phil.uni-sb.de/fun/jargon/index.html

Summary: This is a huge index of jargon, especially tech-speak. After a few hours here you'll sound like you know what you're talking about.

The Mortgage Calculator

Type: WWW

Address: http://ibc.wustl.edu/mort.html

Summary: Back in the days when text-based DOS programs ruled the PC world like primitive insects, I had a utility for everything. In fact, I sometimes had several different programs for the same job. Then Windows came along, and disk space became as precious to me as Manhattan real estate. Thanks to behemoth programs like Word and Excel, not to mention Windows itself, there was no longer room for directories full of little one-job tools. Fortunately a wealth of simple utilities is available on the Net, and this flexible mortgage calculator is a good example. I find it quicker to click over to this URL via a bookmark than to load up a local copy of Excel!

NewsHound

Type: e-mail

Address: newshound-support@sjmercury.com (send a message requesting information)

Summary: This is an electronic version of a clipping service. You tell them what you're interested in, and NewsHound keeps an eye out for articles that match your search criteria. It then sends you the information via e-mail. There is a monthly charge.

Stanford Netnews Filtering Service

Type: WWW

Address: http://woodstock.stanford.edu:2000

Summary: This is an interesting service for those who don't have access to a Usenet news server or who don't want to weed through the thousands of newsgroups looking for what they want. The Stanford Netnews Filtering Service lets you specify areas of interest; it then sends you Usenet postings, via e-mail, based on those criteria.

Taxing Times

Type: WWW

Address: http://www.scubed.com/tax/tax.html

Summary: The only things that are certain in life are death, hard disk crashes, and taxes. This site can help you with one of those.

Xerox PARC Map Viewer

Type: WWW

Address: http://pubweb.parc.xerox.com/map

Summary: Another great example of how hypermedia can be used effectively on the Web. You are presented with a map of the world. Click on an area and it zooms in. Click again and it zooms in some more. You can also search by keyword. This is a well-designed tool that's great for putting geography in perspective.

WEATHER

National Weather Service Forecasts

Type: Gopher

Address: gopher://wx.atmos.uiuc.edu

Summary: Weather reports by geographical region as well as by weather type.

[More] National Weather Forecasts

Type: Gopher
Address: gopher://downwind.sprl.umich.edu
Path: Weather Text, U.S. City Forecasts
Summary: Daily weather information for cities all over the country. Pick a state, then a city.

WEB INFO

A Beginner's Guide to HTML

Type: WWW
Address: http://www.ncsa.uiuc.edu/General/Internet/WWW/HTMLPrimer.html
Summary: Once I started cruising the Web, it wasn't long before I wanted to start putting up my own pages. The HTML markup language that's used to create Web documents is not at all difficult, especially with some of the specialized editing tools. And to help you get started, NCSA provides an excellent hypermedia tutorial. You'll be creating simple documents in a matter of hours.

Building a Corporate Web

Type: WWW
Address: http://www.webcom.com/~wordmark/sem_1.html#home
Summary: Wordmark Associates has put together this informative and well thought out hypermedia seminar for corporations wanting to establish a presence on the Web. I recommend that you read this information *before* designing your commercial Web pages.

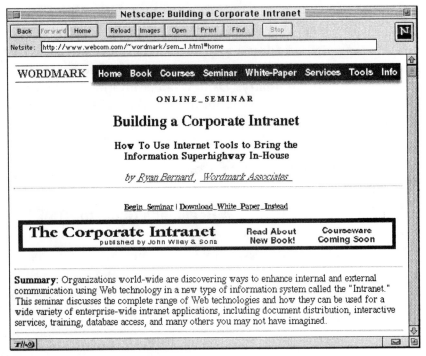

Building a Corporate Web.

The CGI Page

Type: WWW

Address: http://www.yahoo.com/Computers/World_Wide_Web/CGI_Common_Gateway_Interface

Summary: CGI scripts are programs on a Web server that process or manipulate data transmitted by a Web user via forms in an HTML document. Often written in PERL, CGI scripts are useful for many commercial applications on the Web, from collecting demographic information to selling products; they can also be used for more fun applications like presenting the user with a randomly selected fortune. This is a good starting place for learning about CGI.

Imagemaps Made Simple

Type: WWW

Address: http://www.ccsf.caltech.edu/clickmap.html

Summary: If you've explored the Web for more than half an hour, you've probably encountered imagemaps. These are pictures that can launch you to other documents depending where you click. If you've already learned the basics of creating Web pages, this is the best place to get information on developing your own clickable imagemaps.

The PERL Page

Type: WWW

Address: http://www.cis.ufl.edu/cgi-bin/plindex

Summary: PERL stands for Practical Extraction and Report Language. It is a flexible and fairly easy-to-use programming language that's especially suited to manipulating text. It is often used for developing CGI gateways on Web servers. This site will get you started on creating your own PERL scripts.

Talker

Type: WWW

Address: http://www2.infi.net:80/talker/

Summary: For those of you who can't get enough of yaking online, here's another interesting Web-based chat program. Looks interesting.

Virtual "Separator Bar" Collection

Type: WWW

Address: http://inls.ucsd.edu/y/OhBoy/bars.html

Summary: No, this is not a hotlist of virtual drinking establishments. The bars we are talking about here are the horizontal rules that most HTML authors use to break up sections of their document. Instead of letting Web browsers display their default plain-vanilla line when you specify an <hr> tag in your page, why not ship a colorful, interesting, beautiful graphic bar instead? This site includes more horizontal rules than you'll ever use.

WebChat

Type: WWW

Address: http://www.irsociety.com/webchat.html

Summary: WebChat is an exciting new Web-based facility for live conferencing or chatting. You can see a .GIF picture of the person you are chatting with, and you can place .GIFs and Web hotlinks in your messages.

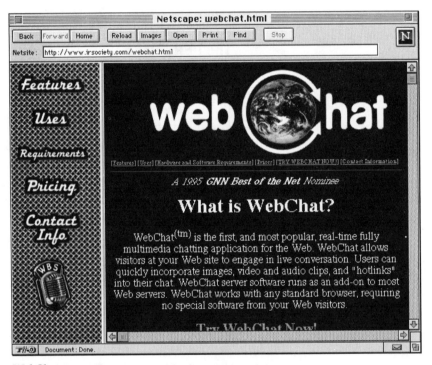

WebChat.

Web Page Design and Layout

Type: WWW

Address: http://www.yahoo.com/Computers/World_Wide_Web/Page_Design_and_Layout

Summary: This is a great place to start if you're looking for ideas and advice on designing your own HTML home page.

The Worst Web Page

Type: WWW

Address: http://www.panix.com/~clays/biff/

Summary: With a little bit of design sense and a willingness to learn, almost anybody can create a decent home page. It takes a special talent, though, to create a truly hideous one. The author of this page has taken many of the annoying interface problems found in typical Web pages and thrown them all together into one ugly mess. While this site is very funny, it is actually more useful than it sounds. As you start designing your own Web documents it's a great place to learn what *not* to do.

Wow, The Web is BIG

Type: WWW

Address: http://www.mit.edu:8001/afs/sipb/user/ mkgray/ht/wow-its-big.html

Summary: This site offers frequently updated statistics on the size of the World Wide Web, based mainly on the flow of traffic. You'll be surprised at how popular the Web really is!

The WWW FAQ

Type: WWW

Address: http://www.boutell.com/faq/

Summary: This list of frequently asked questions is one of the best places to start learning about the Web. It is thorough, well-organized, and updated frequently. A good place to visit if you feel lost or confused or if you simply want a fuller understanding of how the Web works.

Appendix A
About Netscapepress.com

Netscapepress.com is where you will find the most up-to-date information about Netscape Press. Please visit the site at **http://www.netscapepress.com/**. Netscapepress.com features a catalog of other Netscape Press titles, technical support information, and updates to the book as needed.

Netscapepress.com is the home of *Navigate!,* the official electronic publication of Netscape Press. *Navigate!* is a monthly online publication that offers a wide range of articles and reviews aimed at Netscape users. *Navigate!* features interviews with industry icons and experts, as well as articles excerpted from upcoming Netscape Press titles. Learn how to improve your Web site or to use the best search engines online. Stay abreast of the latest technological innovations and impress your friends with your intimate knowledge of the world's most popular Internet browser.

Netscape Press is a joint effort between Ventana Communications Group, Inc., and Netscape Communications Corp., and serves as the publishing arm of Netscape.

Appendix B
About the Companion CD-ROM

The CD-ROM included with your copy of The *Official Netscape Navigator 3.0 Book* contains a licensed copy of Netscape Navigator 3.0 for Macintosh.

Loading the CD-ROM is pretty straightforward:

1. Insert the CD into your CD-ROM drive.

2. After the NetPress icon appears on the desktop, double-click on it just like you would to open any other device on the desktop.

3. After you have read the ReadMe.TXT file to learn about the latest changes or about any other special last-minute information, double-click on Viewer. The CD will launch.

NAVIGATING THE CD-ROM

Your choices for navigating the CD-ROM appear on the opening screen. You can Quit the CD, install Netscape Navigator 3.0 by clicking on the Software button, browse the contents of Chapter 12, "Our Favorite Net Resources," electronically by clicking on From the Book; learn more about Netscape Press, browse the Hot Picks, or learn more about Ventana.

When you click on From the Book, you will be presented with two choices: Locate Browser and Launch Browser. You must click on Locate Browser first, and help the program find your Web browser. You will not have to perform this step again unless you move your Web browser to another directory or another hard drive. You can then click on Launch Browser and your browser will launch and open up a fully hyperlinked version of Chapter 12.

TECHNICAL SUPPORT

Technical support is available for installation-related problems only. The technical support office is open from 8:00 A.M. to 6:00 P.M. Monday through Friday and can be reached via the following methods:

Phone: (919) 544-9404 extension 81

Faxback Answer System: (919) 544-9404 extension 85

E-mail: help@vmedia.com

FAX: (919) 544-9472

World Wide Web: **http://www.vmedia.com/support**

America Online: keyword *Ventana*

LIMITS OF LIABILITY & DISCLAIMER OF WARRANTY

The authors and publisher of this book have used their best efforts in preparing the CD-ROM and the programs contained in it. These efforts include the development, research, and testing of the theories and programs to determine their effectiveness. The authors and publisher make no warranty of any kind expressed or implied, with regard to these programs or the documentation contained in this book.

The authors and publisher shall not be liable in the event of incidental or consequential damages in connection with, or arising out of, the furnishing, performance, or use of the programs, associated instructions, and/or claims of productivity gains.

Appendix C
The Netscape Administration Kit

If there are several people in your organization who use or want to use Netscape Navigator 3.0, and if you're responsible for making sure they install and configure the software correctly, you need the Netscape Administration Kit. This add-on product, which you can purchase directly from Netscape, is a good example of preventive medicine: it will save you from some serious headaches down the road.

The Netscape Administration Kit lets you lock in certain settings for every user on your LAN or WAN. With the Administration Kit installed, Netscape Navigator 3.0 will not run unless it finds a valid *enterprise data file* on the network. Since everyone uses settings from this same file, it's easy to ensure a standard throughout your organization. It's also easy to change a particular setting for everyone all at once.

And what settings can you lock in company-wide using the Netscape Administration Kit? Using this tool you can:

- Ensure that every user has the same proxy server settings.
- Configure the same SMTP and POP mail servers for every employee.
- Setup your entire organization with the correct NNTP news server address.

But that's not all. The Netscape Administration Kit lets you customize the look and feel of the program so that it meets your company's needs. For instance, you can:

- Specify the home page that appears for every user at program startup.

- Redefine the Directory buttons so that they refer to URLs that are important to your organization. For instance, instead of the usual What's New? button you may create one labeled Shifts. When users click it, they get an updated HTML list of who is working which shift.

- Customize the Directory menu. This allows for even more predetermined links to information that's useful throughout the organization.

- Customize the Help menu. Instead of information on plugins or Netscape's own release notes, Acme Widget employees could access the company's personnel policies right from this menu.

The combination of Netscape Navigator 3.0 and the Netscape Administration Kit provides a powerful way to standardize software within an organization. For more information on the Administration Kit, please see the URL http:// home.netscape.com/comprod/products/navigator/version_3.0/ enterprise/index.html.

Glossary

access privileges—A user's rights on a host. Typically users are allowed to create or edit files only in their home directories, though they can run programs from public directories.

account—An agreement with an organization allowing you to take advantage of various services. For instance, an account on an e-mail server lets you log on to send and receive e-mail. Accounts are often protected by *authentication*, requiring that you type in a user name and password.

acronym—A word made up of the first letters of the words in a phrase, such as *ROM* (read-only memory).

activate—To make a window the active one by clicking on it.

active window—The window with the highlighted title bar, where the user is currently interacting with a program.

ACU—*Automatic Call Unit*. Fancy word for a modem.

addressing—The assignment of unique names or numbers to every node on a network so that information doesn't get misdelivered.

agents—Search tool that automatically seeks out online information based on your queries. Also called intelligent agents, knowbots, and droids.

alert box—A box that appears unbidden on the screen, announced by one or more beeps, to give you information. Alert boxes don't require any information from you. A *bomb* is one example. Some people simply call them alerts.

algorithm—The step-by-step process a software program uses to produce its results.

alias—An alternate name used in place of a "real" one. Rather than using your real name to log in to a system, you probably use a shorter alias. Commands can also have aliases. For instance, you can create command files on a UNIX system so that instead of typing *ls -al* to see all the files in your directory, you could just type *dir*. Macintosh System 7.5 automatically establishes aliases for your most frequently-used applications and documents, placing them in the Apple Menu for your convenience.

American Standard Code for Information Interchange—*See ASCII.*

anchor—In HTML, the target of a link. It is sometimes also used to mean any link.

Apple menu — The menu which contains shortcut commands to any number of control panels, applications, system extensions, and desk accessories. The Apple menu can be configured to become your "mission control" point for efficient operation of your system. The menu is designed with the Apple symbol in the far left corner of the menu bar.

application protocol—A *protocol* that "sits on top of" the underlying transport layer of a communications system. For example, *FTP* and *Telnet* are application protocols that format data in particular ways and use the services of the lower-level *TCP/IP* transport layer.

Archie—A network service used for locating files available at *FTP* sites that accept anonymous logins.

ARP—*Address Resolution Protocol.* Protocol used on a network for mapping Ethernet addresses to IP addresses.

ARPAnet—A wide area network developed in the 1960s by the Advanced Research Projects Agency of the U.S. Department of Defense. It links government and academic networks around the world.

ASCII—*American Standard Code for Information Interchange.* This standard assigns a binary value to common text and control characters. ASCII is used for manipulating text in a program and for transmitting text to other devices or systems.

ASCII file—A human-readable file made up only of letters, numbers, and symbols. An ASCII file contains no formatting except tabs, linefeeds, and carriage returns. Also known as a *text file*.

assigned numbers—The usual port numbers for well-known Internet services such as *Telnet*, *FTP*, and so on. For instance, hosts usually wait for Telnet connections on TCP port 23, for World Wide Web connections on port 80, and for Usenet news connections on port 119. These assigned port numbers are how the host knows what kind of connection is being requested.

asynchronous transmission—The transmission of data without special timing information. Each character you transmit is made up of several bits of information. In asynchronous communications, the characters are "packaged," usually by special start and stop bits, so that the receiving hardware or software knows when it has received an entire character. This way, the interval *between* characters doesn't have to be fixed, and information can arrive at any time. *See also synchronous transmission.*

attribute (text)—The display characteristics of text. Text attributes include bold, italic, underlined, and so on. In *World Wide Web* documents, text may be tagged with a wide variety of attributes using *HTML*.

AU sound—Audio format developed by Sun and used for sound files on the Web. Netscape browsers play AU files using the helper program NAPLAYER.

authentication—The process of identifying a user to determine if he or she should have access to a particular computer system. Name and password prompts are a form of authentication.

authoring software—Any software that lets you create HTML or other multimedia documents.

bandwidth—The range of frequencies that can be transmitted over a network, limited by the hardware. Higher bandwidth allows more information on the network at one time.

baud rate—The number of signal changes per second as data is transmitted from one device to another. For instance, 110 transitions per second from a high frequency to a low frequency on a phone line would be 110 baud. Each signal change may signify one bit of data (for instance, high frequency to low could signify 1, low to high could signify 0); if a signal changes in multiple ways (frequency, amplitude, etc.), it may signify multiple bits of data. In the first case, baud rate would equal *bits per second*; in the second case, bits per second would be higher than the baud rate. The difference between baud rate and bits per second is a common icebreaker at nerd parties.

BBS—*See bulletin board system.*

binary—Numbers composed of combinations of two different digits, specifically 1 and 0. In the context of this book, binary data means information that may contain the full range of combinations of binary digits in a *byte*, as opposed to information that contains only the limited range of information that is displayable as text. Bytes of *ASCII* text contain only seven significant *data bits*, as in 1011001, while programs, graphics, spreadsheet files, and so on, contain eight significant data bits per byte, as in 10011011. Any files that cannot be read as text are considered binary files.

BIND—*Berkeley Internet Name Domain* server. This is the DNS server on BSD and related UNIX systems. *See also DNS.*

BinHex—A file format, used mainly in the Macintosh world, for storing and transmitting binary data as *ASCII* text. This format is useful for transferring 8-bit data over 7-bit networks or data paths, or for including binary files as part of mail messages. Among UNIX and PC users, *uuencoding* is more common.

bit—A *bi*nary dig*it*, the smallest piece of information that a computer can hold. A bit is always one of two values, written as 1 or 0 and corresponding to the on/off state of a digital switch or the high/low state of electrical impulses. Combinations of bits are used to represent more complex information, such as *ASCII* text or commands to the computer.

bitmap—A representation of an image as an array of bits.

bit rate—The rate at which bits are transmitted, usually expressed as a certain number of *bits per second*, or bps. *See also baud rate.*

bits per second—*See bit rate.*

bookmarks—In Netscape browsers, a means of permanently storing the *URL*s for sites you want to revisit.

bridge—(1) A device or a combination of hardware and software for connecting networks together. (2) Something that goes over troubled water. *See also internet*.

bulk cipher—An *encryption* method used to encrypt large quantities of information.

bulletin board system (BBS)—An electronic version of the old cork bulletin board—a place to leave and collect messages and files. A modern BBS is really like a whole collection of bulletin boards, with different sections covering different areas of interest. Users can generally exchange public as well as private messages, and many BBSes include extensive areas for distributing shareware or public domain software.

button — On the Mac's screen, an outlined area in a dialog box that you click on to choose, confirm or cancel a command.

byte—A combination of *bits* used to represent a single character. In the world of personal computers, a byte is eight bits long.

cable—A bundle of wires or fiber strands wrapped with insulation and used to connect devices.

cache—An area of memory or a file used to store frequently accessed instructions or data. A memory cache is used to reduce hard disk access time. Memory and file caches are also used by Web browsers and other online programs to store images or data that rarely change; thus, a large home page does not have to be re-sent each time a connection is established.

carrier—A steady background signal on a communication channel used to indicate that the system is ready for the transmission of data. The carrier is then modified to represent the data transmitted.

CCITT—*Consultative Committee on International Telegraphy and Telephony*. This is an international standards-setting body that makes recommendations for international communications technologies.

Certifying Authorities—Organizations that distribute *Digital Certificates*.

CGI—*Common Gateway Interface*. A standardized technique that lets Web clients pass information to Web servers, and then on to other programs that process the information. When a Web site accepts the information you enter into a form, it uses CGI.

character entities—In HTML, special symbols that stand for other characters. Character entities begin with an ampersand (&) and end with a semicolon (;). For example, > in an HTML document would appear on your screen as > (greater than).

check box—A control box that lets you choose a particular option by clicking. Once you click, an X or checkmark appears in the check box; click again and it is cleared.

CIX—*Commercial Internet Exchange*. CIX is an agreement among Internet service providers allowing them to make the Internet available to commercial traffic.

Clear To Send—A signal from a *DCE* to a *DTE* indicating that circuits are ready for data transmission. *See also DCE; DTE.*

clickable image—In a Web page, an image you can click in order to access a different URL. *See also image map.*

client—A computer or a software program that can access particular services on a network. The machine or the software that provides the service for a client is called a *server*. For instance, an e-mail client would request received mail from an e-mail server.

client pull—A method specific to Netscape products whereby a Web client can request the Web server to send it a particular set of data. *See also server push.*

client/server architecture—A system in which a *client* program establishes a connection with a *server* and then requests information or services. *See also client; server.*

client write key—The software key used to encrypt data written or transmitted by the client in a *client/server* system.

Clipboard or clipboard—An area of memory where objects (data) are placed when a user carries out a Cut or Copy command or chooses a menu option. This data can then be passed to another program.

command —The generic name for anything you tell a computer program to do. On the Mac, commands are usually listed on menus, or are generated by holding down the Ctrl (command) key while striking one or more other keys. To choose a command from a menu, you drag down the menu until the command you want is highlighted, then release the mouse button.

command prompt—A set of characters or a symbol that indicates where you type in commands. The DOS C:\ prompt is an example of a command prompt.

computer name—On Microsoft networks, a unique name of up to 15 characters that identifies a particular computer on the network.

connect time—The amount of time you're connected to a host or to a service provider.

connection—A link between two computers for the purpose of transferring or sharing information.

container—Any screen object that holds other objects; for instance, a folder.

content-type—The MIME name for particular types of files to be transferred by e-mail or the Web. For instance, the content-type for a GIF file is *image/gif*. *See also MIME*.

control—Any window object that lets you interact with a program by selecting an action, inputting data, and so on.

crawler—*See spider*.

CSLIP—A common variant of the SLIP protocol that uses compressed IP headers. *See also SLIP*.

cyberspace—A slightly dated term referring to the entire world of online information and services. It was originally coined by the writer William Gibson.

daemon—UNIX-speak for a program that's always running on a server machine, waiting for requests for a particular service. For instance, an FTP server daemon sits and waits for an FTP client to connect and request files.

data—Information used or processed by a software program.

data bits—Bits that carry information as opposed to control information. For example, the bits in the middle of a *byte* might signify a text character and are, therefore, data bits, while the bits at the beginning and end of the byte merely mark the beginning and end of the data.

Data Carrier Detect (DCD or CD)—A signal from a *DCE*, such as a modem, to a *DTE*, such as a PC, indicating that a communication channel has been established with a remote device. *See also DCE; DTE*.

data-file object—An object representing a data file (spreadsheet, document, image, sound clip, etc.) in the file system.

Data Terminal Ready (DTR)—A signal from a DTE to a DCE indicating that it's ready to receive and transmit data. Usually, a modem keeps DTR high as long as it's turned on. *See also DCE; DTE.*

DCE—*Data Communication Equipment.* A device used by a *DTE* to transmit and receive information. Your modem is a DCE.

DDE—*See dynamic data exchange.*

default—In software, the "out of the box" value of a configuration option. The software will use this value unless the user explicitly indicates a different one in a setup program, property sheet, or .INI file.

default button—What you get if you don't specify anything different. The default button has a heavy border around it, to indicate that all you need to do is hit the return key.

desktop—The visual work area that fills your screen and holds the objects you interact with, such as icons, the task bar, and so on. The desktop is a container (or folder) that can also be used as a convenient place to access files.

destination directory—The directory to which you copy, move, or download a file or files.

device driver—A program used by the system to access devices such as video cards, printers, and mice.

dialog box—A box that appears on your screen requesting your input; it engages you in a *dialogue* with the software. It may contain edit fields, check boxes, list boxes, radio buttons, and so on, and it stays on your screen until you click its Cancel or OK button.

dial-up networking—A facility built into Open Transport that allows users to link to a network or to the Internet using phone lines. Similar to *Remote Access Dialer* in Windows NT.

Digital Certificate—A unique electronic key that identifies you and authorizes you to access secure Web sites.

dimmed—A button, menu item, or other control is dimmed or *grayed* (displayed in light gray instead of black) to indicate it represents an option or command that is not currently available.

direct connection—A permanent connection between a computer and the Internet as opposed to a temporary dial-up or *SLIP/PPP* connection.

directory—A structure on a disk that contains files or other subdirectories. Also sometimes referred to as a folder.

directory tree—A hierarchical display of a disk's directories and subdirectories.

DNS—*Domain Name Service.* An Internet service that returns the appropriate *IP address* when queried with a *domain-name address*.

dock—To configure a toolbar so that it no longer floats, but lines up with the edge of a window or pane.

document (World Wide Web)—On the *World Wide Web,* a file or set of related files that can be transferred from a *Web server* to a Web *client.* The document may contain text, graphics, sound, or hyperlinks to other documents.

document encoding—*See encoding.*

document window—A window that lets you view the contents of a document.

domain—A collection of associated computers on the Internet, given a specific domain name that is used as part of the Internet address.

domain-name address—The "plain English" address of a computer on the Internet, as opposed to its numeric *IP address.* For instance, www.echonyc.com is a domain-name address.

download—To get a file or files from a remote computer; the opposite of *upload.*

drag—To move a mouse while pressing and holding one of its buttons. Dragging is used to move or resize objects on the screen.

droids—*See agents.*

drop-down list—A control that displays a current text selection, but that can be opened to display the entire list of choices.

drop-down menu—A menu that is displayed from a menu bar.

DSU—*Digital Services Unit.* The piece of equipment that enables transmission of data in synchronous digital connections to the Net.

DTE—*Data Terminal Equipment*. A device that serves as the originating point or the final destination of information. Typically, a computer or a terminal is a DTE.

dynamic data exchange (DDE)—The exchange of data between programs such that any change in the data in one program affects that same data in the other program. For instance, if spreadsheet data are shared via DDE by Word and Excel, any changes made to the data in Excel will also appear in the Word document.

edit field—*See text box*.

electronic mail—A network service for transmitting messages from one computer to another. Also called *e-mail*.

ellipsis—The "..." added to a menu item or button label to show that the command needs more information to be completed. When you choose a command with an ellipsis, a dialog box appears so you can enter additional information.

encoding—The technique used for storing or expressing data. For instance, text may be stored via ASCII encoding or some form of encoding that uses compression (such as ZIP). In Web browsers, document encoding refers to the translation of incoming characters into display fonts. For instance, you may set Netscape browsers to Japanese encoding so that information in a Japanese HTML document will be correctly displayed.

encryption—A method of *encoding* information for secure transmission. The data can be read in its original form only after it has been decoded. *See also public-key encryption*.

Ethernet—A hardware system and a protocol that is commonly used to connect computers on a LAN. A common alternative to AppleTalk.

external viewer—A separate program used by a *World Wide Web* browser to display graphics or to play sound or video files. After downloading a particular media file, the Web browser launches the external viewer program appropriate to the type of file. In order for this to work, you must configure your Web browser with the names of the external viewer programs you have on your system. Another term for external viewer is *helper application*.

extension—The period and characters at the end of a file or directory name, often used to indicate the type of file or directory. For instance, INDEX.HTML includes the .HTML extension to indicate it is an HTML document.

e-zine—A zine, or small non-mass-market magazine in electronic format. Some e-zines are text files distributed via electronic mail or posted on a BBS; others are Web pages with extensive graphics and even sounds.

FAQ—Abbreviation for *frequently asked question*. FAQs are lists of frequently asked questions (and their answers) in a particular topic area. For instance, a MacOS FAQ would help users understand the basics of using the Macintosh Operating System by providing answers to common questions. Most mailing lists and network newsgroups regularly provide updated FAQs. It is important to read the FAQ for a particular newsgroup before beginning to post messages.

file—A named collection of *ASCII* or *binary* information stored on a disk or other storage device. Files include text, programs, databases, spreadsheets, graphics, and so on.

file server—A computer that provides storage space for files and applications that may be shared by network users.

file menu—On the desktop, in the menu bar, the second menu from the left. Within applications it contains commands for saving, opening, printing, and closing documents, quitting the application, and so forth. In the Finder, the File menu contains commands for opening and closing windows, duplicating icons, ejecting disks, and so forth.

file system—In an operating system, the structure used for storing, organizing, and naming files.

file transfer protocol—Any *protocol* for transferring files from one computer to another. A file transfer protocol usually includes provisions for making sure the data was transferred without errors and for resending any blocks of information that were corrupt.

finger—A UNIX program that lets you retrieve basic information about an Internet user or host. Finger is available via the Web at various sites.

flag—A characteristic of a file that may restrict its use in particular ways. A file may be flagged read-only, for instance.

flame—A public message on any electronic forum, such as a *BBS* or online service, that personally attacks another user. Usually a flame is in response to an earlier message. If the user who has been flamed responds with another flame, or if other users jump into the fray, a "flame war" ensues. Flaming, though common in *Usenet* newsgroups, is generally considered an obnoxious waste of other users' time and of network bandwidth.

folder—A container that holds and organizes objects, typically files or other folders. On the desktop, a folder may represent a directory in the file system; other folders within it are equivalent to subdirectories.

font—A particular style for displayed or printed characters, including the shape, weight, slant, and so on.

font size—The size of a *font*; typically represented in units of measurement called *points*.

FQDN—*Fully Qualified Domain Name.* The full domain name of a computer on the Internet, including both the host name and the domain name. *See also domain-name address.*

frame—A portion of a Web browser window that may contain a different document from other frames within the same window.

FTP—Abbreviation for *File Transfer Protocol.* A particular file transfer protocol that is common on the Internet. It is also used as a verb, as in, "FTP me that file, wouldya?"

full duplex—A communications link in which both ends can transmit data simultaneously, as in a telephone conversation. In situations where you are working interactively online, full duplex communication lets a remote host echo back to you each character you type so that you can see what you're writing as you work. *See also half duplex.*

FYI—*For Your Information.* A series of technical documents on various Internet-related topics, available at many public FTP sites. *See also RFC.*

gateway—A device or the software that links networks that use different protocols. For instance, a Novell network might have an Internet gateway that "packages" information into the *TCP/IP* packets required for Internet communication. The term *gateway* is also used in a very specialized sense to mean a program on a *World Wide Web* host that accepts and processes information sent by a Web client. For instance, a document on a *Web server* might display a form in which you can type your name; the gateway program would then enter your name in a database.

Get Info window—The window that appears when you choose *Get Info* from the File Menu. It tells you the size of the selected file, folder, or disk you have highlighted, when it was created and last modified, and where it resides. There is also space for entering comments, and the capability to adjust the amount of RAM that your system will use, in the case of applications.

GIF—(Pronounced "jiff.") Abbreviation for *Graphic Interchange Format*. This is a format for compressed graphic files developed by CompuServe and Unisys.

Gopher—A menu-based client/server system for exploring information resources on the Internet. A Gopher client is seamlessly built into Web browsers, so you don't need a separate Gopher client program.

GopherSpace—All of the information presented by a *Gopher* server, in the form of directory and file menus.

grayed—*See dimmed.*

half duplex—A communications link in which both ends can transmit and receive data, but not at the same time. Half duplex communication is like two-way radio or CB, where only one person speaks at a time. In situations where you are working interactively online in half duplex, you will not see characters you type echoed to the screen unless you set your communications program to echo them locally. *See also full duplex.*

handle—An interface element added to an object to enable the user to move, resize, or reshape it.

handshaking—The initial negotiation and the exchange of control information between a *DCE* and a *DTE* or between two DTEs in a communications link. Handshaking is necessary to make sure both devices are ready to transfer data and can "understand" each other. *See also Data Carrier Detect; Data Terminal Ready; XOFF; XON.*

hardware handshake—A protocol whereby a *DTE* tells the connected computer to start or stop sending data. Typically, hardware handshaking is implemented by raising and lowering the voltage on the DTR (*Data Terminal Ready*) line in the cable that connects the *DTE* and *DCE*. *See also XOFF; XON.*

helper applications—Programs that a Web browser such as Netscape Navigator 3.0 uses to perform tasks such as displaying particular types of graphics, playing sounds, or initiating Telnet sessions.

highlight—To emphasize text or some other display element, usually by selecting it with the mouse.

history list—In Netscape Navigator 3.0, the list of Web documents you've displayed during the current session.

home page—The *HTML* document you choose to display when you open a *Web browser* such as Netscape Navigator 3.0. It may be located on your own hard drive or on a remote *Web server*. Home page can also refer to the top-level document at a particular Web site.

host computer—A computer that a user can connect to in order to access information or run programs. A user may log in locally using a *terminal* or remotely using a computer and phone lines or the Internet.

host name—The name clients use to access your Web server or other Internet server. For instance, your Web server's host name might be www.acme.com.

hotlist—In a *Web browser*, a user-built list of frequently accessed *World Wide Web* sites. Also, an *HTML* document consisting of hotlinks to Web sites or other Internet resources.

HTML—Abbreviation for *Hypertext Markup Language*. A "markup language" for indicating attributes and links in a Web document. An HTML *tag* may tell a Web browser program how to display a piece of text or a graphic, or it may direct the browser to another file or document.

HTTP—*Hypertext Transfer Protocol*. The *protocol* that World Wide Web *clients* and *servers* use to communicate with each other.

hypermedia—*Hypertext* that also includes nontext information such as graphics, video, or sound.

hypertext—Text that is organized by means of links, or jumps, from one piece of information to another. The reader can move among related topics by clicking on tagged words or phrases.

IAB—*Internet Architecture Board*. The organization that decides on Internet standards.

icon—An image used to represent an object such as a file or program.

image map—A graphic in a Web document that lets you click on certain portions in order to activate particular *URLs*. It has an associated map file that identifies these hot spots. *See also clickable image.*

inactive window—A window with which you are not currently interacting. Its title bar is not highlighted, and it receives no keyboard or mouse input. *See also active window.*

inline images—Graphic images contained within *World Wide Web* documents. An inline image displays automatically as part of a document when it is retrieved; a non-inline image must be retrieved by clicking on a *hotlink*.

intelligent agents—*See agents.*

internet—A larger network made up of two or more connected LANs (*local area networks*) or WANs (*wide area networks*).

Internet—The huge worldwide Internet made up of cooperative networks and using *TCP/IP* protocols to offer a variety of services.

Internet access provider—A business or organization that provides Internet access to consumers, often via dial-up *SLIP* or *PPP* connections. Also known as an *ISP*, or Internet service provider.

Internet address—*See IP address.*

Internet presence provider—An Internet-connected business that provides equipment and services to customers without equipment or technical expertise.

IP address—Also called *Internet address*. The unique address for each computer on the Internet. The IP address appears as a set of four numbers separated by periods.

ISDN—*Integrated Services Digital Network*. The telecommunications standard that supports digital transmission of voice, video, and data over phone lines.

ISOC—*Internet Society.* Organization that was formed to support a worldwide information network. The ISOC sponsors the *IAB.*

ISP—*Internet Service Provider.* Another term for an *Internet access provider.*

IPP—*See Internet Presence Provider.*

Java—An object-oriented programming language developed by Sun Microsystems. It allows developers to create applications that may be run from within Web browsers such as Netscape Navigator 3.0.

JavaScript—A set of commands that can be added to HTML files to add functionality to Web documents. JavaScript is useful for scrolling text, data validation in forms, etc.

JPEG—A format for compressed graphics files. JPEG graphics are commonly used as part of *World Wide Web* documents.

kbyte—*See kilobyte.*

kilobyte (K)—1024 (2^{10}) *bytes* of data. Thus, a 64K file consists of 65,536 bytes.

knowbot—A software program that can retrieve information from a variety of electronic sources when you give it a set of search parameters. Same as *agent.*

LAN—*See local area network.*

link—A special hidden *tag* in an HTML document on the Web. It includes the *URL* for another file or document, or for another anchor point within the same document. When you click a word, phrase, or graphic that's tagged as a link, Netscape Navigator 3.0 automatically retrieves the appropriate target.

list box—A control that displays a scrollable list of choices.

Live3D—Netscape's *VRML* technology.

LiveConnect—Netscape technology that allows Navigator plug-ins, Java applets, and JavaScript to communicate with each other.

local area network (LAN)—A group of computers connected together by cable or wireless transceivers so that users can share resources such as database files, programs, printers, and so on. *See also wide area network.*

log file—A file that is automatically generated by software and indicates occurrances such as errors, attempts to access your server, etc.

log in—To identify yourself to a remote system or network by typing in your login name and password.

login name—The name you use for security verification when you call into a remote system.

login prompt—The prompt (usually *login:* or *name:*) a remote host uses to tell you it's ready for you to type in your *login name*.

logon script—A file containing simple commands that automate the process of logging on to a server, *SLIP* or *PPP* account, or other computer.

log off—To tell a remote host system or a network, using the appropriate commands, that you are terminating interaction. In many cases, logging off will also break the communications link to the remote machine.

log on—To tell a remote system or network, using the appropriate commands, that you are initiating a session.

maximize—To expand a window to its maximum size. *See also minimize.*

maximize button—The button used to maximize a window. On Macintosh systems, it is the button on the right in the title bar.

megabyte (MB)—1024 *kilobytes*, or 1,048,576 bytes.

menu bar—A horizontal bar at the very top of the screen (above the title bar and the rest of the window) that contains menu choices. *See also drop-down menu.*

menu button—A command button that displays a menu.

menu item—A choice on a menu.

message box—A window that appears to inform you of something, for instance that a connection has been established or that an error occurred.

MIME—*Multipurpose Internet Mail Extensions.* MIME is a convention for identifying different types of *binary* information, such as images or sounds, and thereby indicating the appropriate programs for viewing or playing this information. MIME is used in attaching binary files to e-mail messages so that they can be displayed or played automatically when received.

minimize—To minimize the size of a window; in some cases, this means to hide the window. *See also maximize.*

minimize button—The button used to minimize a window.

modem—Short for *mo*dulator/*dem*odulator. A hardware device that connects your computer to other computers using analog telephone lines.

modem command—An instruction, typed from the keyboard or transmitted automatically by a software program, that tells a modem to perform some action. For instance, the command ATH0 tells a modem to hang up the line.

Mozilla—This word stands for "Mosaic meets Godzilla." It is the name for the early Netscape products and for the Netscape-specific extensions to the HTML language. It has also become the Netscape mascot. The word and the associated image appear frequently in Netscape products.

MPEG—*Moving Pictures Expert Group.* MPEG is a standard format for compressed video files, sometimes known as "desktop movies." MPEG files may be part of *World Wide Web* documents, but they require a special *helper application* for viewing.

MUDs and MOOs—Text-based multiuser interactive games, accessed using specialized software or via *Telnet*.

multiple selection list box—A special list box that's used for multiple independent selections.

multiuser system—An operating system, such as UNIX, that lets more than one user at a time access services.

NCSA—*National Center for Supercomputing Applications.* NCSA is the department of the University of Illinois where the Web browser Mosaic was developed. Mosaic was the forerunner of all modern graphically based Web browsers.

network—A collection of interconnected computers. Each attached computer runs its own software processes, whereas in an unnetworked *multiuser system*, users run all processes on the central host computer and use terminals simply to interact. A network lets users share information as well as devices such as printers, disks, and modems.

network administrator—In an organization, the individual who is responsible for configuring and maintaining the network. This is the person to talk to if you have problems with a direct "hard-wired" connection to the Internet.

NFS—*Network File System*. NFS is a set of protocols developed by Sun Microsystems for allowing computers running different operating systems to share files and disk storage.

NIC—*Network Information Center*. The organization responsible for supplying information about the Internet.

NOC–*Network Operations Center*. The organization in charge of the day-to-day operations of a network on the Internet.

node—Any computer or other device on a network that has its own unique network address.

object—An entity that you manipulate in some way to perform a task. (Is that vague enough?) Typical objects are *icons* or *folders* on the *desktop*.

offline—Not currently connected to a remote computer.

online—Currently connected to a remote computer.

option button—A control that allows a user to select one choice from a set of mutually exclusive choices (also known as a *radio button*). *Compare check box.*

packet—A block of information that has been "packaged" with address information, error-checking information, and so on, for transmission on a *network* or on the *Internet*.

parameter—A variable that affects the results of a command. For instance, in the command *dir /p*, /p is a parameter.

parity—A crude system of error-checking used in data communications. For most scenarios these days, your communications software should be set to "no parity."

parsed HTML—HTML files that are read and manipulated by separate software on a server machine after the server software has answered a client request for the document. Using parsed HTML, for instance, a program could customize a Web document based on who requested it. Parsed HTML is also known as server-parsed HTML and SHTML. Often HTML files that will be parsed end with the extension .SHTML instead of .HTML.

Perl—*Practical Extraction and Report Language.* A programming language first developed by Larry Wall for UNIX systems. Because of its power in pattern matching and in handling strings, it is often the language of choice for creating *CGI* programs.

pixel—The smallest unit of graphic information on a computer screen. Graphic images are usually measured in pixels, and a pair of pixel coordinates can indicate an exact point within an image.

POP—*Point of Presence.* The local dial-up node an Internet access provider makes available for its customers.

POP3—*Post Office Protocol, version 3.* The protocol used by Netscape Navigator 3.0 and other e-mail programs to retrieve messages from your e-mail server. *See also SMTP.*

pop-up menu—A menu that appears right at the location of a selected object (sometimes called a *shortcut or a context menu*). The menu contains items related to the selection.

pop-up window—A window with no title bar that appears next to an object and provides information about that object.

port—(1) A hardware connector on the back panel of a computer where you can plug in a serial, parallel, or network *cable.* (2) A unique number assigned to a particular Internet *service* on a host machine. For instance, most *MUDs* and *MOOs* require that you Telnet to a host using a specific port different from the standard Telnet port number. You can usually specify a port number as part of an Internet address, as in *lambda.parc.xerox.com 8888.*

POTS—*Plain Old Telephone Service.* What it sounds like—the current analog phone system, as distinguished from ISDN and other digital technologies.

PPP—*Point-to-Point Protocol*. This is a protocol that lets a computer link to the *Internet* by calling in to a service provider using a modem and a standard telephone line.

properties—Characteristics of an object defining its state, appearance, or value. Often used to mean a program's settings.

property inspector—A viewer that displays the properties of the current selection.

protocol—A set of rules for interaction between software programs on a network. Protocols may include requirements for formatting data, for passing control information back and forth, and for error checking.

public-key encryption—An *encryption* method that requires two unique software keys (one public and one private) for decrypting the data, making it secure across public networks. Pretty Good Privacy (PGP) is a well-known public-key encryption system.

query string—The word or phrase you pass to a Web search engine.

QuickTime—A multimedia file format developed by Apple. It is often used for video clips or "movies."

radio button— A group of buttons only one of which can be set to on at the same time. If you select one radio button, any other that's selected automatically deselects.

random access memory (RAM)—Computer memory that temporarily stores information; for instance, software code that you've loaded by launching a program or data that you're processing. Generally, the more of it, the better!

read-only memory (ROM)—Computer memory containing data that cannot be changed by the user and that remains even when the computer is turned off. ROM is used for storing your computer's BIOS, for instance, which is the code that lets you boot up and performs a variety of low-level functions.

refresh—In Netscape Web browsers such as Navigator 3.0, the command that reloads a document into the browser window from a disk or memory *cache*.

reload—In Netscape Web browsers such as Navigator 3.0, the command that reloads a document into the browser window from its original local or remote source.

remote—Any system that you can connect to by using only communications devices rather than just local wiring.

Remote Access Dialer—A program for connecting via ordinary phone lines or *ISDN* to a remote computer, often used for *SLIP* or *PPP* connectivity.

remote computer—A computer you link to via telephone lines, satellite, or other communication links.

resolution—The density of an image, expressed in dots per inch.

restore button—The button that replaces the maximize button once a window has been maximized. It lets you return the window to the size it was before maximizing.

reverse lookup—The process of looking up the domain name of an Internet-connected computer when all that's known is the numeric IP address. For instance, you may have a numeric IP address assigned by a *SLIP* or *PPP* access provider, but no associated domain name. When you try to log in to certain security-conscious FTP sites, the host software looks up your domain name via DNS reverse lookup. If it can't find one, you are not allowed on the system. *See also domain-name address.*

RFC—*Request for Comments.* An RFC is a proposal or report electronically distributed via the Internet, usually for the purpose of elucidating or helping to define a new Internet technical standard.

robot—*See spider.*

RS-232—The standard used by your serial port. RS-232 lines are the individual pins and wires that make up the hardware interface, such as the send data line, the receive data line, and the various hardware handshaking (or hardware flow control) lines.

RTF—*Rich Text Format.* A file format that can be read by many word processing programs across all platforms.

RTS/CTS—*Ready to Send/Clear to Send.* In an RS-232 serial port, the two lines that allow two devices to signal each other when they are ready to send or receive data. This process is known as *hardware handshaking* or hardware flow control. *See also RS-232.*

script—A software program that doesn't need to be compiled. It is run by another program "as is," in human-readable form. *See also logon script.*

scroll bar—The control that lets you move the image or text within a window either horizontally or vertically to view data that is not currently visible.

search engine—A program on the Net that lets users search for online information. Typical search engines include Infoseek and Alta Vista, both available from Netscape's Search page.

server—A computer or a program that provides a particular service on a network or on the Internet. Typical services include file access, printing, e-mail, *FTP*, and so on. The computers and software that access servers are called *clients*.

server—*See parsed HTML.*

server push—A technique specific to Netscape products whereby a Web server can initiate the transmission of data to the Web *client*. Server push is often used for animation or sound. *See also client pull.*

server write key—The software key used to encrypt data written or transmitted by the server in a *client/server* system. *See also client write key.*

service—A specialized function or utility provided by a *server*.

service provider—An organization, usually commercial, that provides connections to the Internet.

session—A connection between two machines on a network or on the Internet.

SGML—*Standard Generalized Markup Language.* A high-level standard for the electronic publication of information. *HTML* is a subset of SGML.

shell account—An account with an access provider that lets you access a text-based system for performing routine Internet tasks. You connect to a shell account via Telnet or a dial-up terminal emulation program. Some Internet access providers let you put your own Web pages on their server using a shell account.

shortcut—A desktop icon that can be used as a quick way to launch a program or document. Another word for *hotlink* in a WWW document.

SHTML—*See parsed HTML.*

signature—A text file that contains any information that you want to attach regularly to your e-mail messages and network news posts. A signature is usually less than five lines long and contains contact information.

single selection list box—A list box that lets you choose only a single item from a list.

slider—A control that displays a continuous range of values and lets you choose one.

SLIP—*Serial Line Internet Protocol.* Like *PPP*, this is a protocol that lets a computer link to the Internet by calling in to a service provider using a modem and a standard telephone line.

SMTP—*Simple Mail Transfer Protocol.* The most common protocol for sending e-mail messages over the Internet. *See also POP3.*

snail mail—A form of messaging that utilizes carbon-based materials to create and address human-readable data, which is then transmitted over a complex network of streets and air routes by human entities known as "postal employees."

sockets—A software mechanism that allows programs to communicate locally or remotely by setting up endpoints for sending and receiving data. The application programmer does not have to worry about the nuts-and-bolts details of how the data travels from one point to the other, as that is taken care of by the operating system or other resident software. The Windows Sockets API (*Winsock*) uses this concept.

spider—A program that wanders around the Web looking for new content. Links to new sites that it finds may then be added to large directory documents such as Yahoo. Spiders are also known as robots, wanderers, crawlers, and WebCrawlers.

spin box—A control that displays a limited range of values and lets you choose one.

SSL—*Secure Sockets Layer.* A version of the *HTTP* protocol that includes encryption. SSL allows for the secure transfer of sensitive information across the Net, as in financial transactions.

string—Geek-speak for a set of characters. Your name, for instance, is a string.

symbolic link—A name that does not refer to an actual object but points to another name. For instance, on an FTP site, a directory list might include the entry WINDOWS, even though there is no WINDOWS directory at this level. The WINDOWS entry could be a symbolic link to a directory buried much deeper in the file system, such as /pub/micro/pc/GUI/windows. Symbolic links provide convenient shortcuts to actual objects.

synchronous transmission—A method of transmitting data that uses a special timing signal to ensure a set time interval between any two characters. *See also asynchronous transmission.*

tag—A special code used in an *HTML* document to indicate how a piece of text or a graphic should be displayed by a Web browser; it may also establish a *hotlink* to another document.

TCP/IP—*Transmission Control Protocol/Internet Protocol.* TCP/IP is a set of protocols that applications use for communicating across networks or over the Internet. These protocols specify how packets of data should be constructed, addressed, checked for errors, and so on.

Telnet—A program that lets you log in to a remote *host computer* and access its data and services as if you were using a text-based *terminal* attached locally.

terminal—A keyboard and display screen used to access a *host computer*.

terminal emulation—A software program that lets you use a personal computer to communicate with a *host computer*. It transmits special commands and interprets incoming data as if it were a terminal directly connected to the host.

text box—A control that lets you enter and edit text.

text file—*See ASCII file.*

text-only—Containing no visual information other than human-readable *ASCII* text. When you *Telnet* into a UNIX system, for instance, your user interface is text-only, as distinguished from the graphical user interface of systems like Windows.

thread—A software process or task. Operating systems allow for many threads to occur simultaneously.

title bar—The horizontal bar at the top of a window that includes the window name. The title bar also acts as a handle that can be used to drag the window.

title bar icon—The small icon at the top-right corner of the application menu bar. You can use it to display a drop down menu which permits you to switch between open applications.

toolbar—A control that provides a defined area for a set of other controls such as icon buttons, drop-down list boxes, and so on.

traffic—Data traveling across a network or across the Internet.

tree control—A control that lets you display a set of hierarchical objects in an expandable outline format.

upload—To send a file to a remote system; the opposite of *download*.

URL—*Uniform Resource Locator*. A URL is a specially formatted address that a Web browser uses to locate, retrieve, and display a document. The URL includes the Internet address of the data, where it is located on the Web server machine, and what kind of transport protocol is required to retrieve it. URLs are contained in the *hotlinks* within *HTML* documents; they may also be specified by the user of a Web browser "on the fly."

Usenet—A large collection of networked users who communicate using the UNIX-to-UNIX Copy Protocol (UUCP) rather than *TCP/IP*. Usenet is connected to the Internet by gateways, and many Internet users are familiar with its broad range of discussion forums known as newsgroups.

UUCP—*UNIX to UNIX copy*. An older set of network commands for sending and receiving data on dial-up networks.

UUENCODING—A standard for encoding binary data that allows it to be transmitted as 7-bit ASCII information; it is then *UUDECODED* into its original binary form.

virtual server—A server that appears like a separate server to clients but actually runs on the same machine and uses the same server software as other servers. For instance, the Netscape FastTrack server lets you set up www.server1.com, www.server2.com, and www.server3.com all at once. Somebody logging onto www.server2.com would access different information from somebody logging onto www.server1.com.

VRML—*Virtual Reality Modeling Language*. VRML is a specialized language that allows for the creation of three dimensional user interfaces that can be accessed via Web browsers such as Netscape Navigator 3.0.

WAIS—*Wide-Area Information Server*. WAIS is a specialized Internet client/server system for researching information in Internet databases.

WAN—*See wide area network.*

wanderer—*See spider.*

Web—Short for *World Wide Web.*

Web browser—A program for retrieving and viewing *HTML* documents on the *World Wide Web*. Also known as a Web *client*.

WebCrawler—*See spider.*

Web document—Any document available on the *World Wide Web*.

Webmaster—The individual in charge of developing or administering a Web site.

Web server—A computer that stores Web documents and allows *Web browsers* to retrieve them over the Internet using the *HTTP* protocol. Also, the software that makes this possible.

wide area network—A group of computers and/or networks connected to one another by means of long-distance communication devices such as telephone lines and satellites, rather than just through local wiring. *See also local area network.*

widget—In HTML geek-speak, an object in a Web document that accepts user input. Examples are check boxes, radio buttons, drop-down lists, and so on.

workgroup—On Microsoft networks, a collection of grouped computers with a unique name.

World Wide Web (WWW)—An Internet service used for browsing hypermedia documents; the "Internet within the Internet" formed by all the Web servers and *HTML* documents currently online.

XOFF—A special character that's used to control the flow of information between a *DCE* and a *DTE*. When one device receives an XOFF character from the other, it stops transmitting until it receives an *XON*.

XON—A special character used to control the flow of data between a *DCE* and a *DTE*. *See also XOFF*.

Index

the online magazine for Netscape™ users

Empower

yourself with up-to-date tools for navigating the Net—in-depth reviews, where to find them and how to use them.

Enhance

your online experience—get to know the latest plug-ins that let you experience animation, video, virtual reality and sound...live, over the Internet.

Enliven

your Web pages—tips from experienced Web designers help you create pages with punch, spiced with multimedia and organized for easy navigation.

Enchant

your Web site visitors—learn to create interactive pages with JavaScript applets, program your own Internet applications and build added functionality into your site.

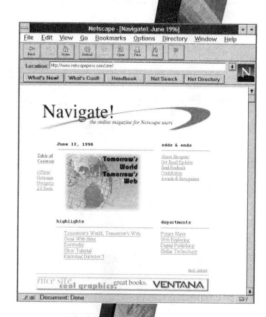

Add Power to Web Pages

Official Netscape JavaScript Book

$29.99, 520 pages, illustrated, part #: 465-0

Add life to Web pages—animated logos, text-in-motion sequences, live updating and calculations—quickly and easily. Sample code and step-by-step instructions show how to put JavaScript to real-world, practical use.

Java Programming for the Internet

$49.95, 806 pages, illustrated, part #: 355-7

Create dynamic, interactive Internet applications. Expand the scope of your online development with this comprehensive, step-by-step guide to creating Java applets. Includes four real-world, start-to-finish tutorials. The CD-ROM has all the programs, samples and applets from the book, plus shareware. Continual updates on Ventana's *Online Companion* will keep this information on the cutting edge.

The Comprehensive Guide to VBScript

$34.99, 408 pages, illustrated, part #: 470-7

The only encyclopedic reference to VBScript and HTML commands and features. Complete with practical examples for plugging directly into programs. The companion CD-ROM features a hypertext version of the book, along with shareware, templates, utilities and more.

 Books marked with this logo include a free Internet *Online Companion*™, featuring archives of free utilities plus a software archive and links to other Internet resources.

Make it Multimedia

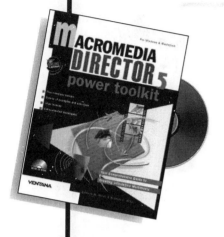

Macromedia Director 5 Power Toolkit

$49.95, 800 pages, illustrated, part #: 289-5

Macromedia Director 5 Power Toolkit views the industry's hottest multimedia authoring environment from the inside out. Features tools, tips and professional tricks for producing power-packed projects for CD-ROM and Internet distribution. Dozens of exercises detail the principles behind successful multimedia presentations and the steps to achieve professional results. The companion CD-ROM includes utilities, sample presentations, animations, scripts and files.

Shockwave!

$49.95, 400 pages, illustrated, part #: 441-3

Breathe new life into your web pages with Macromedia Shockwave. Ventana's *Shockwave!* teaches you how to enliven and animate your Web sites with online movies. Beginning with step-by-step exercises and examples, and ending with in-depth excursions into the use of Shockwave Lingo extensions, *Shockwave!* is a must-buy for both novices and experienced Director developers. Plus, tap into current Macromedia resources on the Internet with Ventana's *Online Companion.* The companion CD-ROM includes the Shockwave player plug-in, sample Director movies and tutorials, and much more!

The Comprehensive Guide to Lingo

$49.99, 700 pages, illustrated, part #: 463-4

Master the Lingo of Macromedia Director's scripting language for adding interactivity to presentations. Covers beginning scripts to advanced techniques, including creating movies for the Web and problem solving. The companion CD-ROM features demo movies of all scripts in the book, plus numerous examples, a searchable database of problems and solutions, and much more!

Web Favorites

Looking Good Online 🌐

$39.99, 400 pages, illustrated, part #: 469-3

Create well-designed, organized web sites—
incorporating text, graphics, digital photos, backgrounds
and forms. Features studies of successful sites and design
tips from pros. The companion CD-ROM features samples
from online professionals; buttons, backgrounds, templates
and graphics.

News Junkies Internet 500 🌐

$24.99, 500 pages, illustrated, part #: 461-8

Quench your thirst for news with this comprehensive listing
of the best news and most useful sites and sources on the
Web. Includes business, international, sports, weather,
law, finance, entertainment, politics and more. Plus rated
reviews of site strengths, weaknesses, design and
navigational properties.

Walking the World Wide Web, Second Edition 🌐

$39.95, 800 pages, illustrated, part #: 298-4

More than 30% new, this book now features 500 listings
and an extensive index of servers, expanded and
arranged by subject. This groundbreaking bestseller
includes a CD-ROM enhanced with Ventana's exclusive
PerpetuWAVE technology; updated online components that
make it the richest resource available for web travelers;
Netscape Navigator; and a hypertext version of the book.

To order any Ventana title, complete this order form and mail or fax it to us, with payment, for quick shipment.

TITLE	PART #	QTY	PRICE	TOTAL

SHIPPING

For all standard orders, please ADD $4.50/first book, $1.35/each additional.
For software kit orders, ADD $6.50/first kit, $2.00/each additional.
For "two-day air," ADD $8.25/first book, $2.25/each additional.
For "two-day air" on the kits, ADD $10.50/first kit, $4.00/each additional.
For orders to Canada, ADD $6.50/book.
For orders sent C.O.D., ADD $4.50 to your shipping rate.
North Carolina residents must ADD 6% sales tax.
International orders require additional shipping charges.

SUBTOTAL = $ _____

SHIPPING = $ _____

TAX = $ _____

TOTAL = $ _____

**Or, save 15%—order online.
http://www.vmedia.com**

Mail to: Ventana • PO Box 13964 • Research Triangle Park, NC 27709-3964 ☎ 800/743-5369 • Fax 919/544-9472

Name _____

E-mail _____ Daytime phone _____

Company _____

Address (No PO Box) _____

City_____ State_____ Zip_____

Payment enclosed ____VISA ____MC ____ Acc't # _____Exp. date_____

Signature _____ Exact name on card _____

Check your local bookstore or software retailer for these and other bestselling titles, or call toll free: **800/743-5369**

All technical support for this product is available from Ventana.
The technical support office is open from 8:00 A.M. to 6:00 P.M. (EST) Monday through Friday and can be reached via the following methods:

World Wide Web: http://www.netscapepress.com/support

E–mail: help@vmedia.com

Phone: (919) 544-9404 extension 81

FAX: (919) 544-9472

America Online: keyword **Ventana**

MACROMEDIA End-User License Agreement PLEASE READ THIS DOCUMENT CAREFULLY BEFORE BREAKING THE SEAL ON THE MEDIA PACKAGE. THIS AGREEMENT LICENSES THE ENCLOSED SOFTWARE TO YOU AND CONTAINS WARRANTY AND LIABILITY DISCLAIMERS. BY BREAKING THE SEAL ON THE MEDIA ENVELOPE, YOU ARE CONFIRMING YOUR ACCEPTANCE OF THE SOFTWARE AND AGREEING TO BECOME BOUND BY THE TERMS OF THIS AGREEMENT. IF YOU DO NOT WISH TO DO SO, DO NOT BREAK THE SEAL. INSTEAD, PROMPTLY RETURN THE ENTIRE PACKAGE, INCLUDING THE UNOPENED MEDIA PACKAGE, TO THE PLACE WHERE YOU OBTAINED IT, FOR A FULL REFUND.

1. Definitions

    (a) "Macromedia« Software" means the software program included in the enclosed package, and all related updates supplied by Macromedia.

    (b) "Macromedia Product" means the Macromedia Software and the related documentation and models and multimedia content (such as animation, sound and graphics), and all related updates supplied by Macromedia.

2. License. This Agreement allows you to:

    (a) Use the Macromedia Software on a single computer.

    (b) Make one copy of the Macromedia Software in machine-readable form solely for backup purposes. You must reproduce on any such copy all copyright notices and any other proprietary legends on the original copy of the Macromedia Software.

    (c) Certain Macromedia Software is licensed with additional rights as set forth in the Supplementary Rights Addendum that may be included in the package for this Macromedia Product.

3. Supplementary Licenses

Certain rights are not granted under this Agreement, but may be available under a separate agreement. If you would like to enter into a Site or Network License, please contact Macromedia.

4. Restrictions

You may not make or distribute copies of the Macromedia Product, or electronically transfer the Macromedia Software from one computer to another or over a network. You may not decompile, reverse engineer, disassemble, or otherwise reduce the Macromedia Software to a human-perceivable form. You may not modify, rent, resell for profit, distribute or create derivative works based upon the Macromedia Software or any part thereof. You will not export or reexport, directly or indirectly, the Macromedia Product into any country prohibited by the United States Export Administration Act and the regulations thereunder.

5. Ownership

The foregoing license gives you limited rights to use the Macromedia Software. Although you own the disk on which the Macromedia Software is recorded, you do not become the owner of, and Macromedia retains title to, the Macromedia Product, and all copies thereof. All rights not specifically granted in this Agreement, including Federal and International Copyrights, are reserved by Macromedia.

6. Limited Warranties

    (a) Macromedia warrants that, for a period of ninety (90) days from the date of delivery (as evidenced by a copy of your receipt): (i) when used with a recommended hardware configuration, the Macromedia Software will perform in substantial conformance with the documentation supplied as part of the Macromedia Product; and (ii) that the media on which the Macromedia Software is furnished will be free from defects in materials and workmanship under normal use. EXCEPT AS SET FORTH IN THE FOREGOING LIMITED WARRANTY, MACROMEDIA DISCLAIMS ALL OTHER WARRANTIES, EITHER EXPRESS OR IMPLIED, INCLUDING THE WARRANTIES OF MERCHANTABILITY, FITNESS FOR A PARTICULAR PURPOSE AND NON-INFRINGEMENT. IF APPLICABLE LAW IMPLIES ANY WARRANTIES WITH RESPECT TO THE MACROMEDIA PRODUCT, ALL SUCH WARRANTIES ARE LIMITED IN DURATION TO NINETY (90) DAYS FROM THE DATE OF DELIVERY. No oral or written information or advice given by Macromedia, its dealers, distributors, agents or employees shall create a warranty or in any way increase the scope of this warranty.

(b) SOME STATES DO NOT ALLOW THE EXCLUSION OF IMPLIED WARRANTIES, SO THE ABOVE EXCLUSION MAY NOT APPLY TO YOU. THIS WARRANTY GIVES YOU SPECIFIC LEGAL RIGHTS AND YOU MAY ALSO HAVE OTHER LEGAL RIGHTS WHICH VARY FROM STATE TO STATE.

7. Exclusive Remedy

Your exclusive remedy under Section 6 is to return the Macromedia Software to the place you acquired it, with a copy of your receipt and a description of the problem. Macromedia will use reasonable commercial efforts to supply you with a replacement copy of the Macromedia Software that substantially conforms to the documentation, provide a replacement for the defective media, or refund to you your purchase price for the Macromedia Software, at its option. Macromedia shall have no responsibility with respect to Macromedia Software that has been altered in any way, if the media has been damaged by accident, abuse or misapplication, or if the non conformance arises out of use of the Macromedia Software in conjunction with software not supplied by Macromedia.

8. Limitations of Damages

(a) MACROMEDIA SHALL NOT BE LIABLE FOR ANY INDIRECT, SPECIAL, INCIDENTAL OR CONSEQUENTIAL DAMAGES (INCLUDING DAMAGES FOR LOSS OF BUSINESS, LOSS OF PROFITS, OR THE LIKE), WHETHER BASED ON BREACH OF CONTRACT, TORT (INCLUDING NEGLIGENCE), PRODUCT LIABILITY OR OTHERWISE, EVEN IF MACROMEDIA OR ITS REPRESENTATIVES HAVE BEEN ADVISED OF THE POSSIBILITY OF SUCH DAMAGES AND EVEN IF A REMEDY SET FORTH HEREIN IS FOUND TO HAVE FAILED OF ITS ESSENTIAL PURPOSE.

(b) Macromedia's total liability to you for actual damages for any cause whatsoever will be limited to the greater of $500 or the amount paid by you for the Macromedia Software that caused such damages.

(c) SOME STATES DO NOT ALLOW THE LIMITATION OR EXCLUSION OF LIABILITY FOR INCIDENTAL OF CONSEQUENTIAL DAMAGES, SO THE ABOVE LIMITATION OR EXCLUSION MAY NOT APPLY TO YOU.

9. Basis of Bargain

The limited warranty, exclusive remedies and limited liability set forth above are fundamental elements of the basis of the bargain between Macromedia and you. Macromedia would not be able to provide the Macromedia Software on an economic basis without such limitations.

10. Government End Users

The Macromedia Product is "Restricted Computer Software."

RESTRICTED RIGHTS LEGEND

Use, duplication or disclosure by the Government is subject to restrictions as set forth in subparagraph (c)(1)(ii) of the Rights in Technical Data and Computer Software clause at DFARS 252.227-7013. Manufacturer: Macromedia, Inc., 600 Townsend, San Francisco, CA 94103

11. General

This Agreement shall be governed by the internal laws of the State of California. This Agreement contains the complete agreement between the parties with respect to the subject matter hereof, and supersedes all prior or contemporaneous agreements or understandings, whether oral or written. All questions concerning this Agreement shall be directed to: Macromedia, Inc., 600 Townsend Street, San Francisco, CA 94103, Attention: Chief Financial Officer.

Macromedia is a registered trademark of Macromedia, Inc.

Suzanne Porta
Publisher Programs Associate
Macromedia, Inc. 600
Townsend Street, Suite 310
San Francisco, CA, 94103 USA
email: sporta@macromedia.com